La Macarena
Pages 88–95

GUADALQUIVIR

LA MACARENA

EL ARENAL

SANTA CRUZ

PARQUE MARIA LUISA

D0060386

Santa Cruz
Pages 74–87

El Arenal
Pages 66–73

Parque María Luisa
Pages 96–103

JAEN

Jaén

ALMERIA

Granada

GRANADA

Almería

Málaga

0 km   50

0 miles   50

Granada and Almería
Pages 188–209

EYEWITNESS TRAVEL

SEVILLE
& ANDALUSIA

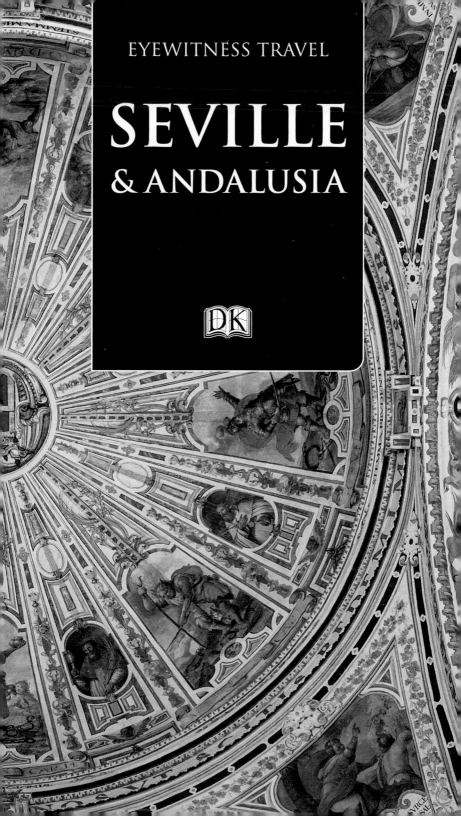

EYEWITNESS TRAVEL

SEVILLE
& ANDALUSIA

DK

LONDON, NEW YORK,
MELBOURNE, MUNICH AND DELHI
www.dk.com

Project Editor Anna Streiffert
Art Editor Robert Purnell
Editors Marcus Hardy, Jane Oliver
US Editors Mary Sutherland, Kathleen Kent
Designers Malcolm Parchment, Katie Peacock
Picture Research Monica Allende, Naomi Peck
DTP Designers Samantha Borland, Sarah Martin

Main Contributors
David Baird, Martin Symington, Nigel Tisdall

Photographers
Neil Lukas, John Miller, Linda Whitwam

Illustrators
Richard Draper, Isidoro González-Adalid Cabezas
(Acanto Arquitectura y Urbanismo S.L.), Steven Gyapay,
Claire Littlejohn, Maltings, Chris Orr, John Woodcock

Printed and bound by L. Rex Printing Co. Ltd., China

First American Edition 1996
15 16 17 10 9 8 7 6 5 4 3

Published in the United States by DK Publishing, 345 Hudson Street,
New York, New York, 10014

**Reprinted with revisions 1997, 1998, 1999,
2000, 2001, 2002, 2003, 2004, 2006, 2008, 2010, 2012, 2014**

Copyright © 1996, 2014 Dorling Kindersley Limited, London
A Penguin Random House Company

A catalog record for this book is available from the Library of Congress.
Published in Great Britain by Dorling Kindersley Limited.

ISSN 1542-1554
ISBN 978-1-4654-1134-1

Floors are referred to throughout in accordance with
European usage; i.e, "first floor" is one flight up.

MIX
Paper from
responsible sources
FSC™ C018179

**The information in this
DK Eyewitness Travel Guide is checked regularly.**

Every effort has been made to ensure that this book is as up-to-date as possible
at the time of going to press. Some details, however, such as telephone numbers,
opening hours, prices, gallery hanging arrangements and travel information are
liable to change. The publishers cannot accept responsibility for any consequences
arising from the use of this book, nor for any material on third party websites, and
cannot guarantee that any website address in this book will be a suitable source of
travel information. We value the views and suggestions of our readers very highly.
Please write to: Publisher, DK Eyewitness Travel Guides, Dorling Kindersley,
80 Strand, London, WC2R 0RL, UK, or email: travelguides@dk.com.

Front cover main image: The Alhambra, Granada

◀ Magnificent domed ceiling of the Museo de Bellas Artes, Seville

Contents

Bible illustration in Moorish style
dating from the 10th century

Introducing
Seville and
Andalusia

Horse and carriage at Plaza de
España, Parque María Luisa

Zahara de la Sierra, one of Andalusia's traditional *pueblos blancos* (white towns)

Tiled street sign for Plaza de San Francisco, Estepona

Mixed green olives

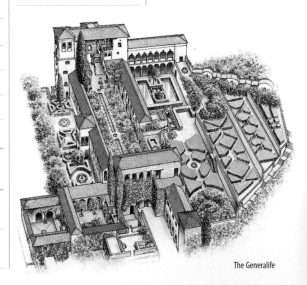

The Generalife

HOW TO USE THIS GUIDE

This guide helps you to get the most from your stay in Seville and Andalusia. It provides both expert recommendations and detailed practical information. *Introducing Seville and Andalusia* maps the region and sets it in its historical and cultural context. *Seville Area by Area* and *Andalusia Area by Area* describe the important sights, with maps, pictures and detailed illustrations. Suggestions on what to eat and drink, accommodation, shopping and entertainment are in *Travellers' Needs*, and the *Survival Guide* has tips on everything from transport to using Spanish telephones.

Seville Area by Area

The centre of Seville has been divided into four sightseeing areas. *Across the River* makes up a fifth area. Each area has its own chapter, which opens with a list of the sights described. All the sights are numbered and plotted on an Area Map. The detailed information for each sight is presented in numerical order, thereby making it easy to locate within the chapter.

A locator map shows where you are in relation to other areas of the city centre.

All pages relating to central Seville have red thumb tabs.

Sights at a Glance lists the chapter's sights by category: Churches, Museums and Galleries, Historic Buildings, Streets and Plazas, etc.

1 Area Map For easy reference, the sights are numbered and located on a map. The sights are also shown on the *Street Finder* on pages 116–21.

2 Street-by-Street Map This gives a bird's-eye view of the heart of each sightseeing area.

A suggested route for a walk covers the more interesting streets in the area.

Stars indicate the sights that no visitor should miss.

3 Detailed information on each sight All the sights in Seville are described individually. Addresses and practical information are provided. The key to the symbols used in the information block is shown on the back flap.

CÓRDOBA AND JAÉN

Córdoba, with its magnificent mosque and pretty Moorish patios, is northern Andalusia's star attraction. Córdoba province encompasses the Montilla and Moriles wine towns and gateways to the province's beautiful Renaissance towns of Úbeda and Baeza, and to the great wildlife reserves of the north.

Córdoba, on Andalusia's great river Guadalquivir, was a Roman provincial capital over 2,000 years ago, but its golden age came with the Moors. In the 10th century it was the western capital of the Islamic empire, rivalling Baghdad in wealth, power and sophistication. Today it is an atmospheric city, its ancient quarters and buildings reflecting a long and glorious history.

Running across the north of Córdoba and Jaén provinces is the Sierra Morena. Deer and boar shelter in the forest and scrub of this broad mountain range. The sierra dominates Jaén province. The great Río Guadalquivir springs to life as a sparkling trout stream in the Sierra de Cazorla, the craggy wilderness along its eastern border.

The city of Jaén, with its attractive old town

Introduction
1 The landscape, history and character of each region is described here, showing how the area has developed over the centuries and what it offers the visitor today.

Andalusia Area by Area

In this book, Andalusia has been divided into four distinct regions, each of which has a separate chapter. The most interesting sights to visit have been numbered on a Regional Map.

Each area of Andalusia has colour-coded thumb tabs.

Regional map
2 This shows the main road network and provides an illustrated overview of the whole region. All entries are numbered and there are also some useful tips on getting around the region by car, bus and train.

Detailed information on each entry
3 All the important towns and other places to visit are dealt with individually. They are listed in order, following the numbering given on the Regional Map. Within each town or city, there is detailed information on important buildings and other sights.

Features give information on topics of particular interest.

The Visitors' Checklist provides a summary of the practical information you need to plan your visit.

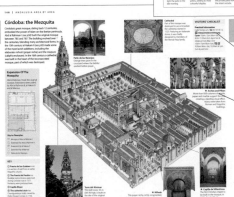

The top sights
4 These are given two or more full pages. Historic buildings are dissected to reveal their interiors; museums and galleries have colour-coded floorplans to help you locate the most interesting exhibits.

INTRODUCING
SEVILLE AND
ANDALUSIA

DISCOVERING SEVILLE AND ANDALUSIA

The following tours have been designed to take in as many of Andalusia's highlights as possible, while keeping long-distance travel to a minimum. First comes a two-day tour of Seville, the region's alluring capital, followed by a three-day tour, ideal if you're going to be spending a long weekend in the city. A one-week tour covers some of the highlights of Andalusia and also contains suggestions for expanding it to a ten-day tour if desired. Finally, there is a two-week tour, which rounds up all of the region's most celebrated attractions, including the Mezquita in Córdoba and Granada's magical Alhambra. Pick, combine and follow your favourite tours, or simply dip in and out and be inspired.

La Giralda
Named after *giraldillo*, its bronze weathervane which depicts Faith, La Giralda, the belltower of Seville's cathedral, can be climbed by visitors to enjoy magnificent views over the city.

A week in Seville and Andalusia

- Be enchanted by the Andalusian capital of **Seville**, crowned by an exquisite minaret-cum-belltower, La Giralda, and a superb royal palace.

- Walk the ancient streets of **Cádiz**, one of the oldest cities in Spain, and relax on its perfect beaches.

- Stroll around the vibrant little city of **Ronda**, draped around a steep gorge and still boasting a wealth of fine 18th-century architecture.

- Hang out with the jet set in chic **Marbella**, which combines glamorous yacht-filled marinas with plenty of old-fashioned charm.

- Visit the famous Museo de Picasso in **Málaga**, and enjoy the city's excellent shopping and nightlife.

- Soak up the spirit of Al Andalus in **Córdoba**, its whitewashed old quarter still dominated by the magnificent Mezquita.

Espiel

Cazalla de la Sierra

Córd

Aracena

El Pedroso

Nerva

Palma Del Río

Écija

Carmona

Seville

Huelva

Osuna

Utrera

El Rocío

Golfo de Cádiz

Jerez de la Frontera

Arcos de la Frontera

Ronda

Cádiz

Gaucín

Marbell

Jimena de la Frontera

Vejer de la Frontera

Parque Natural de los Alcornocales

Zahara de los Atunes

Tarifa

0 kilometres   50

0 miles   50

Two Weeks in Seville and Andalusia

- Explore the region's beautiful capital, **Seville**, famed for its superb art and architecture.

- Listen to flamenco and try some sherry in the delightful little city of **Jerez de la Frontera**.

- Visit the wonderful, whitewashed town of **Vejer de la Frontera** before heading to the picturesque, golden-sand beaches nearby.

- Drive through hills carpeted in cork trees and olive groves, admiring a string of **Pueblos Blancos** (white villages).

- Take a night tour around the magical palace of the Alhambra in **Granada**, the last city to fall to the Christian Monarchs in the 15th century.

- Admire the exquisite little Renaissance cities of **Baeza** and **Úbeda**, miraculously unchanged for centuries.

- Drive through the mountain villages of **Las Alpujarras**, which preserve their distinct architecture and local traditions.

- Enjoy one of the last stretches of unspoilt coastline on the Mediterranean in the **Parque Natural de Cabo de Gata**.

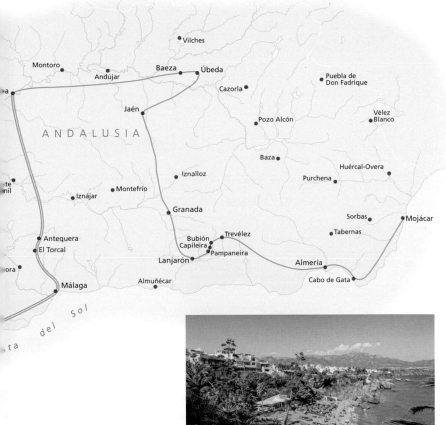

Key

— A week in Seville and Andalusia

— Two weeks in Seville and Andalusia

Nerja Beach, Málaga
The fashionable resort of Nerja, east of Málaga, is popular with locals and visitors alike and boasts a protected sandy beach at the foot of Sierra de Almijara.

2 days in Seville

- **Arriving** Arrive at Seville airport, 10 km (6 miles) northeast of the city centre, and linked by a shuttle bus.
- **Transport** This itinerary can be done entirely on foot.
- **Booking ahead** Not necessary.

Day 1

Morning Begin by visiting the city's most famous landmark, the **Cathedral** and its belltower, known as **La Giralda** (*pp82–3*). Explore the vast dim interior, which contains Columbus's tomb, and climb the belltower, which is virtually unchanged since it functioned as a minaret, to enjoy breathtaking views of the city. Next, plunge back into Seville's history at the magnificent **Real Alcázar** (*pp86–7*), a lavish royal palace.

Afternoon Escape the city heat in the **Parque María Luisa** (*pp102–3*), an elegantly landscaped 19th-century garden full of charming, colourful tiled benches and fountains. Once you've enjoyed a stroll, peek into the museums, one dedicated to Andalusian folk art and the other to archaeological finds. In the evening, cross the river to have dinner in the traditional **Triana** neighbourhood (*pp106–7*).

Day 2

Morning Get lost in the whitewashed lanes of the enchanting **Santa Cruz** district (*pp76–7*), full of enticing courtyards and pretty squares. Perhaps drop in to the **Archivo de Indias** (*p84*) or peek into the **Hospital de los Venerables** (*p85*), before visiting the ravishing **Casa de Pilatos** (*p81*) with its blissful secret garden.

Afternoon Spend a couple of hours at the wonderful **Museo de Bellas Artes** (*pp70–71*), a fine art collection displayed in a handsomely remodelled 17th-century convent. Then enjoy a spot of shopping along

One of the pretty narrow streets in the labyrinthine Santa Cruz district, Seville

the pedestrianized **Calle Sierpes** (*p78*), and a delicious tapas supper at one of the many bars in the area.

3 days in Seville

- **Arriving** Arrive at Seville airport, 10 km (6 miles) northeast of the city centre, and linked by a shuttle bus.
- **Transport** This itinerary can be done on foot, but use the city's bus system if you get tired of walking.
- **Booking ahead** Not necessary.

Day 1

Morning Make your first port of call Seville's beautiful Gothic **cathedral** and its belltower, **La Giralda** (*pp82–3*), which is visible from almost anywhere in

the city. After admiring the fantastic, city-wide views from the top of the belltower, look at its beautiful 12th-century base from the **Plaza Virgen de los Reyes** (*p84*), or perhaps drop in to the **Hospital de los Venerables** (*p85*) to view the artworks.

Afternoon While away an enjoyable hour or two in the **Museo de Bellas Artes** (*pp70–71*), then stroll down to the river to see the **Plaza de Toros de la Maestranza** (*p68*) and the **Torre del Oro** (*p69*). Enjoy dinner overlooking the river, perhaps at one of the restaurants on the **Calle Betis**, many of which have terraces with lovely views.

Day 2

Morning Throw away the map and explore the whitewashed lanes of the magical **Santa Cruz** neighbourhood (*pp76–7*), its wrought-iron balconies overflowing with scarlet geraniums. Explore the exquisite noble mansion known as the **Casa de Pilatos** (*p81*), its salons gleaming with burnished tiles. Relax over a long lunch overlooking one of the pretty squares.

Afternoon Delve into the **Archivo de Indias** (*p84*), where documents relating to Spain's conquest of the Americas are gathered in a spectacular 16th-century library. Follow it up with a visit to the beautiful **Real Alcázar**

Exquisite Mudéjar carved arches at Real Alcázar royal palace, Seville

Stunning mountain views over the Sierra de Grazalema nature reserve, Ronda

(pp86–7), richly decorated with stucco and tiles by local artisans. Then take a stroll in the **Jardines de Murillo** (p85).

Day 3:
Morning Go for a wander in **La Macarena** (pp90–91), one of Seville's most appealing, traditional neighbourhoods, which is named for a much-venerated statue of the Virgin held in the **Basilica de la Macarena** (p93). Visit the **Palacio de Lebrija** (p78), an aristocratic mansion containing a wealth of archaeological treasures, then stop for lunch at one of the arty cafés near the **Alameda de Hércules** (p92).

Afternoon Enjoy a peaceful stroll in the elegant **Parque María Luisa** (pp102–3), with its leafy avenues and tiled benches and fountains. The park contains a pair of fine museums, both well worth a visit: the **Museo de Artes y Costumbres Populares** (p103) and the **Museo Arqueológico** (p103). In the evening, head to the vibrant **Triana** area and take a tour of the many traditional tapas bars.

A week in Seville and Andalusia

- **Arriving** Arrive at Seville airport, 10 km (6 miles) northeast of the city centre, and linked by a shuttle bus.

- **Transport** The Seville section can be done on foot, but a car is essential for the rest of this itinerary.

- **Booking ahead** Not necessary.

Days 1 and 2: Seville
Follow the two-day itinerary on p12.

Day 3: Cádiz
Take the A4/E5 motorway south of Seville and drive to **Cádiz** (pp168–9). Spend the day exploring this enchanting ancient city, which is piled up on a long, narrow isthmus. Amble through the narrow lanes of the **historic quarter** (pp170–1), visiting the atmospheric market and the vast cathedral. Climb the **Torre Tavira** (p169), which contains an enjoyable Camera Oscura, to soak up the splendid views, and then spend an hour or two soaking up the sunshine and atmosphere on one of the city's great beaches.

> **To extend your trip…**
> Head south down the coast towards **Tarifa** (p179). Spend the night there, then head up through the hills of the **Parque Natural de Los Alcornocales** via **Jimena de la Frontera** (p178) and **Gaucín** (p178) to **Ronda**.

Day 4: Ronda
Drive inland, stopping at the beautiful, whitewashed town of **Arcos de la Frontera** (p179), crowned by a ruined castle, then cross the northeastern swathe of the **Sierra de Grazalema** nature reserve (p24) to **Ronda** (pp180–181). This exquisite little city straddles a deep gorge, spanned by a handsome 18th-century bridge, the **Puente Nuevo** (p180). Explore the elegant streets, flanked by palaces and churches, and visit its historic bullring, considered to be the home of bullfighting.

Day 5: Marbella
An easy 40-minute drive will bring you to **Marbella** (pp186–7), which preserves a picturesque historic quarter and a fine main square shaded by orange trees. Long the resort of choice for aristocrats and celebrities, it remains one of the most chic towns on the Costa del Sol.

Day 6: Málaga
A fast motorway links Marbella with Málaga, about 60 km (37 miles) up the coast. **Málaga** (pp184–5) is a vibrant and dynamic city which boasts two exceptional museums – the **Museo de Picasso** (p181) and the **Museo Carmen Thyssen** (pp184–5) – both are well worth a visit. Following your museum stint, scramble up to the striking clifftop fortress, the **Alcazaba** (p185), to enjoy the fabulous views and an interesting local history museum.

The Museo de Artes y Costumbres Populares in the Parque María Luisa, Seville

To extend your trip...
Spend the morning exploring **Antequera**, (*p183*) then go hiking amid the rugged limestone crags of **El Torcal** (*p183*) in the afternoon. Spend the night in Antequera.

Day 7: Córdoba
Drive north to **Córdoba** (*pp144–5*), an enticing city still suffused with the spirit of old Al Andalus. The highlight is the astounding **Mezquita** (*pp148–9*), the vast mosque-turned-church which dates back 12 centuries. Explore the twisting lanes of the **Judería** (*p144*), and visit the impressive **Alcázar de los Reyes Cristianos** (*p146*), set in enchanting gardens.

2 weeks in Seville and Andalusia

- **Arriving** Arrive at Seville airport, 10 km (6 miles) northeast of the city centre, and linked by a shuttle bus.

- **Transport** A car is essential for this tour.

- **Booking ahead**
  Book Alhambra tickets in advance, particularly if you want to do the night visit. **Tel:** 90 288 80 01, or 93 492 37 50 from abroad, or online at **W** ticketmaster.es. More information at: **W** alhambragranada.org

Resplendent arches and pillars adorning the Mezquita, Córdoba

Day 1: Seville
Pick some highlights from the two-day itinerary on p12.

Day 2: Seville to Cádiz
Potter down to **Jerez de la Frontera** (*p166*), cradle of flamenco and home to some fine, sherry-producing *bodegas* (*p167*). Continue on to the enchanting, sun-bleached city of **Cádiz** (*pp168–9*), the oldest continually inhabited city in Spain. Explore the dilapidated yet charming historic quarter (*pp170–71*), and tuck into some delicious seafood in one of its traditional restaurants.

Day 3: Tarifa and the Costa de la Luz
Follow the coast south, stopping at hilltop **Vejer de la Frontera** (*p172*) and perhaps enjoy an hour or two on the beaches at **Zahara de los Atunes** (*p172*). **Tarifa** (*p173*), at the tip of Spain, is the country's kite- and wind-surfing capital, with a delightful, whitewashed old quarter and fabulous white-sand beaches.

Day 4: Pueblos Blancos to Ronda
Drive up through the forested hills of the **Parque Natural de Los Alcornocales** (*p173*), visiting some of the area's **Pueblos Blancos** (white villages, *p178*) on the way. **Jimena de la Frontera** and **Gaucín** are two of the prettiest. Spend the night in **Ronda** (*pp180–81*), a handsome town perched over a deep gorge.

Day 5: Ronda to Marbella
After a morning spent strolling the elegant streets of Ronda, drive to **Marbella** (*pp186–7*), one of the most attractive towns on the Costa del Sol. A favourite with the jet set, it boasts glossy marinas and fine beaches, but its appealing historic quarter, with white-washed lanes and orange trees, is still its best charming feature.

Day 6: Marbella to Málaga
Drive up the coast to the vibrant city of **Málaga** (*pp184–5*), which boasts great beaches and nightlife as well as a host of cultural attractions. These are spearheaded by the excellent **Museo de Picasso** (*p181*) and the **Museo Carmen Thyssen** (*pp184–5*), but don't miss a visit to the clifftop **Alcazaba** (*p185*), an ancient fortress that contains an interesting history museum and offers sublime views over the city.

Day 7: Málaga to Córdoba
Drive north to the market town of **Antequera** (*p183*), where you can pick up some picnic supplies before heading into the surreally beautiful, if arid, landscape of **El Torcal** (*p183*) for a hike. Then continue north to **Córdoba** (*pp144–5*), where you should spend the night.

Day 8: Córdoba
Córdoba was once the capital of a rich and powerful caliphate, and, although its influence has long since waned, it remains one

Garden views of the Palacio del Partal, the oldest palace at the Alhambra, Granada

of the most beautiful and stirring cities in Spain. The vast, dazzling **Mezquita** (*pp148–9*) continues to dominate the city, as it has for more than 12 centuries. The heart of Córdoba is the **Judería** (*p144*), a delightful maze of whitewashed lanes and pretty squares which overflow with flowers in spring.

Day 9: Córdoba to Úbeda
Drive east from Córdoba to reach **Baeza** (*pp156–7*), a perfect little Renaissance time capsule, full of splendid palaces and churches. Enjoy lunch on one of the elegant squares, then head to **Úbeda** (*pp158–9*), another graceful Renaissance town, which, like Baeza, has been inscribed on UNESCO's list of World Heritage Sites. Spend the night in Úbeda.

Day 10: Úbeda to Granada
Head south to **Jaén** (*pp138–9*), a sprawling city surrounded by olive groves. Spend the morning strolling around the upper part of Jaén, visiting the **Castillo de Santa Catalina** (*p148*), which enjoys impressive views, and the extravagantly decorated **Catedral** (*p148*). After a lazy lunch, continue driving to Granada where you should spend the night.

Day 11: Granada
Granada (*pp194–9*), set against the backdrop of the Sierra Nevada, is perhaps the city which most deeply evokes Al Andalus. The whitewashed lanes

Holiday-makers sunbathing on a sandy beach, Marbella

of the **Albaícin** (*pp196–7*) cling steeply to one hillside, while the the **Alhambra** (*pp198–9*), a spellbinding palace set in the perfumed gardens of the **Generalife** (*p202*), crowns another. Other unmissable sights include the vast **cathedral** (*p194*) and the **Capilla Real** (*p194*), which contains the tombs of Ferdinand and Isabella, known as the Catholic Monarchs, who conquered Granada in 1492. Ideally, spend a couple of days in Granada – not least to enjoy the city's famous tapas bars.

Day 12: A drive through Las Alpujarras
Spread along the southern flanks of the Sierra Nevada, **Las Alpujarras** (*pp204–5*) is a beautiful, forested region dotted with tiny villages that preserve their distinctive local

architecture and traditions. Head south of Granada to **Lanjarón** (*p193*), famous for its mineral waters, and then follow the narrow mountain roads east. Stop at any of the villages which take your fancy – perhaps **Pampaneira**, **Bubion** and **Capileira** (*see* **Poqueira Valley**, *p203*), or **Trevélez** (*p204*), which is famous across the country for its superb cured hams. Spend the night in the mountains before continuing to **Almería**.

Day 13: Las Alpujarras to Almería
Continue driving through increasingly flat and arid countryside to **Almería** (*pp206–7*), a large port city crowned by a 1000-year-old fortress. Explore the time-worn historic centre, with its flat-roofed houses and palm trees reminiscent of North Africa.

Day 14: Cabo de Gata and Mojácar
Stock up on picnic goodies and head southeast of Almería to explore the **Parque Natural de Cabo de Gata** (*p208*), an enticing wilderness of rugged hills, secret coves and beautiful beaches. There are few towns and villages, and you may need to scramble down cliffs to reach some of the most alluring little bays. Continue along the coast to reach **Mojácar** (*p209*), a picturesque town of white, cube-shaped houses arranged around more gorgeous beaches.

The picturesque village of Mojácar with its white, cube-shaped houses

Putting Seville and Andalusia on the Map

Andalusia is Spain's southernmost region, bordered by Extremadura and Castilla-La Mancha to the north and Murcia to the northwest. Its long coastline faces the Atlantic to the west and the Mediterranean to the south and east. One of Spain's largest regions, it covers an area of 87,267 sq km (33,693 sq miles) and has a population of 6.8 million. Seville is the province's capital.

Key

══ Motorway

── Major road

━━ International border

── Provincial border

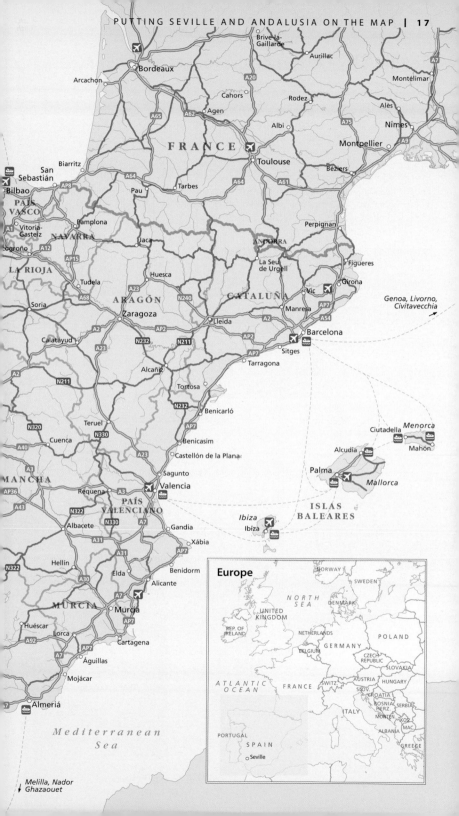

Seville City Centre and Greater Seville

Seville city centre is a compact maze of old, narrow streets, with most sights within walking distance. A couple of wide, busy avenues cut through the centre, dividing it into separate areas. This book focuses on these areas, starting with the historic neighbourhoods on each side of Avenida de la Constitución. To the west, along the river, is El Arenal with the Plaza de Toros; and to the east lies the old Jewish quarter of Santa Cruz, dominated by the massive cathedral and the Reales Alcázares. In the north lies La Macarena with its many churches, while the Parque María Luisa stretches out beyond the Universidad, south of the historic centre.

El Arenal: Teatro de la Maestranza and Torre del Oro

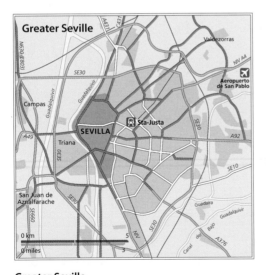

Greater Seville

West of the Guadalquivir river lies the Isla de la Cartuja, former site of Expo '92, and the picturesque Triana quarter. Modern residential areas surround the town centre.

Parque María Luisa: the Plaza de España, built for the 1929 Exposition

La Macarena: Sevillian façades with window grilles lining Calle Santa Clara

Santa Cruz: Horses and carriages at Plaza del Triunfo by the cathedral

Key

- ◼ Major sight
- ◼ Seville city centre
- ◻ Built-up area
- ═ Motorway
- ▬ Major road
- ═ Minor road
- — Railway

0 métres   400
0 yards   400

For map symbols *see back flap*

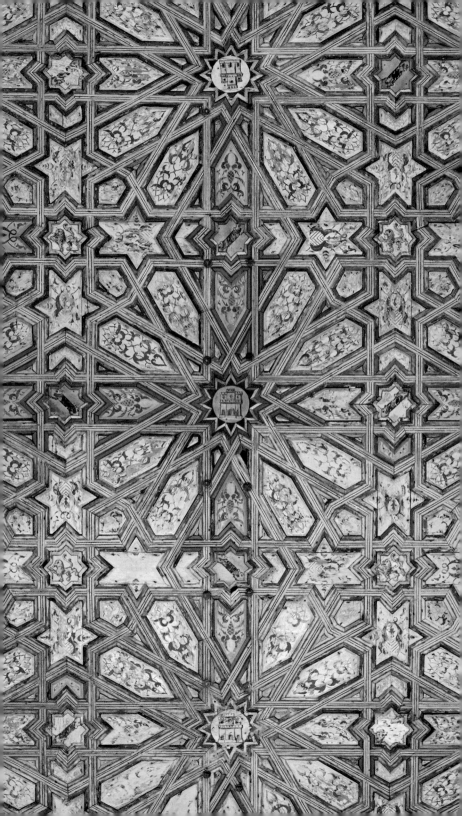

A PORTRAIT OF ANDALUSIA

Andalusia is where all Spain's stereotypes appear to have come together. Bullfighters, flamenco dancers, white villages and harsh sierras are all there in abundance. But they form only part of an intricate tapestry. Beneath the surface, expect to find many contradictions. Wherever you travel, particularly when you escape from the tourist-engulfed coast, you will come across the unexpected, whether it is a local *fiesta* or a breathtaking view.

Until the 1950s, Andalusia had changed scarcely at all since the middle of the 19th century, when the English traveller, Richard Ford, described it as "a land bottled for antiquarians" – almost a feudal society, with attendant rigid social strata.

Today, four-lane highways stretch where not so long ago there were only dirt tracks. Children whose parents are illiterate play with computers and plan university careers. Agriculture is still important, but there are also factories turning out cars and aircraft. As in other European countries, the service industries, tourism especially, predominate. In 2005, they accounted for 68.7 per cent of the region's GNP compared with 8.7 per cent for agriculture and fishing. Yet the 7.9 million inhabitants retain their characteristic love of talk and folklore, their indifference to time and their abundant hospitality.

The Moorish Legacy

The Andalusian character is complex because it reflects a complex history. Successive invaders, including the Phoenicians, Romans, Visigoths and Moors, have all left their indelible mark. Although the Christian rulers of Spain ejected both Jews and Moors from their kingdom, they could not remove their influences on the country – let alone on Andalusia. Look at the face of an Andalusian man or woman and you will catch a glimpse of North Africa. Centuries of Moorish occupation *(see pp50–51)* and the inevitable mingling of blood have created a race and culture different from any in Europe.

As you travel around the region, you will find much physical evidence of the Moorish legacy: in the splendour of the Alhambra *(see pp198–9)* and the

Musicians, singers and dancers continuing a flamenco tradition that dates from the 18th century *(see p32)*

◄ Historic wooden ceiling, Real Alcázar

Mezquita *(see pp148–9)* in Córdoba, and in ruined fortresses and elaborate tilework. Workshops across the region still practise crafts handed down from great Moorish kingdoms. Many of the irrigation networks in use today follow those laid out by the Moors, who built *norias* (waterwheels), *aljibes* (tanks for collecting the rain), *albercas* (cisterns), and *acequias* (irrigation channels).

Sevillanos enjoying a pre-dinner drink and some tapas *(see pp224–5)*

As these words show, the Moors also left a strong linguistic legacy, not only of agricultural terms, but also of words for foods – *naranja* (orange), for example, and *aceituna* (olive).

Moorish influence may also account for Andalusians' love of poetry and fine language. It is no coincidence that Spain's finest poets, including among them Nobel prize winners, come from this region.

People and Culture

Sevillanos work hard to sustain their reputation for flamboyance and hedonism. A 13th-century Moorish commentator noted that they were "the most frivolous and most given to playing the fool". Living up to that image is a full-time occupation, but the visitor should not be deceived by the exuberant façade.

One surprising aspect of both Seville and Andalusia is that although the society may appear open and extrovert, it is, in fact, one that also values privacy.

The Andalusian concept of time can also be perplexing. Progressive business types may try to adjust to the rigorous demands of Europe, but in general, northern Europeans' obsession with time is an object of mirth here. The moment is to be enjoyed and tomorrow will look after itself. A concert will often begin well after the advertised time, and lunch can feasibly take place at any time between 1pm and 4:30pm.

Attitudes to women in Andalusia are changing, as elsewhere in western Europe, though southern Spain's tradition for *machismo* means that there is still some way to go. The number of women, for example, who work outside the

Penitents parading a giant float, Semana Santa *(see p42)*

Barren, remote countryside, one of the many faces of Andalusia's varied landscape *(see pp24–5)*

home is still lower than in other countries of the West. Although many women have a job in their twenties, they still give up work when they marry in order to have children and look after the house.

Paradoxically, the mother is an almost sacred figure in Andalusia, where family ties are written in blood. Although new affluence and a steady movement to the cities is now beginning to erode old values, Andalusia remains a traditional rural society with a distinct emphasis on personal relationships.

Catholicism is Spain's dominant religion, and adoration of the Virgin is a striking feature of Andalusia. Apart from a purely religious devotion,

Sevillian lady in traditional Semana Santa dress *(see p42)*

the Virgin is also subject to a peculiar admiration from the male population.

A man who never attends Mass may be ecstatic about the Virgin of his local church; when she emerges from the church in procession, he feels fiercely possessive of her. If you try to think of the gorgeously robed figure as a pagan earth mother or fertility goddess, the phenomenon is much easier to understand.

As a society, Andalusia is unafraid of its emotions, which are almost always near the surface. There is no shame in the singing of a *saeta*, the "arrow" of praise launched at the Virgin in Semana Santa (Holy Week), nor is there any ambivalence in the matador's desire to kill his antagonist, the bull. The quintessence of this is flamenco; the pain and passion of its songs reflect not just the sufferings and yearnings of gypsies and the poor, but also Andalusia's soul.

Decorative tilework in the Palacio de Viana *(see p146)*

Nun with convent jams

The Landscape of Andalusia

Each year, several million visitors are drawn to the high-rise resorts along Andalusia's Mediterranean coast. Away from these, however, are empty, windswept Atlantic shores and expansive areas of wetland wilderness. Inland there are rugged mountain ranges clothed with forests of pine, cork and wild olive. Also typical of the landscape are the undulating hills awash with vines, cereals and olive trees. Of Andalusia's total land area, some 17 per cent has been designated national parks or nature reserves in order to protect the region's unique abundance of animal and plant life.

The fertile plains of the Guadalquivir valley are watered by the river and have been the bread basket of Andalusia since Moorish times. Fields of cereals alternate with straight lines of citrus trees.

0 kilometres 50
0 miles 25

SIERRA DE ARACENA

S I E R R A M O R

Córdoba

Río Guadalquivir

Sevilla

Río Genil

Huelva

Embalse del Guadalhorce

Río Guadalete

Río Guadalhorce

Málag

Cádiz

SERRANÍA DE RONDA

The Atlantic beaches, where pine trees grow behind the sand dunes, are less developed than the Mediterranean *costas*. Fishing fleets from Cádiz and Huelva operate offshore.

The Río Guadalquivir runs through the wetlands of Coto Doñana *(see pp134–5)* before finally entering the Atlantic Ocean.

The Costa del Sol and the rest of the Mediterranean coast are mainly characterized by arid cliffs draped in bougainvillea and other subtropical shrubs. The beaches below are either pebbly or of greyish sand.

Craggy mountains around Ronda encompass the nature reserve of Sierra de Grazalema. The area is home to a diverse wildlife, including griffon vultures and three species of eagle, and a forest of the rare Spanish fir.

Key

- Desert
- Marshland
- Forest
- Cultivated land

Endless olive groves give the landscape in the provinces of Córdoba and, in particular, Jaén a distinct, crisscrossed pattern. These long-living trees are of great importance to the local economy, for their oil *(see p152)* as well as their beautiful wood.

Andalusian Wildlife

Southern Spain is blessed with some of the richest and most varied flora and fauna in Europe, including some species which are unique to the area. The best time to appreciate this is in spring when wild flowers bloom and migratory birds stop en route from Africa to northern Europe.

Vast forests, mainly of Corsican pine, cover the craggy sierras of Cazorla, Segura and Las Villas *(see p160)* in one of Spain's largest nature reserves.

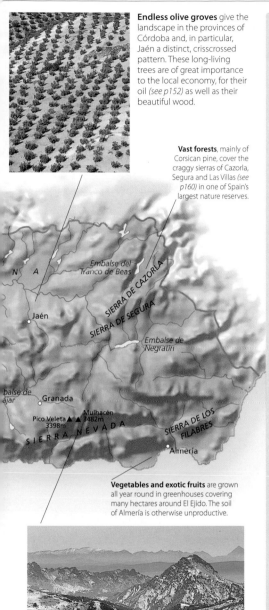

Cork oak grows mainly in the province of Cádiz. Its prized bark is stripped every ten years.

The Cazorla violet, which can only be found in Sierra de Cazorla *(see p161)*, flowers in May.

A mouflon is a nimble and agile wild sheep that was introduced to mountainous areas in the 1970s.

Vegetables and exotic fruits are grown all year round in greenhouses covering many hectares around El Ejido. The soil of Almería is otherwise unproductive.

Flamingos gather in great flocks in the wetlands of Coto Doñana and the Río Odiel delta in Huelva.

The Sierra Nevada, Spain's highest mountain range, reaches 3,482 m (11,420 ft) at the peak of Mulhacén. Although only 40 km (25 miles) from the Mediterranean beaches, some areas are snow-capped all year round. The skiing season starts in December and lasts until spring. In summer the area is perfect for hiking and climbing.

Moorish Architecture

The first significant period of Moorish architecture arrived with the Cordoban Caliphate. The Mezquita was extended lavishly during this period and possesses all the enduring features of the Moorish style: arches, stucco work and ornamental use of calligraphy. Later, the Almohads imported a purer Islamic style, which can be seen at La Giralda *(see p82)*. The Nasrids built the superbly crafted Alhambra in Granada, while the *mudéjares (see p28)* used their skill to create beautiful Moorish-style buildings such as the Palacio Pedro I, part of Seville's Real Alcázar *(see also pp50–53)*.

Reflections in water combined with an overall play of light were central to Moorish architecture.

Moorish domes were often unadorned on the outside. Inside, however, an intricate lattice of stone ribs supported the dome's weight. Like this one in the Mezquita *(see pp148–9)*, they were inlaid with multi- coloured mosaics featuring flower or animal motifs.

Defensive walls

Moorish gardens were often arranged around gently rippling pools and channels.

Development Of Moorish Architecture

Pre-Caliphal era 710–929	Caliphal era 929–1031	Almoravid and Almohad era 1091–1248	Nasrid era 1238–1492
	1031–91 Taifa period *(see p50)*		**c.1350** Alhambra palace

700	800	900	1000	1100	1200	1300	1400
	785 Mezquita in Córdoba begun			**1184** La Giralda in Seville begun		**c.1350** Palacio Pedro I	
		936 Medina Azahara near Córdoba begun			**Mudéjar era, after c.1215**		

Azulejos *(see p80)* were used for wall decorations. Patterns became increasingly geometric, as on these tiles in the Palacio Pedro I *(p86)*.

Moorish Arches

The Moorish arch was developed from the horseshoe arch that the Visigoths used in the construction of churches. The Moors modified it and used it as the basis of great architectural endeavours, such as the Mezquita. Subsequent arches show more sophisticated ornamentation and the slow demise of the basic horseshoe shape.

Caliphal arch, Medina Azahara *(see p142)*

Almohad arch, Patio del Yeso *(see p87)*

Mudéjar arch, Salón de Embajadores *(see p87)*

Nasrid arch, the Alhambra *(see p199)*

Moorish Palace

The palaces of the Moors were designed with gracious living, culture and learning in mind. The imagined palace here shows how space, light, water and ornamentation were combined to harmonious effect.

Clay tiles

Moorish baths made use of steam and hot water; like Roman baths, they often had underfloor heating.

Entrance halls were complex to confuse unwanted visitors.

Arcaded galleries provided shade around courtyards.

Water cooled the Moors' elegant courtyards and served a contemplative purpose. Often, as here in the Patio de los Leones *(see p199)*, water had to be pumped from a source far below.

Elaborate stucco work typifies the Nasrid style of architecture. The Sala de los Abencerrajes *(see p199)* in the Alhambra was built using only the simplest materials, but it is nevertheless widely regarded as one of the most outstanding monuments of the period of the Moorish occupation.

Post-Moorish Architecture

The Christian reconquest was followed by the building of new churches and palaces, many by *mudéjares (see p52)*. Later, prejudice against the Moors grew as Christians began to assert their faith. Gothic styles from northern Europe filtered into Andalusia, though Mudéjar influences survived into the 18th century. In the 16th century, Andalusia was the centre of the Spanish Renaissance; and a uniquely Spanish interpretation of the Baroque emerged in the 18th century.

Mudéjar tower, Iglesia de Santa Ana *(see p196)*

The Reconquest (Mid-13th to Late 15th Century)

Moorish craftsmen working on Christian buildings created a hybrid Christian Islamic style known as Mudéjar. Mid-13th-century churches, such as the ones built in Seville and Córdoba, show a varying degree of Moorish influence, but the Palacio Pedro I in the Real Alcázar *(see pp86–7)* is almost exclusively Moorish in style. By the early 15th century, pure Gothic styles, which are best exemplified by Seville Cathedral *(see pp82–3)*, were widespread. After the fall of Granada in 1492 *(see p52)*, a late Gothic style, called Isabelline, developed.

The Iglesia de San Marcos
(see p94) is a typical example of a Christian church built at the time of the Reconquest. Mudéjar features include the portal and minaret-like tower.

Bell towers were often added later; this one is a Baroque addition.

Windows are framed by Islamic-style, marble columns.

Window openings become progressively narrower towards ground level.

Islamic-style decoration on the main entrance is characteristic of many Mudéjar churches.

Mudéjar portal, Nuestra Señora de la O *(see p166)*

Classical arches, a motif of the transitional Isabelline style, look forward to Renaissance architecture.

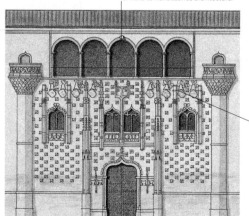

Gothic window, Seville Cathedral

Heavily worked stone reliefs, as decoration on façades of buildings, have their roots in the Gothic style.

The Palacio Jabalquinto
(see p156) has a highly ornate façade. Its coats of arms and heraldic symbols, typical of Isabelline buildings, reveal a strong desire to establish a national style.

The Renaissance (16th Century)

Early Renaissance architecture was termed Plateresque because its fine detailing resembled ornate silver-work. (*Platero* means silversmith.) The façade of the Ayuntamiento *(see p78)* in Seville is the best example of Plateresque in Andalusia. A High Renaissance style is typified by the Palacio Carlos V. The end of the 16th century saw the rise of the austere Herreran style, named after Juan de Herrera, who drafted the initial plans of the Archivo de Indias *(see p84)*.

Plateresque detail on Seville's Ayuntamiento

Courtyard, with Herreran proportions, in the Archivo de Indias

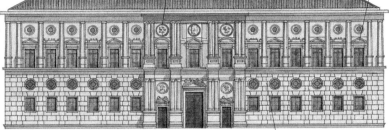

Stone roundels were used as decoration; the central ones would bear the emperor's coat of arms.

Classical pediments adorn the windows.

Rusticated stonework gives the lower level a solid appearance.

The Palacio Carlos V, begun in 1526, is located in the heart of the Alhambra *(see p199)*. Its elegant, grandiose style reflects Carlos V's power as Holy Roman Emperor.

Baroque (17th and 18th Centuries)

Early Spanish Baroque tended to be austere. The 18th century, however, gave rise to the Churrigueresque, named after the Churriguera family of architects. Although the family's own style was fairly restrained, it had many flamboyant imitations. Priego de Córdoba *(see p154)* is a showcase of the Baroque; La Cartuja *(p195)* in Granada contains a Baroque sacristy.

Flamboyant Baroque sacristy of La Cartuja, Granada

Palacio del Marqués de la Gomera, Osuna *(p137)*

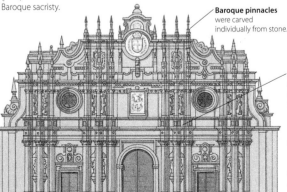

Baroque pinnacles were carved individually from stone.

Repeated string courses define the church's storeys and contribute to the complex decoration of the façade.

Guadix Cathedral *(see p204)* comprises a Renaissance building fronted by a Baroque façade. Such a combination of styles is very common in Andalusia.

The Art of Bullfighting

Bullfighting is a sacrificial ritual in which men (and some women) pit themselves against an animal bred for the ring. In this "authentic religious drama", as poet García Lorca described it, the spectator experiences vicariously the fear and exaltation of the matador. Some Spaniards oppose it (and it is now banned in Catalunya), but it remains popular in Andalusia.

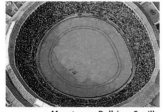

Maestranza Bullring, Seville
This is regarded, with Las Ventas in Madrid, as one of the top venues for bullfighting in Spain.

Bull Breeding
Well treated at the ranch, the *toro bravo* (fighting bull) is bred specially for aggressiveness and courage.

The matador wears a *traje de luces* (suit of light), a colourful silk outfit embroidered with gold sequins.

The passes are made with a *muleta*, a scarlet cape stiffened along one side.

Fiesta!

Bullfighting is an essential and highly popular part of many *fiestas* in Spain. An enthusiastic and very knowledgeable audience, often in traditional dress, fills the arenas from the start of the season in April until its end in October (see pp42–3).

Fiesta wear

The Bullfight

The *corrida* (bullfight) has three stages, called *tercios*. In the first one, the *tercio de varas*, the matador and *picadores* (horsemen with lances) are aided by *peones* (assistants). In the *tercio de banderillas*, banderilleros stick pairs of darts in the bull's back. In the *tercio de muleta* the matador makes a series of passes at the bull with a *muleta* (cape). He then executes the kill, the *estocada*, with a sword.

The matador plays the bull with a *capa* (red cape) in the *tercio de varas* to gauge its intelligence and speed. *Peones* then draw it towards the *picadores*.

Today, horses are heavily padded

Picadores goad the bull with steel-pointed lances, testing its bravery as it charges their horses. The lances weaken the animal's shoulder muscles.

The Bullring

The *corrida* audience sits in the *tendidos* (stalls) or in the *palcos* (balcony), where the *presidencia* (president's box) is. Opposite are the *puerta de cuadrillas*, through which the matador and team arrive, and the *arrastre de toros* (exit for bulls). Before entering the ring, the matadors wait in a corridor *(callejón)* behind the *barreras* and *burladeros* (ringside barriers). Horses are kept in the *patio de caballos* and the bulls wait in the *corrales*.

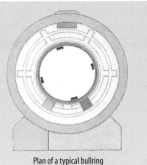

Plan of a typical bullring

Key

- ☐ Tendidos
- ▨ Palcos
- ▨ Presidencia
- ▨ Puerta de cuadrillas
- ■ Arrastre de toros
- ▨ Callejón
- ▨ Barreras
- ▨ Burladeros
- ▨ Patio de caballo
- ☐ Corrales

Banderillas, barbed darts, are thrust into the bull's already weakened back muscles.

Manolete

Regarded as one of the greatest matadors ever, Manolete was gored to death by the bull Islero at Linares, Jaén, in 1947.

The bull may go free if it shows courage – spectators wave white handkerchiefs, asking the *corrida* president to let it leave the ring alive.

Julian López (El Juli)

El Juli debuted at the age of 16. He is renowned for his fierce courage and his flair with the *capa* and the *muleta*.

Banderilleros enter to provoke the wounded bull in the *tercio de banderillas*, gauging its reaction to punishment by sticking pairs of *banderillas* in its back.

The bull weighs about 500 kg (1,100 lb)

The matador makes passes with the cape in the *tercio de muleta*, then lowers it to make the bull bow its head, and thrusts in the sword for the kill.

The estocada recibiendo is a difficult kill that is rarely seen. The matador awaits the bull's charge rather than moving forwards to meet it.

Flamenco, the Soul of Andalusia

More than just a dance, flamenco is a forceful artistic expression of the sorrows and joys of life. Although it has interpreters all over Spain and even the world, it is a uniquely Andalusian art form, traditionally performed by gypsies. There are many styles of *cante* (song) from different parts of Andalusia, but no strict choreography – dancers improvise from basic movements, following the rhythm of the guitar and their feelings. Flamenco was neglected in the 1960s and '70s, but serious interest has once again returned. Recent years have seen a revival of traditional styles and the development of exciting new forms.

Sevillanas, a folk dance that is strongly influenced by flamenco, is danced by Andalusians in bars and at social events (see p244).

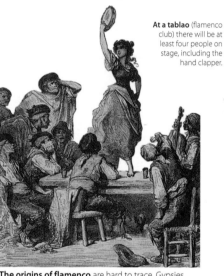

At a tablao (flamenco club) there will be at least four people on stage, including the hand clapper.

The origins of flamenco are hard to trace. Gypsies may have been the main creators of the art, mixing their own Indian-influenced culture with existing Moorish and Andalusian folklore, and with Jewish and Christian music. There were gypsies in Andalusia by the early Middle Ages, but only in the 18th century did flamenco begin to develop into its present form.

The Spanish Guitar

The guitar has a major role in flamenco, traditionally accompanying the singer. The flamenco guitar developed from the modern classical guitar, which evolved in Spain in the 19th century. Flamenco guitars have a lighter, shallower construction and a thickened plate below the soundhole, used to tap rhythms. Today, flamenco guitarists often perform solo. One of the greatest, Paco de Lucía, began by accompanying singers and dancers, but made his debut as a soloist in 1968. His slick, inventive style, which combines traditional playing with Latin, jazz and rock elements, has influenced many musicians outside the realm of flamenco, such as the group Ketama, who play flamenco-blues.

Classical guitar

Soloist Paco de Lucía playing flamenco guitar

Singing is an integral part of flamenco, and the singer often performs solo. Camarón de la Isla (1952–92), a gypsy born near Cádiz, is among the most famous contemporary *cantaores* (flamenco singers). He began as a singer of *cante jondo* (literally, "deep songs"), from which he developed his own, rock-influenced style. He has inspired many singers.

Where To Enjoy Flamenco

Flamenco festivals *pp38–43, p244*
Flamenco guitar *pp38–41, p244*
Flamenco in Sacromonte *p197*
Flamenco singing *pp38–41, p244*
Flamenco tablaos *p244*
Flamenco dress *p239*

Eva Yerbabuena is a *bailaora* (female dancer) renowned for her amazing footwork and intensity. Sara Baras is another dancer famous for her personal style. Both lead their own acclaimed flamenco companies. Other international flamenco stars include Juana Amaya.

The proud yet graceful posture of the *bailaora* seems to suggest a restrained passion.

A harsh, vibrating voice is typical of the singer.

Traditional polka-dot dress

The bailaor (male dancer) plays a less important role than the *bailaora*. However, many have achieved fame, including Antonio Canales. He has introduced a new beat through his original foot movements.

The Flamenco Tablao

These days it is rare to come across spontaneous dancing at a tablao, but if dancers and singers are inspired, an impressive show usually results. Artists performing with duende ("magic spirit") will hear appreciative olés from the audience.

Flamenco rhythm

The unmistakable rhythm of flamenco is created by the guitar. Just as important, however, is the beat created by hand-clapping and by the dancer's feet in high-heeled shoes. The *bailaoras* may also beat a rhythm with castanets; Lucero Tena (born in 1939) became famous for her solos on castanets. Graceful hand movements are used to express the dancer's feelings of the moment – whether pain, sorrow or happiness. Hand and body movements are choreographed, but styles vary from person to person.

Castanets made of wood

Flamenco hand movements, intricate and complex

The Land of Sherry

The Phoenicians introduced the vine to the Jerez region 3,000 years ago. Later, Greeks, then Romans, exported wine from these gentle hills bordering the Atlantic. However, the foundations of the modern sherry trade were laid by British merchants who settled here after the Reconquest *(see pp52–3)*. They discovered that the chalky soil, climate and local grapes produced fine wines, particularly if fortified with grape spirit. The connection persists today with companies such as John Harvey still under British ownership.

Preparing soil to catch the winter rain

Grapes thriving in the chalky soil near Jerez

Sanlúcar de Barrameda

Jerez de la Frontera

Rota

Rio Guadalete

El Puerto de Santa María

Cadiz

Puerto Real

San Fernando

Chiclana de la Frontera

Sherry Regions

Sherry is produced at bodegas, or wineries, in the towns of Jerez de la Frontera, Sanlúcar de Barrameda and El Puerto de Santa María. It is also produced in smaller centres such as Rota and Chiclana de la Frontera.

0 km — 10
0 miles — 5

Key

▨ Sanlúcar de Barrameda
▨ Jerez de la Frontera
▨ El Puerto de Santa María
— Delimited sherry-producing region

Different Types of Sherry

Three months after pressing, and before the fortification process, all sherry is classified as one of five principal types.

Amontillado is *fino* aged in the barrel. The "dying" flor (yeast) imparts a strong, earthy taste. Some brands are dry, others slightly sweetened.

Fino is by far the favoured style in Andalusia. Dry, fresh, light and crisp, it is excellent as an apéritif or with tapas. It should always be served chilled.

Oloroso (which in Spanish means fragrant) is a full, ruddy-coloured sherry, with a rich, nutty aroma. It is sometimes sweetened.

Manzanilla is similar to *fino*, but comes exclusively from Sanlúcar. Light, dry and delicate, it has a highly distinctive, salty tang.

Cream sherry is a full, dark, rich blend of *oloroso* with Pedro Ximénez grapes. As the sweetest type, it is often drunk as a dessert wine.

How Sherry is Made

Sherry is mixed from two principal grape varieties: Palomino, which produces a drier, more delicate sherry; and Pedro Ximénez, which is made into a fuller, sweeter sherry type.

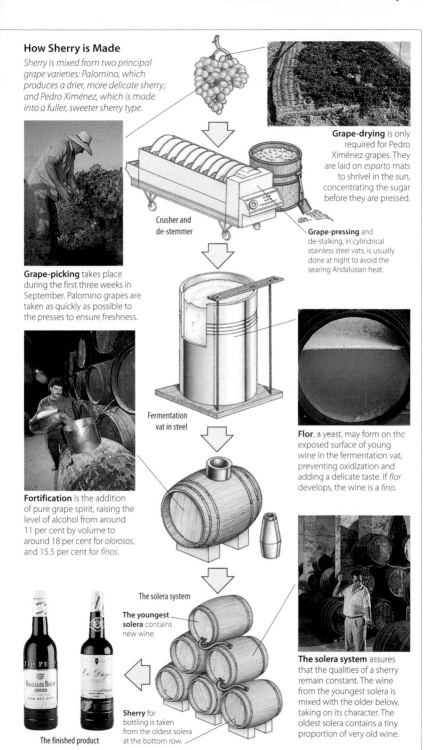

Grape-drying is only required for Pedro Ximénez grapes. They are laid on *esparto* mats to shrivel in the sun, concentrating the sugar before they are pressed.

Crusher and de-stemmer

Grape-picking takes place during the first three weeks in September. Palomino grapes are taken as quickly as possible to the presses to ensure freshness.

Grape-pressing and de-stalking, in cylindrical stainless steel vats, is usually done at night to avoid the searing Andalusian heat.

Fermentation vat in steel

Flor, a yeast, may form on the exposed surface of young wine in the fermentation vat, preventing oxidization and adding a delicate taste. If *flor* develops, the wine is a *fino*.

Fortification is the addition of pure grape spirit, raising the level of alcohol from around 11 per cent by volume to around 18 per cent for *olorosos*, and 15.5 per cent for *finos*.

The solera system

The youngest solera contains new wine.

Sherry for bottling is taken from the oldest solera at the bottom row.

The finished product

The solera system assures that the qualities of a sherry remain constant. The wine from the youngest solera is mixed with the older below, taking on its character. The oldest solera contains a tiny proportion of very old wine.

Beach Life and Leisure in Andalusia

Thanks to its subtropical climate with an average of 300 days' sunshine a year, the coastline of Andalusia – in particular the Costa del Sol – has become one of the most favoured playgrounds for those looking for fun and relaxation. In the 1950s, there was nothing more than a handful of fishing villages *(see p187)*. Now the area attracts several million tourists a year who are well catered for by the vast array of hotels and apartments along the coast. The varied coastline lends itself perfectly to the whole gamut of water sports *(see p246)*, while just inland golf courses have become a major feature of the landscape *(see p246)*. Some of the most popular golf courses are shown on this map, together with a selection of the beaches most worth a visit.

Sunbathing on one of Marbella's beaches, Costa del Sol

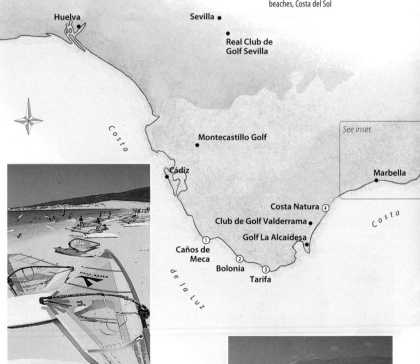

Huelva

Sevilla ●

● Real Club de Golf Sevilla

Costa

● Montecastillo Golf

Cádiz

See inset

Marbella ●

Costa Natura ④

Club de Golf Valderrama ●

Golf La Alcaidesa ●

Costa

Caños de Meca ①

Bolonia ②

Tarifa ③

de la Luz

Costa de la Luz in western Andalusia is a stretch of largely unspoiled beaches, refreshingly free from crowds and tower blocks. Atlantic winds make it a wind- and kitesurfer's paradise.

Costa Tropical is punctuated by pretty coves, ideal for scuba diving. The water is warmer and clearer than on Costa de la Luz, while the sand is coarse and stony.

```
0 kilometres          50
0 miles          25
```

Andalusia's Best Beaches

① **Caños de Meca**
Charming white, sandy beach sheltered by cliffs and sand dunes.

② **Bolonia**
Picturesque beach with Roman ruins close by.

③ **Tarifa**
Sweeping white sands, and winds and waves perfect for skilled windsurfers.

④ **Costa Natura**
Popular nudist beach just outside Estepona.

⑤ **Babaloo Beach**
Trendy spot just off Puerto Banús. Gym and jetskiing.

⑥ **Victor's Beach**
A classic Marbella beach for stylish barbecue parties.

⑦ **Don Carlos**
Perhaps Marbella's best beach, shared by the exclusive Don Carlos beach club.

⑧ **Cabopino/Las Dunas**
Nudist beach and sand dunes beside modern marina. Not too crowded.

⑨ **Rincón de la Victoria**
Nice unspoiled family beach area just east of Málaga.

⑩ **La Herradura**
A stony but picturesque bay west of Almuñécar.

⑪ **Playa de los Genoveses**
One of the unspoilt beaches between Cabo de Gata and the village of San José.

⑫ **Playa Agua Amarga**
Excellent sand beach in secluded fishing hamlet turned exclusive resort.

Costa de Almería is famous for its picturesque fishing villages, and rocky landscapes, which come to life in the breathtaking sunsets. Beaches tend to have escaped overdevelopment, in particular those in the nature reserve of Cabo de Gata, such as San José, here.

Agua Amarga ⑫

Playa de los Genoveses ⑪

Almería ●

La Herradura ⑩

Rincón de la Victoria ⑨

Málaga ●

Costa Tropical

Costa de Almería

del Sol

Costa del Sol

Apart from the crowds of holiday-makers, half a million foreign residents have chosen to live on the Costa del Sol. Complementing the luxury and high life of Marbella are a number of popular beaches and more than 30 of Europe's finest golf courses, including the prestigious Club de Golf Valderrama, host of the 1997 Ryder Cup tournament.

Málaga ●

Club de Campo de Málaga ●

Torremolinos ●
Golf
● Torrequebrado

Club Milas Golf ●
La Cala Golf ●

Club de Golf Las Brisas ●

Club Dama de Noche ●

Guadalmina Golf ●
Monte Mayor
Golf

Marbella
⑥
Victor's
Beach

Golf Rio Real
Marbella Golf
⑦
Don
Carlos

⑤
Babaloo
Beach

⑧
Cabopino and
Las Dunas

Player on the green at the high-profile Marbella Golf

ANDALUSIA THROUGH THE YEAR

Festivals and cultural events fill Andalusia's calendar. Every town and village has an annual *feria* (fair) with stalls, dancing, drinking, fireworks and bullfights. These are held from April to October throughout Andalusia. There are also many *fiestas*, all exuberant occasions when religious devotion mixes with *joie de vivre*. Spring is an ideal time to visit; the countryside is at its most beautiful, the climate is mild and *ferias* and *fiestas* celebrate the

ending of winter. Summer brings heat to the interior and crowds to the *costas*. Autumn is greeted with more *fiestas* and heralds the opening of music and theatre seasons. In winter, jazz, pop and classical concerts can be enjoyed in the cities. The first snow on the Sierra Nevada marks the start of the skiing season. Note that dates for all events, especially *fiestas*, may change from year to year; check with the tourist board *(see p255)*.

Almond trees in blossom on the lush hillsides of Andalusia

Spring

Few parts of the world can match the beauty of spring in Andalusia. After winter rains, the hills and plains are green and lush, and water cascades along riverbeds and irrigation channels. Country roads are a riot of wild flowers; almond blossom covers the hillsides and strawberries are harvested. Popular festivals abound, many of them religious, though often linked with pagan ceremonies marking the end of winter.

March
Cristo de la Expiración *(Friday, nine days before Palm Sunday)*, Orgiva *(see p204)*. One of Andalusia's most ear-splitting *fiestas*; shotguns are fired and rockets, gunpowder and firecrackers are set off.
Semana Santa *(Palm Sunday– Good Friday)*. Seville celebrates

this event spectacularly *(see p42)*, and there are processions in every town and village. On Holy Wednesday in Málaga *(see pp184–5)*, a prisoner is freed from jail and in gratitude joins in one of the processions. This tradition began two centuries ago, when prisoners, braving a plague, carried a holy image through the city's streets. In Baena *(see p151)*, the streets vibrate to the sound of thousands of drums.

April
Fiesta de San Marcos *(25 April)*, Ohanes, Sierra Nevada. Accompanying the image of San Marcos through the streets are young men leading eight bulls. The bulls are persuaded to kneel before the saint.
Feria de Abril *(two weeks after Easter)*, Seville *(see p42)*.
Romería de Nuestra Señora de la Cabeza *(last Sunday in April)*, Andújar *(see p43)*. Major pilgrimage.

May
Día de la Cruz *(first week of May)*, Granada *(see pp194–202)* and Córdoba *(see p42)*.
Feria del Caballo *(first week of May)*, Jerez de la Frontera *(see p166)*. Horse fair.
Festival Internacional de Teatro y Danza *(throughout May)*, Seville. World-class companies perform in Teatro de la Maestranza *(see pp72–3)*.
Festival de los Patios *(second week in May)*, Córdoba *(see p42)*. Patios are on display.
Romería de San Isidro *(15 May)*. *Romerías* are held in many towns, including Nerja *(see p184)*, for San Isidro.
Concurso Nacional de Flamenco *(second week in May; every third year: 2013, 2016)*, Córdoba. National flamenco competition.
Feria de Mayo *(last week of May)*, Córdoba *(see p42)*.
Romería del Rocío *(late May or early June)*, El Rocío *(see p42)*.

Feria del Caballo, held in Jerez de la Frontera in May

Average Daily Hours of Sunshine

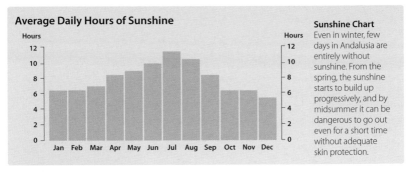

Hours

Jan Feb Mar Apr May Jun Jul Aug Sep Oct Nov Dec

Sunshine Chart
Even in winter, few days in Andalusia are entirely without sunshine. From the spring, the sunshine starts to build up progressively, and by midsummer it can be dangerous to go out even for a short time without adequate skin protection.

Bullrunning during the Lunes de Toro *fiesta* in Grazalema

Summer

During the hot summer months, the *siesta* (afternoon nap) comes into its own. Many people finish work at lunch time and most of the entertainment takes place in the cool of evening. Foreign tourists flocking to the coasts are joined by thousands of Spaniards. Large pop concerts are held in coastal towns.

June

Corpus Christi *(late May or early June)* is commemorated in Granada *(see p43)*. In Seville, the *seises*, young boys dressed in doublet and hose, dance before the cathedral altar. At Zahara, near Ronda, *(see p178)* houses and streets are decked out with greenery.
Noche de San Juan *(23, 24 June)*. The evening of 23 June sees dancing, drinking and singing around bonfires on beaches across Andalusia in honour of St John the Baptist.

Lanjarón *(see p193)* celebrates with a water battle in its streets in the early hours of 24 June.
Romería de los Gitanos *(third Sunday in June)*, Cabra *(see p151)*. A procession made up of thousands of gypsies' heads for a hilltop shrine.
Festival Internacional de Música y Danza *(mid-June–early July)*, Granada *(see pp194–202)*. Performers come to Granada from all over the world. Many events are held in the Alhambra *(see pp198–9)*.

July

Festival de la Guitarra *(first two weeks of July)*, Córdoba *(see pp144–50)*. Guitar festival presenting all musical styles, from classical to flamenco.
Fiesta de la Virgen del Carmen *(around 15 July)*. This Virgin is honoured by many coastal communities by regattas and other sporting events. In the evening, the Virgin's image is put aboard a fishing boat, which parades across the sea

accompanied by fireworks.
Lunes de Toro *(Around 17 July)*, Grazalema *(see p178)*. Bullrunning daily for a week.

August

Fiestas Colombinas *(Around 3 August)*, Huelva *(see p131)*. A Latin American dance and music festival in celebration of Columbus's voyage. It is dedicated to a different Latin American country every year.
Fiestas Patronales de Santa María de la Palma *(15 August)*, Algeciras *(see p174)*. A saint's image is rescued from the sea. It is cleaned, before being carried in a procession of boats to a beach. Afterwards it is returned to the sea.
Feria de Málaga *(two weeks in mid-August, see p43)*.
Fiestas de la Exaltación del Río Guadalquivir *(third week in August)*, Sanlúcar de Barrameda *(see p166)*. Horse races are held on the beach.
Feria de Almería *(last week in August, see p43)*.

The Costa del Sol – popular with tourists and with the Spanish

Average Monthly Rainfall

Rainfall Chart
Rain can be heavy in early spring, but summer is almost dry. Humidity and rainfall increase through September until October. In 2008, a severe drought has fortunately been followed by several years of above-average rainfall.

Chirimoya harvest on the subtropical coast at Almuñécar *(see p193)*

Autumn

This is a most pleasant time to visit Andalusia. The weather is settled, but without the searing summer heat, and the holiday crowds are easing. Grape harvests are in full swing and being celebrated in towns and villages. The theatres start to open for drama and concerts. Along the subtropical coast of the Mediterranean, sweet potatoes and *chirimoyas* (custard apples) are harvested. Inland, mushrooms, freshly picked, feature on menus.

Moros y Cristianos
fiesta, Válor *(see p205)*

September

Feria de Pedro Romero *(first two weeks in September)*, Ronda *(see pp180–81)*. This *fiesta* celebrates the founder of modern bullfighting *(see p181)*. All participants in the Corrida Goyesca wear costumes reflecting the era of Goya, a great bullfighting fan.

Fiestas Patronales de la Virgen de la Piedad *(6 September)*, Baza *(see p204)*. A bizarre *fiesta* in which a figure known as Cascamorras comes from neighbouring Guadix to try to steal a statue of the Virgin. Youths covered with oil taunt him and chase him out of town. He is sent back to Guadix empty-handed, where he receives further punishment for his failure.

Moros y Cristianos *(15 September)*, Válor *(see p205)*. Re-creation of the Reconquest battles.

Fiesta de la Vendimia *(second or third week of September)*, La Palma del Condado *(see p133)*. A lively *fiesta* to bless the first grape juice.

Romería de San Miguel *(last Sunday of September)*, Torremolinos *(see p186)*. One of the largest *romerías* in Andalusia.

Bienal de Arte Flamenco *(last two weeks of September, even-numbered years)*, Seville.

A fabulous opportunity for enthusiasts to see world-class flamenco artists, such as Cristina Hoyos.

Sevilla en Otoño *(September–November)*, Seville. A variety of cultural events, including dance, theatre and exhibitions, and, in addition, sports.

October

Fiesta del Vino *(5–9 October)*, Cadiar *(see p205)*. A feature of this *fiesta* in the mountains of the Alpujarras is the construction of a fountain, which gushes forth wine.

Festival Iberoamericano de Teatro *(last two weeks of October)*, Cádiz *(see pp168–9)*. Latin American theatre festival.

November

Festival Internacional de Jazz *(early November)*, Granada *(see pp194–202)* and Seville.

Festival de Cine Ibero-americano *(last two weeks of November)*, Huelva *(see p131)*. Latin American film festival.

Oil-covered youths chasing Cascamorras in Baza

Average Monthly Temperature

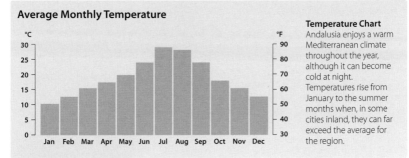

Temperature Chart
Andalusia enjoys a warm Mediterranean climate throughout the year, although it can become cold at night. Temperatures rise from January to the summer months when, in some cities inland, they can far exceed the average for the region.

Medieval music at the Fiesta de los Verdiales in Málaga

Winter

At this time of year the ripe olives are harvested in abundance. The restaurants serve venison, wild boar and partridge dishes as this is the hunting season. Skiers flock to the Sierra Nevada. Though winter is the rainy season and it is cold at night, many days have sunshine. By February, almond blossom and strawberries begin to appear again.

December

La Inmaculada Concepción *(8 December)*, Seville. The *tuna*, groups of wandering minstrels, take to the streets around the Plaza del Triunfo and Santa Cruz *(see pp76–7)*.
Fiesta de los Verdiales *(28 December)*, Málaga *(see pp184–5)*. On Spain's equivalent of April Fool's Day, *El Día de los Santos Inocentes*, thousands of town and country folk gather at the Venta del Túnel, on the outskirts of Málaga. They come to hear

pandas (bands) compete in performing *verdiales*, wild, primitive music from Moorish times, played on medieval instruments.

January

Día de la Toma *(2 January)*, Granada *(see pp194–202)*. This *fiesta* recalls the ousting of the Moors in 1492 *(see p52)*. Queen Isabel's crown and King Fernando's sword are paraded through the streets, and the royal standard flies from the balcony of the Ayuntamiento.
Día de Reyes *(6 January)*. On the evening before this public holiday, the Three Kings arrive, splendidly dressed, to parade through town centres across Andalusia. They ride in small carriages that are drawn either by tractors or horses and, during processions, throw sweets to the excited children.
Certamen Internacional de Guitarra Clásica Andrés Segovia *(first week of January)*, Almuñécar *(see p193)*. Classical guitar competition in homage to the master.

February

Los Carnavales *(second or third week in February)*. Carnival is widely celebrated, most spectacularly in Cádiz *(see p43)* and Isla Cristina *(see p130)*.
Festival de Música Antigua *(February and March)*, Seville. Early music is performed on historic instruments.
Jerez Annual Flamenco Festival *(end February/early March)*, Jerez *(see p166)*. Flamenco performances and workshops.

Public Holidays

New Year's Day (1 Jan)
Epiphany (6 Jan)
Día de Andalucía (28 Feb)
Easter Thursday and Good Friday (variable)
Labour Day (1 May)
Assumption (15 Aug)
National Day (12 Oct)
All Saints' Day (1 Nov)
Constitution Day (6 Dec)
Immaculate Conception (8 Dec)
Christmas Day (25 Dec)

Ski station on the snow-covered slopes of the Sierra Nevada *(see p203)*

Fiestas in Andalusia

There is nothing quite like a Spanish *fiesta* or *feria,* and those of Andalusia are among the most colourful. *Fiestas* may commemorate an historic event or a change of season. More often they mark a religious occasion; Semana Santa (Holy Week), for example, is celebrated all over Andalusia. Feasting, dancing, singing, drinking – often right around the clock – are all integral to a *fiesta*. At a *feria* there will often be a decorated fairground, revellers dressed in traditional flamenco attire, and processions of horses and carriages. Throughout Andalusia you will also come across *romerías,* in which processions carry holy effigies through the countryside to a shrine.

Horsemen and women in their finery at Seville's Feria de Abril

Seville

Semana Santa, or Holy Week (Palm Sunday–Good Friday) is celebrated in flamboyant style in Seville. More than 100 *pasos* (floats bearing religious effigies) are carried through the streets of the city. They are accompanied by *nazarenos,* members of some 50 brotherhoods dating back to the 13th century, wearing long robes and tall pointed hoods. As the processions sway through the streets, appointed singers burst into *saetas,* shafts of song in praise of the Virgin. Emotion reaches fever-pitch in the early hours of Good Friday, when the Virgen de La Macarena is paraded, accompanied by 2,500 *nazarenos (see p93).*

During their Feria de Abril, the spring fair held around two weeks after Easter, the *sevillanos* go on a spree for a week. Daily, from about 1pm, elegant

horsemen and women wearing brightly coloured flamenco dresses show off their finery in a parade known as the *Paseo de Caballos*. At night, *casetas* (temporary marquees) throb to *sevillanas,* a popular dance that has a flamenco accent (out of a thousand *casetas,* about a quarter are open to the public). There are bullfights in the Maestranza bullring *(see p72).*

Huelva and Sevilla

One of Spain's most popular *fiestas,* the Romería del Rocío, is held during Pentecost. More than 70 brotherhoods trek to the shrine of El Rocío *(see p133)* amid Las Marismas, the marshlands at the mouth of the Guadalquivir. They are joined by pilgrims travelling on horseback, on foot or by car. All pay homage to the Virgen del Rocío, also called the White Dove or the Queen of the Marshes. There is drinking and dancing for several days and nights, until the early hours of Monday morning when the Virgin is brought out of the shrine. Young men from the nearby town of Almonte carry her through the crowds for up to 12 hours, fighting off anybody who tries to get near.

Córdoba and Jaén

May is a nonstop *fiesta* in Córdoba *(see pp144–50).* The Día de la Cruz – the Day of the Cross – is held on the first three days of the month. Religious brotherhoods and neighbourhoods compete with each other to create the most colourful, flower-decorated crosses, which are set up in squares and at street corners. Following this is the Festival de los Patios (around 5–15 May), when the

Pilgrims taking part in the Romería del Rocío in Huelva province

patios of the city's old quarter are thrown open for visitors to come and admire. Crowds go from patio to patio, at each one launching into flamenco dance or song.

During the last week of May, Córdoba holds its lively *feria*. It is as colourful as the Feria de Abril in Seville, but more accessible to strangers. This festival, with roots in Roman times, welcomes the spring.

The Romería de Nuestra Señora de la Cabeza takes place on the last Sunday in April at the Santuario de la Virgen de la Cabeza *(see p155)*, a remote shrine in the Sierra Morena. Over 250,000 people attend, some making the pilgrimage on foot or on horseback. At the site, flames shoot up day and night from a torch fed by candles lit by the faithful. Then the Virgin, known as La Morenita, is borne through the crowd to cries of *¡Guapa, guapa!* (beautiful, beautiful!).

Penitents at the Romería de Nuestra Señora de la Cabeza in April

Cádiz and Málaga

For two weeks in February, Los Carnavales (Carnival) is celebrated with more flair and abandon in Cádiz *(see p168)* than anywhere else in Andalusia. Some say it rivals the carnival in Río de Janeiro. Groups of singers practise for months in advance, composing outrageous satirical ditties that poke fun at anything from the current fashions to celebrities, especially politicians. Often sumptuously costumed, they perform their songs in the Falla Theatre in a competition lasting for several days. Then they

Costumed revellers at the February Carnival (Los Carnavales) in Cádiz

take part in a parade. The whole city puts on fancy dress and crowds of revellers throng the narrow streets of the city's old quarter, shouting, singing, dancing and drinking.

The Feria de Málaga in the middle of August each year, celebrates the capture of the city from the Moors by the Catholic Monarchs *(see p52)*. Eager to outdo Seville, Málaga *(see pp184–5)* puts on a fine show. The residents, famous for their ability to organize a good party, put on traditional costume and parade, along with decorated carriages and elegant horsefolk, through the fairground. The entertainment goes on for a week nonstop, and top bullfighters perform at the city's bullring *(see p185)* in La Malagueta.

Granada and Almería

Corpus Christi, held in late May or early June, is one of the major events in Granada *(see pp194–202)*. On the day before Corpus a procession of bigheads (costumed caricatures with outsized heads) and giants parades through the city, led by the *tarasca*, a woman on a huge dragon. The next day, the *custodia*, or monstrance, is carried from the cathedral all through the streets. For a week afterwards there is bullfighting, flamenco and general revelry.

The *feria* in Almería *(see pp206–7)*, which is held at the end of August, is in honour of the Virgen del Mar. There are funfairs, processions, sporting events and bullfights. The city's Virgin dates back to 1502, when a coastguard on the lookout for Berber pirates found an image of the Virgin washed up on a beach.

Feria de Málaga, celebrating the capture of the city from the Moors

THE HISTORY OF SEVILLE AND ANDALUSIA

Andalusia's early history is an extraordinary tale of ancient cities – Cádiz *(see pp168–9)*, founded in 1100 BC, is the oldest city in Europe – and waves of settlers, each one contributing new ideas and customs.

Hominids first inhabited the region about one million years ago. *Homo sapiens* had arrived by 25,000 BC, and by the Iron Age a strong Iberian culture had emerged. Later, trade and cultural links developed first with the Phoenicians, then with the Greeks and Carthaginians. These ties and the abundance of natural raw materials, such as iron, gold and copper ore, made this part of Iberia one of the wealthiest areas of the Mediterranean.

Attracted by its riches, the Romans made their first forays into southern Spain in 206 BC. They ruled for almost 700 years. Their place was eventually taken by the Visigoths as the Western Roman Empire crumbled in the 5th century AD. The Moors, who followed, flourished first in Córdoba, then in Seville, and, towards the end of their almost 800-year rule, in the Nasrid kingdom of Granada.

After the fall of Granada to the Christians in 1492, Spain entered an era of expansion and prosperity. The conquest of the New World made Seville one of the most affluent cities in Europe, but much of this wealth was squandered on wars by the Habsburg kings. By the 18th century, Spain had fallen into economic decline; in the 19th and early 20th centuries poverty led to political conflict and, ultimately, to the Civil War.

The years after the Civil War saw continuing poverty, though mass tourism in the 1960s and 1970s did much to ease this. With Franco's death and Spain's entry into the EU, the Spanish began to enjoy increasing prosperity and democratic freedoms. Andalusia still lagged behind, however. The Expo '92 was part of government policy to foster its economic growth.

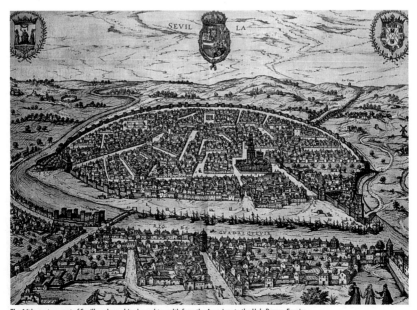

The 16th-century port of Seville, where ships brought wealth from the Americas to the Holy Roman Empire

◀ 18th-century lithograph of the Puerta de la Justicia in the Alhambra *(see pp198–9)*

Early Andalusia

Neanderthals inhabited Gibraltar around 50,000 BC. *Homo sapiens* arrived 25,000 years later and Neolithic tribespeople from Africa settled in Spain from about 7000 BC. By the time the Phoenicians arrived to trade in precious metals, they were met by a sophisticated Iberian culture. They later established trading links with the semi-mythical Iberian kingdom of Tartessus. The Greeks, already settled in northeastern Spain, started to colonize the south from about 600 BC. Meanwhile, Celts from the north had mixed with Iberians. This culture, influenced by the Greeks, created beautiful works of art. The Carthaginians arrived in about 500 BC and, according to legend, destroyed Tartessus.

Areas of influence

☐ Greek ■ Phoenician

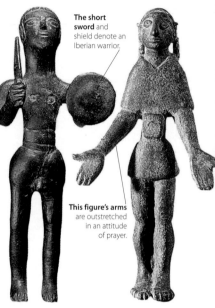

The short sword and shield denote an Iberian warrior.

This figure's arms are outstretched in an attitude of prayer.

Burial Sight at Los Millares
Los Millares (*see p207*) was the site of an early metal-working civilization in about 2300 BC. Up to 100 corpses were buried on a single site; the huge burial chambers were covered with earth to make a gently sloping mound.

Cave Paintings
From approximately 25,000 BC, people painted caves in Andalusia. They portrayed fish, land animals, people, weapons and other subjects with a skilful naturalism.

Iberian bronze figures

These bronze figurines from the 5th–4th centuries BC are votive offerings to the gods. They were discovered in a burial ground near Despeñaperros in the province of Jaén. The Romans regarded the Iberians who crafted them as exceptionally noble.

1,000,000–750,000 BC Stones worked by hominids at Puerto de Santa María, Cádiz		25,000–18,000 BC *Homo sapiens* make cave paintings and rock engravings	4000 BC Burials at Cueva de los Murciélagos in Granada leave Neolithic remains; esparto sandals, religious offerings and other items
Stone tool			4500 BC Farmers begin to grow crops and breed cattle
1,000,000 BC	50,000 BC	10,000 BC 8000 BC	6000 BC 4000 BC
50,000 BC Neanderthals inhabit Gibraltar		7000 BC Neolithic colonists arrive, perhaps from North Africa. Farming begins on Iberian Peninsula	*Neolithic ochre pot* 

Goddess Astarte

The Phoenicians founded Cádiz in about 1100 BC. They brought their own goddess, Astarte, who became popular across Andalusia as the region absorbed eastern influences.

The headdress shows this is a votaress, devoted to her god.

The hand of this priestess is raised in benediction.

Greek Urn

The ancient Greeks imported many artifacts from home; their style of decoration had a strong influence on Iberian art.

Where to see Early Andalusia

Cave paintings can be seen in the Cueva de la Pileta near Ronda la Vieja (p179). At Antequera (p183) there are Bronze Age dolmens dating from 2500 BC; at Los Millares (p207) there are burial chambers dating from the Copper Age. The replicas of the famous Tartessian Carambolo Treasure are in the Museo Arqueológico in Seville (p101) and Iberian stone carvings from Porcuna are exhibited in Jaén (p153).

The Toro de Porcuna (500–450 BC) was found at Porcuna near Jaén with other sculptures.

Dama de Baza

This female figure, dating from around 500–400 BC, may represent an Iberian goddess. It is one of several such figures found in southern Spain.

Carambolo Treasure

Phoenician in style, this treasure is from Tartessus. Although many artifacts have been uncovered, the site of this kingdom has yet to be found.

2300 BC Beginning of the Bronze Age; dolmen-style burials take place at Los Millares (see p207)

800–700 BC Kingdom of Tartessus at its height, influenced by the Phoenicians

Tartessian buckle

241 BC First Punic War between Carthage and Rome

219 BC Carthaginians take Sagunto, eastern Spain

2000 BC	1000 BC	800 BC	600 BC	400 BC

1100 BC Foundation of Cádiz by the Phoenicians

800 BC Celts from northern Europe move southwards

600 BC Greek colonists settle on the coasts of Andalusia

500 BC Carthage colonizes southern Spain

Greek helmet

Romans and Visigoths

The Romans came to Spain during a war against Carthage in 206 BC. Attracted by the wealth of the peninsula, they stayed for 700 years; in 200 years they conquered Spain and split it into provinces. Baetica, with Corduba (Córdoba) as its capital, corresponded roughly to what is now Andalusia. Cities were built, while feudal lords created vast estates, exporting olive oil and wheat to Rome. Baetica became one of the wealthiest of Rome's provinces with a rich, Ibero-Roman culture. The Visigoths who followed continued to assert Roman values until the Moors arrived in AD 711.

Roman Territory AD 100
- Roman Roman Baetica
- Other provinces

Hadrian
Emperors Hadrian and Trajan were born in Baetica. A great many politicians, writers and philosophers from the province also moved to Rome, some enjoying great fortune.

Private villas — Paved streets — Temple

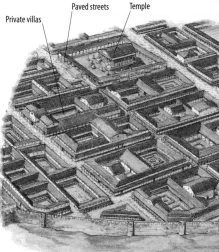

Roman Mosaics in Andalusia
Private houses, temples and public buildings all had mosaic floors. Many themes, from the gods to hunting, were represented.

Italica reconstructed
Scipio Africanus founded Itálica (see p136) in 206 BC after his defeat of the Carthaginians. The city reached its height in the 2nd and 3rd centuries AD and was the birthplace of the emperors Hadrian and Trajan. Unlike Córdoba, it was not built over in post-Roman times and today Itálica is a superbly preserved example of a Roman city.

206 BC Scipio Africanus gains victory against the Carthaginians at Alcalá del Río; Itálica is founded

55 BC Birth of Seneca the Elder in Córdoba

AD 27 Andalusia is named Baetica

Suicide of Seneca

65 Suicide of Seneca the Younger after plotting against Nero

117 Hadrian is crowned Emperor

200 BC	100 BC	AD 1	100	200

200 BC Romans conquer southern Spain and reach Cádiz

61 BC Julius Caesar is governor of Hispania Ulterior (Spain)

Julius Caesar

98–117 Trajan, from Itálica, is emperor. Spanish senators enjoy influence in Rome

69–79 Emperor Vespasian grants Roman status to all towns in Hispania

Harvesting Olives
Carved on a Roman sarcophagus, this scene shows an olive harvest. Olives were grown extensively in the Guadalquivir valley from Córdoba to Seville. Thousands of amphoras of olive oil were shipped to Rome.

The amphitheatre was a standard feature of Roman towns. The one in Itálica is said to have been the third largest in the Roman Empire.

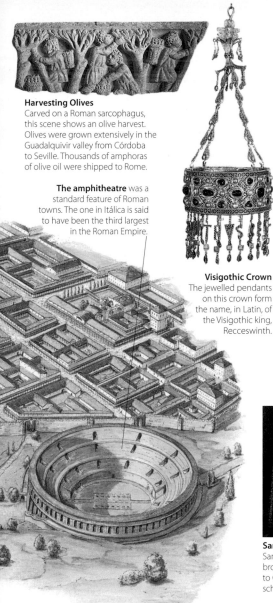

Visigothic Crown
The jewelled pendants on this crown form the name, in Latin, of the Visigothic king, Recceswinth.

Where to see Roman and Visigothic Andalusia

Extensive Roman remains can be seen at the sights of Itálica (see p136), Carmona (p136) and Ronda la Vieja (p179); in Málaga there is a partially excavated Roman amphitheatre, and Roman columns can be seen at the Alameda de Hércules in Seville (p92). The Museo Arqueológico in Seville (p101), Córdoba (p147) and Cádiz (p168) all have Roman artifacts on display. Visigothic pillars and capitals can be viewed in the Mezquita in Córdoba (pp148–9).

The Roman ruins at Itálica (see p136) are situated 9 km (5.5 miles) north of Seville.

San Isidoro and San Leandro
San Isidoro (560–635) of Seville, like his brother, San Leandro, converted Visigoths to Christianity; he also wrote a great scholastic work, *Etymologies*.

415 Visigoths arrive in Spain from northern Europe

446 Tarraconensis in north still Roman; Rome attempts to win back rest of Spain

Illuminated cover of Etymologies by San Isidoro

632 Death of Prophet Muhammad

| 300 | 400 | 500 | 600 |

409 Vandals sack Tarraconensis (Tarragona)

Theodosius

476 Visigoths control whole of Spain

589 Third Council of Toledo in central Spain. Visigothic King Reccared converted from Arianism to Catholicism

635 Death of San Isidoro of Seville

The Moorish Conquest

Called in to resolve a quarrel among the Visigoths, the Moors first arrived in 710. They returned in 711 to conquer Spain; within 10 years, the north alone remained under Christian control. The Moors named their newly conquered territories Al Andalus and in 929 they established an independent caliphate. Córdoba, its capital, was the greatest city in Europe, a centre for art, science and literature. In the 11th century the caliphate collapsed into 30 feuding *taifas* (party states). Almoravids, tribesmen from North Africa, invaded the region in 1086, and in the 12th century Almohads from Morocco ousted the Almoravids and designated Seville their capital.

Moorish Domain AD 800
☐ Al Andalus

Abd al Rahman III receives the Byzantine envoy.

Apocalypse
An 11th-century account of an 8th-century text, *Commentaries on the Apocalypse* by Beato de Liébana, this illustration shows Christians going to war.

Bronze Stag
This 10th-century caliphal-style bronze is from Medina Azahara.

The Court of Abd al Rahman III

Abd al Rahman III began his palace of Medina Azahara (see p142) in 936. This 19th-century painting by Dionisio Baixeres shows a Byzantine envoy presenting the caliph with the works of the Greek scientist Dioscorides. The Moors of Córdoba possessed much knowledge of the ancient world, which was later transmitted to Europe. The Medina was sacked by Berber mercenaries in 1010.

Visigothic king and Moorish chief

756 Abd al Rahman I reaches Spain and asserts himself as ruler, declaring an independent emirate based around Córdoba

936 Construction of Medina Azahara begins *(see pp142–3)*

929 Abd al Rahman III proclaims caliphate in Córdoba

700	800	900

711 Invasion under Tariq ben Ziyad

710 First Moorish intervention in Spain

785 Construction of the Mezquita *(see pp148–9)* begins at Córdoba

822–52 Rule of Abd al Rahman II

Coin from the reign of Abd al Rahman III

912–61 Rule of Abd al Rahman III

961–76 Al Hakam II builds great library at Medina Azahara; expands Mezquita

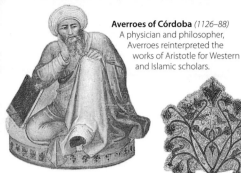

Averroes of Córdoba *(1126–88)*
A physician and philosopher, Averroes reinterpreted the works of Aristotle for Western and Islamic scholars.

Horseshoe arches were a major feature here, as in the Mezquita *(see pp148–9)* at Córdoba.

Mozarabic Bible
Moorish society integrated Jews and Mozarabs (Christians living an Islamic lifestyle). Illustrations like this one, from a 10th-century Bible, are in a Moorish decorative style.

Clerics prepare the manuscript to be given to Abd al Rahman III.

Cufic Script
Islamic artists, forbidden to use representations of the human figure, made ample use of calligraphy for decoration.

Where to see Moorish Andalusia

The Mezquita in Córdoba *(see pp148–9)* and the ruins of the palace at Medina Azahara *(p142)* are the most complete remnants of Spain's Moorish caliphate. Artifacts found at Medina Azahara can be seen in the Museo Arqueológico in Córdoba *(see p147)*. The Alcazaba at Almería *(see p206)* dates from the 10th century, when this city was still part of the caliphate, while the Alcazaba at Málaga *(see p185)* was built during the ensuing Taifa period. The Torre del Oro *(see p73)* and La Giralda *(see p82)* in Seville are both Almohad structures.

The Alcazaba in Almería *(p206)*, dating from the 10th century, overlooks the old town.

Irrigation in Al Andalus
The water wheel was vital to irrigation, which the Moors used to grow newly imported crops such as rice and oranges.

Al Mansur

1012 *Taifas* emerge as splinter Moorish states

1031 Caliphate ends

1086 Almoravids invade

1120 Almoravid power starts to wane

1126 Birth of Averroes, Arab philosopher

1147 Almohads arrive in Seville; build Giralda and Torre del Oro

1000	1100	1200

976–1002 Al Mansur, military dictator, comes to power

1085 Fall of Toledo in north to Christians decisively loosens Moorish control over central Spain

1010 Medina Azahara sacked by Berbers

1135 Maimónides, Jewish philosopher, born in Córdoba

1175–1200 Height of Almohad power. Previously lost territory won back from Christians

Maimónides

The Reconquest

The war between Moors and Christians, which started in northern Spain, arrived in Andalusia with a landmark Christian victory at Las Navas de Tolosa in 1212; Seville and Córdoba fell soon afterwards. By the late 13th century only the Nasrid kingdom of Granada remained under Moorish control. Meanwhile, Christian monarchs such as Alfonso X and Pedro I employed Mudéjar *(see p28)* craftsmen to build churches and palaces in the reconquered territories – Mudéjar literally means "those permitted to stay". Granada eventually fell in 1492 to Fernando and Isabel of Aragón and Castilla, otherwise known as the Catholic Monarchs.

Moorish Domain in 1350
☐ Nasrid kingdom

The Catholic Monarchs enter Granada; Fernando and Isabel were awarded this title for their services to Christendom.

Boabdil

Cantigas of Alfonso X
Alfonso X, who won back much of Andalusia from the Moors, was an enlightened Christian monarch. His illuminated *Cantigas* are a vivid account of life in Reconquest Spain.

The Fall of Granada
This relief by Felipe de Vigarney (1480 – c.1542), in Granada's Capilla Real (see p194), shows Boabdil, the last Moorish ruler, surrendering the city in 1492. Trying to establish a Christian realm, the Catholic Monarchs converted the Moors by force and expelled the Jews. The same year, Columbus got funds for his voyage to America (see p131).

Almohad Banner
This richly woven tapestry is widely believed to be the banner captured from the Moors by the Christians at the battle of Las Navas de Tolosa.

1226 Fernando III takes Baeza

1236 Fernando III conquers Córdoba

1252–84 Alfonso X reconquers much of Andalusia. Toledo Translators' School in the north continues to translate important works of Moorish literature

Pedro I of Castilla

1333 Moors add tower to the 8th-century Keep *(see p176)* on Gibraltar

1220

1260

1300

1340

1212 Almohad *(see p46)* power broken by Christian victory at Las Navas de Tolosa

1248 Fernando III takes Seville

1238 Nasrid dynasty established in Granada. Alhambra *(see p198)* begins

1350–69 Reign of Pedro I of Castilla, who rebuilds Seville Alcázar in Mudéjar style. His lack of Spanish patriotism provokes civil war against Henry II of Trastámara

Alfonso X

Chivalry
The Moors lived by chivalric codes –
this jousting scene is in the Sala de
los Reyes in the Alhambra *(see p198)*.

Nasrid warriors

Crown
This Mudéjar-style crown,
bearing the coats of
arms of Castilla and León,
is made of silver, ivory
and coral.

Astrolabe
As this 15th-century
navigation tool shows,
the Moors had great
technical expertise.

Boabdil's Demise
Legend has it that Boabdil
wept as he left Granada.
He moved to Laujar de
Andarax *(see p203)* until
1493, then later to Africa.

Where to see Reconquest Andalusia

Many of the Reconquest
buildings in Andalusia are
Mudéjar in style *(see p28)*. The
most notable are the Palacio
Pedro I in the Real Alcázar
(p87) and parts of the Casa de
Pilatos *(p81)*, both in Seville.
Christian churches built in
Andalusia during the 13th, 14th
and 15th centuries are also either
completely Mudéjar in style or
have Mudéjar features such as a
minaret-like bell tower or portal;
as, for example, the Iglesia de San
Marcos *(p94)* in Seville. During this
period the Nasrids of Granada
built the most outstanding
example of Moorish architecture
in Spain, the Alhambra and
Generalife *(pp198–202)*. Seville
Cathedral *(pp82–3)* was
constructed in the 15th century
as a high Gothic assertion of the
Catholic faith.

The Palacio Pedro I *(see p87)* in
Seville is considered to be the
most complete example of
Mudéjar architecture in Spain.

1369 Henry II of Trastámara
personally kills Pedro I; lays seeds
of monolithic Castilian regime

*La Pinta, one of
Columbus's ships*

1492 Columbus
sails to America

1492 Fall of Granada to
the Catholic Monarchs

| 1380 | 1420 | 1460 |

1469 Marriage of Fernando of
Aragón to Isabel of Castilla

1474 Isabel proclaimed queen in Segovia

1479 Fernando becomes king of
Aragón; Castilla and Aragón united

*Forced baptism
of the Moors*

Seville's Golden Age

The 16th century saw the rise of a monolithic Spanish state, led by the Catholic Monarchs. Heretics were persecuted and the remaining Moors treated so unjustly that they often rebelled. In 1503 Seville was granted a monopoly on trade with the New World and Spain entrusted with "converting" the Indians by the pope. In 1516 the Habsburg Carlos I came to the throne, later to be elected Holy Roman Emperor; Spain became the most powerful nation in Europe. Constant war, however, consumed the wealth that its main port, Seville, generated. By the 1680s the Guadalquivir had silted up, trade had passed to Cádiz and Seville declined.

Spanish Empire in 1700
Spanish territories

La Giralda *(see p82)*, once an Almohad minaret, is now the belfry of Seville's cathedral.

Carlos I *(1516–56)*
Carlos I of Spain was made Holy Roman Emperor Carlos V in 1521. His election enabled the Holy Roman Empire to gain access to the immense wealth that Spain, Seville in particular, generated at this time.

Map of Central America
Within 30 years of Columbus's first voyage, the distant lands and seas of Central America had become familiar territory to Spanish navigators.

Seville in the 16th Century

This painting by Alonso Sánchez Coello (1531–88) shows Seville at its height. With the return of treasure fleets from the New World, astonishing wealth poured into the city and it became one of the richest ports in Europe. The population grew, religious buildings proliferated and artistic life found new vigour. Despite the prosperity of the city, poverty, crime and sickness were endemic.

1502 Moors rebel in Las Alpujarras *(see pp204–5)*; they are baptized or expelled by the Inquisition

1516 Death of Fernando

Seville Inquisition banner

1519 Hernán Cortés conquers Mexico

1559 Inquisition persecutes Protestants in Seville

1588 Spanish Armada fails in attack on England

1587 Cádiz raided by Drake

1580 Seville becomes largest city in Spain

1500   **1525**   **1550**   **1575**

1516–56 Reign of Carlos I, later Holy Roman Emperor

1506 Death of Isabel

1532 Pizarro conquers Peru

1519 Magellan sails from Sanlúcar de Barrameda on first circumnavigation of the world

1556–98 Reign of Felipe II

1558 Second Moorish rebellion in Las Alpujarras

Ferdinand Magellan (1480–1521)

Inquisition
Fears of heresy laid the ground for the Spanish Inquisition to be set up in the 15th century. In the 16th century autos-da-fé (trials of faith) were held in Seville in the Plaza de San Francisco (see p78).

Unloading and loading took place virtually in the heart of the city.

Velázquez
Born in Seville in 1599, Diego Velázquez painted his earliest works in the city, but later became a court painter in Madrid. This crucifix is a detail of a painting he made at the behest of Felipe IV.

Ships from other parts of Europe brought goods to the city; this merchandise would be traded later in the New World.

The Last Moors
The last Moors were expelled in 1609; this destroyed southern Spain's agriculture, which had taken over 700 years to develop.

Where to see the Golden Age in Andalusia

The Isabelline style (see p28), lasting testament to nationalistic fervour of the early 16th century, can be seen in the Capilla Real (p194) in Granada and the Palacio de Jabalquinto in Baeza (pp156–7). Baeza and Úbeda (pp158–9) both prospered during the Renaissance in Spain and contain some of the best architecture of this period in Andalusia. The Plateresque (p29) façade of the Ayuntamiento (pp78–9) in Seville is a good example of the style, and the Palacio Carlos V (p195) in Granada is the best example of Classical Renaissance architecture in Spain. The Archivo de Indias (pp84–5) was built according to the principles of Herreran style (p29). The Hospital de la Caridad (p73) is a fine 17th-century Baroque building.

The Capilla Real (see p194) in Granada was built to house the bodies of the Catholic Monarchs, Fernando and Isabel.

1598–1621 Reign of Felipe III

1608 Cervantes, active in Madrid and Seville, publishes *Don Quixote*

1609 Expulsion of Moors by Felipe III

Original edition of Don Quixote

1649 Plague in Seville kills one in three

1600	1625	1650	1675

1599 Velázquez born in Seville

1596 Sack of Cádiz by the English fleet

1617 Murillo born in Seville

1630 Madrid becomes Spain's largest city. Zurbarán moves to Seville

1665–1700 Carlos II, last of the Spanish Habsburgs

Young beggar by Murillo (1617–82)

Bourbon Kings

The 13-year War of the Spanish Succession saw Bourbons on the throne in place of the Habsburgs and, under the Treaty of Utrecht, the loss of Gibraltar to the British *(see pp176–7)*. Later, ties with France dragged Spain into the Napoleonic Wars: following the Battle of Trafalgar, the Spanish king Carlos IV abdicated and Napoleon Bonaparte placed his brother Joseph on the Spanish throne. The Peninsular War ensued and, with British help, the French were driven out of Spain. After the Bourbon restoration, Spain, weakened by further strife, began to lose her colonies. Andalusia became one of Spain's poorest regions.

Spain in Europe (1812)
- Napoleonic dependencies
- Napoleonic rule

Romantic Andalusia
Andalusia's Moorish legacy helped to establish it as a land of beauty and myth, making it popular with travellers of the Romantic era.

The Constitution is proclaimed to the people of Cádiz.

Carlos III
A Bourbon monarch of the Enlightenment and an innovator in matters of society and science, Carlos III tried to establish colonies of farm workers in the sparsely populated sierra Morena.

The 1812 Constitution

During the Peninsular War, Spain's Parliament met in Cádiz, and in 1812 produced an advanced liberal constitution. However, after the Bourbon restoration in 1814, Fernando VII banned all liberal activity. Ironically, during the First Carlist War, Fernando's daughter, Isabel II, contesting her right to the throne against her uncle Don Carlos, turned to the liberals for support.

1701 Felipe V of Bourbon begins his reign

1717 American trade moves to Cádiz

1726 Spain tries to retake Gibraltar

1779–83 Great Siege of Gibraltar

1700

1725

1750

1775

1701–13 War of the Spanish Succession

1713 Treaty of Utrecht; Gibraltar ceded to Britain

1724 Felipe V abdicates but is reinstated

1746–59 Reign of Fernando VI

1759–88 Carlos III

1771 Royal Tobacco Factory in Seville is completed

1788–1808 Carlos IV

Battle of Bailén
In 1808, at Bailén, a Spanish army comprising local militias beat an experienced French army, taking 22,000 prisoners.

Battle of Trafalgar
In 1805, the Spanish, allied at the time to Napoleon, lost their fleet to the British admiral, Nelson.

Support for the constitution came from a wide section of society, including women.

Where to see Bourbon Andalusia

Eighteenth-century Baroque architecture can be seen all over Andalusia. The prime examples in Seville are the former Royal Tobacco Factory, now the city's Universidad (see pp100–101), and the Plaza de Toros de la Maestranza (p72). Osuna (p137), Écija (p137) and Priego de Córdoba (p154) all have fine examples of the style. The lower levels of Cádiz Cathedral (p168) are the most complete example of a Baroque church found in Spain. The Puente Isabel II (p107) is a fine example of 19th-century *arquitectura de hierro* (iron architecture).

The Puente Isabel II is an example of the architecture of Andalusia's "industrial" age.

Washington Irving
In *Tales of the Alhambra (1832)* the American diplomat Washington Irving perpetuated a highly romanticized view of Andalusia.

Seville's Tobacco Factory
Carmen (1845), by Prosper Mérimée (see p100), was inspired by the women – more than 3,000 of them – who worked in the tobacco factory.

1808 Joseph Bonaparte made king of Spain. Battle of Bailén	**1812** Liberal constitution drawn up in Cádiz	*Isabel II*		**1870–73** Reign of King Amadeo	**1873–4** First Republic
	1814–33 (Bourbon restoration) Reign of Fernando VII			**1868** Isabel II loses her throne in "glorious" revolution	
1800	**1825**		**1850**		**1875**
1805 Battle of Trafalgar	**1814** South American colonies begin struggle for independence	**1843** Isabel II accedes to throne	**1846–9** Second Carlist War	**1872–6** Third Carlist War	
				1874 Second Bourbon restoration: Alfonso XII made king	
1808–14 Peninsular War	**1833** First Carlist War			*Alfonso XII*	

The Seeds of Civil War

Andalusia continued to decline, remaining so deeply feudal that by the early 20th century social protest was rife. The 1920s brought dictator General Primo de Rivera and relative, but short-lived, social order. In 1931, a Republican government, initially comprising liberals and moderate socialists, came to power. A rigid social order made real reforms slow to arrive, however, and 1931–36 saw growing conflict between extreme left and right wing (including the Falange) elements. Finally, in 1936, the Nationalist General Franco, leading a Moroccan garrison, invaded Spain, declaring war on the Republic.

Andalusia in 1936
- Nationalist territory
- Republican territory

Moorish Revival
By the late 19th century, regionalism, *andalucismo*, led to a revival of Moorish-style architecture. An example is Seville's Estación de Córdoba.

Women fought alongside men against the Nationalist army.

Picasso
Pablo Picasso, shown in this self-portrait, was born in Málaga in 1881. His most famous work, *Guernica*, depicts the tragic effects of the Civil War.

The Republican Army
In Andalusia, Franco attacked the Republican army at the very start of the war. Cádiz and Seville fell to Nationalists, but other Andalusian towns held out longer. Franco seized Málaga in 1937, executing thousands of Republicans.

1876 Composer Manuel de Falla born in Cádiz

1882–1912 Growing militancy of farm workers

1885–1902 Regency of María Cristina

Spanish soldiers, Cuban War

1895–8 Cuban War

1880

1890

1900

1881 Pablo Picasso born

1893 Guitarist Andrés Segovia born near Jaén

1885 Anarchist group *Mano Negra* active in Andalusia

1898 Cuba gains independence with US aid; Cádiz and Málaga begin to decline

1902–31 Reign of Alfonso XIII

Casas Viejas
In 1933, peasants were massacred after an uprising by anarchists at Casas Viejas in the province of Cádiz. The incident further served to undermine the Republican government.

Where to see Early 20th-Century Architecture in Andalusia

This period is characterized by architectural revivals. The regionalist style can be seen at the Plaza de España (see p102), the Museo Arqueológico (p103), and the Museo de Artes y Costumbres Populares (p103), all in the Parque María Luisa. The Teatro Lope Vega (p101) is in a Neo-Baroque style.

The Pabellón Real (see p103) in the Parque María Luisa is a pastiche of the late Gothic, Isabelline (see p28) style.

1929 Exposition
This trade fair was intended to boost Andalusia's economy. Unfortunately, it coincided with the Wall Street Crash.

Arms were supplied to the Republican army by the then Soviet Union.

Federico García Lorca
This poster is for Lorca's play, *Yerma*. The outspoken poet and playwright was murdered by local Falangists in his home town, Granada, in 1936.

General Queipo de Llano
Queipo de Llano broadcast radio propaganda to Seville as part of the Nationalists' strategy to take the city.

1923–30 Dictatorship of General Primo de Rivera

1929 Ibero-American Exposition, Seville

1933 Massacre at Casas Viejas

Republican poster

1936 Civil War starts

¡ATACAD!

1910

1920

1930

1940

1917–20 Bolshevik Triennium; communists lead protests in Andalusia

José Antonio Primo de Rivera

1931–39 Second Republic

1933 Falange founded by José Antonio Primo de Rivera; later supports Franco

1936 Franco becomes head of state

1939 Civil War ends

Modern Andalusia

By 1945 Spain remained the only Nationalist state in Europe. When Franco died in 1975 and Juan Carlos I came to the throne, the regions clamoured for devolution from Franco's centralized government. In 1982, the Sevillian Felipe González came to power and, in the same year, Andalusia became an autonomous region. Spain joined the European Union in 1986 and benefitting from European investors, the 1990s saw economic growth. This continued until the global financial meltdown in 2008; Spain entered into a recession in 2009 and by 2013 unemployment had reached 25 per cent of the population.

Autonomous regions
Present-day Andalusia

Feria
Despite the repressive regime that Franco established, the spirit of the Andalusian people remained evident in events such as the *feria* in Seville.

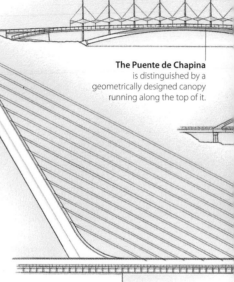

The Puente de Chapina
is distinguished by a geometrically designed canopy running along the top of it.

The Hungry Years
After the Civil War, Spain was isolated from Europe and after World War II, received no aid; amid widespread poverty and rationing, many Andalusians left to work abroad.

New bridges
Despite its autonomy, Andalusia still lagged behind much of the rest of Spain economically. Funds were provided by central government to build the new infrastructure needed to support Expo '92. Five bridges, all of the most innovative, modern design, were built over the Guadalquivir river.

1940 Franco refuses to allow Hitler to attack Gibraltar from Spanish territory

1953 Spain is granted economic aid in return for allowing US bases on Spanish soil

1966 Palomares incident: two US aircraft collide and four nuclear bombs fall to earth, one in the sea, but do not explode. The Duchess of Medina Sidonia, "the red duchess", leads protest march on Madrid

1976 Adolfo Suárez appointed prime minister and forms centre-right government

| 1940 | 1950 | 1960 | 1970 | 198 |

1940–53 The Hungry Years
Franco meets American President Eisenhower (1953)

1962 Development of Costa del Sol begins

1969 Spain closes its border with Gibraltar

1975 Franco dies. Third Bourbon restoration; Juan Carlos I accedes to the throne

Franco's Funeral *(1975)*
Franco's death was mourned as much as it was welcomed; most people, though, saw the need for democratic change.

Package Holidays
Buildings for mass tourism transformed Andalusia's coast.

Where to see modern Andalusia

The most striking buildings of modern Andalusia were built in the early part of the 1990s. Expo '92 left Seville with five new bridges over the Guadal-quivir river, while at La Cartuja *(see p108)* Expo's core pavilions still stand, soon to be the site of new attractions. The Teatro de la Maestranza *(pp72–3)*, in El Arenal, was also built during this period.

The Omnimax cinema on the former Expo '92 site was originally built as part of the Pavilion of Discoveries.

The Puente del Alamillo (Harp) has a single upward arm supporting its weight.

The Puente de la Barqueta, a unique suspension bridge supported by a single overhead beam, spans 168 m (551 ft).

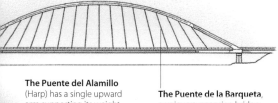

FYD●'O:

Felipe González
In 1982, the year after an attempted coup by the Civil Guard colonel Antonio Tejero, Felipe González, leader of the socialist PSOE, claimed a huge electoral victory.

Expo '92
Hosted by Seville, Expo '92 placed Andalusia at the centre of a world stage. However, the city was left in debt for several years.

1982 Felipe González elected prime minister; Andalusia becomes an autonomous region	**1996** In the general election González loses to a coalition led by Aznar	**2004** The Spanish Socialist Workers' Party wins the general elections, a result that defies most predictions	
1985 Spain-Gibraltar border opens		**2006** Seville FC are the UEFA Cup champions	**2012** Spanish unemployment reaches record high, youth unemployment stands at 50 per cent
1990	**2000**	**2010**	**2020**
1981 Colonel Tejero attempts coup and holds Spanish Parliament hostage; Juan Carlos intervenes	**2002** Spain converts to the euro	**2009** Andalusia's first subway system opens in Seville	
Colonel Tejero	**2006** In March, the Basque terrorist organization ETA announces a permanent ceasefire	**2007** Madrid to Málaga high-speed AVE train line opens	

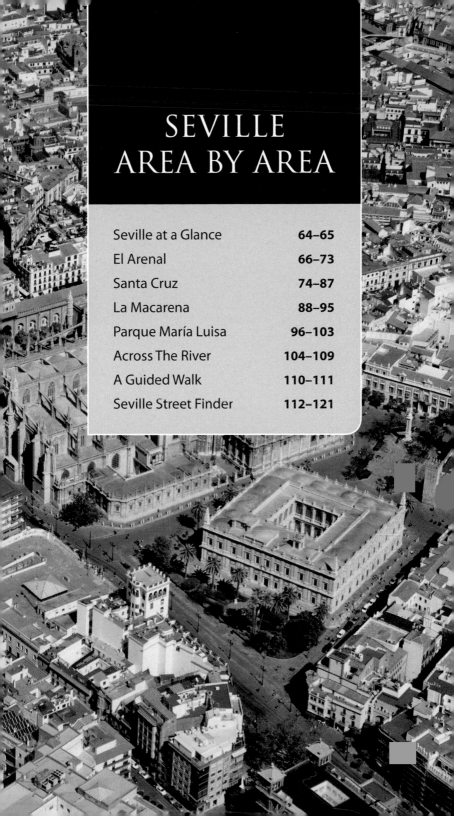

SEVILLE
AREA BY AREA

Seville at a Glance

The capital of Andalusia is a compact and relaxing city with a rich cultural heritage. Conveniently, many of its principal sights can be found within or very near the city centre, which is set on the east bank of the Río Guadalquivir. Most visitors head straight for the cathedral and La Giralda, Real Alcázar and Museo de Bellas Artes. Among other highly popular monuments are the exquisite Renaissance palace of Casa de Pilatos and Seville's bullring, the Plaza de Toros de la Maestranza. There are, however, many other churches, monuments and neighbourhoods to discover in the four central areas described in this section, and more, further afield, across the river.

The splendid ceiling of Museo de Bellas Artes *(see pp70–71)*

El Arenal
Pages 66–73

La Giralda rising above the massive Gothic cathedral *(see pp82–3)*

Plaza de Toros de la Maestranza seen from the river *(see p72)*

The Moorish Torre del Oro, built to defend Seville *(see p73)*

Aerial view of Santa Cruz area, with La Giralda, Real Alcázar and Archivo de Indias in foreground

La Macarena
Pages 88–95

Santa Cruz
Pages 74–87

**Parque
Maria Luisa**
Pages 96–103

One of many elaborate floats in the Basílica de la Macarena, during Easter Week in Seville *(see p93)*

The impressive wooden structure of the Metropol Parasol, located in La Encarnación square, acts as a grand gateway to La Macarena *(see p89)*

Roman relief of Leda and the Swan, Casa de Pilatos *(see p81)*

Sumptuous Mudéjar arches and decor in Salón de Embajadores, Real Alcázar *(see pp86–7)*

Plaza de España in the green oasis of Parque María Luisa *(see pp102–3)*

Patio of Real Fábrica de Tabacos, today the Universidad *(see p100)*

EL ARENAL

Bounded by the Río Guadalquivir and guarded by the mighty 13th-century Torre del Oro, El Arenal used to be a district of munitions stores and shipyards. Today, this quarter is dominated by the dazzling white bullring, Plaza de Toros de la Maestranza, where the Sevillians have been staging *corridas* for more than two centuries. The many classic bars and wine cellars in neighbouring streets get extra busy during the summer bullfighting season.

Once central to the city's life, the influence of the Guadalquivir declined as it silted up during the 17th century. By then, El Arenal had become a notorious underworld haunt clinging to the city walls. After being converted into a canal in the early 20th century, the river was restored to its former

navigable glory just in time for Expo '92. The east riverfront was transformed into a tree-lined, shady promenade with excellent views of Triana and La Cartuja across the river *(see pp108–9)*. Boat trips and sightseeing tours depart from the Torre del Oro. Close by is the smart Teatro de la Maestranza, where opera, classical music and dance take place before well-informed audiences.

The Hospital de la Caridad testifies to the city's continuing love affair with the Baroque. Its church is filled with famous paintings by Murillo, and the story of the Seville School is told with pride in the immaculately restored Museo de Bellas Artes further north. The city's stunning collection of great works by Zurbarán, Murillo and Valdés Leal is reason enough to visit Seville.

Sights at a Glance

Historic Buildings
❸ Plaza de Toros de la Maestranza
❺ Hospital de la Caridad
❻ Torre del Oro

Museums
❶ Museo de Bellas Artes *pp70–71*

Churches
❷ Iglesia de la Magdalen

Theatres
❹ Teatro de la Maestranza

☐ **Restaurants** *p228*
1 El Aguador de Velazquez
2 Bodeguita Casablanca
3 La Brunilda Tapas
4 El Burladero
5 El Cabildo
6 Enrique Becerra
7 Taberna del Alabardero

0 metres 400
0 yards 400

See also Street Finder maps 1, 3, 5

◀ The striking Baroque domed ceiling of the Museo de Bellas Artes   **For map symbols** *see back flap*

Street-by-Street: El Arenal

Once home to the port of Seville, El Arenal also housed the artillery headquarters and ammunition works. Now its atmosphere is set by Seville's bullring, the majestic Plaza de Toros de la Maestranza, which is located here. During the bullfighting season *(see pp30–31)* bars and restaurants are packed, but for the rest of the year the backstreets remain quiet. The riverfront is dominated by one of Seville's best-known monuments, the Moorish Torre del Oro, while the long, tree-lined promenade beside Paseo de Cristóbal Colón is the perfect setting for a romantic walk along the Guadalquivir.

❸ ★ Plaza de Toros de la Maestranza
Seville's 18th-century bullring, one of Spain's oldest, has a Baroque façade in white and ochre.

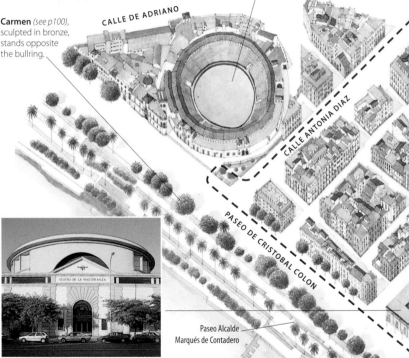

Carmen *(see p100)*, sculpted in bronze, stands opposite the bullring.

CALLE DE ADRIANO

CALLE ANTONIA DIAZ

PASEO DE CRISTOBAL COLON

Paseo Alcalde
Marqués de Contadero

❹ Teatro de la Maestranza
This showpiece theatre and opera house opened in 1991. Home of the Orquesta Sinfónica de Sevilla, it also features international opera and dance companies.

| 0 metres | 75 |
| 0 yards | 75 |

The Guadalquivir
The river used to cause catastrophic inundations. After floods in 1947, a barrage was constructed. Today, peaceful boat trips start from the Torre del Oro.

El Buzo
This is one of many traditional restaurants situated on or just off Calle Arfe. Nearby lies Mesón Sevilla Jabugo I, where *jamón ibérico (see p225)* is served.

Locator Map
See Street Finder, maps, 3, 5–6

El Postigo is an arts and crafts market.

GARCIA VINUESA

To Seville Cathedral

On Plaza del Cabildo, a well-hidden square, convent-made sweets are sold in El Torno.

AVENIDA DE LA CONSTITUCION

TOMAS DE IBARRA

5 ★ Hospital de la Caridad
The Baroque church of this hospice for the elderly is lined with paintings by Bartolomé Esteban Murillo and Juan de Valdés Leal.

DE MAYO

TEMPRADO

To Real Alcázar

Key
— Suggested route

CALLE SANTANDER

Maestranza de Artillería

6 ★ Torre del Oro
Built in the 13th century in order to protect the port, this crenellated Moorish tower now houses a small maritime museum.

❶ Museo de Bellas Artes

The former Convento de la Merced Calzada has been restored to create one of the finest art museums in Spain. The convent, which was completed in 1612 by Juan de Oviedo, is built around three patios, which today are adorned with flowers, trees and *azulejos (see p80)*. The museum's impressive collection of Spanish art and sculpture extends from the medieval to the modern, focusing on the work of Seville School artists such as Bartolomé Esteban Murillo, Juan de Valdés Leal and Francisco de Zurbarán.

♿ ♿ for disabled

★ **San Hugo en el Refectorio** *(1655)*
One of several works by Zurbarán for the monastery at La Cartuja *(see p109)*, this scene depicts the Carthusian Order of monks first renouncing the eating of meat.

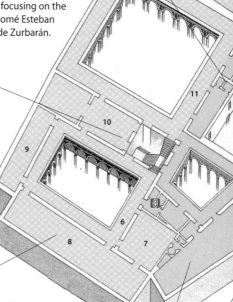

11

10

9

6

8

7

First floor

La Inmaculada
This stirring *Inmaculada* (1672), by Valdés Leal (1622–90) is in Sala 8, a gallery devoted to the artist's forceful religious paintings.

Gallery Guide

Signs provide a self-guided chronological tour through the museum's 14 galleries, starting by the Claustro del Aljibe. Works downstairs progress from the 14th century through to Baroque; those upstairs from the Baroque to the early 20th century.

The Claustro de los Bojes is enclosed by Tuscan-style arches.

4

3

2

★ **San Jerónimo** *(1528)*
Sculpted by the Florentine Torrigiano, this masterpiece in terracotta brought the vitality of the Italian Renaissance to Seville.

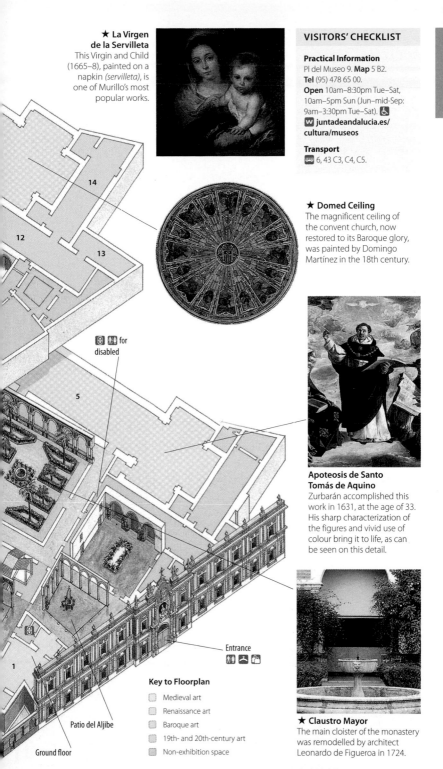

★ La Virgen de la Servilleta
This Virgin and Child (1665–8), painted on a napkin (servilleta), is one of Murillo's most popular works.

VISITORS' CHECKLIST

Practical Information
Pl del Museo 9. **Map** 5 B2.
Tel (95) 478 65 00.
Open 10am–8:30pm Tue–Sat,
10am–5pm Sun (Jun–mid-Sep:
9am–3:30pm Tue–Sat). ♿
Ⓦ juntadeandalucia.es/
cultura/museos

Transport
🚌 6, 43 C3, C4, C5.

★ Domed Ceiling
The magnificent ceiling of the convent church, now restored to its Baroque glory, was painted by Domingo Martínez in the 18th century.

🛗 🚻 for disabled

5

Apoteosis de Santo Tomás de Aquino
Zurbarán accomplished this work in 1631, at the age of 33. His sharp characterization of the figures and vivid use of colour bring it to life, as can be seen on this detail.

14

12

13

Entrance
🚻 ♨ 📷

Key to Floorplan

- ☐ Medieval art
- ☐ Renaissance art
- ☐ Baroque art
- ☐ 19th- and 20th-century art
- ☐ Non-exhibition space

Patio del Aljibe

Ground floor

1

★ Claustro Mayor
The main cloister of the monastery was remodelled by architect Leonardo de Figueroa in 1724.

Madonna and Child in the Baroque Iglesia de la Magdalena

❷ Iglesia de la Magdalena

Calle San Pablo 10. **Map** 3 B1 (5 B2). 🚇 Plaza Nueva. **Tel** 95 422 96 03. **Open** 7:30–11am, 6:30–9pm Mon–Sat; 7:30am–1:30pm, 6:30–9pm Sun.

This immense Baroque church by Leonardo de Figueroa, completed in 1709, has gradually been restored to its former glory. In its southwest corner is the Capilla de la Quinta Angustia, a Mudéjar chapel with three cupolas. This chapel survived from an earlier church where the great Spanish painter Bartolomé Murillo (see pp70–71) was baptized in 1618. The font, which was used for his baptism stands in the baptistry of the present building. The sheer west front is surmounted by a belfry painted in vivid colours.

Among the religious works in the church are a painting by

Francisco de Zurbarán, St Dominic in Soria, housed in the Capilla Sacramental (to the right of the south door), and frescoes by Lucas Valdés above the sanctuary depicting The Allegory of the Triumph of Faith. On the wall of the north transept is a cautionary fresco, which depicts a medieval auto-da-fé (trial of faith).

❸ Plaza de Toros de la Maestranza

Paseo de Colón 12. **Map** 3 B2 (5 B4). 🚇 Prado de San Sebastian. 🚌 Archivo de Indias. 🚍 C3, C4. **Tel** 95 421 03 15. **Open** 9:30am–7pm daily (to 8pm May–Oct); 9:30am–3pm on bullfight days. 🎫 📷 **W** realmaestranza.com

Seville's famous bullring is arguably the finest in the whole of Spain and is a perfect venue for a first experience of the corrida, or bullfight (see pp30–31). Although the art of the matador (bullfighter) is now declining in popularity, the sunlit stage, with its whitewashed walls, blood red fences and merciless circle of sand, remains crucial to the city's psyche. Even if you dislike the idea of bullfighting, this arcaded arena, dating from 1761 to 1881, is an aesthetic marvel and well worth a visit.

The bullring accommodates as many as 12,500 spectators. Guided tours start from the main entrance on Paseo de Colón. On the west side is the Puerta del Príncipe (Prince's Gate), through which the very best of the matadors are carried

triumphant on the shoulders of admirers from the crowd.

Passing the enfermería (emergency hospital), visitors reach a museum which details the history of the bullfight in Seville. Among its collection of costumes, portraits and posters are scenes showing early contests held in the Plaza de San Francisco. The tour continues to the chapel where matadors pray for success, and then on to the stables where the horses of the picadores (lance-carrying horsemen) are kept.

The bullfighting season starts on Easter Sunday and continues intermittently until October. Most corridas are held on Sunday evenings. Tickets can be bought from the taquilla (booking office) at the bullring itself.

Entrance with 19th-century ironwork, Teatro de la Maestranza

❹ Teatro de la Maestranza

Paseo de Colón 22. **Map** 3 B2 (5 C5). 🚇 Prado de San Sebastian. 🚌 Puerta Jerez. 🚍 C3, C4. **Tel** 95 422 65 73 (information). **Open** for performances. 🎫 ♿ **W** teatromaestranza.com

Close to the Plaza de Toros, and with echoes of its circular bulk, is Seville's 1,800-seat opera house and theatre. It opened in 1991 and many international opera companies perform here (see p245). Like many of the edifices built in the run-up to Expo '92 (see pp60–61), it was designed in a rather austere

Arcaded arena of the Plaza de Toros de la Maestranza, begun in 1761

Finis Gloriae Mundi by Juan de Valdés Leal in the Hospital de la Caridad

style by architects Luis Marín de Terán and Aurelio del Pozo. Ironwork remnants of the 19th-century ammunition works that first occupied the site decorate the river façade. Tickets are sold from the box office in the adjacent Jardín de la Caridad.

❺ Hospital de la Caridad

Calle Temprado 3. **Map** 3 B2 (5 C5). 🅜 Prado de San Sebastian. 🚎 Puerto Jerez. 🚌 C3, C4. **Tel** 95 422 32 32. **Open** 9am–7:30pm Mon–Sat, 9am–12:30pm Sun & public hols. 🅿

Founded in 1674, this charity hospital is still used today as a sanctuary for the elderly and the infirm. In the gardens opposite the entrance stands a statue of its benefactor, Miguel de Mañara. The complex was designed by Pedro Sánchez Falconete. The façade of the hospital church, with its whitewashed walls, terracotta stonework and framed *azulejos* (*see p80*) provides a glorious example of Sevillian Baroque.

Inside are two square patios adorned with plants, 18th-century Dutch *azulejos* and fountains with Italian statues depicting Charity and Mercy. At their northern end a passage to the right leads to another patio, where a 13th-century arch from the city's shipyards survives. A bust of Mañara stands amid rose bushes. Inside the church there are many original canvases by

some of the leading artists of the 17th century, despite the fact that some of its greatest artworks were looted by Marshal Soult at the time of the Napoleonic occupation of 1810 (*see p57*). Immediately above the entrance is the ghoulish *Finis Gloriae Mundi* (The End of the World's Glories) by Juan de Valdés Leal, while opposite hangs his morbid *In Ictu Oculi* (In the Blink of an Eye). Many of the other works are by Murillo, including *St John of God Carrying a Sick Man*, portraits of the Child Jesus, *St John the Baptist as a Boy* and *St Isabel of Hungary Curing the Lepers*. Looking south from the hospital's entrance you can

see the octagonal Torre de Plata (Tower of Silver) rising above Calle Santander. Like the Torre del Oro nearby, it dates from Moorish times and was built as part of the city defences.

❻ Torre del Oro

Paseo de Colón s/n. **Map** 3 B2 (5 C5). 🅜 Plaza de Cuba. 🚎 Puerta Jerez. 🚌 C3, C4, C5. **Tel** 95 422 24 19. **Open** 9:30am–1:30pm Tue–Fri, 10:30am–1:30pm Sat & Sun. **Closed** Aug. 🅿 (free Tue).

In Moorish times the Tower of Gold formed part of the walled defences, linking up with the Real Alcázar (*see pp82–3*) and the rest of the city. It was built as a defensive lookout in 1220, when Seville was under the rule of the Almohads (*see pp46–7*), and had a companion tower on the opposite river bank. A mighty chain would be stretched between the two to prevent ships from sailing upriver. In 1760 the turret was added. The gold in the tower's name may refer to gilded *azulejos* that once clad its walls, or to New World treasures unloaded here. The tower has had many uses, but is now the Museo Marítimo, exhibiting maritime maps and antiques.

The Torre del Oro, built by the Almohads

Don Juan of Seville

Miguel de Mañara (1626–79), founder and subsequent benefactor of the Hospital de la Caridad, is frequently linked with Don Juan Tenorio. The amorous conquests of the legendary Sevillian seducer were first documented in 1630 in a play by Tirso de Molina. They have since inspired works by Mozart, Molière, Byron and Shaw. Mañara is thought to have led an equally dissolute life prior to his conversion to philanthropy – apparently this was prompted by a premonition of his own funeral which he experienced one drunken night.

The legendary Don Juan with two of his conquests

SANTA CRUZ

The Barrio de Santa Cruz, Seville's old Jewish quarter, is a warren of white alleys and patios that has long been the most picturesque corner of the city. Many of the best-known sights are grouped here: the cavernous Gothic cathedral with its landmark Giralda; the splendid Real Alcázar with the royal palaces and lush Jardines del Alcázar; and the Archivo de Indias, whose documents tell of Spain's exploration and conquest of the New World.

Spreading northeast from these great monuments is an enchanting maze of whitewashed streets. The artist Bartolomé Esteban Murillo lived here in the 17th century while his contemporary, Juan de Valdés Leal, decorated the Hospital de los Venerables with fine Baroque frescoes.

Further north, busy Calle de las Sierpes is one of Seville's favourite shopping streets. Its adjacent market squares, such as the harming Plaza del Salvador, provided backdrops for Cervantes' stories. Nearby, the ornate façades and interiors of the Ayuntamiento and the Casa de Pilatos, a gem of Andalusian architecture, testify to the great wealth and artistry that flowed into the city in the 16th century.

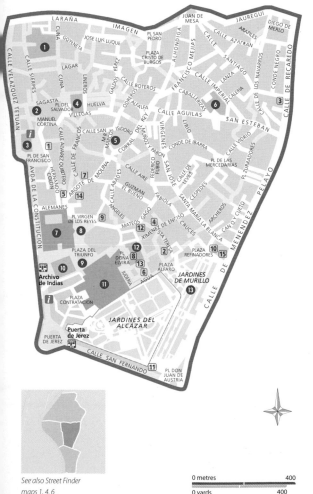

Sights at a Glance

Gardens
2. Calle Sierpes
4. Iglesia del Salvador
8. Plaza Virgen de los Reyes
9. Plaza del Triunfo
13. Jardines de Murillo

Churches
7. Seville Cathedral and La Giralda pp82–3

Historic Buildings
1. Palacio de Lebrija
3. Ayuntamiento
5. Museo del Baile Flamenco
6. Casa de Pilatos
10. Archivo de Indias
11. Real Alcázar pp86–7
12. Hospital de los Venerables

☐ **Restaurants** pp228–9

1. Albarama
2. La Albahaca
3. Berrecita
4. Casa Plácido
5. Casa Robles
6. Corral del Agua
7. Don Raimundo
8. Doña Elvira
9. El Giraldillo
10. El Modesto
11. Ergaña Oriza
12. San Marco
13. Santa Cruz
14. Santo
15. Vineria San Telmo

See also Street Finder maps 1, 4, 6

0 metres 400
0 yards 400

◀ Baths of Doña María de Padilla, beneath the Patio del Crucero, in the Real Alcázar

For map symbols see back flap

Street-by-Street: Santa Cruz

The maze of narrow streets to the east of Seville cathedral and the Real Alcázar represents Seville at its most romantic and compact. As well as the expected souvenir shops, tapas bars and strolling guitarists, there are plenty of picturesque alleys, hidden plazas and flower-decked patios to reward the casual wanderer. Once a Jewish ghetto, its restored buildings, with characteristic window grilles, are now a harmonious mix of up-market residences and tourist accommodation. Good bars and restaurants make the area well worth a visit.

⑧ Plaza Virgen de los Reyes
Horse carriages line this plaza which has an early 20th-century fountain by José Lafita.

Palacio Arzobispal, the 18th-century Archbishop's Palace, is still used by Seville's clergy.

Convento de la Encarnación *(see p84)*

AVENIDA DE LA CONSTITUCIÓN

MATEC

ROMERO MURU

❼ ★ Seville Cathedral and La Giralda
This huge Gothic cathedral and its Moorish bell tower are Seville's most popular sights.

SANTO TOMAS

MIGUEL MAÑARA

❿ Archivo de Indias
Built in the 16th century as a merchants' exchange, the Archive of the Indies now houses documents relating to the Spanish colonization of the Americas.

❾ Plaza del Triunfo
A Baroque column celebrates the city's survival of the great arthquake of 1755. Opposite is a modern statue of the Immaculate Conception.

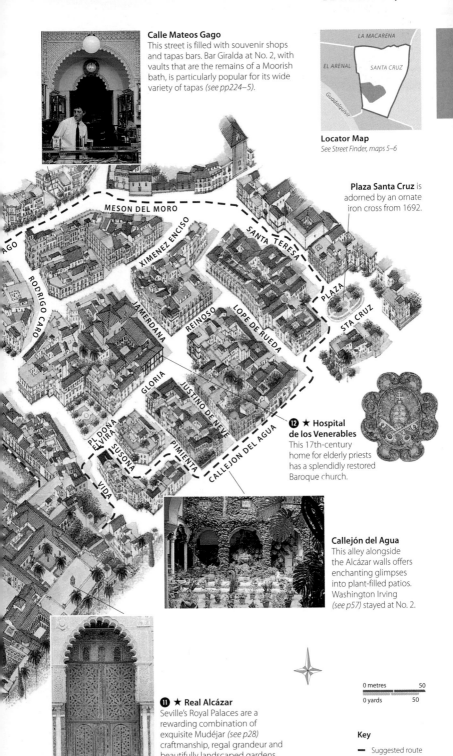

Calle Mateos Gago
This street is filled with souvenir shops and tapas bars. Bar Giralda at No. 2, with vaults that are the remains of a Moorish bath, is particularly popular for its wide variety of tapas *(see pp224–5)*.

Locator Map
See Street Finder, maps 5–6

Plaza Santa Cruz is adorned by an ornate iron cross from 1692.

⓬ ★ Hospital de los Venerables
This 17th-century home for elderly priests has a splendidly restored Baroque church.

Callejón del Agua
This alley alongside the Alcázar walls offers enchanting glimpses into plant-filled patios. Washington Irving *(see p57)* stayed at No. 2.

⓫ ★ Real Alcázar
Seville's Royal Palaces are a rewarding combination of exquisite Mudéjar *(see p28)* craftsmanship, regal grandeur and beautifully landscaped gardens.

0 metres   50
0 yards   50

Key
— Suggested route

Mosaic, from Itálica *(see p136)*, in the Palacio de Lebrija

❶ Palacio de Lebrija

Calle Cuna 8. **Map** 1 C5; 3 C1 (5 C2). **Tel** 95 422 78 02. **Open** 10:30am–7:30pm Mon–Fri, 10am–2pm & 4–6pm Sat, 10am–2pm Sun. 🐾 🖼 ⓦ **palaciodelebrija.com**

The home of the family of the Countess Lebrija, this mansion illustrates palatial life in Seville. The ground floor houses Roman and medieval exhibits. A guided tour of the first floor features a library and art, such as the Moorish inspired *azulejos* *(see p80)*.

The house itself dates from the 15th century and has some Mudéjar *(see p28)* features, including the arches around the main patio. Many of its Roman treasures were taken from the ruins at Itálica *(see p136)*, including the mosaic floor in the main patio. The *artesonado* ceiling above the staircase came from the palace of the Dukes of Arcos in Marchena, near Seville. Ancient roman glass ware, coins and later examples of marble from

Medina Azahara *(see p142)* are displayed in rooms off the main patio.

❷ Calle Sierpes

Map 3 C1 (5 C3).

The street of the snakes, running north from Plaza de San Francisco, is Seville's main pedestrianized shopping promenade. Long-established stores selling the Sevillian essentials – hats, fans and the traditional *mantillas* (lace headdresses) stand alongside clothes boutiques, souvenir shops, bargain basements and lottery kiosks. The best time to stroll along it is when the *sevillanos* themselves do – during the early evening *paseo*.

The parallel streets of Cuna and Tetuán on either side also offer some enjoyable window-shopping. Look out for the splendid 1924 tiled advert for Studebaker automobiles *(see p80)* at Calle Tetuán 9.

At the southern end of Calle Sierpes, on the wall of the Banco Central Hispano, a plaque marks the site of the Cárcel Real (Royal Prison), where the famous Spanish writer Miguel de Cervantes (1547–1616) *(see p55)* was incarcerated. Walking north from here, Calle Jovellanos to the left leads to the Capillita de San José. This small, rather atmospheric chapel, built in the 17th century, contrasts sharply with its commercial surroundings. Further on, at the junction with Calle Pedro Caravaca, you can take a look back into the

anachronistic, upholstered world of the Real Círculo de Labradores, a private men's club founded in 1856. Right at the end of the street, take the opportunity to peruse Seville's best-known *pastelería* (cake shop), La Campana.

Plateresque doorway, part of the façade of Seville's Ayuntamiento

❸ Ayuntamiento

Plaza Nueva 1. **Map** 3 C1 (5 C3). 🚇 Plaza Nueva. **Tel** 95 547 02 64. **Open** 5:30 & 6pm Tue–Thu. 🖼

Seville's city hall stands between the historic Plaza de San Francisco and the modern expanse of Plaza Nueva.

In the 15th–18th centuries, Plaza de San Francisco was the venue for autos-da-fé, public trials of heretics held by the Inquisition *(see p55)*. Those found guilty would be taken to the Quemadero and burnt alive. (This site is now the Prado de San Sebastián, north of Parque María Luisa, *see pp102–3*.) These days, Plaza de San Francisco is the focus of activities in Semana Santa and Corpus Christi *(see pp38–9)*.

Plaza Nueva was once the site of the Convento de San Francisco. In its centre is an equestrian statue of Fernando III, who liberated Seville from the Moors and was eventually canonized in 1671 *(see p52)*.

The Ayuntamiento, begun in 1527, was finished in 1534. The east side, looking on to Plaza de San Francisco, is a fine example of the ornate Plateresque style

Tables outside La Campana, Seville's most famous *pastelería*

(see p29) favoured by the architect Diego de Riaño. The west front is part of a Neo-Classical extension built in 1891. It virtually envelops the original building, but richly sculpted ceilings survive in the vestibule and in the lower Casa Consistorial (Council Meeting Room). This room contains Velázquez's *Imposition of the Chasuble on St Ildefonso*, one of many artworks in the building. The upper Casa Consistorial has a dazzling gold coffered ceiling and paintings by Zurbarán and Valdés Leal *(see pp70–71)*.

❹ Iglesia del Salvador

Pl del Salvador. **Map** 3 C1 (6 D3). **Tel** 95 421 16 79. **Open** 10am– 5:30pm Mon–Sat, 3–7pm Sun. 🖼

This church has been completely restored. Its cathedral-like proportions result in part from the desire of Seville's Christian conquerors to outdo the Moors' architectural splendours. A mosque first occupied the site; part of the Moorish patio survives beside Calle Córdoba, boxed in by arcades incorporating columns embellished with Roman and Visigothic capitals.

By the 1670s the mosque, long since consecrated for Christian worship, had fallen into disrepair. Work started on a new Baroque structure, designed by Esteban García. The church was completed in 1712 by Leonardo de Figueroa. Inside, the nave is by José

Baroque façade of the Iglesia del Salvador on the Plaza del Salvador

Granados, architect of Granada cathedral *(see p194)*. In the Capilla Sacramental there is a fine statue, *Jesus of the Passion*, made in 1619 by Juan Martínez Montañés (1568–1649). In the northwest corner, a door leads to the ornate Capilla de los Desamparados and a Moorish patio. Over the exit on Calle Córdoba, the bell tower rests on part of the original minaret.

Adjacent to the church is the Plaza del Salvador, a meeting place for Seville's youngsters. The bronze statue

commemorates the sculptor Montañés. On the east side of the church, the Plaza Jesús de la Pasión is given over to shops catering to weddings – the Iglesia del Salvador is a favourite among *sevillanos* for getting married.

❺ Museo del Baile Flamenco

Calle Manuel Rojas Marcos 3. **Map** 3 C1 (6 D3). **Tel** 95 434 03 11. **Open** 9am–7pm daily. 🖼 🖼 **W** museoflamenco.com

Although flamenco was supposedly born across the river, in Triana, the Barrio de Santa Cruz has become its de facto home in Seville. This museum of flamenco dance, occupying a restored 18th-century house on a small street between the Plaza del Alfalfa and the cathedral, is intended as an introduction of the art form to the visitor. As much as a space for exhibits in the traditional sense, it is a venue for live performances of flamenco and a school offering classes in flamenco music and dance.

The Sign of Seville

The curious abbreviation "no8do" is emblazoned everywhere from the venerable walls of the Ayuntamiento to the sides of the municipal buses. It is traditionally said to stand for *"No me ha dejado"* ("She has not deserted me"). These words were reputedly uttered by Alfonso the Wise, after the city remained loyal to him in the course of a dispute with his son Sancho during the Reconquest *(see pp52–3)*. The double-loop symbol in the middle represents a skein of wool, the Spanish word for which is *madeja*, thus *no (madeja) do*.

The traditional emblem of Seville, here in stone on the Ayuntamiento

The Art of Azulejos

Cool in summer, durable and colourful, glazed ceramic tiles have been a striking feature of Andalusian façades and interiors for centuries. The techniques for making them were first introduced by the Moors – the word *azulejo* derives from the Arabic *az-zulayj* or "little stone". Moorish *azulejos* are elaborate mosaics made of unicoloured stones. In Seville the craft flourished and evolved in the potteries of Triana *(see pp106–7)*. A later process, developed in 16th-century Italy, allowed tiles to be painted in new designs and colours. The onset of the Industrial Revolution enabled *azulejos* to be mass-produced in ceramics factories including, until 1980, the famous "Pickman y Cia" at the monastery of La Cartuja *(see p109)*.

Mudejar-Style Azulejos

The Moors created fantastic mosaics of tiles in sophisticated geometric patterns as decoration for their palace walls. The colours used were blue, green, black, white and ochre.

16th-century Mudéjar tiles, Casa de Pilatos

Interlacing motifs, Patio de las Doncellas

Mudéjar tiles in the Patio de las Doncellas, Real Alcázar

Sign for the Royal Tobacco Factory (now part of the Universidad, *(see pp100–1)* made in painted glazed tiles in the 18th century

Azulejos for Commercial Use

As techniques for making and colouring azulejos improved, their use was extended from interior decor to decorative signs and shop façades. Even billboards were produced in multicoloured tiles. The eye-catching results can still be seen all over Andalusia.

Contemporary glazed ceramic beer tap

Azulejo billboard advertising the latest model of Studebaker Motor Cars (1924), situated on Calle Tetuán, off Calle de las Sierpes *(see p78)*

Genoan fountain and Gothic balustrades in the Mudéjar Patio Principal of the Casa de Pilatos

❻ Casa de Pilatos

Plaza de Pilatos 1. **Map** 4 D1 (6 E3).
Tel 95 422 52 98. 🕐 9am–6pm daily.
🎫 📷 1st floor. ♿ ground floor.
🌐 **fundacionmedinaceli.org**

In 1518 the first Marquess of Tarifa departed on a Grand Tour of Europe and the Holy Land. He returned two years later, enraptured by the architectural and decorative wonders of High Renaissance Italy. He spent the rest of his life creating a new aesthetic, which was very influential. His palace in Seville, called the House of Pilate because it was thought to resemble Pontius Pilate's home in Jerusalem, became a luxurious showcase for the new style.

Over the centuries, subsequent owners added their own embellishments. The Casa de Pilatos is now the residence of the Dukes of Medinaceli and is still one of the finest palaces in Seville.

Visitors enter it through a marble portal, commissioned by the Marquess in 1529 from Genoan craftsmen. Across the arcaded Apeadero (carriage yard) is the Patio Principal. This courtyard is essentially Mudéjar (*see p28*) in style with *azulejos* and intricate plasterwork. It is

Lantern in the entrance portal

surrounded by irregularly spaced arches capped with delicate Gothic balustrades. In its corners stand three Roman statues, Minerva, a dancing muse and Ceres, and a Greek fourth statue, a 5th century BC original of the goddess Athena. In its centre is a fountain imported from Genoa. To the right, through the Salón del Pretorio with its coffered ceiling and marquetry, is the Corredor de Zaquizamí. Among the antiquities in adjacent rooms are a bas-relief of *Leda and the Swan* and two Roman reliefs commemorating the Battle of Actium of BC 31. Further along, in the Jardín Chico there is a pool with a bronze of Bacchus.

Coming back to the Patio Principal, you turn right into the Salón de Descanso de los Jueces. Beyond this is a rib-vaulted chapel, which has a sculpture dating from the 1st century AD, *Christ and the Good Shepherd*. Left through the Gabinete de Pilatos, with its small central fountain, is the Jardín Grande. The Italian architect, Benvenuto Tortello, created the loggias in the 1560s.

Returning once more to the main patio, behind the statue of Ceres, a tiled staircase leads to

the apartments on the upper floor. It is roofed with a wonderful *media naranja* (half orange) cupola built in 1537. There are Mudéjar ceilings in some rooms, which are filled with family portraits, antiques and furniture. Plasterwork by Juan de Oviedo and frescoes by Francisco de Pacheco still survive in rooms, which bear these artists' names.

West of the Casa de Pilatos, the Plaza de San Ildefonso is bounded by the Convento de San Leandro, famous for the *yemas* (sweets made from egg yolks) sold from a *torno* (drum). Opposite the convent is the Neo-Classical Iglesia de San Ildefonso, which has statues of San Hermenegildo and San Fernando by Pedro Roldán.

Escutcheons in the coffered ceiling of the Salón del Pretorio

For hotels and restaurants in this region see pp216–19 and pp228–37

❼ Seville Cathedral and La Giralda

Seville's cathedral occupies the site of a great mosque built by the Almohads *(see pp50–51)* in the late 12th century. La Giralda, its bell tower, and the Patio de los Naranjos are a legacy of this Moorish structure. Work on the Christian cathedral, the largest in Europe, began in 1401 and took just over a century to complete. As well as enjoying its Gothic immensity and the works of art in its chapels and Treasury, visitors can climb La Giralda for superb views over the city, and enjoy views of the city from the cathedral rooftop (reservations necessary).

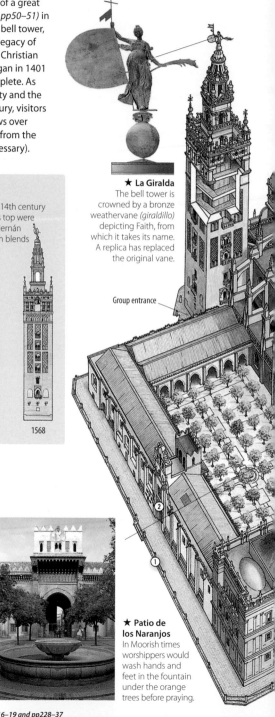

★ **La Giralda**
The bell tower is crowned by a bronze weathervane *(giraldillo)* depicting Faith, from which it takes its name. A replica has replaced the original vane.

Group entrance

The Rise of La Giralda

The minaret was finished in 1198. In the 14th century the original Muslim bronze spheres at its top were replaced by Christian symbols. In 1568 Hernán Ruiz added the Renaissance belfry, which blends perfectly with the Moorish base.

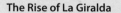

| 1198 | 1400 | 1557 (plan) | 1568 |

KEY

① **Roman pillars** brought from Itálica *(see p136)* surround the cathedral steps.

② **Puerta del Perdón**

③ **The Sacristía Mayor** houses many works of art, including paintings by Murillo.

④ **The Tomb of Columbus** dates from the 1890s. His coffin is carried by bearers representing the kingdoms of Castile, León, Aragón and Navarra *(see p52)*.

⑤ **Puerta del Bautismo**

⑥ **Iglesia del Sagrario**, a large 17th-century chapel, is now used as a parish church.

★ **Patio de los Naranjos**
In Moorish times worshippers would wash hands and feet in the fountain under the orange trees before praying.

Retablo Mayor
Santa María de la Sede, the cathedral's patron saint, sits at the high altar below a waterfall of gold. The 44 gilded relief panels of the *retablo* were carved by Spanish and Flemish sculptors between 1482 and 1564.

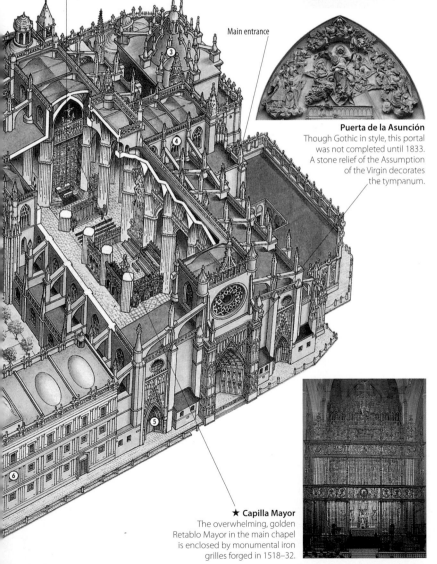

Main entrance

Puerta de la Asunción
Though Gothic in style, this portal was not completed until 1833. A stone relief of the Assumption of the Virgin decorates the tympanum.

★ **Capilla Mayor**
The overwhelming, golden Retablo Mayor in the main chapel is enclosed by monumental iron grilles forged in 1518–32.

Upper part of the Baroque doorway of the Palacio Arzobispal

❽ Plaza Virgen de los Reyes

Map 3 C2 (6 D4). Palacio Arzobispal **Closed** to the public. Convento de la Encarnación **Closed** to the public.

The perfect place to pause for a while and admire the Giralda (see pp82–3), this plaza presents an archetypal Sevillian tableau: horse-drawn carriages, orange trees, gypsy flower-sellers and religious buildings. At its centre is an early 20th-century monumental lamppost and fountain by José Lafita, with grotesque heads copied from Roman originals in the Casa de Pilatos (see p81).

At the north of the square is the Palacio Arzobispal (Archbishop's Palace), begun in the 16th century, finished in the 18th, and commandeered by Marshal Soult during the Napoleonic occupation of 1810 (see pp56–7). A fine Baroque palace, it has a jasper staircase and paintings by Zurbarán and Murillo. On the opposite side of

the square is the whitewashed Convento de la Encarnación, which was founded in 1591. The convent stands on grounds that have also been the site of a mosque and of a hospital.

The Plaza Virgen de los Reyes was once home to the Corral de los Olmos, a rogues' inn which features in the writings of Miguel de Cervantes (see p55) – on one of the convent walls a plaque bears an inscription testifying to this.

❾ Plaza del Triunfo

Map 3 C2 (6 D4).

Lying between the cathedral (see pp82–3) and the Real Alcázar (see pp86–7), the Plaza del Triunfo was built to celebrate the triumph of the city over an earthquake in 1755. The quake devastated the city of Lisbon, over the border in Portugal, but caused comparatively little damage in Seville – a salvation attributed to the city's great devotion to the Virgin Mary. She

Decorative Giralda relief on the Archivo de Indias

is honoured by a Baroque column beside the Archivo de Indias. In the centre of the Plaza del Triunfo a monument commemorates Seville's belief in the Immaculate Conception.

In Calle Santo Tomás, off the southeastern corner of the Plaza del Triunfo, lies a building used by the Archivo de Indias. Formerly the Museo de Arts Contemporáneo – now in the Monasterio de Santa Mariá de las Cuevas (see p109) – the building is no longer open to the public. Dating from 1770 it was once a barn where tithes collected by the Church were stored. Parts of the Moorish city walls were uncovered during the renovation of the building.

❿ Archivo de Indias

Avda de la Constitución s/n. **Map** 3 C2 (6 D5). 🚇 Archivo de Indias. 🚍 Prado de San Sebastian. **Tel** 95 450 05 28. **Open** 9:30am–5pm Mon–Sat, 10am–2pm Sun. 🔳 mcu.es/archivos

Façade of the Archivo de Indias by Juan de Herrera

The archive of the Indies punches home Seville's pre-eminent role in the colonization and exploitation of the New World. Built between 1584–98 to designs by Juan de Herrera, co-architect of El Escorial near Madrid, it was originally a lonja (exchange), where merchants traded. In 1785, Carlos III had all Spanish documents relating to the "Indies" collected under one roof, creating a fascinating archive. It contains letters from Columbus, Cortés, Cervantes, and George Washington, the first American president, and the extensive correspondence of Felipe II. The vast collection amounts to some 86 million handwritten pages and 8,000 maps and drawings. An extensive programme of document digitization is ongoing.

Visitors to the Archivo de Indias climb marble stairs to library rooms where drawings and maps are exhibited in a reverential atmosphere. Displays change on a regular basis; one might include a watercolour map from the days when the city of Acapulco was little more than a castle, drawings recording a royal *corrida* (bullfight) held in Panama City in 1748 or designs and plans for a town hall in Guatemala.

⓫ Real Alcázar

See pp86–7.

⓬ Hospital de los Venerables

Plaza de los Venerables 8. **Map** 3 C2 (6 D4). ☷ Archivo de Indias. **Tel** 95 456 26 96. **Open** 10am–1:30pm, 4–7:30pm daily. ▨ except Sun evening. ⬧ ⬚

Located in the heart of the Barrio de Santa Cruz, the Hospital of the Venerables was founded as a home for elderly priests. It was begun in 1675 and completed around 20 years later by Leonardo de Figueroa. It was restored as a cultural centre by FOCUS (Fundación Fondo de Cultura de Sevilla).

It is built around a central, sunken patio. The upper floors, along with the infirmary and the cellar, are used as galleries for exhibitions. A separate guided tour visits the hospital church, a showcase of Baroque splendours, with frescoes by Juan de Valdés Leal and his son Lucas Valdés.

Other highlights include the sculptures of St Peter and St Ferdinand by Pedro Roldán, flanking the east door; and The Apotheosis of St Ferdinand by Lucas Valdés, top centre in the *retablo* of the main altar. Its frieze (inscribed in Greek) advises visitors to "Fear God and Honour the Priest".

In the sacristy, the ceiling has an effective *trompe l'oeil* depicting *The Triumph of the Cross* by Juan de Valdés Leal.

⓭ Jardines de Murillo

Map 4 D2 (6 E5).

These formal gardens at the southern end of the Barrio de Santa Cruz once used to be orchards and vegetable plots in the grounds of the Real Alcázar. They were donated to the city in 1911. Their name commemorates Seville's best-known painter, Bartolomé Murillo (1617–82), who lived in nearby Calle Santa Teresa. A long promenade, Paseo de Catalina de Ribera, pays tribute to the founder of the Hospital de las Cinco Llagas, which is now the seat of the Parlamento de Andalucía *(see p93)*. Rising

Monument to Columbus in the Jardines de Murillo

above the garden's palm trees is a monument to Columbus, incorporating a bronze of the *Santa María*, the caravel that bore him to the New World in the year of 1492 *(see p131)*.

Fresco by Juan de Valdés Leal in the Hospital de los Venerables

⑪ Real Alcázar

In 1364 Pedro I *(see p52)* ordered the construction of a royal residence within the palaces built by the city's Almohad *(see pp50–51)* rulers. Within two years, craftsmen from Granada and Toledo had created a jewel box of Mudéjar patios and halls, the Palacio Pedro I, which now forms the heart of Seville's Real Alcázar. Later monarchs added their own distinguishing marks – Isabel I *(see p53)* despatched navigators to explore the New World from her Casa de la Contratación, while Carlos V *(see p54)* had grandiose, richly decorated apartments built.

Gardens of the Alcázar
Laid out with terraces, fountains and pavilions, these gardens provide a delightful refuge from the heat and bustle of Seville.

★ **Salones de Carlos V**
Vast tapestries and lively 16th-century *azulejos* decorate the vaulted halls of the apartments and chapel of Carlos V.

KEY

① **Patio del Crucero** lies above the old baths.

② **Jardín de Troya**

③ **Casa de la Contratación**

④ **The façade** of the Palacio Pedro I is a unique example of Mudéjar style.

⑤ **The Patio de la Montería** was where the court met before hunting expeditions.

★ **Patio de las Doncellas**
The Patio of the Maidens boasts plasterwork by the top craftsmen of Granada.

★ **Salón de Embajadores**
Built in 1427, the dazzling dome of the Ambassadors' Hall is made up of carved and gilded, interlaced wood.

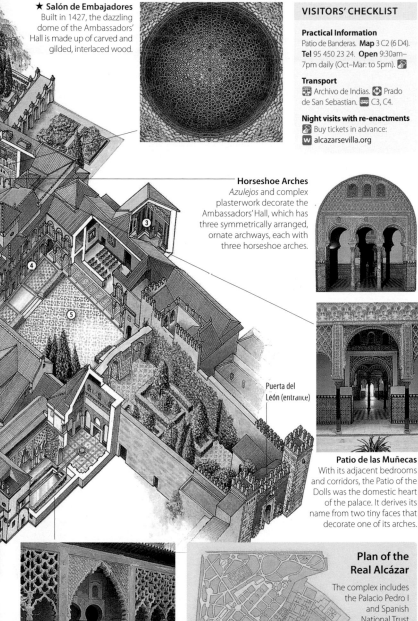

Horseshoe Arches
Azulejos and complex plasterwork decorate the Ambassadors' Hall, which has three symmetrically arranged, ornate archways, each with three horseshoe arches.

Puerta del León (entrance)

Patio de las Muñecas
With its adjacent bedrooms and corridors, the Patio of the Dolls was the domestic heart of the palace. It derives its name from two tiny faces that decorate one of its arches.

Plan of the Real Alcázar

The complex includes the Palacio Pedro I and Spanish National Trust offices. The palace's upper floor is used by the Spanish royal family during visits to the city.

Patio del Yeso
The Patio of Plaster, a garden with flower beds and a water channel, retains features of the earlier, 12th-century Almohad Alcázar.

Key

☐ Area illustrated above

☐ Gardens

LA MACARENA

The north of Seville, often overlooked by visitors, presents a characterful mix of decaying Baroque and Mudéjar churches, old-style neighbourhood tapas bars and washing-filled back streets. Its name is thought to derive from the Roman goddess, Macaria, the daughter of the hero Hercules. La Macarena is a traditional district and the power of church and family is still strong there.

Metropol Parasol creates a grand gateway to this neighbourhood, and from there head north up Calle Feria to the Basílica de la Macarena, an important shrine to Seville's much-venerated Virgen de la Esperanza Macarena. Beside this modern church stands

a restored entrance gate and remnants of defensive walls, which enclosed the city during the Moorish era.

Among many churches and convents in this quarter, the Monasterio de San Clemente and Iglesia de San Pedro retain the spirit of historic Seville, while the Convento de Santa Paula offers a rare opportunity to peep behind the walls of a closed religious community. The 13th-century Torre de Don Fadrique in Convento de Santa Clara is a notable sight to the west of the area. Further north is the former Hospital de las Cinco Llagas, now restored as the seat of Andalusia's Parliament.

Sights at a Glance

Churches and Convents
1. Monasterio de San Clemente
2. Torre de Don Fadrique
4. Basílica de la Macarena
6. Parlamento de Andalucía
8. Iglesia de San Marcos
9. Convento de Santa Paula
10. Iglesia de San Pedro
11. Iglesia de Santa Catalina

Boulevards
3. Alameda de Hércules

Historic Buildings
5. Camera Obscura

Monuments
7. Murallas

Modern Architecture
12. Metropol Parasol

☐ **Restaurants** *p229*
1. Con Tenedor
2. Eslava

*See also Street Finder
maps 2, 5, 6*

```
0 metres        500
0 yards         500
```

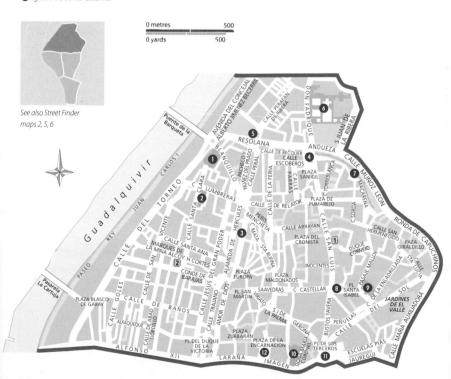

◀ Revered weeping statue of the Virgen de la Esperanza Macarena, Basílica de la Macarena

Street-by-Street: La Macarena

A stroll in this area provides a glimpse of everyday life in a part of Seville that has so far escaped developing the rather tourist-oriented atmosphere of Santa Cruz. Calle de la Feria, the main street for shopping and browsing, is best visited in the morning when there is plenty of activity and its market stalls are filled with fresh fish and vegetables. Early evening, meanwhile, is a good time to discover the area's large number of fine churches, which are open for Mass at that time. It is also the time when local people visit the bars of the district for a drink and tapas.

Palacio de las Dueñas
Boxed in by the surrounding houses, this 15th-century Mudéjar palace has an elegant patio. It is the private residence of the Dukes of Alba, whose tiled coat of arms can be seen above the palace entrance.

Calle de la Feria
On Thursday mornings, El Jueves, Seville's oldest market, takes place on this street full of shops.

Iglesia San Juan de la Palma is a small Mudéjar church. Its brickwork belfry was added in 1788.

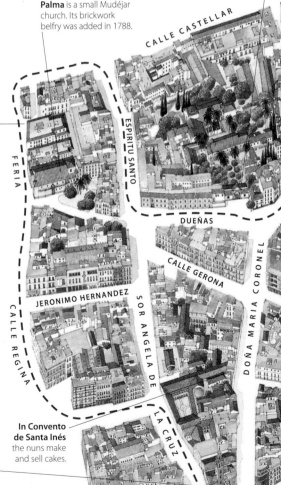

CALLE CASTELLAR

ESPIRITU SANTO

FERIA

DUEÑAS

CALLE GERONA

JERONIMO HERNANDEZ

SOR ANGELA DE

DOÑA MARIA CORONEL

CALLE REGINA

LA CRUZ

❿ ★ Iglesia de San Pedro
The church where Velázquez was baptized is a mix of styles, from Mudéjar to these modern tiles on its front.

In Convento de Santa Inés the nuns make and sell cakes.

Key

— Suggested route

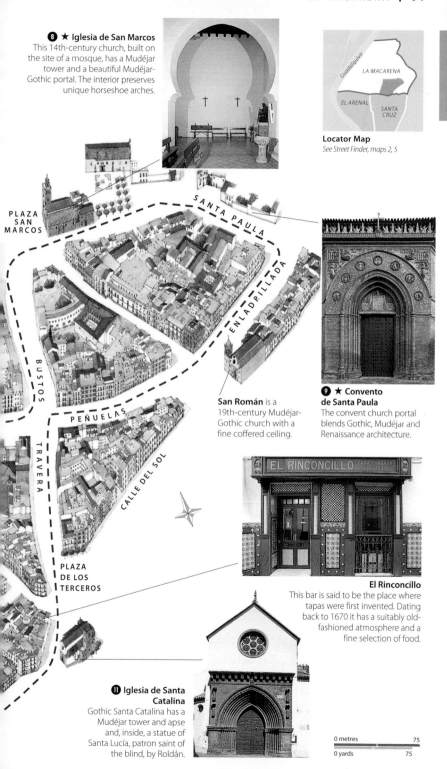

8 ★ Iglesia de San Marcos
This 14th-century church, built on the site of a mosque, has a Mudéjar tower and a beautiful Mudéjar-Gothic portal. The interior preserves unique horseshoe arches.

Locator Map
See Street Finder, maps 2, 5

PLAZA SAN MARCOS

SANTA PAULA

ENLADRILLADA

BUSTOS

PEÑUELAS

TRAVERA

CALLE DEL SOL

PLAZA DE LOS TERCEROS

San Román is a 19th-century Mudéjar-Gothic church with a fine coffered ceiling.

9 ★ Convento de Santa Paula
The convent church portal blends Gothic, Mudéjar and Renaissance architecture.

El Rinconcillo
This bar is said to be the place where tapas were first invented. Dating back to 1670 it has a suitably old-fashioned atmosphere and a fine selection of food.

11 Iglesia de Santa Catalina
Gothic Santa Catalina has a Mudéjar tower and apse and, inside, a statue of Santa Lucía, patron saint of the blind, by Roldán.

| 0 metres | 75 |
| 0 yards | 75 |

❶ Monasterio de San Clemente

Calle Reposo 9. **Map** 1 C3. 🚌 C3, C4. **Tel** 95 437 80 40. Church **Open** for Mass only: 8am Mon–Sat, 10am Sun & public hols. W sanclementesevilla.com

Behind the ancient walls of the Monasterio de San Clemente is a tranquil cloister with palms and fruit trees, and an arcade with a side entrance to the monastery's church.

This atmospheric church can also be entered through an arch in Calle Reposo. Its features range from the 13th to 18th centuries, and include a fine Mudéjar *artesonado* ceiling, *azulejos (see p80)* dating from 1588, a Baroque main *retablo* by Felipe de Rivas and early 18th-century frescoes by Lucas Valdés.

❷ Torre de Don Fadrique

Convento de Santa Clara, Calle Santa Clara 40. **Map** 1 C4. **Tel** 955 47 13 02. **Open** by appointment only.

One of the best-preserved historical surprises in Seville, this 13th-century tower stands like a chess-piece castle in the Convento de Santa Clara. This is

Marble columns at the southern end of Alameda de Hércules

entered from Calle Santa Clara, passing through an arch to a sleepy patio with orange trees and a fountain. To the left is a second courtyard, where the tower is hidden away. The Gothic entrance to the courtyard was built during the 16th century as part of Seville's first university and transplanted here in the 19th century.

Constructed in 1252, the tower formed part of the defences for the palace of the Infante Don Fadrique. On the façade Romanesque windows sit below Gothic ones. More than 80 steps lead to the upper floor, from which there are impressive views across the city towards La Giralda and Puente de la Barqueta.

The convent of Santa Clara was founded in 1260, though the present buildings date from the 15th century. The Mannerist entrance portico is by Juan de Oviedo. Inside, the nave has a Mudéjar coffered ceiling and an outstanding main *retablo* sculpted by Juan Martínez Montañés in 1623.

Gargoyle on the Torre de Don Fadrique

❸ Alameda de Hércules

Map 2 D4.

This tree-lined boulevard was originally laid out in 1574. The former marshy area was thus turned into a fashionable promenade for use by *sevillanos* of the Golden Age *(see pp54–5)*. Since the relocation of the Sunday morning flea market to Charco de la Pava *(see p108)*, efforts have been made to improve the Alameda, and these days it is a trendy, clean area with a certain bohemian charm. At the southern end of the boulevard stand two marble columns. They were brought here from a Roman temple dedicated to Hercules in what is now Calle Mármoles (Marbles Street), where three other columns remain. Time-worn statues of Hercules and Julius Caesar cap the Alameda's columns.

The area boasts an eclectic mix of bars, restaurants and cafes.

Torre de Don Fadrique in the patio of Convento de Santa Clara

❹ Basílica de la Macarena

Calle Bécquer 1. **Map** 2 D3. 🚌 C1, C2, C3, C4. **Tel** 95 437 01 95. **Open** 9am–2pm, 5–9pm daily. Treasury **Open** 9:30am–1:30pm, 5–8:30pm daily. **Closed** Easter hols. 🅿

The Basílica de la Macarena was built in 1949 in the Neo-Baroque style by Gómez Millán as a new home for the much-loved Virgen de la Esperanza Macarena. It butts on to the 13th-century Iglesia de San Gil, where the Virgin was housed until a fire in 1936.

The image of the Virgin stands above the main altar amid waterfalls of gold and silver. It has been attributed to Luisa Roldán (1656–1703). The wall-paintings by Rafael Rodríguez Hernández have themes focusing on the Virgin.

In the museum housed in the Treasury there are magnificent processional garments as well as gowns made from *trajes de luces* (suits of lights), donated by famous and no doubt grateful bullfighters. The floats used in Semana Santa (see p42), among them La Macarena's elaborate silver platform, can also be admired.

Float of the Virgen de la Macarena in Semana Santa processions

❺ Camera Obscura

C/ Resolana s/n. **Open** 11:30am–7pm Tue–Sun. **Tel** 679 09 10 73. 🆆 torredelosperdigones.com

The Camera Obscura at the Tower of Perdigones, located in Seville's old quarter, has fantastic views of the 1992 World Expo fairground, Cartuja Island and the Guadalquivir River. It projects real time images, with movement, by using mirrors and magnifying glasses over a periscope.

Virgen De La Macarena

Devotions to the Virgen de la Macarena reach their peak during Semana Santa (see p42), when her statue is borne through the streets on a canopied float decorated with swathes of white flowers, candles and ornate silverwork. Accompanied by hooded penitents and cries of *¡guapa!* (beautiful!) from her followers, the virgin travels along a route from the Basílica de la Macarena to the cathedral (see pp82–3) in the early hours of Good Friday.

Renaissance façade and Baroque portal of Parlamento de Andalucía

❻ Parlamento de Andalucía

C/ Parlamento de Andalucia s/n. **Map** 2 E3. **Open** By written application or call the protocol office. **Tel** 954 59 22 88. 🅿 🆆 parlamentodeandalucia.es

The Parliament of Andalusia has its seat in an impressive Renaissance building, the Hospital de las Cinco Llagas (five wounds). The hospital, founded in 1500 by Catalina de Ribera, was originally sited near Casa de Pilatos. In 1540 work began on what was to become Europe's largest hospital. Designed by a succession of architects, its south front has a Baroque central portal by Asensio de Maeda.

The hospital was completed in 1613, and admitted patients until the 1960s. In 1992 it was restored for the Parliament.

At the heart of the complex, the Mannerist church, built by Hernán Ruiz the Younger in 1560, has today been turned into a debating chamber.

Virgen de la Macarena – the main reredos in Basílica de la Macarena

❼ Murallas

Map 2 E3.

A section of the defensive walls that once enclosed Seville survives along calles Andueza and Muñoz León. It runs from the rebuilt Puerta de la Macarena at the Basílica de la Macarena (*see p93*) to the Puerta de Córdoba some 400 m (1,300 ft) further east.

Dating from the 12th century, it was constructed as a curtain wall with a patrol path in the middle. The original walls had over 100 towers; the Torre Blanca is one of seven that can be seen here. At the eastern end stands the 17th-century Iglesia de San Hermenegildo, named after the Visigothic king who was allegedly martyred on the site. On the southern corner of this church remains of Moorish arches can be seen.

❽ Iglesia de San Marcos

Plaza de San Marcos. **Map** 2 E5 (6E1). **Tel** 95 450 26 16. **Open** 7:30–8:30pm Mon–Sat.

This 14th-century church retains several Mudéjar features, notably its Giralda-like tower (based on the minaret of an earlier mosque) and the decoration on the Gothic portal on Plaza de San Marcos. The restoration of the interior, gutted by fire in 1936, has highlighted unique horseshoe arches in the nave. A statue of St Mark with book and quill pen, attributed to Juan de Mesa, is in the far left corner. In the plaza at

The Gothic-Mudéjar portal of the 14th-century Iglesia de San Marcos

the back of the church is the Convento de Santa Isabel, founded in 1490. It became a women's prison in the 19th century. The church dates from 1609. Its Baroque portal, facing onto Plaza de Santa Isabel, has a bas-relief of *The Visitation* sculpted by Andrés de Ocampo.

❾ Convento de Santa Paula

C/ Santa Paula 11. **Map** 2 E5 (6 F1). **Tel** 95 453 63 30. **Open** 10am–1pm Tue–Sun.

Seville has many enclosed religious complexes, but few are accessible. This is one of them, a convent set up in 1475 and still home to 40 nuns. The public is welcome to enter through two different doors in the Calle Santa Paula. Bang on the brown one, marked No. 11, to have a look at the convent museum. Steps lead to two galleries crammed with religious paintings and artifacts. The

windows of the second look onto the nuns' cloister, which echoes with laughter in the afternoon recreation hour. The nuns make a phenomenal range of marmalades and jams, which visitors may purchase in a room near the exit.

Ring the bell by a brick doorway nearby to visit the convent church, reached by crossing a meditative garden. Its portal vividly combines Gothic arches, Mudéjar brickwork, Renaissance medallions, and ceramics by the Italian artist, Nicola Pisano. Inside, the nave has an elaborate wooden roof carved in 1623. Among its statues are St John the Evangelist and St John the Baptist, carved by Juan Martínez Montañés.

St John the Baptist by Montañés in the Convento de Santa Paula

---

Sevillian Bell Towers

Bell towers rise above the rooftops of Seville like bookmarks flagging the passing centuries. The influence of La Giralda (*see p82*) is seen in the Moorish arches and tracery adorning the 14th-century tower of San Marcos, and the Mudéjar brickwork which forms the base for San Pedro's belfry. The churches of Santa Paula and La Magdalena reflect the ornate confidence of the Baroque period, while the towers of San Ildefonso illustrate the Neo-Classical tastes of the 19th century.

San Marcos   San Pedro   Santa Paula

Intricate pattern on a chapel door in the Iglesia de San Pedro

⑩ Iglesia de San Pedro

Plaza San Pedro. **Map** 2 D5 (6 E2). **Tel** 95 422 91 24. **Open** 8:30–11:30am, 7–8:30pm Mon–Sat; 9:30am– 1:30pm, 7–8:30pm Sun. ♿

The church where the painter Diego Velázquez was baptized in 1599 presents a typically Sevillian mix of architectural styles. Mudéjar elements survive in the lobed brickwork of its tower, which is surmounted by a Baroque belfry. The principal portal, facing Plaza de San Pedro, is another Baroque adornments added by Diego de Quesada in 1613. A statue of St Peter looks disdainfully down at the heathen traffic below.

The poorly lit interior has a Mudéjar wooden ceiling and west door. The vault of one of its chapels is decorated with exquisite geometric patterns formed of interlacing bricks. Behind the church, in Calle Doña María Coronel, cakes and biscuits are sold from a revolving drum in the wall of the Convento de Santa Inés. An arcaded patio fronts its restored church, with frescoes by Francisco de Herrera and a nun's choir separated from the public by a screen. The preserved body of Doña María Coronel, the convent's 14th-century founder, is honoured in the choir every 2 December.

⑪ Iglesia de Santa Catalina

Plaza Ponce de Léon. **Map** 2 D5 (6 E2). **Tel** 95 421 74 41. **Closed** for restoration; end date not known.

Built on the former site of a mosque, this 14th-century church has a Mudéjar tower modelled on La Giralda (see p78) (best viewed from Plaza Ponce de Léon) which has been spared the customary Baroque hat. On the west side, by Calle Alhóndiga, the Gothic portal is originally from the Iglesia de Santa Lucía, which was knocked down in 1930. Within its entrance is a horseshoe arch. At the far left end of the nave, the Capilla Sacramental is by Leonardo de Figueroa. On the right, the Capilla de la Exaltación has a decorative ceiling, circa 1400, and a figure of Christ by Pedro Roldán.

⑫ Metropol Parasol

Plaza de la Encarnación. **Map** 2 D5 (6 D2). **Tel** 606 635 214. **Open** Observation decks & skywalks: 10:30am–10:30pm Sun–Thu, 10:30am–12:30am Fri & Sat; Museum: 10am–8pm Tue–Sat, 10am–2pm Sun & public hols. ♿

This ultra-modern structure, commonly referred to as "Las Setas" (The Mushrooms), is a striking contrast of modern architecture and astounding archeological find: the Observation Deck on top provides a soaring view of the city, with skywalks circling around the core of trendy gastrobars, while the first floor has an open air plaza, which hosts cultural events and social functions. The local market buzzes with life on the ground floor, and the Antiquarium Museum, housed in the basement, showcases the archaeological remains that were found when this project began in 1973, with extensive Roman ruins from the Tiberius era (c 30 AD–600 AD), and a Moorish house from the 12th and 13th century.

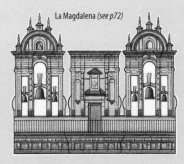

La Magdalena (see p72)

San Ildefonso (see p81)

PARQUE MARÍA LUISA

The area south of the city centre is dominated by the extensive, leafy Parque María Luisa, Seville's principal green area. A great part of it originally formed the grounds of the Baroque Palacio de San Telmo, dating from 1682. Today the park is devoted to recreation; with its fountains, flower gardens and mature trees it provides a welcome place to relax during the long, hot summer months. Just north of the park lies Prado de San Sebastián, the former site of the *quemadero*, the platform where many victims of the Inquisition *(see p51)* were burnt to death. The last execution took place here in 1781.

Many of the historic buildings situated within the park were erected for the Ibero-American Exposition of 1929. This international jamboree sought to reinstate Spain and Andalusia on the world map. Exhibitions from Spain, Portugal and Latin America were displayed in attractive, purpose-built pavilions that are today used as museums, embassies, military headquarters and also cultural and educational institutions. The grand five-star Hotel Alfonso XIII and the crescent-shaped Plaza de España are the most striking legacies from this surge of Andalusian pride.

Nearby is the Royal Tobacco Factory, forever associated with the fictional gypsy heroine, Carmen, who toiled in its halls. Today it is part of the Universidad, Seville's university.

Sights at a Glance

Museums
- ❻ Museo de Artes y Costumbres Populares
- ❼ Museo Arqueológico

Theatres
- ❹ Teatro Lope de Vega

Gardens
- ❺ Parque María Luisa pp98–9

Historic Buildings
- ❶ Hotel Alfonso XIII
- ❷ Palacio de San Telmo
- ❸ Universidad

☐ **Restaurants** *p229*
1 San Fernando

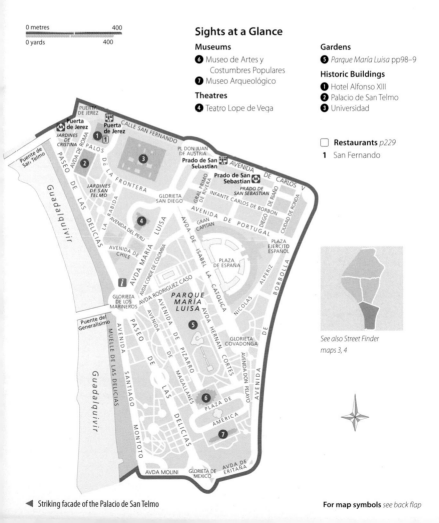

See also Street Finder maps 3, 4

◀ Striking facade of the Palacio de San Telmo

For map symbols see back flap

Street-by-Street: Around the Universidad

South of the Puerta de Jerez, a cluster of stately buildings stands between the river and Parque María Luisa. The oldest ones owe their existence to the Guadalquivir itself – the 17th-century Palacio de San Telmo was built as a training school for mariners, while the arrival of tobacco from the New World prompted the construction of the monumental Royal Tobacco Factory, today the Universidad de Sevilla. The 1929 Ibero-American Exposition added pavilions in various national and historic styles and also the opulent Hotel Alfonso XIII, creating an area of proud and pleasing architecture that will entertain visitors as they walk towards the Parque María Luisa.

To Triana

Paseo de las Delicias
This riverside walk flanks the Jardines de San Telmo. Its name means the "walk of delights".

Pabellón de Chile is now the Escuela de Artes Aplicadas (School of Applied Arts).

Pabellón de Perú
Modelled on the Archbishop's Palace in Lima, this pavilion has a vividly carved façade. It is typical of the nationalistic designs used for the Exposition buildings.

Pabellón de Uruguay

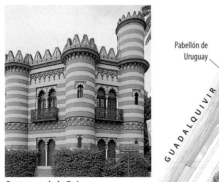

Costurero de la Reina
Today it serves as the municipal tourist office, but the "Queen's sewing box" used to be a garden lodge.

0 metres   75
0 yards   75

Key
— Suggested route

Monument to El Cano, who completed the first world circumnavigation in 1522 after Magellan was killed on route.

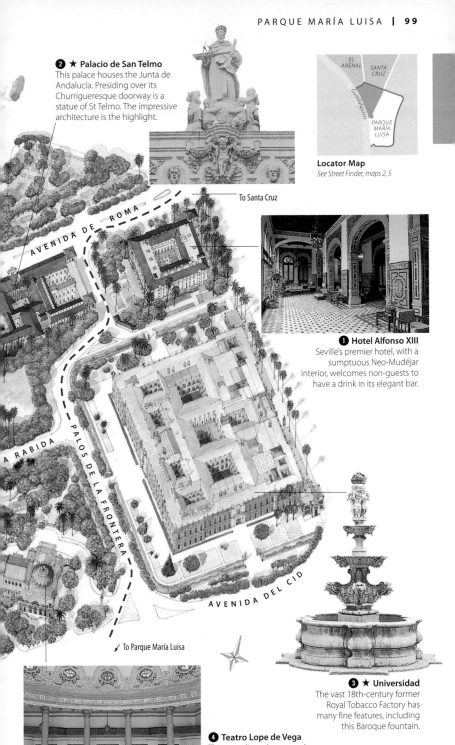

2 ★ **Palacio de San Telmo**
This palace houses the Junta de Andalucía. Presiding over its Churrigueresque doorway is a statue of St Telmo. The impressive architecture is the highlight.

Locator Map
See Street Finder, maps 2, 5

To Santa Cruz

AVENIDA DE ROMA

A RABIDA

PALOS DE LA FRONTERA

AVENIDA DEL CID

To Parque María Luisa

1 **Hotel Alfonso XIII**
Seville's premier hotel, with a sumptuous Neo-Mudéjar interior, welcomes non-guests to have a drink in its elegant bar.

3 ★ **Universidad**
The vast 18th-century former Royal Tobacco Factory has many fine features, including this Baroque fountain.

4 **Teatro Lope de Vega**
This grandiose theatre and casino, the 1929 Pabellón de Sevilla, is now a major venue for staging concerts and shows.

❶ Hotel Alfonso XIII

Calle San Fernando 2. **Map** 3 C3 (6 D5).
🚇 Puerta Jerez. 🚌 Prado de San
Sebastian. **Tel** 95 491 70 00.
♿ except toilets.
🌐 **hotel-alfonsoxiii-sevilla.com**

At the southeast corner of
Puerta de Jerez is Seville's best-
known luxury hotel, named
after King Alfonso XIII *(see p58)*,
who reigned 1902–31, when
Spain became a republic. It was
built between 1916–28 for
visitors to the 1929 Ibero-
American Exposition *(see p59)*.
The building is in Regionalista
style, decorated with *azulejos*
(see p80), wrought iron and
ornate brickwork. Its centrepiece
is a grand patio with a fountain
and orange trees. Non-residents
are welcome to visit one of the
hotel's bars or restaurants.

Central patio with fountain in the elegant Hotel Alfonso XIII

Churrigueresque adornments of the portal
of Palacio de San Telmo

❷ Palacio de San Telmo

Avenida de Roma s/n. **Map** 3 C3.
🚇 Puerta Jerez. 🚌 Plaza de Cuba.
Tel 95 500 10 10. **Open** Thu, Sat & Sun
by appointment only. 🈯 ♿ 📷
🌐 **juntadeandalucia.es**

This imposing palace was built
in 1682 to serve as a marine
university, training navigators
and high-ranking officers. It is
named after St Telmo, patron
saint of navigators. In 1849 the
palace became the residence
of the Dukes of Montpensier –
until 1893 its vast grounds

included what is now the
Parque María Luisa *(pp102–3)*.
The palace became a seminary
in 1901, and today it is the
presidential headquarters of
the regional government.

The palace's star feature is the
exuberant Churrigueresque portal
overlooking Avenida de Roma by
Antonio Matías de Figueroa,
completed in 1734. Surrounding
the Ionic columns are
allegorical figures of the Arts
and Sciences. St Telmo
can be seen holding a
ship and charts,
flanked by the sword-
bearing St Ferdinand
and St Hermenegildo
with a cross. The north
façade, which is on
Avenida de Palos de la
Frontera, is crowned by a
row of Sevillian
celebrities. These sculptures were
added in 1895 by Susillo. Among
them are representations of
several notable artists.

Façade detail of the
Universidad

❸ Universidad

Calle San Fernando 4. **Map** 3 C3.
🚇 Puerta Jerez. 🚌 Prado de San
Sebastian. **Tel** 95 455 10 00.
Open 8am–8:30pm Mon–Fri.
Closed public hols. 🌐 **us.es**

The former Real Fábrica de
Tabacos (Royal Tobacco Factory)
is now part of Seville University.
It was a popular attraction for
19th-century travellers in
search of Romantic Spain.
Three-quarters of
Europe's cigars were
then manufactured
here, rolled on the
thighs of over 3,000
cigarreras (female
cigar-makers), who
were said "to be more
impertinent than
chaste", as the writer
Richard Ford observed
in his 1845 *Handbook for Spain*.
The factory complex is the
largest building in Spain after El
Escorial in Madrid and was built

Carmen

The hot blooded *cigarreras*
working in Seville's Royal Tobacco
Factory inspired the French author,
Prosper Mérimée, to create his
famous gypsy heroine, *Carmen*.
The short story he wrote in 1845
tells the tragic tale of a sensual
and wild woman who turns her
affections from a soldier to a
bullfighter and is then murdered
by her spurned lover. Bizet based
his famous opera of 1875 on this
impassioned drama, which
established Carmen as an
incarnation of Spanish romance.

Carmen and Don José

between 1728–71. The moat and watchtowers show the importance given to protecting the king's lucrative tobacco monopoly. To the right of the main entrance is the former prison where workers caught smuggling tobacco were kept. To the left is the chapel, now used by university students.

The discovery of tobacco in the New World is celebrated in the principal portal, which has busts of Columbus *(see p131)* and Cortés. This part of the factory was once used as residential quarters – to either side of the vestibule lie small patios with plants and ironwork. Ahead, the Clock Patio and Fountain Patio lead to the former working areas. The tobacco leaves were first dried on the roof, then shredded by donkey-powered mills below. Production now takes place in a modern factory situated on the other side of the river, by the Puente del Generalísimo.

Baroque fountain in one of the patios in the Universidad

❹ Teatro Lope de Vega

Avenida María Luisa s/n. **Map** 3 C3. 🚊 & 🚇 Prado de San Sebastian. **Tel** 95 547 28 28 (ticket office). **Open** for performances. ♿ 🌐 **teatrolopedevega.org.**

Lope de Vega (1562–1635), often called "the Spanish Shakespeare", wrote more than 1,500 plays. This Neo-Baroque theatre which honours him was opened in 1929 as a casino and theatre for the Ibero-American Exposition *(see p59)*. Its colonnaded and domed buildings are still used to stage performances and plays

Dome of the Neo-Baroque Teatro Lope de Vega, opened in 1929

(see pp244–5). Visitors to the Café del Casino can relax and enjoy a coffee amid its faded opulence.

❺ Parque María Luisa

See pp102–3.

❻ Museo de Artes y Costumbres Populares

Pabellón Mudéjar, Parque María Luisa. **Map** 4 D5. **Tel** 95 554 29 51. **Open** 10am–8:30pm Tue–Sat, 10am–5pm Sun (Jun–mid-Sep: 9am–3:30pm Tue–Sat, 10am–5pm Sun). ✉ ♿

Housed in the Mudéjar Pavilion of the 1929 Ibero-American Exposition *(see p59)*, this museum is devoted to the popular arts and traditions of Andalusia. Exhibits in the basement include a series of workshop scenes detailing crafts such as leatherwork, ceramics and cooperage.

There is also an informative account of the history of the *azulejo*. Upstairs is a display of 19th-century costumes, furniture, musical instruments and rural machinery. Romantic images of flamenco, bullfighting, and the Semana Santa and Feria de Abril *(see p42)* are a compendium of the Sevillian cliché.

❼ Museo Arqueológico

Plaza de América, Parque María Luisa. **Map** 4 D5. **Tel** 95 512 06 32. **Open** 10am–8:30pm Tue–Sat, 10am–5pm Sun (Jun–mid-Sep: 9am–3:30pm Tue–Sat, 10am–5pm Sun). ✉ ♿

The Renaissance pavilion of the 1929 Ibero-American Exposition is now Andalusia's museum of archaeology. The basement houses Paleolithic to early-Roman exhibits, such as copies of the remarkable Tartessian Carambolo treasures *(see p47)*. This hoard of 6th-century BC gold jewellery was discovered near Seville in 1958.

Upstairs, the main galleries are devoted to the Roman era, with statues and fragments rescued from Itálica *(see p136)*. Highlights include a 3rd-century BC mosaic from Écija *(see p137)*, sculptures of local-born emperors Trajan and Hadrian. The rooms continue to Moorish Spain via Palaeo-Christian sarcophagi, Visigothic relics and artifacts from Medina Azahara *(see p142)*.

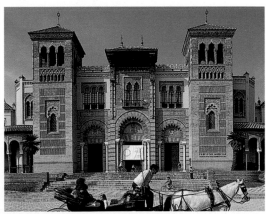

Museo de Artes y Costumbres Populares, the former Mudéjar Pavilion

● Parque María Luisa

This vast park takes its name from Princess María Luisa de Orléans, who donated part of the grounds from the Palacio de San Telmo *(see p100)* to the city in 1893. The area was landscaped by Jean-Claude Forestier, director of the Bois de Boulogne in Paris, who created a leafy setting for the pastiche pavilions of the 1929 Ibero-American Exposition *(see p59)*. The most dazzling souvenirs from this extravaganza are the Plaza de España and Plaza de América, both the work of Anibal González, which set the park's theatrical mood. Sprinkling fountains, flowers and cool, tree-shaded avenues all go to make this park a refreshing retreat from the heat and dust of the city.

★ **Plaza de España**
Tiled benches line this semicircular plaza, centrepiece of the 1929 Exposition.

KEY

① **Glorieta de la Infanta** has a bronze statue honouring the park's benefactress, the Princess María Luisa de Orléans.

② **Glorieta de Bécquer**, is a tribute to the Romantic Sevillian poet, Gustavo Adolfo Bécquer (1836–70). Allegorical figures, depicting the phases of love, add charm to this monument. It was sculpted by Lorenzo Coullaut Valera in 1911.

③ **Starting point for horse and carriage rides**

④ **Pabellón Real**

⑤ **The Monte Gurugú** is a mini-mountain with a tumbling waterfall.

Isleta de los Patos
In the centre of the park is a lake graced by ducks and swans. A gazebo situated on an island provides a peaceful resting place.

Fuente de los Leones
Ceramic lions guard this octagonal fountain, which is surrounded by myrtle hedges. Its design was inspired by the fountain in the Patio de los Leones at the Alhambra *(see p199)*.

❼ ★ Museo Arqueológico
The Neo-Renaissance Pabellón de las Bellas Artes today houses a regional archaeological museum. Many finds from nearby Roman Itálica *(see p136)* are among the exhibits.

❻ ★ Museo de Artes y Costumbres Populares
The pavilions of Plaza de América evoke the triumph of the Mudéjar, Gothic and Renaissance styles. The Pabellón Mudéjar houses a museum of Andalusian folk arts.

Ceramics
Brightly painted Sevillian ceramics from Triana decorate the park in the form of floral urns, tiled benches and playful frogs and ducks placed around the fountains.

ACROSS THE RIVER

On the west bank of the Guadalquivir, old Seville meets the new. Since Roman times, pottery has been made in Triana, an area named after the emperor Trajan. It has traditionally been a working-class district, famous for the bullfighters and flamenco artistes that came from its predominantly gypsy community. With cobbled streets and shops selling ceramics, it still has an authentic, lived-in feel. Iglesia de Santa Ana is a fine Mudéjar-Gothic church. From the riverside restaurants and bars along Calle Betis there are views of Seville's towers and belfries.

In the 15th century, a Carthusian monastery was built in what was then a quiet area north of Triana – hence the name that the district acquired: Isla de la Cartuja. Later Columbus resided here, planning his future exploits. Mainly due to this connection, La Cartuja was the site for Expo '92 (see pp108–9). The monastery buildings were restored and several pavilions of strikingly modern design built. The majority of the pavilions now house offices; a branch of the University of Seville is also here. The Expo site has been redeveloped to include the Isla Mágica theme park (see p108).

Sights at a Glance

Theme Parks
❶ Isla Mágica
❷ Cartuja '93

Traditional Areas
❺ Triana pp102–3

Churches and Monasteries
❹ Monasterio de Santa María de las Cuevas

❻ Iglesia de Nuestra Señora de la O
❼ Iglesia de Santa Ana

Markets
❸ Charco de la Pava Flea Market

Key
- Seville city centre
- Greater Seville
- Motorway
- Major road
- Minor road

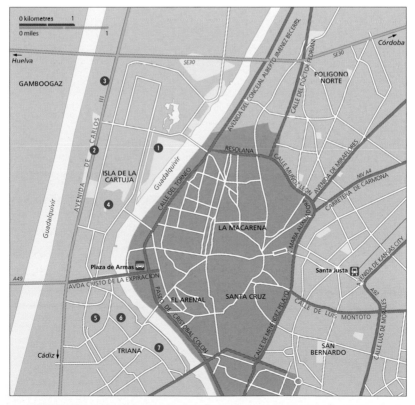

◀ Looking towards Triana district and the bell tower of Iglesia de Santa Ann at sunset

For map symbols see back flap

❺ Triana

Named after the Roman emperor Trajan, this quarter has, since early times, been famous for its potteries. Plenty of workshops still produce and sell tiles and ceramics. Once Seville's gypsy quarter, this *barrio* also has a reputation for producing great bullfighters, sailors and flamenco artists. It remains a traditional working-class district, with compact, flower-filled streets and a tangibly independent atmosphere. Visitors to Triana can buy tiles and wander through its narrow streets during the day, and enjoy the lively bars and romantic views across the Río Guadalquivir at night.

To Nuestra Señora de la O *(see p109)*

Callejón de la Inquisición

CASTILLA

SAN JORGE

PLAZA DEL ALTOZANO

ANTILLANO CAMPOS

COVADONGA

SAN JACINTO

RODRIGO DE TRIANA

Cerámica Santa Ana
Founded in 1870, this is the best known of Triana's tile shops. It sells anything from replicas of 16th-century tiles to ashtrays.

Plaza del Altozano
At the west end of Puente de Isabel II, this plaza features glass-fronted, wrought-iron balconies called *miradores*.

Santa Justa and Santa Rufina as represented by Murillo (c.1665)

Santa Justa and Santa Rufina

Two Christians working in the Triana potteries in the 3rd century have become Seville's patron saints. The city's Roman rulers are said to have thrown the young women to the lions after they refused to join a procession venerating Venus. This martyrdom has inspired many works by Sevillian artists, including Murillo and Zurbarán *(see pp70–71)*. The saints are often shown with the Giralda, which, apparently, they protected from an earthquake in 1755.

Calle Rodrigo de Triana
This street in white and ochre is named after the Andalusian sailor who first caught sight of the New World on Columbus's epic voyage of 1492 *(see p55)*.

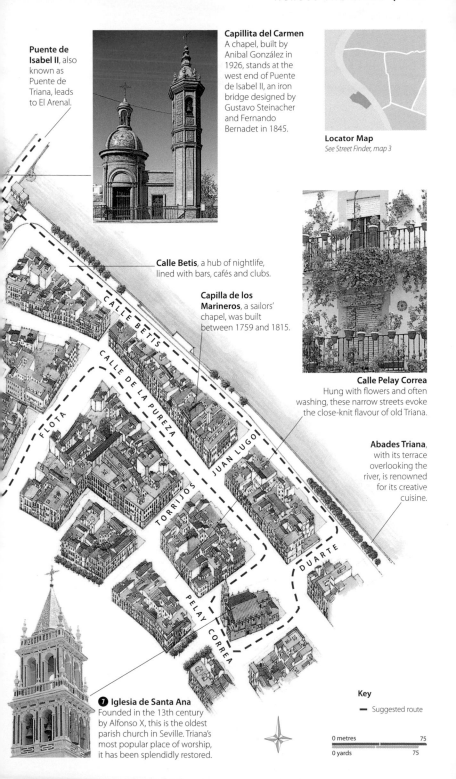

Puente de Isabel II, also known as Puente de Triana, leads to El Arenal.

Capillita del Carmen
A chapel, built by Anibal González in 1926, stands at the west end of Puente de Isabel II, an iron bridge designed by Gustavo Steinacher and Fernando Bernadet in 1845.

Locator Map
See Street Finder, map 3

Calle Betis, a hub of nightlife, lined with bars, cafés and clubs.

Capilla de los Marineros, a sailors' chapel, was built between 1759 and 1815.

Calle Pelay Correa
Hung with flowers and often washing, these narrow streets evoke the close-knit flavour of old Triana.

Abades Triana, with its terrace overlooking the river, is renowned for its creative cuisine.

❼ Iglesia de Santa Ana
Founded in the 13th century by Alfonso X, this is the oldest parish church in Seville. Triana's most popular place of worship, it has been splendidly restored.

Key
— Suggested route

0 metres   75
0 yards   75

A thrill ride at the Isla Mágica theme park

❶ Isla Mágica

Pabellón de España, Isla de la Cartuja.
Map 1 B3. **Tel** 902 16 17 16. **Open**
varies, see website for opening hours
(which change throughout the year)
as well as package deals (hotel and
park entry). 📶 🌐 **islamagica.es**

Opened in 1997, the Isla Mágica
theme park occupies part of
the Isla de la Cartuja site
redeveloped for Expo '92
(see pp60–61), including the
Pabellón de España and the the
dramatically leaning Pabellón
de Andalucía.

The park recreates the
exploits of the explorers who
set out from Seville in the 16th
century on voyages of discovery
to the New World. The
first of the six zones which
visitors experience is Seville,
Port of the Indies, followed by
among others, the Gateway to
the Americas, the World of the
Maya, the Pirate's Lair and El
Dorado. The Jaguar is the most

thrilling ride for visitors – a
rollercoaster hurtling at 85 km/h
(53 mph) along its looping
course, but head also for
The Anaconda, a flume ride,
and The Orinoco Rapids on
which small boats are buffeted
in swirling water. The Fountain
of Youth is designed for
children, with carousels and
fighting pirates.

Shows in the park include
street performances and dance
shows as well as IMAX cinema
screenings. The shows provide
the historical background and
incorporate special effects
and audience participation.
New shows are added every
season with some shows
running throughout and others
featuring for just a few weeks.
Check the Isla Magica website
for up-to-date information.

❷ Cartuja '93

Paseo del Oeste (renamed Calle
Leonardo da Vinci). **Map** 1 A3.

This science and technology
park occupies the western side
of the Expo '92 site. Visitors can
walk along Calle Leonardo da
Vinci and the service roads for
close-up views of some of Expo
'92's most spectacular pavilions.
These buildings, however, now
part of the Andalusian World
Trade Centre, belong to public
and private companies and are
closed to visitors. Groups of
buildings south and east of the
Parque Alamillo are part of Seville

The Pabellón de Andalucía, built on
Isla de la Cartuja for Expo '92

University, which has links with
Cartuja '93. To its south lie the
gardens surrounding the
ancient Monasterio de Santa
María de las Cuevas, now
housing a contemporary art
museum (see p109).

❸ Charco de la Pava Flea Market

Open Sat & Sun am.

Situated beyond the Olympic
Stadium, along the River
Guadalquivir, is the Charco
de La Pava flea market. The
market occupies a large open
space on the far side of the
Cartuja and is held on Sunday
mornings and Saturdays. It is
a popular spot among locals
and tourists who come here
for a leisurely browse through
the bric-a-brac. Stretched out
along the ground are all
manner of goods for sale, from
rusty farming tools to brass
ornaments, paintings and old
photographs. The market was,
for many years, held at
Alameda de Hércules (see p92)
in the La Macarena area to
the north of the city.

Despite its proximity to the
city centre, Charco de la Pava,
and the area immediately
surrounding it, has little in the
way of cafés and restaurants,
so stock up with a hearty
breakfast before heading out
in search of a bargain.

Passenger boat at the Isla Mágica theme park

Main entrance of the Carthusian Monasterio de Santa María de las Cuevas, founded in 1400

❹ Monasterio de Santa María de las Cuevas

Calle Americo Vespucio 2, Isla de la Cartuja. **Map** 1 A4. **Tel** 95 503 70 70. Monastery & Centro Andaluz de Arte Contemporaneo **Open** 11am–9pm Tue–Sat, 11am–3pm Sun & public hols. 🎟 (free Tue–Fri 7–9pm & 11am–9pm Sat). ♿ 📷 🌐 **caac.es**

This huge complex, which was built by the Carthusian monks in the 15th century, is closely tied to Seville's history. Columbus stayed and worked here, and even lay buried in the crypt of the church, Capilla Santa Ana, from 1507 to 1542. The Carthusians lived here until 1836 and commissioned some of the finest works of the Seville School, including masterpieces by Zurbarán and Montañés – these are now housed in the Museo de Bellas Artes *(see pp70–71)*.

In 1841 Charles Pickman, a British industrialist, built a ceramics factory on the site. After decades of successful business, production ceased in 1980 and the monastery was restored as a central exhibit for Expo '92. Also of interest are the Capilla de Afuera by the main gate, and the Casa Prioral, which has an exhibition of the restoration. There is a Mudéjar cloister, made of marble and brick. The chapter house has a number of tombstones of rich patrons of the monastery.

The Centro Andaluz de Arte Contemporáneo features contemporary art exhibitions, as part of the Museo de Arte Contemporaneo. The centre's permanent collection is mostly by 20th century Andalusian artists while its temporary exhibitions include paintings, photographs, installations and performance art by international artists. Past exhibitions have featured everything from sculpture to Internet art.

❺ Triana

See pp106–7.

The colourful belfry of Nuestra Señora de la O in Triana

❻ Iglesia de Nuestra Señora de la O

C/ Castilla. **Map** 3 A1. **Tel** 95 433 75 39. **Open** daily.

The Church of Our Lady of O, built in the late 17th century, has a brightly painted belfry decorated with *azulejos* made locally. Inside, Baroque sculptures include a Virgin and Child with silver haloes, attributed to Duque Cornejo, in the far chapel to the left as you enter. On the other side of the high altar is a fine group by Pedro Roldán depicting St Anne, St Joachim and Mary, the Virgin; a Jesus of Nazareth bearing his cross in the main chapel on the far wall is also by the same sculptor.

The church is in Calle de Castilla, whose name comes from the notorious castle in Triana where the Inquisition had its headquarters from the 16th century. The Callejón de la Inquisición, a nearby alley, leads down to the river.

❼ Iglesia de Santa Ana

C/ de la Pureza 84. **Map** 3 B2. **Tel** 95 427 08 85. **Open** 9am–3pm, 7–9pm daily.

One of the first churches built in Seville after the Reconquest *(see pp52–3)*, Santa Ana was founded in 1276 but has been much remodelled over the centuries. Today it is a focal point for the residents and *cofradias* (the religious brotherhoods) of Triana.

The vaulting of the nave is similar to Burgos cathedral's vaulting, suggesting that the same architect worked on the two churches. The west end of the nave has a 16th-century *retablo*, richly carved by Alejo Fernández. The sacramental chapel in the north wall has a Plateresque entrance.

In the baptistery is the *Pila de los Gitanos*, or Gypsy Font, which is believed to pass on the gift of flamenco song to the children of the faithful.

A 90-Minute Walk in Seville

This walk begins in one of the city's most elegant parks and explores one of its oldest *barrios* (neighbourhoods): the medieval Jewish quarter of Santa Cruz. The tiny alleys and squares of Santa Cruz conceal a museum to one of the city's great painters, Murillo, as well as a host of churches and many crafts galleries and restaurants. The walk then takes you through Seville's grandest square before heading for the Guadalquivir River, a historic bridge and the Triana area, famous for its ceramics district and home of Seville's flamenco culture.

A sun-drenched alley in the neighbourhood of Santa Cruz

Key

••• Walk route

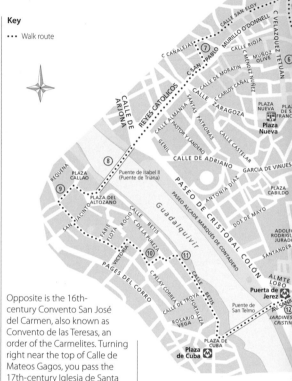

Plaza Santa Cruz to the Rio Guadalquivir

This small square, with its birdcage and garden, sits close to both the Jardines de Murillo ①, where there is a monument to Columbus, and the walls of the Real Alcázar. Take Calle Santa Teresa past the museum and birthplace of painter Bartolomé Esteban Murillo (1618–82) ②; the pieces held here are minor compared to those kept in the Museo des Bellas Artes *(see pp70–72)*.

Patio of a house in the Santa Cruz quarter

Opposite is the 16th-century Convento San José del Carmen, also known as Convento de las Teresas, an order of the Carmelites. Turning right near the top of Calle de Mateos Gagos, you pass the 17th-century Iglesia de Santa Cruz ③ with its triple carillon. Turn left into Calle Guzman El Bueno ("Guzman the Good"), named after the defender of Tarifa during the Moorish invasion. Guzman features some classic town mansions built around spacious interior patios. Cross into the Argote de Molina and walk behind the Palacio Arcobispal ④ down to the gates of the cathedral courtyard, the chief remaining Moorish section of this building; worshippers would wash here before entering the mosque.

Take a sharp right into Calle Hernan Colon, where odd little shops selling collectables jostle with souvenir stores. Colon leads into Plaza de San Francisco and the Ayuntamiento ⑤ (town hall), begun in 1527 by architect Diego de Riaño. It is one of the best examples of Renaissance architecture in Spain. Cross the square to Calle Sierpes, one of Seville's oldest shopping streets. Sierpes is the place to buy fans, mantilla shawls and hats, not least at Maquedano (No. 40) ⑥ which always has an impressive window display. Where Sierpes meets tiny Plaza La Campana, turn left on Calle

The Giralda tower seen from Plaza de San Francisco

Tips for Walkers

Starting point: Plaza Santa Cruz.
Length: 3.5 km (2 miles).
Getting there: Plaza Santa Cruz is a short walk from Calle de Menéndez Pelayo, close to the Real Alcazar and Cathedral.
Stopping-off points: El Faro de Triana, on Puente de Isabel II, has tables overlooking the river and a rooftop terrace. It's a great place to stop for a drink or a seafood meal.

Martin Villa to Plaza del Duque de la Victoria and its statue of Velazquez. Turn right into Calle San Eloy; at its end is the Iglesia de la Magdalena ⑦, a church built in 1709 on the remains of an earlier Arabic mosque. Its interior features works by Zurburan and Valdés, and its exquisite representation of the Virgen del Amparo (protection) is a star of the Easter Semana Santa processions. It is claimed she intervened on behalf of petitioners during the after-shocks of the 1755 earthquake and in the 19th century the church served as a refuge for homeless children. Circle to the front of the church and right into Calle San Pablo, which becomes Reyes Catolicos, leading straight to Puente de Isabel II ⑧. Built in 1852 on the found-ations of a long-lost 12th-century Arab bridge, it's also known as Puente de Triana.

Puente de Isabel II to Puente de San Telmo

The bridge enters the *barrio* of Triana, forever associated with flamenco, bullfighting and

El Faro de Triana restaurant on Puente de Isabel II (Puente Triana)

Azulejos of Santa Ana church in Triana

ceramics (*azulejos*). For workshops and shops, bear right into Calles San Jorge and then left into Antillano ⑨ and Alfareria. This runs into Calle Rodrigo de Triana. Turn left into Calle Victoria and right into Pelay Correa to reach Seville's oldest church, the 13th-century Iglesia Santa Ana ⑩. Its interior features major works by 16th-century sculptors such as Jurate and Ocampo. Behind the church, take a right on Triana's bar-lined riverfront, Calle Betis ⑪, with views across to the Plaza de Toros, the Torre del Oro and, to the left, sculptor Eduardo Chillida's modernist peace monument, *La Tolerancia* (Tolerance). Betis runs to the 1931 Puente de San Telmo, which leads to the Jardines de Cristina ⑫, a major bus hub, and to Calle San Fernando ⑬, which passes the Universidad and continues to the Jardines de Murillo.

⑧ Puente de Isabel II, stretching over the Guadalquivir River

STREET FINDER

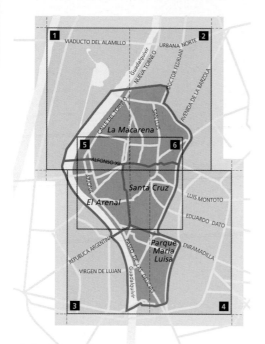

VIADUCTO DEL ALAMILLO
URBANA NORTE
La Macarena
Santa Cruz
El Arenal
Parque María Luisa
REPUBLICA ARGENTINA
VIRGEN DE LUJAN
LUIS MONTOTO
EDUARDO DATO
ENRAMADILLA

Key

- Major sight
- Place of interest
- Other building
- Railway station
- Bus terminus
- River boat boarding point
- P Parking
- i Tourist information
- Hospital
- Police station
- Church
- Convent and Monastery
- Railway line
- Pedestrianized street
- M Metro station
- Metro-Centro tram stop

Scale of Maps 1–2 & 3–4

0 metres	250
0 yards	250

1 : 13,000

Scale of Maps 5–6

0 metres	150
0 yards	150

1 : 8,250

Key to abbreviations used in the Street Finder

Avda	Avenida	d	de, del, de la,	Pl	Plaza	Sra	Señora
C	Calle		de las, de los	Po	Paseo	Sta	Santa

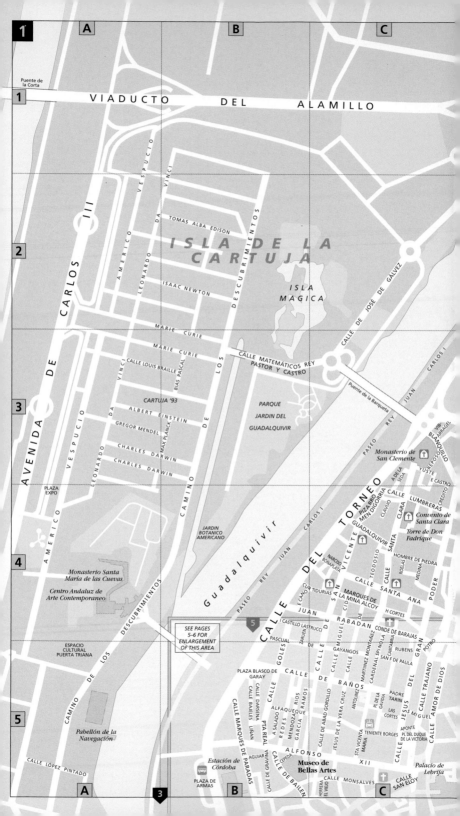

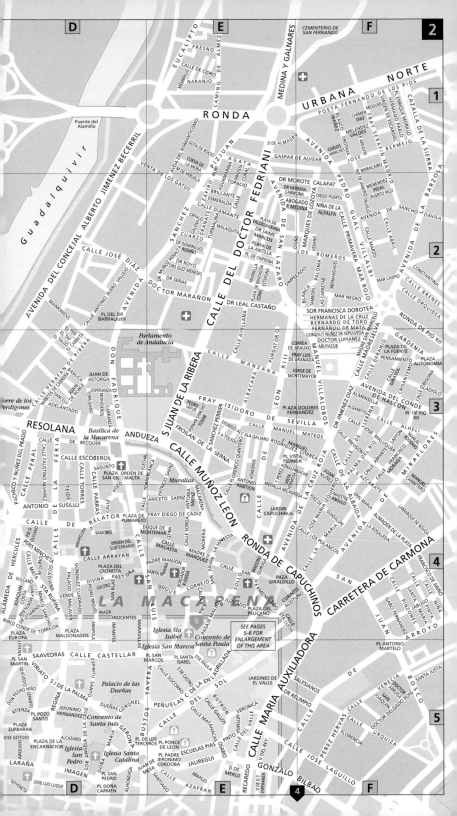

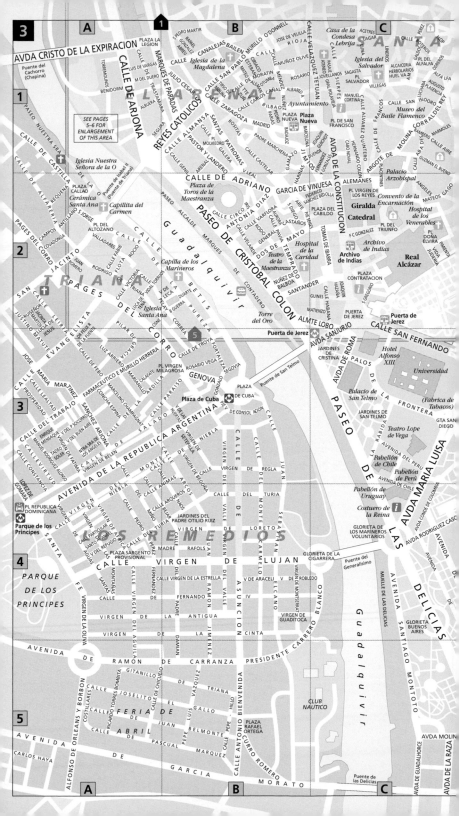

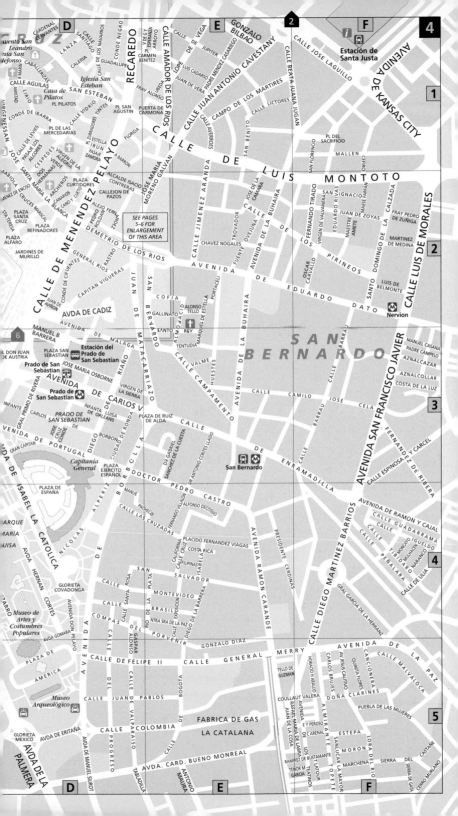

ANDALUSIA AREA BY AREA

Andalusia at a Glance

Andalusia is a region of contrasts where snowcapped mountains rise above deserts and Mediterranean beaches, and Moorish palaces can be found standing next to Christian cathedrals. Its eight provinces, which in this guide are divided into four areas, offer busy towns such as Granada and Córdoba with their astonishing architectural treasures, in addition to sleepy villages, endless olive groves and nature reserves of great beauty.

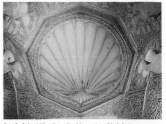

Roof of the Mihrab in the Mezquita, Córdoba's top sight *(see pp148–9)*

The amphitheatre in the Roman city of Itálica *(see p48 and p136),* just outside Seville

CORDOB

Córd

HUELVA

SEVILLA

Jabugo

Seville

Huelva

Golden chalice from the rich treasury of Cádiz cathedral *(see p168)*

Cádiz

MALAG

CADIZ

Los Barrios

Arcos de la Frontera, one of the pretty pueblos blancos (white villages, *see pp178–9*) so typical of Andalusia

◄ Rooftop view of Antequera, Andalusia

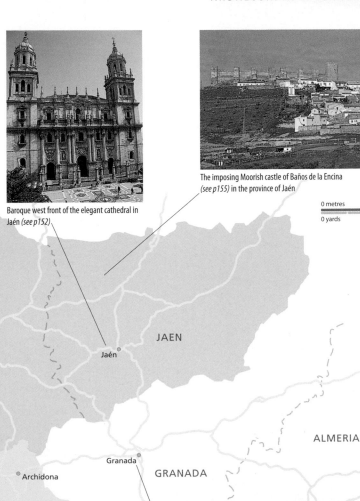

Baroque west front of the elegant cathedral in
Jaén *(see p152)*

The imposing Moorish castle of Baños de la Encina
(see p155) in the province of Jaén

0 metres 50
0 yards 25

JAEN

Jaén

ALMERIA

Granada

Archidona GRANADA

Almería

Málaga

Magical Alhambra overlooking the Albaicín, Granada *(see pp194–202)*

Cabo de Gata, a nature reserve with
excellent beaches *(see p208)*

HUELVA AND SEVILLA

Andalusia's western extremities and the plains surrounding
Seville are rarely explored by travellers in southern Spain.
There are isolated beaches along Huelva province's Atlantic coast
and good walking country in the northern sierras. The Parque Nacional de
Doñana on the Guadalquivir delta is Europe's largest nature reserve; inland,
orange groves straddle the river's valley.

As Roman legions under Scipio Africanus crossed southern Spain on their westward trek in the 3rd century BC, they founded a formidable metropolis, Itálica. Its ruins remain north of Seville. Later, the Moors held the region as part of the Emirate of al Andalus. They peppered it with their whitewashed, fortified towns, of which Carmona, in Sevilla province, is a fine example.

After the Christian Reconquest *(see pp52–3)*, Moorish traditions persisted through Mudéjar architecture *(see pp28–9)*, blending with Baroque and Renaissance in cities such as Osuna, which flourished in the 16th century.

Huelva province is inextricably bound up with another chapter in the history of world conquest – in 1492 Columbus set out on his epic voyage from Palos de la Frontera, which at the time was an important port. He stayed nearby, at the Franciscan Monasterio de la Rábida, built earlier that century. Running along Huelva's northern border is a ridge of mountains, of which the forested Sierra de Aracena forms part. This ridge continues into Sevilla province as the Sierra Norte de Sevilla. Here, goats forage, birds of prey fly overhead and streams gush through chasms. The landscape erupts in a riot of wild flowers in spring, turning brown as the searing summer sets in.

The Parque Nacional de Doñana preserves the dunes and marshlands near the mouth of the Guadalquivir to the south. Here, teeming birdlife and wetland fauna thrive on the mudflats and shallow, saline waters.

Iglesia de Nuestra Señora del Rocío, El Rocío, where many pilgrims converge each Pentecost Sunday

◄ Whitewashed buildings in Sierra de Aracena and Picos de Aroche National Park

Exploring Huelva and Sevilla

Cosmopolitan Seville is the natural base from which to explore the far-flung corners of Huelva and Sevilla provinces, such as the little-visited and awesomely beautiful Sierra de Aracena and the rugged Sierra Norte. The Atlantic coast offers a virtually unbroken stretch of beaches and the Parque Nacional de Doñana features a fascinating marsh landscape abundant in wildlife. Between the coast and the mountains are rolling agricultural plains, interrupted by vineyards in fertile El Condado. Among the region's historic towns are Écija and Osuna, with fine Baroque features, while the history of Columbus can be traced in the towns around Huelva.

The mines of Riotinto, Sierra de Aracena

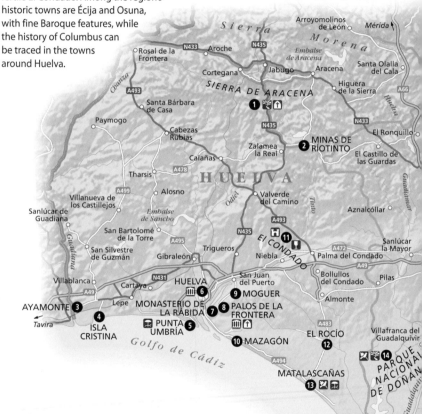

Fishing boats at anchor in the harbour of Punta Umbría

For map symbols *see back flap*

Key

- Motorway
- Major road
- Minor road
- Scenic route
- Main railway
- Minor railway
- International border
- Provincial border

Getting Around

The busy A4 linking Córdoba with Seville slices through the eastern half of the region, bypassing Écija and Carmona, then streaks on down to Jerez de la Frontera and Cádiz as the AP4. Another motorway, the A92, brings traffic from Málaga and Granada. All join a ring-road at Seville, with the A49 continuing to Huelva and Portugal. All these cities are also connected by rail. A complex and inexpensive bus network run by many different companies links most towns. To explore the more remote parts of the region, particularly mountain roads, it is essential to have private transport.

A well-known *bodega* advertisement in the rolling hills of the Sierra de Aracena

Sights at a Glance

A ham shop in Jabugo, Sierra de Aracena

❶ Sierra de Aracena

Huelva. **Road map** A2. 🚉 El Repilado. 🚌 Aracena. ℹ️ Plaza San Pedro s/n, Aracena (959 12 82 06). 🚌 Sat. 🌐 sierradearacena.com

This wild mountain range in northern Huelva province is one of the most remote and least visited corners of Andalusia. Its slopes, covered with cork, oak, chestnut and wild olive, are cut by rushing streams and many tortuous mountain roads.

The main town of the region, Aracena, squats at the foot of a ruined Moorish fortress on a hillside pitted with caverns. One of these, the **Gruta de las Maravillas**, can be entered to see its underground lake in a chamber hung with stalactites. Near the fortress, the **Iglesia del Castillo**, which was built in the 13th century by the Knights Templar, has a Mudéjar tower and foundations.

The village of **Jabugo** also nestles amid these mountains. It is famed across Spain for its tasty cured ham, *jamón ibérico*, or *pata negra (see p223)*.

Gruta de las Maravillas
Pozo de la Nieve. **Tel** 959 12 83 55. **Open** 10am–1:30pm, 3–6pm. 🏛️ 🎫

❷ Minas de Riotinto

Huelva. **Road map** A2. 🚌 Riotinto. **Tel** 959 59 00 25. **Open** 10:30am–3pm, 4–7pm daily (Jul–Sep: to 8pm). **Closed** 1 & 6 Jan, 25 Dec 🏛️ 🎫 🎫 🌐 parquemineroderiotinto.com

A fascinating detour off the N435 between Huelva city and the Sierra de Aracena leads to the opencast mines at Riotinto. These have been excavated since Phoenician times; the Greeks, Romans and Visigoths exploited their reserves of iron, copper, silver and mineral ores.

The lip of the crater overlooks walls of rock streaked with green and red fissures. Below, the trucks at work in the mines appear toy-sized. The **Museo Minero** in the village explains the history of the mines and of the Riotinto Company. At weekends and on public holidays there is a train tour in restored 1900 carriages.

Ⓜ Museo Minero
Plaza del Museo s/n. **Tel** 959 59 00 25. **Open** daily. 🏛️ 🎫 🎫 🎫 🌐 parquemineroderiotinto.com

❸ Ayamonte

Huelva. **Road map** A3. 🚹 18,000. 🚌 ℹ️ Avda Ramon y Cajal, s/n (959 47 09 88). 🚌 Sat morning.

Before the road bridge over the lower Guadiana river was completed in 1992, anyone who was crossing between southern Andalusia and the Algarve coast of Portugal had to pass through Ayamonte. The small, flat-bottomed car ferry across the jellyfish-infested mouth of the Guadiana river still operates and is an alternative for those who are making the journey between the two countries. Visitors can watch the ferry from the tower of Ayamonte's **Iglesia San Francisco**, which has a fine Mudéjar ceiling.

❹ Isla Cristina

Huelva. **Road map** A3. 🚹 18,000. 🚌 ℹ️ Calle San Francisco 12 (959 33 26 94). 🚌 Thu. 🌐 islacristina.org

Once a distinct island, Isla Cristina is now surrounded by marshes. Situated near the mouth of the Guadiana river, it is an important fishing port, home to a fleet of tuna and sardine trawlers. With a fine sandy beach, Isla Cristina is now a popular summer resort. Situated on the main seafront is an excellent choice of restaurants, which serve delicious, freshly landed fish and seafood.

Tuna and sardine trawlers moored for the night in the port of Isla Cristina

Frescoes depicting the life of Columbus at Monasterio de la Rábida

🎨 Museo Provincial

Alameda Sundheim 13. **Tel** 959 65 04 24. **Open** 10am–8:30pm Tue–Sat, 10am–5pm Sun & public hols (Jun–mid-Sep: 9am–3:30pm Tue–Sat, 10am–5pm Sun & public hols). ♿

❼ Monasterio de la Rábida

Huelva. **Road map** A3. 🚌 from Huelva. **Tel** 959 35 04 11. **Open** 10am–1pm, 4–6:15pm Tue–Sun. 🎫 ☑ 🌐 monasteriodelarabida.com

❺ Punta Umbría

Huelva. **Road map** A3. 🚗 14,000. 🚌 ℹ️ Ciudad de Huelva s/n (959 49 51 60). 🚢 Mon.

Punta Umbría is one of the main beach resorts in Huelva province. It sits at the end of a long promontory, with the Marismas del Odiel wetlands to one side and a sandy beach bordering the Gulf of Cádiz to the other. The Riotinto Company first developed the resort in the late 19th century for its British employees. These days, however, it is mainly Spanish holiday-makers who stay in the beachside villas.

Bronze jug, Museo Provincial, Huelva

A long bridge crosses the marshes, giving road access from Huelva. It is more fun to follow a trail blazed by Riotinto expatriates seeking the sun and take the ferry across the bird-rich wetlands.

❻ Huelva

Huelva. **Road map** A3. 🚗 130,000. 🚉 🚌 ℹ️ Avenida Alemania 12 (959 25 74 03). 🚢 Fri.

Founded as Onuba by the Phoenicians, the town had its grandest days as a Roman port. It prospered again in the early days of trade with the Americas, but Seville soon took over. Its decline culminated in 1755, when Huelva was almost wiped out by the great Lisbon earthquake. Today, industrial suburbs sprawl around the Odiel quayside, from which the Riotinto Company once exported its products all over the commercial world.

That Columbus set sail from Palos de la Frontera, across the estuary, is Huelva's main claim to international renown. This fact is celebrated in the excellent **Museo Provincial**, which also has several exhibitions charting the history of the mines at Riotinto. Some archaeological finds from the very early days of mining are cleverly presented.

To the east of the centre the Barrio Reina Victoria is a bizarre example of English suburbia in the very heart of Andalusia. It is a district of bungalows in mock-Tudor style, built by the Riotinto Company for its staff in the early 20th century. South of the town, at Punta del Sebo, the Monumento a Colón, a 1929 bleak statue of Columbus by Gertrude Vanderbuilt Whitney, dominates the Odiel estuary.

In 1491, a dejected Genoese explorer found refuge in the Franciscan friary at La Rábida, which is across the Odiel estuary from Huelva. King Fernando and Queen Isabel had refused to back his plan to sail west to the East Indies. The prior, Juan Pérez, who as the confessor of the queen had great influence, eventually succeeded in getting this decision reversed. The following year, this sailor, by name Columbus, became the first European to reach the Americas since the Vikings.

La Rábida friary, which was built on Moorish ruins in the 15th century, is now a shrine to Columbus. Frescoes painted by Daniel Vásquez Díaz in 1930 glorify Columbus's life. The Sala de las Banderas contains a small casket of soil from every Latin American country. Worth seeing are the Mudéjar cloisters, the lush gardens and the beamed chapterhouse.

Columbus in Andalusia

Cristóbal Colón – Christopher Columbus to the English-speaking world – was born in Genoa in Italy, trained as a navigator in Portugal and conceived the idea of reaching the Indies by sailing westwards. In 1492 he sailed from Palos de la Frontera and later the same year landed on Watling Island in the Bahamas, believing that he had fulfilled his ambition.

Columbus made three further voyages from bases in Andalusia, reaching mainland South America and other islands in what are still termed the West Indies in deference to his mistake. He died at Valladolid in 1506.

Columbus takes his leave before setting sail

Historic map, Casa Museo de Martín Alonso Pinzón, Palos de la Frontera

❽ Palos de la Frontera

Huelva. **Road map** A3. 🗺 12,000. 🚌
ℹ️ Parque Botánico José Celestino Mutis, Paraje de la Rábida (959 53 05 35). 🚢 Sat.

Palos is an unprepossessing agricultural town on the eastern side of the Río Odiel's marshy delta. Yet it is a major attraction on the Columbus heritage trail.

On 3 August 1492, Columbus put out to sea from Palos in his caravel, the *Santa María*, with the *Pinta* and the *Niña*, whose captains were Martín and Vicente Pinzón, brothers from Palos. A statue of Martín Pinzón stands in the town's main square, and his former home has been turned into a small museum of exploration, named the **Casa Museo de Martín Alonso Pinzón**.

The Gothic-Mudéjar **Iglesia San Jorge**, dates from the 15th century. It has a fine portal, through which Columbus left after hearing Mass before his famous voyage. Afterwards, he boarded the *Santa María* at a pier, which is now forlornly silted up.

These days, Palos's prosperity comes from the thousands of hectares of strawberry beds in the surrounding fields, which soak up the sun.

🏛 Casa Museo de Martín Alonso Pinzón
Calle Colón 24. **Tel** 959 10 00 41.
Open 10am–2pm Mon–Fri.

❾ Moguer

Huelva. **Road map** A3. 🗺 15,000. 🚌
ℹ️ Calle Castillo s/n (959 37 18 98).
🚢 Thu. 🌐 aytomoguer.es

A beautiful, whitewashed town, Moguer is a network of shaded courtyards and narrow streets lined with flower boxes. It is a delight to stroll around, exploring treasures such as the 16th-century hermitage of **Nuestra Señora de Montemayor** and the Neo-Classical **Ayuntamiento**. Moguer is also the birthplace of the poet and 1956 Nobel laureate, Juan Ramón Jiménez. The **Museo de Zenobia y Juan Ramón Jiménez**

The 16th-century Nuestra Señora de Montemayor in Moguer

charts the poet's life and work, and is located in his restored former home.

The walls of the 14th-century **Convento de Santa Clara** enclose some splendid, stone-carved Mudéjar cloisters. The nuns' dormitory, kitchen and refectory capture some of the atmosphere of their life inside the enclosure.

The **Monasterio de San Francisco** is worth seeing for its church, with a superb white tower and Baroque portals.

🏛 Museo de Zenobia y Juan Ramón Jiménez
Calle Juan Ramón Jiménez 10.
Tel 959 37 21 48. **Open** Tue–Sun.
Closed Sun pm & public hols. 🎟 📷

⛪ Convento de Santa Clara
Plaza de las Monjas. **Tel** 959 37 01 07.
Open Tue–Sat. **Closed** often closed on Sat for events; public hols. 🎟

Mazagón's sandy beach on the Costa de la Luz

❿ Mazagón

Huelva. **Road map** A3. 🗺 3,500. 🚌
ℹ️ Edificio Mancomunidad, Avda de los Conquistadores s/n (959 37 60 44).
🚢 Fri evening.

One of the more remote beach resorts of the Costa de la Luz, Magazón shelters among pine woods 23 km (14 miles) southeast of Huelva. Virtually deserted in winter, it comes to life in summer when mainly Spanish holiday-makers arrive to fish, sail and enjoy the huge, and often windswept, beach. Visitors to the resort may still take pleasure in the solitude, however, while walking for miles along the endless Atlantic shoreline and among the sand dunes.

Moorish walls surrounding Niebla in El Condado

⓫ El Condado

Huelva. **Road map** B2. 🚌 🚍 Palma del Condado. ℹ Calle Campo Castillo s/n, Niebla Huelva (959 36 22 70).

The rolling, fecund hills to the east of Huelva produce several of Andalusia's finest wines. El Condado, defined roughly by Niebla, Palma del Condado, Bollullos del Condado and Rociana del Condado, is the heart of this wine-growing district.

Niebla is of ancient origin. Its bridge is Roman, but its solid walls are Moorish, as is the now ruined, 12th-century **Castillo de Niebla**, also known as Castillo de los Guzmanes.

Around Niebla, vineyards spread out over the landscape, which is dotted with villages close to the main *bodegas*. These include Bollullos del Condado, which has the largest cooperative winery in Andalusia and also the **Museo del Vino**. Here you can learn about wine-growing techniques and also taste their wines before making your purchase.

Bollullos and Palma del Condado are good examples of the popular young white wines produced in the region.

Palma del Condado is best visited in September when the inhabitants celebrate the year's *vendimia* (grape harvest).

🏰 Castillo de Niebla
C/ Campo Castillo s/n. **Tel** 959 36 22 70. **Open** 10am–2pm, 3–6pm Mon–Sun.

🏛 Museo del Vino
Plaza Idelfonso Pinto s/n, Bollullos del Condado. **Tel** 959 41 05 13. **Open** 10am–2pm, 3–6pm Mon–Sat.

⓬ El Rocío

Huelva. **Road map** B3. 🏔 2,500. 🚍 ℹ Centro Doñana, Avda de la Canaliega s/n. 959 44 38 08. 🛒 Tue.

Bordering the wetlands of the Doñana region (*see pp134–5*), the village of El Rocío is for most of the year a tranquil, rural backwater, which attracts few visitors.

At the Romería del Rocío (*see pp42–3*) in May, however, nearly a million people converge on the village. Many are pilgrims who travel from all over Spain by bus, car, horse, or even on gaudily decorated ox-carts or on foot. They come to **Ermita de Nuestra Señora del Rocío** that has a statue reputed to have been behind miraculous apparitions since 1280. Pilgrims are joined by revellers, who are enticed by the promise of plentiful wine, music and a great party.

⓭ Matalascañas

Huelva. **Road map** A3. 🏔 1,200. 🚍 ℹ Avenida de las Adelfas s/n. 959 43 00 86. 🛒 Thu.

Matalascañas is the largest Andalusian beach resort west of the Guadalquivir river. Thousands holiday here, lying in the sun, riding, sailing or water-skiing by day and dancing to the latest disco beat at night. At Romería del Rocío, the resort overflows with pilgrims and revellers.

Matalascañas is totally self-contained. To one side there are dunes and forests stretching as far as Mazagón, to the other the wild peace of the Doñana (*see pp134–5*).

Iglesia de Nuestra Señora del Rocío in the village of El Rocío

⑭ Parque Nacional de Doñana

The National Park of Doñana is ranked among Europe's greatest wetlands. Together with its adjoining protected areas (Parque Natural de Doñana), the park covers over 50,000 hectares (185,000 acres) of marshes and sand dunes. The area used to be hunting grounds (coto) belonging to the Dukes of Medina Sidonia and was never suitable for human settlers. The wildlife flourished and, in 1969, the area became officially protected. In addition to a wealth of endemic species, thousands of migratory birds stay in winter when the marshes flood again, after months of drought.

Shrub Vegetation
Backing the sand dunes is a thick carpet of lavender, rock rose and other low shrubs.

Prickly Juniper
This species of juniper (Juniperus oxycedrus) thrives in the wide dune belt, rooting deep into the sand. The trees sometimes get buried beneath the dunes.

Palacio del Acebrón

El Rocío

La Rocina

H612

El Acebuche

Matalascañas

Palacio de Doñana

Laguna de Santa Olaya ①

Coastal Dunes
Softly rounded, white dunes, up to 30 m (99 ft) high, fringe the park's coastal edge. The dunes, ribbed by prevailing winds off the Atlantic, shift constantly.

Key

☐ Marshes
▨ Dunes
••• Parque Nacional de Doñana
••• Parque Natural de Doñana
▬ Road
☆ Viewpoint

KEY

① **Monte de Doñana**, the wooded area behind the sand dunes, provide shelter for lynx, deer and boar.

② **Wild cattle** use the marshes as water holes.

Official Tour
Numbers of visitors are controlled very strictly. On official day tours along rough tracks, the knowledgeable guides point out elusive animals while ensuring minimal environmental impact.

For additional map symbols see back flap

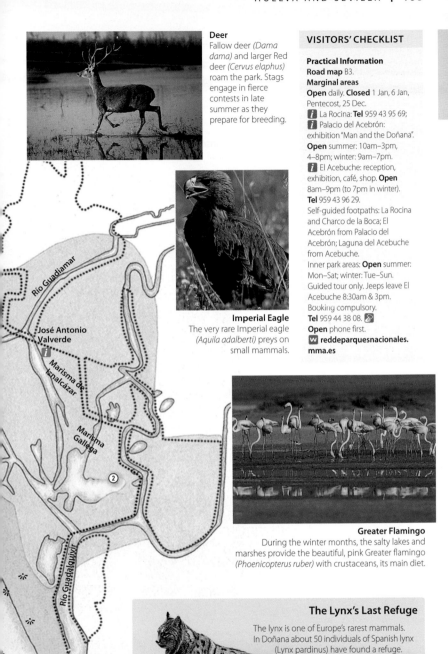

Deer
Fallow deer *(Dama dama)* and larger Red deer *(Cervus elaphus)* roam the park. Stags engage in fierce contests in late summer as they prepare for breeding.

Imperial Eagle
The very rare Imperial eagle *(Aquila adalberti)* preys on small mammals.

VISITORS' CHECKLIST

Practical Information
Road map B3.
Marginal areas
Open daily. **Closed** 1 Jan, 6 Jan, Pentecost, 25 Dec.
ℹ️ La Rocina: **Tel** 959 43 95 69;
ℹ️ Palacio del Acebrón:
exhibition "Man and the Doñana".
Open summer: 10am–3pm, 4–8pm; winter: 9am–7pm.
ℹ️ El Acebuche: reception, exhibition, café, shop. **Open** 8am–9pm (to 7pm in winter).
Tel 959 43 96 29.
Self-guided footpaths: La Rocina and Charco de la Boca; El Acebrón from Palacio del Acebrón; Laguna del Acebuche from Acebuche.
Inner park areas: **Open** summer: Mon–Sat; winter: Tue–Sun.
Guided tour only. Jeeps leave El Acebuche 8:30am & 3pm.
Booking compulsory.
Tel 959 44 38 08. 🚐
Open phone first.
🆆 reddeparquesnacionales.mma.es

Greater Flamingo
During the winter months, the salty lakes and marshes provide the beautiful, pink Greater flamingo *(Phoenicopterus ruber)* with crustaceans, its main diet.

The Lynx's Last Refuge

The lynx is one of Europe's rarest mammals. In Doñana about 50 individuals of Spanish lynx (Lynx pardinus) have found a refuge. They have yellow-brown fur with dark brown spots and pointed ears with black tufts. A research programme is under way to study this shy animal, which tends to stay hidden in scrub. It feeds mainly on rabbits and ducks, but sometimes also deer fawn.

The elusive lynx, only spotted with patience

0 kilometres   5

0 miles   5

Scenic view over the rooftops of Lebrija with their distinctive red tiles

⑮ Lebrija

Sevilla. **Road map** B3. 🏛 24,000. 🚃
🚌 🅸 Casa de Cultura, Calle Tetuán
15 (95 597 40 68). 🏛 Tue.

The pretty, walled town of
Lebrija enjoys panoramic views
over the neighbouring sherry-
growing vineyards of the Jerez
region *(see p226)*.
 Narrow cobbled streets lead
to **Iglesia de Santa María de la
Oliva**. This is a 12th-century
Almohad mosque with many
original Islamic features, which
was consecrated as a church by
Alfonso X *(see p52)*.

⑯ Itálica

Sevilla. **Road map** B2. 🚃 from Plaza de
Armas, Seville. **Tel** 95 512 38 47. **Open**;
Apr–May: 9am–8pm Tue–Sat, 10am–
5pm Sun & pub hols; Jun–mid-Sep:
9am–3:30pm Tue–Sat, 10am–5pm Sun
& pub hols; mid-Sep–Mar: 9am–6:30pm
Tue–Sat, 10am–5pm Sun & pub hols.

Scipio Africanus established
Itálica in 206 BC, as one of the
first cities founded by the
Romans in Hispania. Later, it
burgeoned, both as a military
headquarters and as a cultural
centre, supporting a population
of several
thousand.
Emperors
Trajan and
Hadrian were both
born in Itálica. The
latter bestowed imperial
largesse on the city
during his reign in the
2nd century AD, adding
marble temples and other
fine buildings.

Roman mosaic
from Itálica

Archaeologists have speculated
that the changing course of the
Guadalquivir may have led to
the demise of Itálica. Certainly,
the city declined steadily after
the fall of the Roman Empire,
unlike Seville, which flourished.
 At the heart of the site you
may explore the crumbling
remains of a vast amphitheatre,
which once seated 25,000. Next
to it is a display of finds from
the site, although many of the
treasures are displayed in the
Museo Arqueológico in Seville
(see p101). Visitors can wander
among the traces of streets
and villas. Little remains of
the city's temples or baths, as
most stone and marble was
plundered by builders over
the subsequent centuries.
 The village of **Santiponce** lies
just outside the site. Here, some
better-preserved Roman
remains, including baths and a
theatre, have been unearthed.

⑰ Sierra Norte

Sevilla. **Road map** B2. 🚃 Estación de
Cazalla y Constantina. 🚌 Constantina;
Cazalla. 🅸 Calle Paseo del Moro 2,
Cazalla de la Sierra (95 488 35 62).

An austere mountain range
flanks the northern border of
Sevilla province.
Known as the Sierra
Norte de Sevilla,
it is a part of the
greater Sierra
Morena, which forms
a natural frontier
between Andalusia and
the plains of La Mancha and
Extremadura. The region is

sparsely populated and, as it is
relatively cool in summer, it can
offer an escape from the
relentless heat of Seville. In
winter, you may meet the
occasional huntsman carrying
a partridge or hare.
 Cazalla de la Sierra, the main
town of the area, seems
surprisingly cosmopolitan and is
popular with young *sevillanos* at
weekends. It has made a unique
contribution to the world of
drink, namely Liquor de Guindas.
This is a concoction of cherry
liqueur and aniseed, whose taste
is acquired slowly, if at all.
 Constantina, to the east, is
more peaceful and has superb
views across the countryside.
A romantic aura surrounds the
ruined castle, which is situated
high above the town.

Grazing cow in the empty expanses of the
Sierra Norte de Sevilla

⑱ Carmona

Sevilla. **Road map** B2. 🏛 25,000. 🚃
🅸 Alcázar de la Puerta de Sevilla s/n
(95 419 09 55). 🏛 Mon & Thu.
🆆 **turismo.carmona.org**

Travelling east from Seville
on the NIV E5, Carmona is
the first major town you come
to. It rises above expansive
agricultural plains. Sprawling
suburbs spill out beyond the
Moorish city walls, which can be
entered through the old **Puerta
de Sevilla**. Inside, there is a
dense concentration of
mansions, Mudéjar churches,
squares and cobbled streets.
 The grandeur of Plaza de San
Fernando is characterized by
the strict Renaissance façade
of the old **Ayuntamiento**. The
present town hall, located just
off the square, dates from the

Tomb of Servilia, Necrópolis Romana, Carmona

18th century; in its courtyard are some fine Roman mosaics. Close by lies **Iglesia de Santa María la Mayor**. Built in the 15th century over a mosque, whose patio still survives, this is the finest of the churches. Dominating the town, however, are the imposing ruins of the **Alcázar del Rey Pedro**, once a palace of Pedro I, also known as Pedro el Cruel (the Cruel) *(see p52)*. Parts of it now form a parador.

Just outside Carmona is the **Necrópolis Romana**, the extensive remains of a Roman burial ground. A site museum displays some of the worldly goods buried with the bodies. These include statues, glass and jewellery, as well as urns.

🏛 **Ayuntamiento**
Calle Salvador 2. **Tel** 95 414 00 11. **Open** 8am–3pm Mon–Fri. **Closed** public hols.

🏛 **Necrópolis Romana**
Avenida Jorge Bonsor 9. **Tel** 95 414 08 11. **Open** Tue–Sat. **Closed** public hols.

⓳ Écija

Sevilla. **Road map** C2. 🚗 40,000. 🚌 ⓘ Plaza de España 1, Ayuntamiento (95 590 29 33). 🚍 Thu. 🕸 **turismoecija.com**

Ecija is nicknamed "the frying pan of Andalusia" owing to its famously torrid climate. In the searing heat, the palm trees which stand on the Plaza de España provide some blissful shade. This is an ideal place to sit and observe daily life. It is also the focus of evening strolls and coffee-drinking.

Écija has 11 Baroque church steeples. A good number are adorned with gleaming *azulejos (see p80)* and together they make an impressive sight. The most florid of these is the **Iglesia de Santa María** overlooking Plaza de España. **Iglesia de San Juan**, adorned with an exquisite bell tower, is a very close rival.

The **Palacio de Peñaflor** is also in Baroque style. Its pink marble doorway is topped by twisted columns, while a pretty wrought-iron balcony runs along the front façade.

🏛 **Palacio de Peñaflor**
C/Caballeros 32. **Tel** 95 483 02 73. **Open** daily (courtyard only).

⓴ Osuna

Sevilla. **Road map** C3. 🚗 17,500. 🚌 🚍 ⓘ C/Carrera 82, Antiguo Hospital (95 481 57 32). 🚍 Mon.

Osuna was once a key Roman garrison town before being eclipsed during the Moorish era. The Dukes of Osuna, who wielded immense power, restored the town to prominence in the 16th century. During the 1530s they founded the grand collegiate church, **Colegiata de Santa María**. Inside is a Baroque *retablo*, and paintings by José de Ribera. The dukes were also the founders of the town's **Universidad**, a rather severe building with a beautiful patio.

Some fine mansions, among them the Baroque **Palacio del Marqués de la Gomera**, are also a testament to the former glory of this town.

㉑ Estepa

Sevilla. **Road map** C3. 🚗 12,000. 🚌 ⓘ Carre Aguilar y cano s/n (95 591 27 17). 🚍 Mon, Wed & Fri. 🕸 **estepa.es**

Legend has it that when the invading Roman army closed on Estepa in 207 BC, the townsfolk committed mass suicide rather than surrender. These days, life in this small town in the far southeast of Sevilla province is far less dramatic. Its fame today derives from the production of its renowned biscuits – *mantecados* and *polvorones*. Wander among the narrow streets of iron-grilled mansions, and sit on the main square to admire the beautiful black and white façade of the Baroque church, **Iglesia del Carmen**.

Wall painting on the ornate Baroque façade of Palacio de Peñaflor, Écija

CÓRDOBA AND JAÉN

Córdoba, with its magnificent mosque and pretty
Moorish patios, is northern Andalusia's star attraction.
Córdoba province encompasses the Montilla and Moriles wine towns and
also Baroque treasures such as Priego de Córdoba. Jaén's mountain passes are
gateways to the province's beautiful Renaissance towns of Ubeda and Baeza,
and to the great wildlife reserves of the mountain ranges.

Córdoba, on Andalusia's great river Guadalquivir, was a Roman provincial capital over 2,000 years ago, but its golden age came with the Moors. In the 10th century it was the western capital of the Islamic empire, rivalling Baghdad in wealth, power and sophistication. Today it is an atmospheric city, its ancient quarters and buildings reflecting a long and glorious history.

Córdoba's surrounding countryside is dotted with monuments to its Moorish past – like the Caliph's palace of Medina Azahara. To the south lies the Campiña, an undulating landscape covered in regiments of olives and vines, and green and gold expanses of sunflowers and corn. Here and there are whitewashed villages and hilltop castles with crumbling walls.

Running across the north of Córdoba and Jaén provinces is the Sierra Morena. Deer and boar shelter in the forest and scrub of this broad mountain range. The sierras dominate Jaén province. The great Río Guadalquivir springs to life as a sparkling trout stream in the Sierra de Cazorla, the craggy wilderness along its eastern border. Through the ages, mule trains, traders, highwaymen and armies have used the cleft in Sierra Morena, known as Desfiladero de Despeñaperros, to cross from La Mancha and Castilla to Andalusia.

Ancient castles perched on heights, once strategic outposts on the Muslim/ Christian frontier, now overlook the peaceful olive groves punctuated by historic towns preserving gems of post-Reconquest architecture.

The city of Jaén with its cathedral in the foreground, as viewed from Castillo de Santa Catalina

◀ Córdoba cathedral and mosque

Exploring Córdoba and Jaén

This region of rolling fields and craggy heights is divided by the fertile Guadalquivir valley. On the northern banks of the river is Córdoba with its famous Mezquita. The wild, uninhabited Sierra Morena lies to the north, while southward is a prosperous farming area dotted with historic towns, such as Priego de Córdoba. Further east, amid the olive groves of Jaén, are the Renaissance jewels, Baeza and Úbeda. From these towns it is an easy excursion to the nature reserve of Cazorla, which offers dramatic scenery and a glimpse of deer and wild boar.

Main street of Cabra at siesta time

Belalcázar

Santa Eufemia

Hinojosa del Duque

Zújar

A420

SIERRA MORENA TOUR ❶

Torrecampo

Guadalmez

Puertollano

Alcaracejos

Añora

Pedroche

Conquista

Pozoblanco

Peñarroya-Pueblonuevo

N432

Bélmez

N502

Villanueva de Córdoba

A420

Morena

Cardeña

Fuente Obejuna

Sierra

Espiel

A421

SANTUARIO VIRGEN DE LA CABEZA ❶⑥

Bembézar

Villaviciosa de Córdoba

Embalse de Puente Nuevo

N420

Embalse del Guadalmellato

Embalse del Bembézar

CÓRDOBA

Adamuz

ANDÚJAR ❶⑤

Embalse del Retortillo

Hornachuelos

A433

MEDINA AZAHARA ❹

N432

CÓRDOBA ❺

MONTORO ❻

Villa del Río

Bujalance

Arjona

Posadas

CASTILLO DE ALMODÓVAR DEL RÍO ❸

Guadajoz

A309

Porcuna

A306

A431

PALMA DEL RÍO ❷

La Carlota

A4

NIV

N331

N432

Castro del Río

A305

Fernán Núñez

Espejo

A316

La Rambla

MONTILLA ❼

BAENA ❶❶

Sevilla

Doña Mencía

Alcaudete

AGUILAR ❽

A318

CABRA ❶⓪

A333

A340

A309

A45

A340

LUCENA ❾

PRIEGO DE CÓRDOBA ❶②

Puente Genil

Embalse de Cordobilla

Rute

Benamejí

A331

Iznájar

Genil

Málaga

Olive groves stretching across the countryside

For additional map symbols *see back flap*

Sights at a Glance

The town of Cazorla on the border of the nature reserve

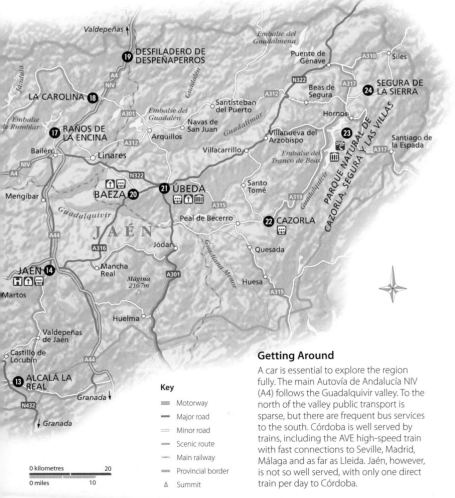

Getting Around

A car is essential to explore the region fully. The main Autovía de Andalucía NIV (A4) follows the Guadalquivir valley. To the north of the valley public transport is sparse, but there are frequent bus services to the south. Córdoba is well served by trains, including the AVE high-speed train with fast connections to Seville, Madrid, Málaga and as far as Lleida. Jaén, however, is not so well served, with only one direct train per day to Córdoba.

Key

━━ Motorway
━━ Major road
⋯⋯ Minor road
━━ Scenic route
⌁⌁ Main railway
━━ Provincial border
△ Summit

0 kilometres   20
0 miles   10

❷ Palma del Río

Córdoba. **Road map** C2. 🏛 19,500.
🚌 🚋 ℹ C/Santa Clara s/n (957 64
43 70). 🎪 Tue. 🌐 **palmadelrio.es**

Remains of the walls built by
the Almohads in the 1100s are a
reminder of the frontier days of
this farming town. The Romans
established a settlement here,
on the main route from
Córdoba to Itálica (see p136),
almost 2,000 years ago.
The Baroque **Iglesia de
la Asunción** dates
from the 18th century.
The monastery of
San Francisco is now
a delightful hotel
(see p218), and
guests dine in
the 15th-century
refectory of the
Franciscan monks.
Palma is the home
town of the late El
Cordobés, one of
Spain's most

Bell tower, La
Asunción

famous matadors. As a youth he
would creep out into the fields
around the town to practise with
the bulls. His biography, Or I'll
Dress You in Mourning, gives a
vivid view of Palma and of the
hardship that followed the end
of the Civil War.

❸ Castillo de Almodóvar del Río

Córdoba. **Road map** C2. **Tel** 957 63 40
55. **Open** Apr–Jun: 11am–2:30pm,
4–7pm daily; Jul: 10am–4pm Mon–Fri
(to 7pm Wed), 10am–8pm Sat & Sun;
Aug–Oct: 11am–2:30pm, 4–7pm daily;
Nov–Mar; 11am–2:30pm, 4–8pm daily.
🅿 🌐 **castillodealmodovar.com**
One of Andalusia's most
dramatic silhouettes breaks
the skyline as the traveller
approaches Almodóvar del
Río. The Moorish castle, with
parts dating back to the 8th
century, overlooks the whitewashed town and surrounding
fields of cotton and cereals.

Detail of wood carving in the main hall of
Medina Azahara

❹ Medina Azahara

Ctra Palma del Rio, km 5.5, Córdoba.
Road map C2. **Tel** 957 10 49 33. **Open**
Apr & May: 9am–8pm Tue–Sat, 10am–
5pm Sun and pub hols; Jun–mid-Sep:
9am–3:30pm Tue–Sat, 10am–5pm
Sun and pub hols; mid–Sep–Mar:
9am–6pm Tue–Sat, 10am–5pm Sun
and pub hols. 🅿 (free for EU citizens).

To the northwest of Palma del
Río lie the remains of a Moorish

❶ Sierra Morena Tour

The austere Sierra Morena runs across northern
Andalusia. This route through Córdoba province
takes in a region of oak- and pine-clad hills, where
hunters stalk deer and boar. It also includes the
open plain of Valle de los Pedroches, where storks
make their nests on church towers. The area,
little visited by tourists, is sparsely populated. Its
individual character is more sober than the usual
image of Andalusia and it makes a delightful
excursion on a day out from Córdoba.

④ **Hinojosa del Duque**
"Catedral de la Sierra", the vast, 15th-century
pile of the Gothic-Renaissance Iglesia
San Juan Bautista, dominates the town.
It has a Churrigueresque retablo.

Rising At Fuente Obejuna

On 23 April 1476, townsfolk
stormed the palace of the hated
lord, Don Fernando Gómez
de Guzmán. He was hurled
from a palace window, then
hacked to pieces in the main
plaza. When questioned by
a judge who committed
the crime, the men and
women replied as one,
"Fuente Obejuna, señor!"
Nobody was punished,
at least according
to Lope de Vega's best-known play, named
after the village.

Lope de Vega
(1562–1635)

② **Peñarroya-
Pueblonuevo**
This was once an
important copper-
and iron-mining
centre.

③ **Fuente Obejuna**
The Plaza Lope de Vega is
often the venue for Lope
de Vega's famous play. The
parish church, Nuestra
Señora del Castillo, was
built in the 15th century.

① **Bélmez**
Remains of a
13th-century castle
crown a hill, from which
there are fine views.

palace built in the 10th century for Caliph Abd al Rahman III, who named it after his wife. More than 10,000 workers and 15,000 mules ferried building materials from as far as North Africa.

The palace is built on three levels and includes a mosque, the caliph's residence and fine gardens. Alabaster, ebony, jasper and marble decoration adorned its many halls.

Unfortunately, the glory was short-lived. The palace was sacked by Berber invaders in 1010. Then, over centuries, it was ransacked for its building materials. Now, the ruins give only glimpses of its former splendour – a Moorish main hall, for instance, with marble carvings and a fine wooden ceiling. The palace is being restored, but progress is slow.

❺ Córdoba

See pp144–50.

❻ Montoro

Córdoba. **Road map** D2. ⚃ 9,600. 🚌 ℹ Plaza de España 8 (957 16 00 89). 🚍 Tue. 🆆 montoro.es

Spread over five hills that span a bend in the River Guadalquivir, Montoro dates from the times of the Greeks and Phoenicians. Today the economy of this rather lethargic town depends on its olive groves. The solid bridge, which was designed by Enrique de Egas, was started in the time of the Catholic Monarchs *(see pp52–3)* and took more than 50 years to finish. The townswomen sold their jewellery to raise funds for the bridge, hence its name: **Puente de las Donadas** (Bridge of the Donors).

Steep streets give the town charm. In Plaza de España are the **Ayuntamiento**, former seat of the ducal rulers, with a Plateresque façade, and the Gothic-Mudéjar **Iglesia de San Bartolomé**.

Leather bags and embossed saddlery are among several enduring crafts that are still produced in Montoro.

The 16th-century bridge spanning the Guadalquivir at Montoro

⑤ Belalcázar
An immense tower, part of a ruined castle built in 1466, dominates the skyline. In around 1480, Sebastián de Belalcázar, conqueror of Nicaragua, was born here.

Tips for Drivers

Length: 190 km (118 miles).
Stopping-off points: There are many shady places to stop along the way to have a picnic. Some of the villages along this route, such as Fuente Obejuna, have restaurants and bars.

⑥ Añora
This town is famous for preserving old customs, such as *Cruces de Mayo* (May Crosses) *(see p42)*.

⑦ Pedroche
A 56-m (184-ft) high granite church tower, with an alarming crack in it, rises above this village.

⑧ Pozoblanco
Pozoblanco entered Spanish folklore on 26 September 1984, when matador Paquirri was fatally gored by a bull.

Key
🚌 Tour route
— Other roads
▲ Mountain peak

Map labels:
⑤ A420, ④ A420, A420, El Viso, A420, Villaralto, CO225, A449, Fuente la Lancha, ⑥, ⑦, A430, ⑥, ⑧, Alcaracejos, ▲ Pelayo, N502, N432, Cordoba

❺ Street-by-Street: Córdoba

The heart of Córdoba is the old Jewish quarter near the Mezquita, known as the Judería. A walk around this area gives the visitor the sensation that little has changed since this was one of the greatest cities in the Western world. Narrow, cobbled streets where cars cannot penetrate, secluded niches, wrought iron gates, tiny workshops where silversmiths create fine jewellery – all appears very much as it was 1,000 years ago. Traffic roars along the riverfront, past the replica of a Moorish water wheel and the towering walls of the Great Mosque. Most of the sights are in this area, while modern city life takes place some blocks north, around the Plaza de las Tendillas.

Sinagoga
Hebrew script covers the interior walls of this medieval synagogue, the only one remaining in Andalusia.

Baños del Alcázar Califales
These 10th century Arab baths now house a museum recreating the history and uses of the baths.

Capilla de San Bartolomé, in Mudéjar style, contains elaborate plasterwork.

★ Alcázar de los Reyes Cristianos
Water terraces and fountains add to the tranquil atmosphere of the gardens belonging to the palace-fortress of the Catholic Monarchs, constructed in the 14th century.

To Barrio de San Basilio

0 metres		75
0 yards		75

Key

— Suggested route

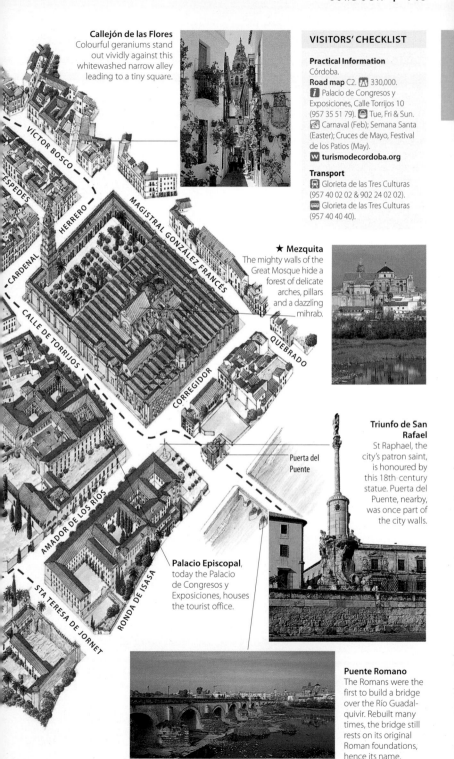

Callejón de las Flores
Colourful geraniums stand out vividly against this whitewashed narrow alley leading to a tiny square.

VISITORS' CHECKLIST

Practical Information
Córdoba.
Road map C2. 330,000.
Palacio de Congresos y Exposiciones, Calle Torrijos 10 (957 35 51 79). Tue, Fri & Sun.
Carnaval (Feb); Semana Santa (Easter); Cruces de Mayo, Festival de los Patios (May).
W turismodecordoba.org

Transport
Glorieta de las Tres Culturas (957 40 02 02 & 902 24 02 02).
Glorieta de las Tres Culturas (957 40 40 40).

★ Mezquita
The mighty walls of the Great Mosque hide a forest of delicate arches, pillars and a dazzling mihrab.

Triunfo de San Rafael
St Raphael, the city's patron saint, is honoured by this 18th-century statue. Puerta del Puente, nearby, was once part of the city walls.

Puerta del Puente

Palacio Episcopal, today the Palacio de Congresos y Exposiciones, houses the tourist office.

Puente Romano
The Romans were the first to build a bridge over the Río Guadalquivir. Rebuilt many times, the bridge still rests on its original Roman foundations, hence its name.

Exploring Córdoba

Córdoba's core is the old city around the Mezquita on the banks of the Guadalquivir. Its origins are probably Carthaginian; the name may be derived from Kartuba, Phoenician for "rich and precious city". Under the Romans it was a provincial capital and birthplace of philosopher Seneca. However, Córdoba's golden age was in the 10th century when Abd al Rahman III created an independent caliphate with Córdoba as its capital. Its influence spread to North Africa and the Balearic Islands. Córdoba was a centre of trade, industry and learning, where Jews and Christians lived alongside Muslims. Civil war *(see pp50–51)* ended the caliphate and the city was pillaged. It declined after falling to Fernando III in 1236, although a number of fine buildings have since been erected.

Naranjas y Limones (Oranges and Lemons) in Museo Julio Romero de Torres

🔼 Mezquita

See pp144–5.

Alcázar de los Reyes Cristianos

C/Caballerizas Reales s/n. **Tel** 957 42 01 51. **Open** mid-Sep–mid-Jun: 8:30am–8:45pm Tue–Fri; mid-Jun–mid Sep: 8:30am–2:30pm Tue–Sun.

This palace-fortress was built in 1328 for Alfonso XI. Fernando II and Isabel stayed here during their campaign to conquer Granada from the Moors *(see p52)*. Later it was used by the Inquisition *(see p55)*, and then as a prison.

The beautiful gardens, with ponds and fountains, are open in the evenings in July and August. Behind the palace's walls are Roman mosaics.

❎ Sinagoga

Calle Judíos 20. **Tel** 957 20 29 28. **Open** 9:30am–2pm, 3:30–5:30pm Tue–Sun.

Constructed around 1315, the small Mudéjar-style synagogue is one of three in Spain preserved from that era. The other two are both in Toledo, just south of Madrid. The women's gallery and decorative plasterwork, with Hebrew script, are of particular interest.

The synagogue lies in the Judería, the Jewish quarter, which has hardly changed since Moorish times. It is a labyrinth of narrow streets, with whitewashed houses and patios. In a small plaza nearby is a bronze statue of Maimónides, a 12th-century Jewish sage.

🏛 Baños del Alcázar Califales

Campo Santo de los Mártires. **Tel** 608 15 88 93. **Open** 8:30am–7:30pm Tue–Fri; 9:30am–4:30pm Sat; 9:30am– 2:30pm Sun & hols. (free 8:30–10:30am Mon–Fri).

Built in the Umayyad Palace under orders from Al-Hakam II in the 10th century, these Arab baths reflect the classical order of Roman baths: cold rooms, warm rooms and hot rooms. They are all vaulted and lit by star-shaped apertures and are remarkably well-preserved. A museum recreates the social and religious history and uses of the baths.

🏛 Museo Julio Romero de Torres

Plaza del Potro 1. **Tel** 957 47 03 56. **Open** 8:30am–8:45pm Tue–Fri, 8:30am–4:30pm Sat; 8:30am–2:30pm Sun & public hols.

Julio Romero de Torres (1874–1930), who was born in this house, captured the soul of Córdoba in his paintings. Many depict nudes in stilted poses; others are painfully mawkish, including the deathbed scene *Look How Lovely She Was* (1895). His unpredictable style varied from the macabre *Cante Hondo* (1930) to the humorous *Naranjas y Limones* (1928).

🏛 Museo de Bellas Artes

Plaza del Potro 1. **Tel** 957 10 36 43. **Open** Jun–mid-Sep: 9am–3:30pm, 10am–5pm Sun & pub hols; mid-Sep–May: 10am–8:30pm Tue–Sat, 10am–5pm Sun & public hols.

Located in a former charity hospital, this museum exhibits sculptures by local artist Mateo Inurria (1867–1924) as well as paintings by Murillo, Valdés Leal and Zurbarán of the Seville School *(see p70)*.

🟥 Plaza de la Corredera

Built in the 17th century in Castilian style, this handsome,

Daily market in the arcaded Plaza de la Corredera

arcaded square has been the scene of bullfights and other public events. The buildings have been restored, but the cafés under the arches still retain an air of the past. A market is held here daily.

⌂ Palacio de Viana

Plaza Don Gome 2. **Tel** 957 49 67 41.
Open 10am–7pm Tue–Sat;
10am–3pm Sun.

Tapestries, furniture, porcelain and paintings are displayed in

Central fountain in the garden of the 17th-century Palacio de Viana

this 17th-century mansion. Purchased by a savings bank in 1981, the former home of the Viana family is kept much as they left it. There are 14 beautiful patios and a delightful garden.

⌂ Museo Arqueológico

Plaza Jerónimo Páez 7. **Tel** 957 35 55 17. **Open** Jun–mid-Sep: 9am–3:30pm Tue–Sat, 10am–5pm Sun & pub hols; mid-Sep–May: 10am–8:30pm Tue–Sat, 10am–5pm Sun & pub hols.

Roman remains, including mosaics and pottery are on display in this Renaissance mansion. Other exhibits include Moorish items such as a 10th century bronze stag found at Medina Azahara *(see p142).*

⌂ Puente Romano

This arched bridge has Roman foundations, but was rebuilt by the Moors. Nearby, south of the Mezquita, stands the Puerta del Puente, designed by Hernán Ruiz in 1571.

Moorish bronze stag in the Museo Arqueológico

⌂ Torre de la Calahorra

Tel 957 29 39 29. **Open** daily.
Oct– Apr: 10am–6pm; May–Sep:
10am– 8:30pm.

At the end of the Puente Romano, this defensive tower was built in the 1300s. It houses a museum about the life, culture and philosophy of 10th-century Córdoba.

Sights at a Glance

1. Sinagoga
2. Baños del Alcázar Califales
3. Alcázar de los Reyes Cristianos
4. Puente Romano
5. Torre de la Calahorra
6. Mezquita
7. Museo Arqueológico
8. Museo Julio Romero de Torres and Museo de Bellas Artes
9. Plaza de la Corredera

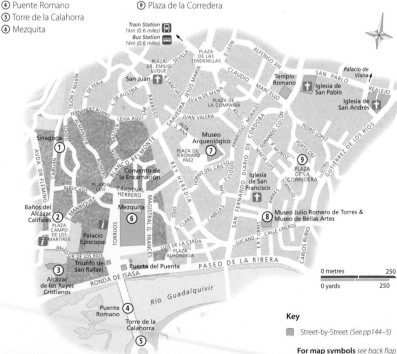

Key

■ Street-by-Street (See pp144–5)

For map symbols see back flap

Córdoba: the Mezquita

Córdoba's great mosque, dating back 12 centuries, embodied the power of Islam on the Iberian peninsula. Abd al Rahman I *(see p50)* built the original mosque between 785 and 787. The building evolved over the centuries, blending many architectural forms. In the 10th century al Hakam II *(see p50)* made some of the most lavish additions, including the elaborate *mihrab* (prayer niche) and the *maqsura* (caliph's enclosure). In the 16th century a cathedral was built in the heart of the reconsecrated mosque, part of which was destroyed.

Patio de los Naranjos
Orange trees grow in the courtyard where the faithful washed before prayer.

Expansion of The Mezquita

Abd al Rahman I built the original mosque. Extensions were added by Abd al Rahman II, al Hakam II and al Mansur.

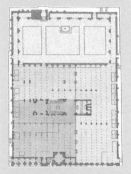

Key to Floorplan

- Mosque of Abd al Rahman I
- Extension by Abd al Rahman II
- Extension by al Hakam II
- Extension by al Mansur
- Patio de los Naranjos

KEY

① **Puerta de San Esteban** is set in a section of wall from an earlier Visigothic church.

② **The Puerta del Perdón** is a Mudéjar-style entrance gate, built during Christian rule in 1377. Penitents were pardoned here.

③ **Capilla Mayor**

④ **The cathedral choir** has Churrigueresque stalls, carved by Pedro Duque Cornejo in 1758.

⑤ **Capilla Real**

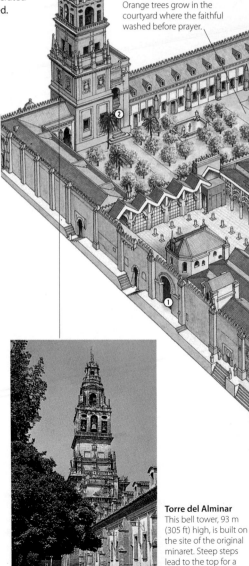

Torre del Alminar
This bell tower, 93 m (305 ft) high, is built on the site of the original minaret. Steep steps lead to the top for a fine view of the city.

Cathedral
Part of the mosque was destroyed to accommodate the cathedral, started in 1523. Featuring an Italianate dome, it was chiefly designed by members of the Hernán Ruiz family.

VISITORS' CHECKLIST

Practical Information
Calle Torrijos s/n. **Tel** 957 47 05 12.
w **mezquitadecordoba.org**
Open 10am–7pm Mon–Sat,
8:30–11:30am & 3–6pm Sun &
religious hols (Mar–Oct:
10am–7pm Mon–Sat). 🎧 ✝
9:30am Mon–Sat; 10:30am & 1pm
Sun & pub hols.

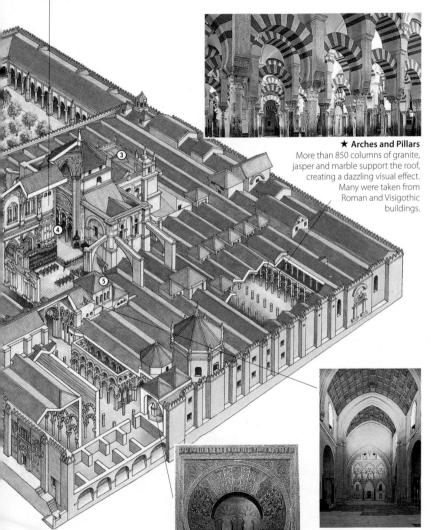

★ **Arches and Pillars**
More than 850 columns of granite, jasper and marble support the roof, creating a dazzling visual effect. Many were taken from Roman and Visigothic buildings.

★ **Capilla de Villaviciosa**
The first Christian chapel to be built in the mosque, in 1371, the Capilla de Villaviciosa has stunning multi-lobed arches.

★ **Mihrab**
This prayer niche, richly ornamented, held a gilt copy of the Koran. The worn flagstones indicate where pilgrims circled it seven times on their knees.

The Patios of Córdoba

Since early times, family and social life in Andalusia have revolved around the courtyard or patio, which is at the heart of the classic Mediterranean house. The sleeping accommodation and living rooms were built round this space, which introduces air and light into the house. Brick arches, colourful tiles, ironwork, orange and lemon trees, and pots full of flowers add to the charm of these cool and tranquil retreats. Córdoba takes pride in all its patio gardens, be they palatial spaces in the grandest residences or tiny courtyards in humble homes, shared by many. There are traditional patios in the San Lorenzo and Judería quarters and in Barrio San Basilio, west of the Mezquita.

Whitewashed walls   Tiled portrait of saint   Orange trees

Festival de los Patios, when scores of patios are thrown open to the public, takes place in early May (see pp42–3). The most beautifully decorated patio wins a prestigious prize.

Andalusian Patio

This scene, painted by García Rodríguez (1863–1925), evokes a style of patio that is still common in Andalusia. The patio walls are usually immaculately whitewashed, contrasting with the colourful display of geraniums and carnations in terracotta pots. Fragrant blooms of jasmine add to the atmosphere.

Moorish-style lamps, which now have electric bulbs, light the patio in the late evening.

Azulejos, a reminder of the region's Moorish past, decorate many patios, adding to their colourful display.

Cancelas are attractively designed iron gates which screen the private patio from the street outside.

A central fountain or well traditionally provided water and remains a feature of many patios today.

❼ Montilla

Córdoba. **Road map** C2. 🚶 23,000.
🚌 🚐 ℹ️ Calle Capitan Alonso de
Vargas 3 (957 65 23 54). 🏛️ Fri.

Montilla is the centre of an
important wine-making region,
but one that finds it difficult to
emerge from the shadow of a
more famous rival. The excellent
white wine is made in the same
way as sherry *(see pp34–5)* and
tastes rather like it but, unlike
sherry, does not need fortifying
with alcohol. Some *bodegas*,
including **Alvear** and **Pérez
Barquero**, are happy to
welcome visitors.

The Mudéjar **Convento de
Santa Clara** dates from 1512
and the **castle** from the 18th
century. The town library is in
the **Casa del Inca**, so named
because Garcilaso de la Vega,
who wrote about the Incas,
lived there in the 16th century.

🏠 **Bodega Alvear**
Avenida María Auxiliadora 1. **Tel** 957 65
01 00. **Open** daily (call first to arrange
visit). **Closed** Sun & public hols.

🏠 **Bodega Pérez Barquero**
Avenida Andalucía 27. **Tel** 957 65 05
00. **Open** phone ahead to make an
appt, or e-mail info@perezbarquero.
com. 🌐 **perezbarquero.com**

The historic crest of the Bodega
Pérez Barquero

❽ Aguilar

Córdoba. **Road map** C2. 🚶 13,500.
🚌 🚐 ℹ️ Cuesta de Jesús 2, Edificio
Antiguo Posito (957 66 15 67). 🏛️ Tue,
Thu & Fri.

Ceramics, wine and olive oil are
important products in Aguilar,
which was settled in Roman times.
There are several seigneurial
houses, and the eight-sided
Plaza de San José. Built in 1810,
it houses the town hall. Nearby is
a Baroque clock tower.

❾ Lucena

Córdoba. **Road map** D2. 🚶 40,000.
🚌 ℹ️ Castillo del Moral s/n (957 51
32 82). 🏛️ Wed. 🌐 **turlucena.com**

Lucena prospers from furniture
making and from its brass and
copper manufactures, and
produces interesting ceramics.
Under the caliphs of Córdoba
(see p50) it was an important
trading and intellectual centre,
with a dynamic, independent,
Jewish community.

Iglesia de Santiago, with a
Baroque turret, was built on the
site of a synagogue in 1503.
The **Torre del Moral** is the only
remaining part of a Moorish
castle. Granada's last sultan,
Boabdil, was captured in 1483,
and imprisoned here. Nearby,
the 15th-century **Iglesia de
San Mateo** has a flamboyant
Baroque sacristy and three
naves with delicate arches.

On the first Sunday in May
Lucena stages an elaborate
ceremony, which honours the
Virgen de Araceli.

❿ Cabra

Córdoba. **Road map** D2. 🚶 21,000.
🚌 ℹ️ Calle del Junquillo, s/n (957 52
34 93). 🏛️ Mon. 🌐 **turismo.cabra.eu**

Set amid fertile fields and vast
olive groves, Cabra was an
episcopal seat in the 3rd century.
On a rise stands the former castle,
which is now a school. There are

Statue of Santo Domingo, Iglesia Santo
Domingo in Cabra

also some noble mansions and
the **Iglesia Santo Domingo** with
a Baroque façade.

Just outside the town, the
Fuente del Río, source of
the Río Cabra, is a pleasantly
leafy spot in which to picnic.

⓫ Baena

Córdoba. **Road map** D2. 🚶 20,000.
🚐 ℹ️ Virrey del Pino 5 (957 67 17 57).
🏛️ Thu. 🌐 **baena.es**

Baena's olive oil has been famed
since Roman times. At the top
of the whitewashed town is
Iglesia Santa María la Mayor.
On the Plaza de la Constitución
stands the handsome, modern
town hall. The **Casa del Monte**,
an arcaded mansion dating
from the 18th century, flanks
it on one side.

Easter week is spectacular,
when thousands of drummers
take to the streets *(see p38)*.

Decoration on façade of the 18th-century Casa del Monte, Baena

⑭ Jaén

The Moors knew Jaén as *geen*, meaning "way station of caravans". Their lofty fortress, later rebuilt as the Castillo de Santa Catalina, symbolizes Jaén's strategic importance on the route to Andalusia from the more austere Castile. For centuries this area was a battleground between Moors and Christians *(see pp52–3)*. The older, upper part of the city holds most interest. Around the cathedral and towards the Barrio San Juan are numerous seigneurial buildings, long winding streets and steep alleys. The city centre is filled with smart shops, and in the evenings the narrow streets near Plaza de la Constitución are filled with people enjoying the *tapeo* in the many bars.

Mighty ramparts of Castillo de Santa Catalina

🏰 Castillo de Santa Catalina
Carretera al Castillo. **Tel** 953 12 07 33 (tourist centre), 953 23 00 00 (parador). **Open** Tue–Sun. **Closed** public hols. 🅿

Hannibal is believed to have erected a tower on this rocky pinnacle, high above the city. Later the Moors established a fortress, only to lose it to the crusading King Fernando III in 1246. A larger castle was then built with huge ramparts. This has been restored and a medieval-style *parador* (inn) built next door.

It is worthwhile taking the sinuous road up to the Torre del Homenaje and the castle chapel. Even more rewarding are the great views of the city, the mountains and the landscape, thick with olive trees.

🏛 Catedral
Plaza de Santa Maria. **Open** 10am–2pm, 4–7pm Mon–Sat, (to 6pm Sat), 10am–midday Sun.

Andrés de Vandelvira, responsible for many of Ubeda's fine buildings *(see pp158–9)*, designed the cathedral in the 16th century. Later additions include two 17th-century towers that flank the west front. Inside are beautifully carved choir stalls and a museum with valuable works of art.

Every Friday, from 10:30am–noon and 5–6pm, worshippers can view the Lienzo del Santo Rostro. St Veronica is said to have used this piece of cloth to wipe Christ's face, which left a permanent impression.

🛁 Baños Arabes
Palacio Villardompardo, Plaza Santa Luisa de Marillac. **Tel** 953 24 80 68. **Open** 9am–9pm Tue–Sat, 9:15am–2:15pm Sun. **Closed** public hols.

These 11th-century baths are known as the baths of Ali, a Moorish chieftain. They were restored during the 1980s. The interior features horseshoe arches, ceilings decorated with tiny star-shaped windows, a hemispherical dome and two earthenware vats in which bathers once immersed themselves. The baths are entered through the Palacio Villardom-pardo, which also houses a museum of local arts and crafts.

🏛 Capilla de San Andrés
Tucked away in a narrow alley next to a college lies this Mudéjar chapel. It was founded

Olive Oil
Olive oil is the life-blood of Jaén and its province. Since the Phoenicians, or possibly the Greeks, brought the olive tree to Spain it has flourished in Andalusia, particularly in Jaén, which today has an annual production of more than 200,000 tonnes of oil. Harvesting, mostly by hand, takes place from December onwards. Quality is controlled by a system known as *Denominación de Origen Controlada*. The best product, virgin olive oil, is made from the first cold-pressing, so that the full flavour, vitamins and nutrients of the oil are preserved.

Harvest time in one of the many olive groves in Andalusia

Horseshoe arches supporting the dome at the Baños Arabes

Shrine of Virgen de la Capilla in Iglesia San Ildefonso

in the 16th century, possibly on the site of a synagogue, by Gutiérrez González, who was treasurer to Pope Leo X and endowed with extensive privileges. A magnificent gilded iron screen by Maestro Bartolomé de Jaén is the highlight of the chapel.

🏛 Iglesia San Ildefonso

This mainly Gothic church has façades in three different styles. One is Gothic, with a mosaic of the Virgin descending on Jaén during a Moorish siege in 1430. A second is partly Plateresque (*see p29*) and the third, by Ventura Rodríguez in the late 18th century, is Neo-Classical. Inside, the high altar is by Pedro and José Roldán. There is also a chapel which enshrines the Virgen de la Capilla, Jaén's patron saint. The museum next door is devoted to the Virgin.

🏛 Real Monasterio de Santa Clara

Founded in the 13th century, just after the Reconquest of the city by Christian forces, Real Monasterio de Santa Clara is one of the most ancient monasteries in Jaén. It has a lovely cloister, which dates from about 1581. The church has an *artesonado* ceiling and shelters a curious 16th-century bamboo image of Christ made in Ecuador. Sweet cakes are offered for sale by the nuns from the convent.

🏛 Museo Provincial

Paseo de la Estación 27. **Tel** 953 10 13 66. **Open** Jun–mid-Sep: 9am–3:30pm

VISITORS' CHECKLIST

Practical Information
Jaén. **Road map** D2. 🗺 115,000.
ℹ Calle Maestra 18 (953 31 32 81). 🚌 Thu. 🎭 Semana Santa (Easter); Festividad de Nuestra Señora de la Capilla (11 Jun); Feria de San Lucas (18 Oct); Romería de Santa Catalina (25 Nov).

Transport
🚉 Paseo de la Estación s/n (902 24 02 02). 🚌 Plaza Coca de la Piñera s/n. 953 25 01 06.

Tue–Sat, 10am–5pm Sun & public hols; mid-Sep–May: 10am–8:30pm Tue–Sat, 10am–5pm Sun & pub hols.

This building incorporates remains of the Iglesia de San Miguel and the façade of a 16th-century granary. A Palaeo-Christian sarcophagus, Roman mosaics and sculptures, and Greek and Roman ceramics are among the articles on display.

A short walk along Paseo de la Estación is the Plaza de las Batallas and a memorial to the defeats of Napoleon at Bailén (*see p57*) and of the Moors at Las Navas de Tolosa (*see p52*).

Sights at a Glance

① Baños Arabes
② Capilla de San Andrés
③ Real Monasterio de Santa Clara
④ Catedral
⑤ Iglesia San Ildefonso

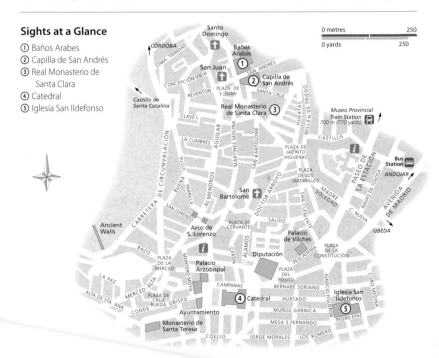

The Moorish Castillo de la Mota and the ruined church crowning the hill above Alcalá la Real

⑫ Priego de Córdoba

Córdoba. **Road map** D2. 🏔 23,000. 🚌
ℹ Carrera de las Monjas 1 (957 70 06 25). 🚃 Sat. 🔲 turismodepriego.com

Priego de Córdoba lies on a fertile plain at the foot of La Tiñosa, the highest mountain in Córdoba province. It is a pleasant small town with an unassuming air, well away from the main routes, and yet it claims to be the capital of Córdoba Baroque. The title is easy to accept in view of the dazzling work of local carvers, gilders and ironworkers.

The town's labyrinthine old quarter was the site of the original Arab settlement. But the 18th century, when silk manufacture prospered, was Priego's golden age. During this time elegant houses were built and money was lavished on fine Baroque architecture, particularly churches.

A restored Moorish fortress, standing on Roman foundations, introduces visitors to the fine medieval quarter, **Barrio de la Villa**. Whitewashed buildings line its narrow streets and flower-decked squares. Paseo Colombia leads to the Adarve, a long promenade with views of the surrounding countryside.

The nearby **Iglesia de la Asunción** is an outstanding structure. Originally Gothic in style, it was converted to a Baroque church by Jerónimo Sánchez de Rueda in the 18th

century. Its *pièce de résistance* is the sacristy chapel, created in 1784 by local artist Francisco Javier Pedrajas. Its sumptuous ornamentation in the form of sculpted figures and plaster scrolls and cornices can be overwhelming. The main altar is in Plateresque style *(see p29)*.

The **Iglesia de la Aurora** is another fine Baroque building. At midnight every Saturday the cloaked brotherhood, Nuestra Señora de la Aurora, parades the streets singing songs to the Virgin and collecting alms.

Silk merchants built many of the imposing mansions that follow the curve around the Calle del Río. Niceto Alcalá Zamora was born at No. 33 in 1877. A brilliant orator, he

Fine statuary ornaments the 16th-century Fuente del Rey at Priego de Córdoba

became Spain's president in 1931, but was forced into exile during the Civil War. Today the house contains an interesting museum about Niceto Alcala Zamora.

At the end of the street is the **Fuente del Rey**, or King's Fountain. This is a Baroque extravaganza, with three pools, 139 spouts gushing water, and includes Neptune among its exuberant statuary.

May is one of the liveliest months to visit Priego. Every Sunday a procession celebrates the town's deliverance from a plague which devastated the population centuries ago.

⑬ Alcalá la Real

Jaén. **Road map** D2. 🏔 22,000. 🚌
ℹ Fortaleza de la Mota (953 10 27 17). 🚃 Tue.

Alcalá was a strategic point held by the military Order of Calatrava during Spain's Reconquest *(see pp52–3)*. On the hilltop of La Mota are the ruins of the Moorish **Fortaleza de la Mota**, built by the rulers of Granada in the 14th century, with later additions. Nearby are ruins of the town's main church. There are splendid views over the countryside and the historic town, with its air of past glories. The Renaissance **Palacio Abacial** and **Fuente de Carlos V** are the chief attractions to be found around the plaza in the centre of the town.

⓮ Jaén

See pp152–3.

⓯ Andújar

Jaén. **Road map** D2. 40,000. Torre del Reloj Plaza de Santa Maria s/n (953 50 49 59). Tue.

This strategically situated town was once the site of Iliturgi, an Iberian town that was destroyed by Scipio's army in the Punic Wars *(see p48)*. A 15-arched bridge built by the Roman conquerors still spans the Guadalquivir river.

In the central plaza is the Gothic **Iglesia San Miguel**, with paintings by Alonso Cano. The **Iglesia Santa María la Mayor** features a Renaissance façade and a splendid Mudéjar tower. Inside is the painting *Christ in the Garden of Olives* (c.1605) by El Greco.

The town is also renowned for its potters, who still turn out ceramics in traditional style. Olive oil *(see p152)*, which is produced in Andújar, figures strongly in the local cuisine.

Roman bridge spanning the Guadalquivir at Andújar

⓰ Santuario Virgen de la Cabeza

Padres Trinitarios. **Road map** D2. **Tel** 953 54 90 15. **Open** 10am–8pm daily. **santuariovirgencabeza.org**

North of Andújar, amid the oak trees and bull ranches of the Sierra Morena, is the Santuario Virgen de la Cabeza. Within this grim stone temple from the 13th century, is a much-venerated Virgin. According to tradition her image was sent to Spain by St Peter.

Much of the building and the original statue of the Virgin were destroyed in 1937 in the Civil War *(see pp58–9)*. For nine months 230 civil guards held out against Republican forces. 20,000 men attacked the sanctuary before it burned down. Captain Santiago Cortés, the commander of the civil guard, died from his battle wounds.

On the last Sunday in April every year, many thousands make a pilgrimage to the sanctuary to pay homage to the Virgin *(see p43)*.

Replica of the statue of the Virgin Mary, Santuario de la Cabeza

⓱ Baños de la Encina

Jaén. **Road map** D2. from Linares & Jaen. **Tel** Callejon del Castillo 1. 953 61 32 29 (Ayuntamiento). **Open** Wed–Sun. **bdelaencina.com**

Caliph al-Hakam II *(see p50)* ordered the construction of this fortress, Castillo de Burgalimar, in the foothills of the Sierra Morena in AD 967. Rising above the village, it is a daunting sight with its 15 towers and soaring ramparts. Its heights give views across pastures and olive groves.

During the spring fair there is a *romería* (see p42) to the town's shrine of the Virgen de la Encina. According to local tradition, the Virgin made a miraculous appearance on an *encina* (holm oak tree).

⓲ La Carolina

Jaén. **Road map** E1. 15,500. Carretera Madrid–Cádiz km 269 (953 68 08 82). Tue & Fri.

Founded in 1767, La Carolina was populated by settlers from Germany and Flanders. This was an ill-fated plan to develop the area and to make it safer for travellers. The person in charge, Carlos III's minister, Pablo de Olavide, had a palace built on the main square. Just outside town is a monument to a battle at Las Navas de Tolosa in 1212. Alfonso VIII, king of Castile, was led by a shepherd over the hills to Las Navas, where he crushed the Moors. His victory began the reconquest of Andalusia *(see pp52–3)*.

Façade of the palace of Pablo de Olavide

⓳ Desfiladero de Despeñaperros

Jaén. **Road map** E1. Visitors Centre, Auto via de Andalucia (A4) km 257 Santa Elena, Jaén (953 66 43 07).

This spectacular pass in the Sierra Morena is the main gateway to Andalusia. Armies, stage-coaches, mule-trains and brigands all used the pass, so hold-ups were common.

The four-lane Autovía de Andalucía and a railway line thread their way through the chasm, which offers view rock formations – *Los O* (the organ pipes) and *del Fraile* (monk's lea

⑳ Street-by-Street: Baeza

Nestling amid olive groves, beautiful Baeza is a small town, unusually rich in Renaissance architecture. In 2003 it was named a UNESCO World Heritage site. Called Beatia by the Romans and later the capital of a Moorish fiefdom, Baeza is portrayed as a "royal nest of hawks" on its coat of arms. It was conquered by Fernando III in 1226 – the first town in Andalusia to be definitively won back from the Moors – and was then settled by Castilian knights. An era of medieval splendour followed, reaching a climax in the 16th century, when Andrés de Vandelvira's splendid buildings were erected. In the early 20th century, Antonio Machado, one of his generation's greatest poets, lived here for some years.

★ **Palacio de Jabalquinto**
An Isabelline *(see p28)* style façade, flanked by elaborate, rounded buttresses, fronts this splendid Gothic palace.

Antigua Universidad
From 1542 until 1825, this Renaissance and Baroque building was the site of one of Spain's first universities.

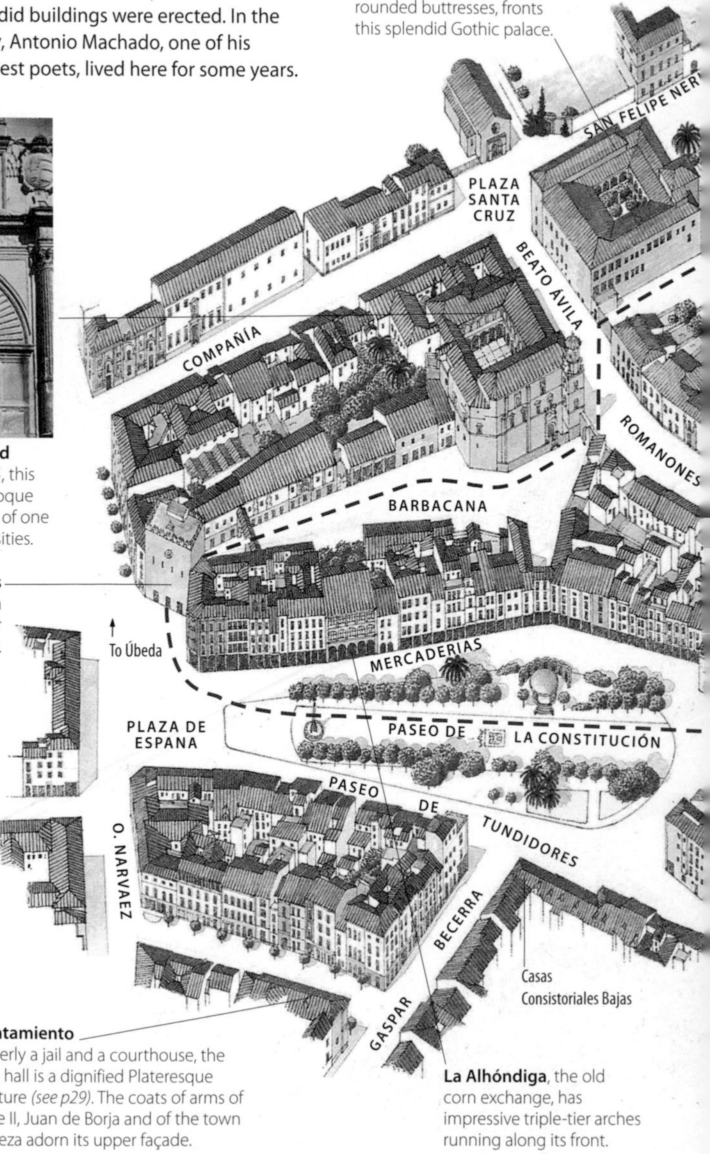

Torre de los Aliatares is a 1,000-year-old tower built by the Moors.

↑ To Úbeda

Ayuntamiento
Formerly a jail and a courthouse, the town hall is a dignified Plateresque structure *(see p29)*. The coats of arms of Felipe II, Juan de Borja and of the town of Baeza adorn its upper façade.

La Alhóndiga, the old corn exchange, has impressive triple-tier arches running along its front.

Casas Consistoriales Bajas

...taurants in this region see pp216–19 and pp228–37

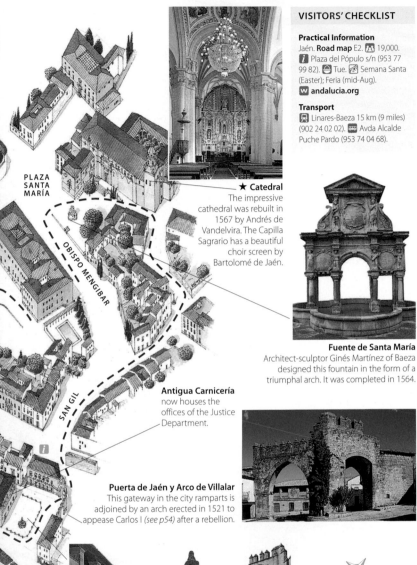

VISITORS' CHECKLIST

Practical Information
Jaén. **Road map** E2. 19,000.
Plaza del Pópulo s/n (953 77
99 82). Tue. Semana Santa
(Easter); Feria (mid-Aug).
w andalucia.org

Transport
Linares-Baeza 15 km (9 miles)
(902 24 02 02). Avda Alcalde
Puche Pardo (953 74 04 68).

★ Catedral
The impressive cathedral was rebuilt in 1567 by Andrés de Vandelvira. The Capilla Sagrario has a beautiful choir screen by Bartolomé de Jaén.

PLAZA SANTA MARÍA

OBISPO MENGIBAR

SAN GIL

Fuente de Santa María
Architect-sculptor Ginés Martínez of Baeza designed this fountain in the form of a triumphal arch. It was completed in 1564.

Antigua Carnicería
now houses the offices of the Justice Department.

Puerta de Jaén y Arco de Villalar
This gateway in the city ramparts is adjoined by an arch erected in 1521 to appease Carlos I *(see p54)* after a rebellion.

To Jaén

Key

Tourist information

— Suggested route

★ Plaza del Pópulo
The Casa del Pópulo, a fine Plateresque palace, now the tourist office, overlooks this square. In its centre is the Fuente de los Leones, a fountain with an Ibero-Roman statue flanked by lions.

| 0 metres | 75 |
| 0 yards | 75 |

㉑ Úbeda

Perched on the crest of a ridge, Úbeda is a showcase of Renaissance magnificence. Thanks to the patronage of some of Spain's most influential men of the 16th century, such as Francisco de los Cobos, secretary of state, and his great nephew, Juan Vázquez de Molina, a number of noble buildings are dotted about the town. The Plaza de Vázquez de Molina is surrounded by elegant palaces and churches and is undoubtedly the jewel in the crown. The narrow streets of the old quarter contrast sharply with modern Úbeda, which expands north of the Plaza de Andalucía. In 2003 Úbeda became a UNESCO World Heritage Site.

Maestro Bartolomé's choir screen at Capilla del Salvador

🏛 Capilla del Salvador

Three architects, Andrés de Vandelvira (credited with refining the Renaissance style), Diego de Siloé and Esteban Jamete helped design this 16th-century landmark. It was built as the personal chapel of Francisco de los Cobos, whose tomb lies in the crypt.

Although the church was pillaged during the Civil War *(see pp58–9)*, it retains a number of treasures. These include a carving of Christ, which is all that remains of an altarpiece by Alonso de Berruguete, Maestro Bartolomé de Jaén's choir screen, and a sacristy by Vandelvira.

Behind the church are two other buildings dating from the 16th century – Cobos's palace, which is graced by a Renaissance façade, and the Hospital de los Honrados Viejos (Honoured Elders). At the end of Baja del Salvador is the Plaza de Santa Lucía. A promenade leads from this point along the Redonda de Miradores, following the line of the old walls and offering views of the countryside.

🏛 Palacio de las Cadenas

Pl de Vázquez de Molina. **Tel** 953 75 04 40. **Open** 8am–3pm, 5–10pm Mon–Fri; 9am–1pm Sat & Sun.

Two stone lions guard Úbeda's town hall, which occupies this palace built for Vázquez de Molina by Vandelvira during the mid-16th century. The building gets its name from the iron chains *(cadenas)* once attached

to the columns supporting the main doorway.

Crowning the corners of the Classical façade are carved stone lanterns. A museum of local pottery is in the basement. The building also houses the tourist information office.

🏛 Parador de Úbeda

Plaza de Vázquez de Molina s/n. **Tel** 953 75 03 45. **Patio Open** to non-guests daily. **W** parador.es

Built in the 16th century but considerably altered in the 17th century, this was the residence of Fernando Ortega Salido, Dean of Málaga and chaplain of El Salvador. The austere palace is now a hotel, which is also known as the Parador Condestable Dávalos in honour of a warrior famed during the Reconquest *(see pp52–3)*.

🏛 Santa María de los Reales Alcázares

Built on the site of an original mosque, this church, mainly dating from the 13th century, is being restored. Inside there is fine ironwork by Maestro Bartolomé. The Gothic cloister, with pointed arches and ribbed vaults, and a Romanesque doorway, are particularly noteworthy.

Near the church is the Cárcel del Obispo (Bishop's Jail), so called because nuns punished by the bishop were confined there. Today the building contains the town's courthouse.

🏛 Iglesia de San Pablo

The three doors of this church all date from different periods. The main entrance is in late Gothic

Stone lions guarding the Palacio de las Cadenas

Statuary on the main entrance of Iglesia de San Pablo

style while the others are in transitional Romanesque and Isabelline. Inside is an apse, which dates from the 13th century and a beautiful 16th-century chapel by Vandelvira. The church is surmounted by a Plateresque tower (1537).

Nearby on Plaza de Vázquez de Molina is a monument to the poet and mystic San Juan de la Cruz (1549–91).

🏛 **Museo Arqueológico**

Casa Mudéjar, C/Cervantes 6. **Tel** 953 10 86 23. **Open** Jun–mid-Sep: 9am–3:30pm Tue–Sat, 10am–5pm Sun & pub hols; mid-Sep–May: 10am–8:30pm Tue–Sat, 10am–5pm Sun & pub hols.

This archaeological museum exhibits artifacts from Neolithic times to the Moorish era. The display includes tombstones from the 1st century AD and Moorish and Mudéjar works in wood and plaster. It is located in the 15th-century Casa Mudéjar, among the many palaces and churches gracing the streets of the old quarter.

🏛 **Hospital de Santiago**

Calle Obispo Cobos s/n. **Tel** 953 75 08 42. **Open** 8am–3pm (to 2:30pm in winter), 5–10pm Mon–Fri, 10am–2:30pm, 5:30–10pm Sat & Sun.

Created on the orders of the Bishop of Jaén around 1562, this colossal former hospital was designed by Vandelvira. The façade is flanked by square towers. Marble columns grace the patio with its central fountain. A staircase leads up to the gallery roofed by a frescoed ceiling.

Today the building houses the Palacio de Congresos y Exposiciones. At the entrance is an information office, and in a corner of the patio there is a stone-vaulted café.

Nearby, on Avenida de la Constitución, is Úbeda's bullring, which is open during the *fiesta*.

Distinctive steeple above the Hospital de Santiago

Sights at a Glance

① Hospital de Santiago
② Museo Arqueológico
③ Iglesia de San Pablo
④ Capilla del Salvador
⑤ Parador de Úbeda
⑥ Palacio de las Cadenas
⑦ Santa María de los Reales Alcázares

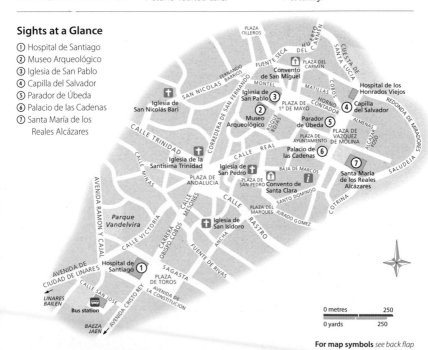

0 metres 250
0 yards 250

For map symbols *see back flap*

Ruins of La Iruela, spectacularly situated above the road outside Cazorla

② Cazorla

Jaén. **Road map** E2. ⛰ 8,500. 🚌 🛈
Paseo del Santo Cristo 17 (953 71 01
02). 🏛 Mon & Sat.

Cazorla was wealthy in ancient
times when the Romans mined
the surrounding mountains for
silver. Today it is better known as
the jumping-off point for those
who wish to visit the Parque
Natural de Cazorla, Segura y
Las Villas.

Modern buildings have
proliferated, but it is pleasant to
stroll along the crooked streets
between the Plaza de la
Corredera and the charming
Plaza Santa María. The ruined
Iglesia de Santa María forms a
picturesque backdrop to this
popular meeting place. Above
stands the **Castillo de la Yedra**
which houses a folklore museum.

On the road leading to the
park are the remains of **La Iruela**,
a much-photographed fortress
atop a rocky spur. On 14 May the
locals pay homage to a former
resident of Cazorla, San Isicio,
one of seven apostles who
preached Christianity in Spain
before the arrival of the Moors.

🏛 **Castillo de la Yedra**
Folklore Museum: **Tel** 953 10 14 02
Open Jun–mid-Sep: 9am–8:30pm
Tue–Sat, 10am–5pm Sun & public
hols; mid-Sep–May: 10am–8:30pm
Tue–Sat; 10am–5pm Sun & pub hols.

② Parque Natural de Cazorla, Segura y Las Villas

Jaén. **Road map** E2. 🚌 Cazorla. 🛈
Paseo del Santo Cristo 17, Cazorla
(953 72 01 02).

First-time visitors are amazed by
the spectacular scenery of this
214,336-ha (529,409-acre)
nature reserve with its thick
woodland, tumbling streams
and abundant wildlife. Bristling
mountains rise over 2,000 m
(6,500 ft) above the source of
the Guadalquivir River. The river
flows north through a delightful
valley before reaching the
Tranco de Beas dam, where
it turns to run down towards
the Atlantic.

Cars are allowed only on
the main road. Many visitors
explore on foot, but horses and
bikes can be hired from the
**Centro de Recepción e
Interpretación de la Naturaleza**,
in the reserve. It provides a lot
of useful information. There are
also opportunities for hunting
and angling.

🏛 **Centro de Recepción e
Interpretación de la Naturaleza**
Carretera del Tranco km 49, Torre del
Vinagre. **Tel** 953 71 30 40. **Open** daily.

② Segura de la Sierra

Jaén. **Road map** E1. ⛰ 2,200. 🚌 🛈
Ayuntamiento, Calle Regidor Juan de
Isla 1 (953 48 02 80).

This tiny village at 1,200 m
(4,000 ft) above sea level is
dominated by its restored
Moorish **castillo** (ask for keys in
the village). From the ramparts
there are splendid views of the
harsh mountain ranges. Below is
an unusual bullring, partly
chipped out of rock. It sees
most action at the *fiesta* in the
first week of October.

Olive oil in the Segura de la
Sierra area is one of four which
bear Spain's prestigious
*Denominación de Origen
Controlada* label *(see p152)*.

Moorish castillo at Segura de la Sierra, surrounded by olive groves

Wildlife in Cazorla, Segura and Las Villas

The nature reserve of Sierra de Cazorla, Segura and Las Villas protects a profusion of wildlife. Most is native to the region, but some species have been introduced or reintroduced for hunting. More than 100 species of birds live in Cazorla, some very rare. It is the only habitat in Spain, apart from the Pyrenees, where the lammergeier can be seen. The extensive forests are home to a range of plant life, such as the indigenous Viola cazorlensis (*see p25*), which grows among rocks.

The golden eagle *(Aquila chrysaetus)*, king of the air, preys on small mammals living in the reserve.

Griffon vultures *(Gyps fulvus)* circle high above the reserve, descending rapidly when they catch sight of their prey.

The lammergeier *(Gypaetus barbatus)* drops bones from a height on to rocks to smash them and eat the marrow.

Landscape

The area's craggy limestone heights and riverside meadows are part of its attraction. Water trickles down the mountains, filling the lakes and brooks of the valley. This lush landscape provides ideal habitats for a diversity of wildlife.

Red deer *(Cervus elaphus)*, reintroduced to the area in 1952, are most commonly seen in the autumn months.

The Spanish ibex *(Capra pyrenaica)* is amazingly sure-footed on the rocky terrain. Today, the few that remain only emerge at dusk in order to feed.

Otters *(Lutra lutra)* live around lakes and streams and are active at dawn and dusk.

Wild boar *(Sus scrofa)* hide in woodland by day and forage at night for anything from acorns to roots, eggs of ground-nesting birds and small mammals.

CÁDIZ AND MÁLAGA

Andalusia's southern provinces offer striking contrasts.
Behind Málaga's suburbs are forested mountains with awesome natural
wonders, such as the Garganta del Chorro. Behind the tourist resorts of the
Costa del Sol is the Serranía de Ronda, habitat of elusive wildlife. Here, white
Moorish towns command strategic hilltop locations. East of Gibraltar are the sherry
towns of Cádiz province and the raw coastal strands of the Costa de la Luz.

In Málaga province the mountains fall steeply to the Mediterranean. The ancient port of Málaga town was a wintering place for English travellers in the 19th century; then in the 1960s, the narrow strip of coast to its east and west was claimed by the nascent tourist industry as the "Costa del Sol".

A rash of high-rise development around the beaches of grey sand at its eastern end soon made the name "Torremolinos" synonymous with the excesses of cheap package holidays for the mass market. Meanwhile, at Marbella, further southwest, an exclusive playground for international film stars and Arab royalty was taking shape. Gibraltar, a geographical and a historical oddity, is a decisive full stop at the end of

the Costa del Sol. The mountains of North Africa loom across the Strait of Gibraltar, and the spirit of the Moors can be felt very clearly in Tarifa and Cádiz – author Laurie Lee's city "sparkling with African light". Between these two towns is the Cádiz section of the Costa de la Luz ("Coast of Light") *(see p36)* which continues up north along the shores of Huelva province. Little developed, it is characterized by long stretches of windswept sand, popular with locals.

North of Cádiz is sherry country, with its hills and large vineyards. To taste sherry visit Jerez de la Frontera – a link in a chain of towns on the frontier of the Christian war to reconquer Andalusia from its Muslim rulers.

Ronda with its 18th-century bridge spanning the Guadalevín river

◀ Whitewashed Moorish town near Estepona, Málaga

Exploring Cádiz and Málaga

With a network of excellent roads across the region, the mountains of Málaga province's interior are easily accessible to holiday-makers who are staying on the Costa del Sol. Day trips can be made from either Marbella or Torremolinos to the glorious Montes de Málaga and Grazalema nature reserves or to the Serranía de Ronda, with lunch stops at classic *pueblos blancos*. In the heart of this characteristic Andalusian landscape lies the captivating town of Ronda, ensouled by clear, stark light and the lingering aura of Moorish times.

Further west, on the Atlantic coast beyond Tarifa where mass-market developers fear to tread, the same spirit lingers. The once great city of Cádiz and the small ports of El Puerto de Santa María, Chipiona and Sanlúcar de Barrameda all make excellent bases for exploring sherry country.

Outside dining at a restaurant close to the cathedral in Málaga

Key

- ▬▬ Motorway
- ▬ Major road
- ═══ Minor road
- ▬ Scenic route
- ┄┄ Main railway
- ─── Minor railway
- ▬▬ International border
- ▬▬ Provincial border

For map symbols *see back flap*

Sights at a Glance

Getting Around

Málaga's international airport *(see p265)* is the busiest airport in Andalusia, and opened a third terminal in 2010. The main highway linking the Costa del Sol resorts is the A7/N340, with the AP7 toll road an option from Fuengirola to Guadiaro. After Algeciras, the road narrows and continues (N340 and A48) to Cádiz. The highway A376 from San Pedro de Alcántara northwards to Ronda is a sensationally beautiful route. The A382 and A385 cut across the north from Jerez towards Antequera. The route then continues as a dual carriageway, known as the A92, to Granada. A railway running along the Costa del Sol links Málaga, Torremolinos and Fuengirola. Another heads north from Málaga, stopping at Álora, El Chorro and Fuente de Piedra. Although you will find it possible to explore remote corners of Cádiz and Málaga provinces using the complex bus network, it requires some patience.

The beach of Nerja, situated at the foot of Sierra de Almijara on the Costa del Sol

Entrance to the Barbadillo *bodega* in Sanlúcar de Barrameda

❶ Sanlúcar de Barrameda

Cádiz. **Road map** B3. 🚹 62,000. 🚌
ℹ️ Calzada del Ejército s/n (956 36 61 10). 🐟 Wed.

A fishing port at the mouth of the Guadalquivir river, Sanlúcar is overlooked by the Moorish **Castillo de Santiago**. The Parque Nacional de Doñana *(see pp134–5)*, over the river, can be reached by boat from the riverside quay. From here Columbus set off on his third trip to the Americas, in 1498, and in 1519 Ferdinand Magellan left the port intending to circumnavigate the globe.

However, Sanlúcar is now best known for its *manzanilla (see p34)*, a light, dry sherry from, among other producers, **Bodegas Barbadillo**.

Visitors can sip a *copita* (little glass) of *manzanilla* and enjoy the local shellfish, *langostinos*. There is also a museum on site, **Museo de Manzanilla**, which traces the history of the drink.

Sights in the town include the **Iglesia de Nuestra Señora de la O** *(see p28)*, which has superb Mudéjar portals.

🏠 **Bodegas Barbadillo**
C/Luis de Eguilaz 11. **Tel** 956 38 55 00. 🕙 11am Tue–Sat. 🚹 👢 🏛️ Museo de Manzanilla: **Open** 10am–3pm Tue–Sat. 🔤 **barbadillo.net**

❷ Chipiona

Cádiz. **Road map** B3. 🚹 17,000. 🚌
ℹ️ Calle Del Castillo 5 (956 92 90 65). 🐟 Mon.

lively little resort town, Chipiona approached through sherry eyards. It has a great beach

and a holiday atmosphere in the summer. Days on the beach are followed by a *paseo* along the quay or the main street of the Moorish old town, where many cafés and ice-cream parlours *(heladerías)* stay open well past midnight. There are also street entertainers and horse-drawn carriages. The **Iglesia de Nuestra Señora de Regla**, the main church, has a natural spring feeding a fountain, and an adjoining cloister decorated with 17th-century *azulejos*.

❸ Jerez de la Frontera

Cádiz. **Road map** B3. 🚹 186,000. ✈️
🚌 🚉 ℹ️ Plaza del Arenal, Edificio Los Arcos (956 33 88 74). 🐟 Mon.
🔤 **turismojerez.com**

Jerez, the capital of sherry production, is surrounded by chalky countryside blanketed with long rows of vines. British merchants have been involved for centuries in producing and shipping sherry, and have created Anglo-Andaluz dynasties like Sandeman and John Harvey – names which can be seen emblazoned over the *bodega* entrances. A tour of a *bodega*, through cellars piled high with *soleras (see p35)*, will enable visitors to learn how to distinguish a *fino* from an *amontillado* and an *oloroso* sherry *(see p34)*.

Jerez has a second claim to world fame, the **Real Escuela Andaluza de Arte Ecuestre** – the school of equestrian art. On selected days, in a display of exquisite dressage, the horses dance to music amid colourful pageantry. Visitors can arrange

to watch horses being trained. Nearby is **La Atalaya Theme Centre**, including two museums: the magical **Palacio del Tiempo**, home to the most impressive clocks in Europe, and **El Misterio de Jerez**, which pays tribute to the history of sherry in the area.

The old city walls flank the Barrio de Santiago. On Plaza de San Juan is the 18th-century **Palacio de Pemartín**, the home of the **Centro Andaluz de Flamenco**, which, through exhibitions and audiovisual shows, offers an insight to this music and dance tradition *(see pp32–3)*. The 16th-century Gothic **Iglesia de San Mateo** is just one of several interesting churches nearby.

The partially restored, 11th-century **Alcázar** includes a well-preserved mosque, now a church. Just to the north of the Alcázar is the **Catedral del Salvador**, whose most interesting sight, *The Sleeping Girl* by Zurbarán, is in the sacristy.

🎭 **Real Escuela Andaluza de Arte Ecuestre**
Avenida Duque de Abrantes s/n.
Tel 956 31 96 35 (information, press 2 for English). Call to arrange visit. 🚹 👢
🔤 **realescuela.org**

🏠 **Alcázar**
Alameda Vieja s/n. **Tel** 956 14 99 55.
Open daily. **Closed** 25 Dec, 1 & 6 Jan.
🚹 🚻

🏛️ **La Atalaya Theme Centre**
Calle Cervantes 3. **Tel** 902 18 21 00.
Open Tue–Sun. 🚹 🚻 👢

🎭 **Palacio de Pemartín**
Centro Andaluz de Flamenco, Plaza de San Juan 1. **Tel** 956 81 41 32. **Open** Mon–Fri. **Closed** public hols.

Antique clock in Palacio del Tiempo, Jerez de la Frontera

❹ El Puerto de Santa María

Cádiz. **Road map** B3. 🔼 76,000. ✈
🚆 🚌 ℹ Calle Luna 22 (956 54 24 13).
🛥 Tue. 🌐 **turismoelpuerto.com**

Sheltered from the Atlantic wind and waves of the Bay of Cádiz, El Puerto de Santa María is a tranquil town which has burgeoned as one of the main ports for the exportation of sherry in Andalusia. A number of sherry companies, such as **Terry** and **Osborne**, have *bodegas* here, which can be visited for tours and tasting.

Among the town's sites are the 13th-century **Castillo San Marcos** and a **Plaza de Toros** – one of the largest and most famous bullrings in Spain. The town's main square, the Plaza Mayor, is presided over by the 13th-century, Gothic **Iglesia Mayor Prioral**, which is worth a look for its unusual choir.

Scattered around the town are several fine old *palacios*, or stately houses, adorned with the coats of arms of wealthy families who prospered in the port during colonial times.

The waterfront is lined with quite a few first-rate seafood restaurants, among them La Resaca (the Hangover), where, when it is dark, gypsies perform fiery flamenco.

🏰 Castillo San Marcos
Plaza Alfonso X, El Sabio. **Tel** 956 85 17 51. **Open** for guided visits with wine-tasting: 11:30am, 12:30pm, 1:30pm Tue (free); 10am, 11am, noon, 1pm, 2pm Wed–Sat (reservations required). 🖋

🎪 Plaza de Toros
Plaza Elias Ahuja s/n. **Tel** 956 54 15 78. **Open** Tue–Sun. ♿

🍷 Bodegas Osborne
Calle de los Moros. **Tel** 956 86 91 00. **Open** Mon–Fri (phone to arrange). **Closed** public hols. ♿ 🖋

🍷 Bodegas Terry
Calle Toneleros s/n. **Tel** 956 85 77 00. **Open** Mon–Fri (phone to arrange). **Closed** pub hols. ♿ 🖋

El Puerto de Santa María's 13th-century Castillo San Marcos

Bodegas of Jerez

Touring *bodegas* and tasting sherry is one of the major reasons for visiting Jerez. The tourist office here will supply a list of *bodegas* offering tours, and a tour time-table. The most comprehensive tours are those that are offered by González Byass, Pedro Domecq and Sandeman.

Real Escuela Andaluza de Arte Ecuestre
Bodegas Sandeman
C. PIZARRO
La Atalyaka Theme Centre
AV. DUQUE DEL ABRANTES
Bodegas Wisdom & Warter
D. PASTORA
Bodegas Garvey
CALLE LEALAS
C. LUIS PÉREZ
DEL OLIVAR
SEVILLA
CALLE
NUÑO DE CAÑAS
SANTO DOMINGO
Bodegas Williams & Humbert
PZA. DE PEDRO ROMERO
Plaza de Toros
C. CIRCO
C. JUAN BELMONTE
C. ANCHA
CALLE PORVERA
C. GAITAN
GUADALETE
MAMELON
SANTO
CALLE ZARAGOZA
C. CONCEDORES
C. PAJARETE
CALLE 29 DE OCTUBRE
C. NUESTRA SEÑORA DE LA PAZ
PLAZA DE LOS ÁNGELES
C. PONCE
CANCILLERIA
Iglesia de San Juan
ℹ
ALAMEDA CRISTINA
PLAZA DE S. ANDRÉS
CALLE ROSARIO
CARACUEL
C. ADEDOS
C. VALIENTES
C. GENERAL MOSCARDO
C. CLAVEL
CALLE MERCED
C. MURO
C. JUSTICIA
Palacio de Pemartin
CALLE ALCALDESA
Convento de Santo Domingo
PLAZA RAFAEL RIVERA
EGUILAR
CALLE BIZCONEROS
C. GASPAR FERNÁNDEZ
CALLE
Bodegas John Harvey
CALLE ARCOS
Iglesia de San Mateo
CALLE FRANCOS
C. CASTEL-LANOS
Iglesia de San Dionisio
PLAZA DE LA ASUNCION
DOCTRINA
CALLE HONDA
RONDA DEL CARACOL
SAN BLAS
C. SAN ILDEFONSO
CAMPANALAS
PLAZA DE LOS PEONES
C. SALVADOR
L. DIEZ
AMARGURA
CALLE LARGA
CONSISTORIO
CALLE MEDINA
Train Station 1.5km (1 mile)
Bus Station 1km (0.6 mile)
Bodegas Pedro Domecq
PUERTA DE ROTA
CUESTA DE LA CHAPARRA
MANUEL MARÍA GONZÁLEZ
Catedral del Salvador
PLAZA DEL ARENAL
CALLE CALZADA
El Alcázar
Bodegas González Byass
CUESTA DE LA ALCUBILLA

| 0 metres | 500 |
| 0 yards | 500 |

Key

🟦 Bodega

For map symbols *see back flap*

❺ Cádiz

Jutting out of the Bay of Cádiz, and almost entirely surrounded by water, Cádiz can lay claim to being Europe's oldest city. Legend names Hercules as its founder, although history credits the Phoenicians with establishing the town of Gadir in 1100 BC. Occupied by the Carthaginians, Romans and Moors in turn, the city also prospered after the Reconquest *(see pp52–3)* on wealth taken from the New World. In 1587 Sir Francis Drake raided the port in the first of many British attacks in the war for world trade. In 1812 Cádiz briefly became Spain's capital when the nation's first constitution was declared here *(see p56).*

Saint Bruno in Ecstasy by Zurbarán in the Museo de Cádiz

Exploring Cádiz

Writers have waxed lyrical over Cádiz for centuries: " … the most beautiful town I ever beheld … and full of the finest women in Spain," gushed Lord Byron in 1809. Modern Cádiz is a busy port, with a few ugly suburbs to get through before arriving at the historic centre. This is situated on a peninsula that juts sharply into the sea, and consists of haphazardly heaped, Moorish-style houses.

The joy of visiting Cádiz is to wander the harbour quayside, with its well-tended gardens and open squares, then plunging into the centre *(see p170–71).*

The old town is full of narrow, dilapidated alleys, where flowers sprout from rusting cans mounted on walls beside religious tile paintings. Markets pack into tiny squares, alive with the bartering of fish and vegetables, and street vendors selling pink boiled shrimps in newspaper.

The pride of Cádiz is Los Carnavales *(see p43).* Under the dictator Franco, Cádiz was the only city where the authorities failed to suppress the anarchy of carnival.

🏛 Catedral

Open 10am–6:30pm Mon–Sat; 1–6:30pm Sun.

Known as the Catedral Nueva (New Cathedral) because it was built over the site of an older one, this Baroque and Neo-Classical church is one of Spain's largest. Its dome of yellow tiles looks like gilt glinting in the sun. The carved stalls inside came from a Carthusian monastery. In the crypt are the tombs of the composer Manuel de Falla (1876–1946) and writer José María Pemán (1897–1981), both natives of Cádiz. The cathedral's treasures are stored in a museum in Plaza Fray Félix and include jewel-studded monstrances of silver and gold and notable paintings.

🏛 Museo de Cádiz

Plaza de Mina s/n. **Tel** 856 10 50 23. **Open** Jun–mid-Sep: 9am–3:30pm Tue–Sat, 10am–5pm Sun; mid-Sep–May: 10am–8:30pm Tue–Sat, 10am–5pm Sun. **Closed** 1 Jan, 1 May, 25 Dec. ♿

On the ground floor there are archaeological exhibits charting the history of Cádiz, including statues of Roman leaders, such as emperor Trajan, and Phoenician stone sarcophagi. Upstairs is one of Andalusia's largest art galleries, displaying works by Rubens, Murillo and Zurbarán, as well as paintings by recognized contemporary Spanish artists. On the third floor is a collection of puppets made for village *fiestas*

Cádiz Cathedral

The cupola was built between 1812 and 1838 by Juan Daura, the last in a long line of architects of this cathedral.

Baroque vaults

Stalls

The presbytery altar was partly sponsored by Isabel II *(see pp56–7).*

Neo-Classical towers

Neo-Classical façade

around Andalusia. There are also some more recent ones satirizing current political figures.

Oratorio de San Felipe Neri

Calle Santa Inés s/n. **Tel** 956 80 70 18. **Open** 10am–1:45pm, 5–9:45pm Tue–Fri, 10am–1:45pm Sat.

On 19 March 1812 a major event took place in this 18th-century Baroque church: the proclamation of a liberal constitution for Spain (see p56). As Napoleon's troops besieged Cádiz during the Peninsular War (see p54), the members of the provisional parliament assembled in the church to draft a document that would inspire radicals throughout Europe. In its limitations of the power of the monarch and its provisions for citizens to enjoy unprecedented rights, the constitution was ahead of its time and ultimately doomed to fail. No sooner had the French been driven out of Spain in 1814 than it was repealed by Fernando VII.

Commemorative plaques on the Oratorio de San Felipe Neri

The Baroque Torre Tavira, the highest watchtower in Cádiz

Torre Tavira

Calle Marqués del Real Tesoro 10. **Tel** 956 21 29 10. **Open** daily. **Closed** 1 Jan & 25 Dec. **W** torretavira.com

In the mid-1700s when much of Spain's trade with the Americas passed through the port of Cádiz, the city's merchants built themselves watchtowers from which to observe the coming and going of vessels – either for commercial interest in the cargoes or for their own amusement. More than 100 such towers remain as part of Cádiz's skyline, but only this one is open to the public.

Baroque in style, the tower rises above what was once the home of the Marqués de Ricaño (now a music academy); it stands in the centre of the Old Town and is its highest point, reaching 45 m (150 ft) above sea level. Its penultimate floor

VISITORS' CHECKLIST

Practical Information
Cádiz.
Road map B4. 150,000. Plaza San Juan de Dios 11 (956 24 10 01). Mon. Los Carnavales (Feb), Semana Santa (Easter). **W** cadizturismo.com

Transport
Plaza de Sevilla s/n (902 24 02 02). Plaza de la Hispanidad s/n (902 19 92 08).

contains the first camera obscura installed in Spain, but it is also worth visiting for the simple pleasure of the views over the rooftops and the sea from its four balconies.

Environs
At the northern lip of the Bay of Cádiz is Rota, a town best known for its Spanish-US naval base but which also claims to have the highest population of chameleons in Spain.

The southern limit of the bay is marked by the small island of Sancti Petri, believed by archaeologists to be the site of a Temple of Hercules built by the Phoenicians in the 12th century BC over the mythical burial site of the hero-turned-god.

Much of the bay lying between these two points forms the Bahía de Cádiz Nature Reserve; a shifting population of migratory wildfowl uses this area as a staging post between the Straits of Gibraltar and the Doñana National Park (see pp134–5).

El Vapor Boat

Rather than drive up the isthmus into Cádiz, you can travel by ferry across the bay from El Puerto de Santa María (see p167). A fast catamaran provides a regular service, but a more charming way to make the trip is on board the wooden-hulled, double-decker vaporcito ("little steamer"), which takes 40 minutes to cross the bay. There are five sailings each way (six in summer). Take the first boat out and the last one back to fit in a full day's sightseeing. **Tel** 629 46 80 14; **W** elvapordelpuerto.com

El Vapor, a steamer crossing the Bay of Cádiz

A 90-Minute Walk Around Historic Cádiz

This walk begins at the Ayuntamiento (town hall) and takes in 3,000 years of Cádiz history, most of which is defined by the surrounding sea. The route starts on the eastern flank over the Bay of Cádiz. It heads into the heart of the city's warren of small alleys and squares before reaching the topiary gardens by the university. You are rarely out of sight of the sea, passing Cádiz's fish market, its most famous fish restaurant, its beach spa and the Atlantic seafront. The walk ends at the city's monumental cathedral, with its golden-coloured dome overlooking the ocean.

A café-lined lane near the central Plaza San Juan de Dios

Plaza San Juan de Dios to Parque Genovés

The palm-lined Plaza San Juan offers many cafés and shops. The Neo-Classical Ayuntamiento ①, built in 1799, is chiefly the work of architect Torcuato Benjumeda. Head north from the square, taking Calle Nueva ②, part of Cádiz's busy shopping district. Nueva runs into Calle San Francisco up to Plaza de San Francisco ③, one

of many tiny neighbourhood squares. Turn right into Isabel La Catolica, which becomes Calle Rafael de la Viesca and, via Doctor Zurita, enters the Plaza de España. The militaristic Monumento a las Cortes ④, erected in 1912, has special resonance for the people of Cádiz, and Spain itself. In 1812, Cádiz was home to a short-lived alternative parliament to Madrid, but this attempt to establish democratic rule was crushed by the monarchy. Across the plaza, turn left into Fernando El Catolico, which leads to the seafront Murallas (walls) de San Carlos ⑤, overlooking the Bay of Cádiz and the town of Puerto de Santa Maria opposite, an interesting destination in its own right. At the Murallas, follow Calle Honduras ⑥ left, hugging Cádiz's sea walls. You pass the Alameda Apodaca ⑦, one of numerous gardens boasting vast dragon trees, and the Baluarte (battlement) de la Candelaria ⑧, now a contemporary arts centre. Turn left again into Avenida Carlos III, passing the Universidad and the lovely Parque Genovés ⑨, with its avenue of symmetrical topiary trees, open-air theatre and café.

⑤ The Murallas de San Carlos, overlooking the Bay of Cádiz

...in leafy Parque Genovés

Tips for Walkers

Starting point: Plaza San Juan de Dios.
Length: 4 km (3 miles)
Getting there: Plaza San Juan de Dios is next to the port and a few minutes' walk from rail and bus stations.
Stopping-off points: The family-owned Terraza on the Plaza de la Catedral s/n has outdoor seating with a fantastic view of the cathedral.

...urants in this region see pp216–19 and pp228–37

Parador to Playa de la Caleta
At the end of the Parque is Cádiz's modern parador hotel, refurbished in 2010 ⑩. From here, you can head into the heart of the Old Town. Turn left into Calle Benito Perez Galdos, passing Plaza de Falla and the gaudy, pink Gran Teatro Falla ⑪, both named after local composer Manuel de Falla, interred in the cathedral. The Neo-Mudéjar theatre was finished in 1919, after 30 years' construction, and is busiest during Cádiz's wild February Carnival *(see p43)*. Calle Galdos

⑱ View from one of the bell towers of the Catedral de Santa Cruz

Alcala Sacramento, turn right into Plaza Topete and the city's bustling market, with stalls preparing delicious fresh seafood snacks. Cross the square to Calle Libertad and into Desamparados, then turn right into the leafy Plaza de la Cruz Verde ⑭, which, via Calle Maria Arteaga, joins Calle Rosa to reach the city's most famous beach, Playa de la Caleta, its 19th-century bathing station ⑮ (now government offices) and a nautical college. The beach overlooks the old harbour and two small forts, one of which, San Sebastián, was once the 1100 BC Phoenician settlement of Gadir and site of a temple to Kronos.

Caleta to Catedral
From Caleta, Calle de Nájera joins the Campo del Sur seafront, but it's worth turning left into Calle Venezuela into the fishermen's quarter and down to San Felix and the most famous fish restaurant in the region, El Faro (open: 1pm) ⑯. Both the restaurant and the tapas bar here live up to the local saying, "Don't leave Cádiz before eating at El Faro." Take Felix up to the seafront and turn left into Campo del Sur ⑰, where pastel-colour buildings stretch to the magnificent Catedral de Santa Cruz ⑱, begun in 1722 and finished only in 1838. Several architects contributed to its mix of Baroque, Rococo and Neo-Classical styles. The views from its bell towers repay the climb. Calle Pelota, opposite, leads back to Plaza San Juan.

Key

••• Walk route

| 0 metres | 300 |
| 0 yards | 300 |

changes name here to Calle Sacramento, the busiest of the shopping streets, and you pass the Oratorio de San Felipe Neri ⑫ and the unusual 18th-century Torre Tavira ⑬, named after its first keeper, Antonio Tavira. At 45 m (150 ft) above sea level, this lookout and camera obscura is the highest viewpoint in the city. At Calle

⑬ View of the cathedral from Torre Tavira

Carved *retablo*, Iglesia de Santa María la Coronada, Medina Sidonia

❻ Medina Sidonia

Cádiz. **Road map** B4. 🏔 11,500. 🚌 ℹ Plaza Iglesia Mayor s/n (956 41 24 04). 🚍 Mon.

As you drive along the N440, between Algeciras and Jerez, Medina Sidonia appears startlingly white atop a conical hill. The town was taken from the Moors in 1264 by Alfonso X, and during the 15th century the Guzmán family were established as the Dukes of Medina Sidonia to defend the territory between here and the Bay of Cádiz. After the Reconquest *(see pp52–3)*, the family grew rich from investments in the Americas, and Medina Sidonia became one of the most important ducal seats in Spain. Many parts of the town's medieval walls still

stand and cobbled alleys nestle beneath them.

The **Iglesia de Santa María la Coronada** is the town's most important building. Begun on the foundations of a castle in the 15th century, after the Reconquest, it is a fine example of Andalusian Gothic. Inside is a collection of religious works of art dating from the Renaissance, including paintings and a charming *retablo* with beautifully carved panels.

❼ Vejer de la Frontera

Cádiz. **Road map** B4. 🏔 13,000. ℹ In Ayuntamiento c/Marques de Tamarón 10 (956 45 17 36). 🅦 vejerdelafrontera.co.uk

Attractively located on a hilltop above Barbate, Vejer de la Frontera was one of the first places occupied by the Muslim invaders in 711, shortly after they had defeated the Visigoths in battle close by (the exact site is not known).

The oldest part of town is enclosed by an irregular wall that is protected by three towers and entered by four gates. Within the walled area are the Arab castle and the parish church, the Iglesia Parroquial del Divino Salvador, which was built on the site of a mosque between the 14th and 16th centuries in a mixture of Gothic and Mudejar architecture. Later buildings

outside the walls include the Palacio del Marqués de Tamaron, which is a 17th- to 18th-century stately home.

The lighthouse on Cabo de Trafalgar, Costa de la Luz

❽ Barbate

Cádiz. **Road map** B4. 🏔 22,000. ℹ C/Vázquez de Mella 2 (956 43 39 62). 🅦 barbate.es

The largest coastal settlement between Cádiz and Tarifa, Barbate stands at the mouth of the eponymous river, in an area of marshes and saltflats. There is not much of interest in the town itself, but two small tourist resorts attached to it are worth visiting.

A short way south down the coast is **Zahara de los Atunes**, which has grown up along one of the coast's best beaches. The epithet of "the tuna fish" is a reminder of an important industry in these waters. Barbate's culinary speciality is *mojama*, tuna that has been cured in the same way as *jamón serrano*. Inland from Zahara, around the main N340 coast road, are large swathes of wind turbines generating electricity for the national grid. The road

fortified walls surrounding the Old Town of Vejer de la Frontera

otels and restaurants in this region see pp216–19 and pp228–37

The characteristic turbines of a windfarm north of Tarifa

Windfarms

North of Tarifa, the wind blows with such reliable force that it is used to drive wind turbines to generate electricity. Spain has the world's second-highest installed capacity of windpower after Germany, and the country aims to meet 20 per cent of its energy needs from renewable resources by 2020. Critics argue that windpower works only when the wind is strong enough and that the turbines are unsightly. Another objection, that the blades of the turbines are a hazard to birds, hasn't been substantiated by evidence.

north out of Barbate (past the fishing port) climbs over a headland fringed by cliffs and planted with dense pine woods to drop down to the small holiday resort of **Los Caños de Meca**, which grew up as a hippy hideaway in the 1970s and still has a carefree feel to it.

On a short sand spit nearby stands a lighthouse marking the **Cabo de Trafalgar** (Cape Trafalgar), which gave its name to the naval battle fought on 21 October 1805. Early in the morning of that day, Britain's Admiral Nelson decided to take on the combined fleet of Spanish and French ships that had left Cádiz two days earlier. The British were outnumbered and outgunned but defeated the enemy without the loss of a single ship. Nelson, however, was struck by a musket ball late in the battle and died soon after.

A statue of Trajan at Baelo Claudia

and gradually grew in importance through trade with North Africa and its fish salting and pickling works.

Emperor Claudius (41–54 AD) elevated Baelo Claudia to the status of municipality, but its prestige was short-lived, since it was effectively destroyed by an earthquake in the 2nd century and finally abandoned in the 6th century. The ruins, which include a theatre, a necropolis and several erect columns, are in a picturesque spot next to a beautiful beach beside the small settlement of Bolonia.

🔟 Tarifa

Cádiz. **Road map** B4. 🗺 16,000. 🚌
ℹ️ Paseo de la Alameda s/n (956 68 09 93). 🚇 Tue. 🌐 tarifaweb.com

Tarifa, Europe's wind- and kite-surfing capital *(see p36)* takes its name from Tarif ben Maluk, an 8th-century Moorish commander.

The 10th-century **Castillo de Guzmán el Bueno** is the site of a legend. In 1292, Guzmán, who was defending Tarifa from the Moors, was told his hostage son would die if he did not surrender. Rather than give in, he threw down his dagger for the captors to use.

🏰 Castillo de Guzmán el Bueno
Calle Guzmán el Bueno. **Tel** 956 68 09 93. **Open** Tue–Sun. 🈹

9️⃣ Baelo Claudia

Bolonia, Cádiz. **Road map** B4. **Tel** 956 10 67 97. **Open** Apr–mid-May: 9am–8pm Tue–Sat, 10am–5pm Sun; Jun–mid-Sep: 9am–3:30pm Tue–Sat, 10am–5pm Sun; mid-Sep–Mar: 9am–6:30pm Tue–Sat, 10am–5pm Sun. 🈹 (free to EU citizens). 🌐 **juntadeandalucia. es/cultura/museos**

The Roman settlement of Baelo Claudia was established on the seashore in the 2nd century BC

1️⃣1️⃣ Parque Natural de Los Alcornocales

Cádiz and Málaga. **Road map** B4.
ℹ️ Visitor's Centre A-2228, km 1 - Parque Natural de los Alcornocales (956 42 05 29). 🌐 **alcornocales.org**

This nature reserve is named after the *alcornocales*, cork oak trees that are prevalent in many parts of it. They are easily identified because they have been stripped of their lower bark, leaving the vivid red heartwood showing. The far south of the natural park is crossed by deep valleys called *canutos*, in which rare vestiges of Europe's ancient fern-rich forests cling on.

Apart from its wildlife, the area has a few towns worth visiting, including Jimena de la Frontera, Castellar de la Frontera and Medina Sidonia *(see p172)*, and several caves holding prehistoric paintings.

Cork trees in the Parque Natural de Los Alcornocales

⑫ Tangier

Tangier is only 45 minutes by fast ferry from Tarifa, making it a perfect day trip. Despite its proximity, this ancient port, founded by the Berbers before 1000 BC, will be a sharp culture shock for those used to life in Europe. Tangier is vibrant with eastern colour, and the vast, labyrinthine Medina, the market quarter, pulsates with noise. From their workshops in back alleys, craftsmen make traditional goods for busy shops and stalls in the crowded streets. Yet behind wrought-iron railings the traveller will see tranquil courts decorated with mosaics, cool fountains and mosques.

View into the labyrinthine Medina from the Grand Socco

Sights at a Glance

① Dar El Makhzen
② Kasbah
③ Hôtel Continental
④ Grand Mosque
⑤ Rue es Siaghin
⑥ Grand Socco
⑦ American Legation

🏛 Dar El Makhzen

Place de la Kasbah. **Tel** 212 39 93 20 97. **Open** Wed–Mon. 📷

Sultan Moulay Ismail, who unified Morocco in the 17th century, had this palace built within the Kasbah. The sultans lived here until 1912. It is now a museum of crafts such as ceramics, embroidery and ironwork. The exhibits are arranged round a central courtyard and in cool rooms with tiled ceilings. There are illuminated Korans in the Fez Room and a courtyard in the style of Andalusian Moorish gardens.

🏯 Kasbah

The Kasbah or citadel, where the sultans once held court, is at the Medina's highest point. It is separated from its alleys by sturdy walls and four massive stone gateways. From the battlements there are views over the Strait of Gibraltar.

The Kasbah encloses the Dar El Makhzen, the treasury house, the old prison and the law courts. Villas once owned by American and European celebrities, such as Paul Bowles, the author of *The Sheltering Sky*, are also within the Kasbah walls.

Façade of the Dar El Makhzen, the museum of Moroccan arts

🅲 Grand Mosque

Green and white minarets rise above this massive edifice built in the 17th century by Sultan Moulay Ismail. An exquisitely carved gateway suggests more treasures within – non-Muslims, however, are forbidden from entering any mosque.

🏯 Grand Socco

Traders from the Rif mountains come to barter their goods at this busy main square at the heart of Tangier. The square's official name, Place du 9 Avril 1947, commemorates a visit by Sultan Muhammad V.

VISITORS' CHECKLIST

Practical Information
Morocco.
Road map B4. 315,000.
Languages: Arabic, French.
Currency: dirhams **Visas:** Visitors
from the UK, Ireland, New Zealand,
Australia, the US or Canada require
no visa for a visit of up to 90 days.

Transport
(fast ferry) from Gibraltar; from
Algeciras by Trasmediterranea
956 58 75 17. *See p265* for more
info on getting to North Africa.
29 Blvd Pasteur (212 39 94 80 50).

The carved façade of Tangier's Grand Mosque

American Legation
Rue du Portugal. **Tel** 212 39 93 53 17.
Open 10am–1pm, 3–5pm Mon–Thu,
10am–noon, 3–5pm Fri, by appt at
weekends. **legation.org**

This former palace was the US'
first diplomatic mission. It was the
American Embassy until 1961 and
is now an art museum.

Hôtel Continental
Rue Dar El Baroud. **Tel** 212 39 93 10 24.
Open daily.
Numerous intrigues have
been played out in this hotel
overlooking the port. Today it is a
fine place to sit and drink tea.

The International Era

From 1932 until its incorporation
into Morocco in 1956, Tangier was
an international zone, tax free and
under the control of a committee
of 30 nations. This was an era that
was characterized by financial
fraud, espionage, large-scale
smuggling, outrageous sexual
licence and profligacy by wealthy
tax exiles, such as heiress Barbara
Hutton. Celebrities such as Henri
Matisse, Jack Kerouac and Orson
Welles added colour to the scene.

Orson Welles, once a familiar sight on
the streets of Tangier

Rue es Siaghin
The Medina's "Silversmith's Street"
was Tangier's main thoroughfare
in the 1930s and still offers a
staggering array of merchandise;
shop owners will offer you mint
tea in a bid to get you to buy.

⑬ Ceuta

Road map C4. 76,000. from
Algeciras. Calle Edrisis, Baluarte de
los Mallorquines (856 20 05 60).
ceuta.es

The closest of Spain's two North
African enclaves to Europe is
worth visiting if you want to dip
your toe into North Africa
without leaving Spain (although
you will need to show an
identity card or passport
on entering), or if are on
your way to Morocco.
Ceuta is only 12 miles
from mainland Spain.
Ceuta is dominated by
a hill called Monte Hacho,
on which there is a fort
occupied by the Spanish
army. The city has
Phoenician and Arab remains,
churches dating from the 17th to
the 19th centuries and several
museums, including the **Museo
de la Legion**, dedicated to the
Spanish Foreign Legion.
Ceuta's shops offer the chance
to indulge in some tax-free
shopping. Both Ceuta and Melilla
are surrounded by high fences,
as they are European entry points
for illegal immigrants from parts
of Africa.

Museo de la Legión
Paseo de Colon. **Tel** 956 51 37 52.
Open 10am–1:30pm, 4–6pm Mon–Sat.

European architectural influence in the
North African enclave of Ceuta

⑭ Melilla

Road map E5. 69,000. from
Málaga or Almería. *See p265* for travel
info Palacio de Exposiciones y
Congresos, Calle Fortuny 21 (952 97
61 90). **melillaturismo.com**

Spain's second North African
enclave, settled by Spain in
1497, is located 150 km (90
miles) due south of Adra (in
Almería), across the sea, on the
Moroccan coast. It takes a little
effort to get there, as Melilla is
a six hour ferry ride from
mainland Spain, but it is worth
it as there is plenty to see,
including the only Gothic
architecture in Africa and
Modernisme, the Catalan
version of Art Nouveau
architecture. Modern-day Melilla
prides itself on being a place of
peaceful co-existence between
its main four component
cultures: Christian, Muslim,
Jewish and Hindu. All the
principal sights are located in
Melilla La Vieja (Old Melilla), a
cluster of four fortified areas
separated by moats or walls,
built in the 14th century on a
hammer-head promontory
jutting out into the sea.
The 19th- and 20th-century
parts of the city, however, are
equally worth strolling around
in, since they include an
abundance of splendid Art
Nouveau and Art Deco
buildings. There are around 900
period edifices in Melilla. There's
also a small beach.

For hotels and restaurants in this region see pp216–19 and pp228–37

⑮ Gibraltar

Native Gibraltarians are descendents of British, Genoese Jews, Portuguese and Spanish who remained after the Great Siege *(see p56)*. Britain seized Gibraltar during the War of the Spanish Succession in 1704, and was granted it "in perpetuity" by the Treaty of Utrecht *(see p56)* nine years later. As the gateway to the Mediterranean, the Rock was essential to Britain in colonial times. Tensions over Gibraltar have now eased, with more co-operation between Spain and Britain expected in the future. Each year, around 4 million people stream across the frontier at La Línea to visit this speck of England bolted on to Andalusia. Pubs, fish and chips, pounds sterling and bobbies on the beat all contrast with Spain.

The Keep
The lower part of this Moorish castle, built in the 8th century, is still used to house Gibraltar's prison population.

Siege Tunnels
Soldiers' barracks and storerooms fill 50 km (31 miles) of tunnels.

KEY

① **The airport runway** currently crosses over the main road from La Línea to Gibraltar.

② **Spanish border and customs**

③ **The Apes' Den** is home to Gibraltar's tailless apes; legend has it that the British will keep the Rock only as long as the apes remain.

④ **Europa Point,** on the southernmost tip, looks across the Strait of Gibraltar to North Africa.

⑤ **The 100-Ton Gun** was put here in 1884; it took two hours to load and it could fire shells weighing 910 kg (2,000 lb).

⑥ **A cable car** runs from the centre of the town to the Top of the Rock, Gibraltar's summit, which, at 450 m (1,475 ft) high, is often shrouded in mist.

St Michael's Cave
During World War II these caves served as a bombproof military hospital. These days classical concerts are performed here.

La Línea de la Concepción, with Gibraltar in the distance

⑯ La Línea de la Concepción

Cádiz. Road map C4. 60,000.
Avenida de 20 Abril s/n (956 78 41 35). Wed.

La Línea is a town on the Spanish side of the border with Gibraltar. Its name, "The Line", refers to the old walls that once formed the frontier, but were demolished during the Napoleonic wars to prevent the French using them for defence. Now it is a lively trading town, with several hotels patronized by people who want to avoid the higher prices of Gibraltar hotels.

The elegant marina at Sotogrande

⑰ Sotogrande

Cádiz. Road map C4. 2,000. San Roque. C/San Felipe s/n (956 69 40 05). Sun.

Just above Gibraltar, on the Costa del Sol, Sotogrande is an exclusive residential seaside town, popular with wealthy Gibraltarians, who commute daily to the Rock and live in exclusive villas. The marina is filled with expensive yachts and lined with excellent seafood restaurants.

Nearby there are several immaculately manicured golf courses (see p36).

Gibraltar Museum
This museum, built on the foundations of Moorish baths, houses an exhibition of Gibraltar's history under British rule.

⓲ A Tour Around the Pueblos Blancos

Instead of settling on Andalusia's plains, where they would have fallen prey to bandits, some Andalusians chose to live in fortified hilltop towns and villages. The way of life in these *pueblos blancos* – so called because they are whitewashed in the Moorish tradition – has barely changed for centuries. Touring the *pueblos blancos*, which crown the mountains rising sharply from the coast, will show visitors a world full of references to the past. Yet today they are working agricultural towns, not just tourist sights.

③ **Zahara de la Sierra** This fine *pueblo blanco*, a tightly huddled hillside village below a castle ruin, has been declared a national monument.

④ **Grazalema** At the heart of the Parque Natural de la Sierra de Grazalema, this village has the highest rainfall in Spain. Lush vegetation fills the park.

② **Ubrique**
This town, nestling at the foot of the Sierra de Ubrique, has become a flourishing producer of leather goods.

Sevilla

Cadiz, Jerez

El Bosque

Benamahoma

Embalse de Zahara

A372

A373

Benaocaz

A374

Embalse de los Hurones

Parque Natural Sierra de Grazalema

① **Arcos de la Frontera**
This strategically positioned town has been fortified for centuries. From the commanding heights of this stronghold, there are views over the Guadalete valley.

Charco de los Hurones

CA5221

Sierra de Ubrique

Cortes de la Frontera

A373

⑧ **Jimena de la Frontera**
An expanse of cork and olive trees blankets the hills leading up to this village. A ruined Moorish castle, which is open to visitors, overlooks the surroundings where wild bulls graze peacefully.

CA503

A375

Río Hozgárganta

Parque Natural de los Alcornocales-Sierra del Aljibe

Río Guadiaro

La Sauceda

CA3331

A369

⑦ **Gaucín**
From here there are unsurpassed vistas over the Mediterranean, the Atlantic, the great hump of Gibraltar and across the strait to the Rif mountains of North Africa.

0 km

0 miles   05

⑤ Setenil
The streets of this white town are formed from the ledge of a gorge, carved from tufa rock by the river Trejo.

⑥ Ronda
With the Tajo gorge as an efficient moat, Ronda was one of the last towns recaptured from the Moors. It later became the cradle of modern bullfighting *(see pp176–7)*.

Key

━━ Tour route
━ Other roads

Tips for Drivers

Tour length: 205 km (135 miles).
Stopping-off points: Ronda has a wide range of hotels and restaurants. Arcos de la Frontera has a parador *(see p218)*, other hotels and restaurants. Gaucín, Jimena de la Frontera and Zahara de la Sierra also have places to stay and eat. Grazalema has a resort for families and Setenil a couple of bars and a hotel. Ubrique has a hotel.

⑲ Arcos de la Frontera

Cádiz. **Road map** B3. 🗺 30,000.
🚌 🚇 Plaza del Cabildo s/n (956 70 22 64). 🛍 Fri.
🌐 **ayuntamientoarcos.org**

Arcos has been inhabited since prehistoric times. Its strategic position encouraged settlement, first as the Roman town of Arcobriga, and later as the stronghold of Medina Arkosh under the Caliphate of Córdoba *(see p50)*. It was captured by Alfonso X's *(see p52)* Christian forces in 1264.

An archetypal white town, it has a labyrinthine Moorish quarter that twists up to its ruined castle. At its centre is the Plaza de España, one side of which gives views across sunbaked plains. Fronting the square are the superb **Parador de Arcos de la Frontera** *(see p218)* and the **Iglesia de Santa María de la Asunción**, a late Gothic-Mudéjar building worth seeing for its extravagant choir stalls and altarpiece. A small museum displays the church treasures. More striking is the massive, Gothic **Parroquia de San Pedro**. Its thick-set tower provides a view over the sheer drop down to the Guadalete river. Nearby is the **Palacio del Mayorazgo** with an ornate, Renaissance façade. The **Ayuntamiento** is also worth seeing, particularly to view its beautiful Mudéjar ceiling.

🏛 **Palacio del Mayorazgo**
Calle San Pedro 2. **Tel** 956 70 30 13 (Casa de Cultura). **Open** 8am–2pm Mon–Fri. ♿

🏛 **Ayuntamiento**
Plaza del Cabildo 1. **Tel** 956 70 49 50. **Open** Mon–Fri. **Closed** public hols.

Roman theatre set amid the ruins of Acinipo (Ronda la Vieja)

⑳ Ronda la Vieja

Málaga. **Road map** C3. 🚉 🚌 Ronda.
Tel 952 21 36 40 & 630 42 99 49.
ℹ Avenida de Blas Infante, s/n (952 16 93 11). **Open** 9am–3:30pm Wed–Sat, 10am–3pm Sun. **Cuevas de la Pileta** by guided tour (twice daily).
🌐 **turismoderonda.es**

Ronda la Vieja is the modern name for the remains of the Roman city of Acinipo, 12 km (7 miles) northwest of Ronda *(see pp180–81)*. An important town in the 1st century AD, it later declined, unlike the growing town of Ronda, which was called Arunda by the Romans.

The ruins are beautifully sited on a hillside where only a fraction of the town has been excavated. The town's most important sight is the theatre, but lines of stones also mark foundations of houses, and of the forum and other public buildings.

Along the C339, 22 km (12 miles) from Ronda la Vieja, are the Cuevas de la Pileta, the site of prehistoric cave paintings dating from about 25,000 BC *(see p47)*.

The Gothic-Mudéjar Iglesia de Santa María de la Asunción

㉑ Street-by-Street: Ronda

One of the most spectacularly located cities in Spain, Ronda sits on a massive rocky outcrop, straddling a precipitous limestone cleft. Because of its impregnable position this town was one of the last Moorish bastions, finally falling to the Christians in 1485. On the south side perches a classic Moorish *pueblo blanco (see p178)* of cobbled alleys, window grilles and dazzling whitewash – most historic sights are in this old town. Across the gorge in El Mercadillo, the newer town, is one of Spain's oldest bullrings.

★ Puente Nuevo
Building the "New Bridge" over the nearly 100 m (330 ft) deep Tajo gorge was a feat of civil engineering in the late 18th century.

To El Mercadillo, Plaza de Toros and Parador de Ronda *(see p219)*

Convento de Santo Domingo was the local headquarters of the Inquisition.

Casa del Rey Moro
From this 18th-century mansion, built on the foundations of a Moorish palace, 365 steps lead down to the river.

Key

— Suggested route

0 metres 75
0 yards 75

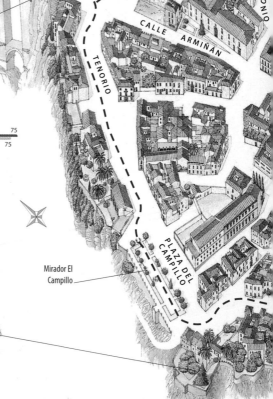

SANTO DOMINGO

CALLE ARMIÑAN

TENORIO

ANTONIO

PLAZA DEL CAMPILLO

Mirador El Campillo

★ Palacio Mondragón
Much of this palace was rebuilt after the Reconquest *(see pp52–3)*, but its arcaded patio is adorned with original Moorish mosaics and plasterwork.

Palacio del Marqués de Salvatierra
Bizarre images of biblical scenes and South American Indians embellish the façade of this palace, built in Renaissance style in the 18th century.

To Puente Viejo, Baños Arabes

Santa María la Mayor
A minaret and a Muslim prayer niche survive from the 13th-century mosque that once stood on the site of this church.

Minarete San Sebastián
is all that remains of a 14th-century mosque.

MARQUÉS DE SALVATIERRA

CARMEN

ESCALERA

ARMIÑAN

PLAZA DUQUESA DE PARCENT

VISITORS' CHECKLIST

Practical Information
Málaga. **Road map** C3. 34,000. Paseo de Blas Infante, s/n (95 218 71 19). Sun. Fiesta Romeria Virgen de la Cabeza (May), Feria de Málaga (Aug), Feria de Pedro Romero (Sep). Casa del Rey Moro: **Open** gardens only. Palacio del Marqués de Salvatierra: **Closed** to the public. Palacio Mondragón: **Open** daily. Plaza de Toros and Museo Taurino: **Open** daily. Baños Arabes: **Open** daily.
w turismoderonda.es

Transport
Avda Andalucía s/n (902 24 02 02). Pl Concepción García Redondo s/n (95 287 22 62).

Ayuntamiento
The town hall was remodelled in the 20th century and incorporates parts of older buildings. It has a two-tier arcaded façade and Mudéjar ceiling.

Bullfighting At Ronda

Ronda's Plaza de Toros is the spiritual home of bullfighting. Inaugurated in 1785, it is one of the oldest, most important bullrings in Spain. Aficionados travel from all over the country for the singular atmosphere of the Corrida Goyesca (see p40); millions watch the spectacle on television. It is the dream of every aspiring matador to fight at Ronda. The classic Ronda style (more severe than the exuberant School of Seville) was developed by Pedro Romero. Born in 1754, he is known as the father of modern bullfighting.

Romero, who killed over 6,000 bulls

㉒ Parque Natural Sierra de las Nieves

Road map C3. *i* C/ Espíritu Santo 37 (95 287 07 39).

One of Andalusia's least accessible areas, this UNESCO biosphere reserve southeast of Ronda extends between Parauta (to the east), Tolox (west), El Burgo (north) and Istán (south). Interestingly, it features both extreme highs and lows, reaching up to the peak of Torrecilla (1,919 m/ 6,295 ft) and down to one of the world's deepest potholes, GESM, which is 1,100 m (3,608 ft) deep. The sierra is popular for caving and rock climbing, and it also has some moderate to difficult signposted walking trails.

A short way south, near Ojén, is the beauty spot of Refugio de Juanar, which offers gentle walks through mixed woodland to a viewpoint overlooking the coast.

Olive groves between the villages of Álora and Antequera

㉓ Álora

Málaga. **Road map** C3. 🚌 13,000. 🚊 🚌 *i* Plaza Baja de la Despedía (95 249 55 77). 🗓 Mon. 🌐 **alora.es**

Situated in the Guadalhorce River valley, Álora is an important agricultural centre.

The Garganta del Chorro, rising high above the Guadalhorce river

It is a classic white town (*pueblo blanco, see pp178–9*), perched on a hillside overlooking an expanse of wheat fields, citrus orchards and olive groves.

The town's cobbled streets radiate from the 18th-century **Iglesia de la Encarnación**. At the weekly market, stalls of farm produce and clothing fill nearby streets. On the higher of Álora's twin hills stands the **Castillo**, with a cemetery of niche tombs set in neat blocks.

🏛 Castillo Árabe
Calle Ancha. **Tel** 95 249 55 77 (tourist office). **Open** daily.

㉔ Garganta del Chorro

Málaga. **Road map** C3. 🚊 El Chorro. 🚌 Parque Ardales. *i* Avenida Constitución s/n (95 249 55 77).

Up the fertile Guadalhorce valley, 12 km (7 miles) on from Álora, is one of the geographical wonders of Spain. The Garganta del Chorro is an immense gaping chasm 180 m (590 ft) high, slashing through a limestone mountain. In some places, where the Guadalhorce river hurtles through the gorge, waters foaming white, it is only 10 m (30 ft) wide. Below the gorge is a hydroelectric plant, which detracts slightly from the wildness and impressive beauty of the place.

The nearby village of **El Chorro** offers a wide range of outdoor activities.

㉕ Fuente de Piedra

Málaga. **Road map** C3. 🚊 🚌 *i* C/Castillo 1 (95 273 54 53).

The largest of several lakes in an expanse of wetlands north of Antequera, the Laguna de la Fuente de Piedra teems with bird life, including huge flocks of flamingos. In March, every year, up to 25,000 of them arrive to breed before migrating back to West Africa. Visitors should be aware that if there is drought in the region, there will be fewer birds breeding.

Apart from flamingos, you will also be able to admire cranes, herons, bee-eaters, snow-white egrets, as well as many species of ducks and geese. Their numbers have been on the increase since conservation and anti-hunting laws were introduced and the area declared a sanctuary. A road off the N334 leads to the lake side, from where visitors can watch the birds. Be advised that restraint is required: it is forbidden to join the waders in the lake. Information is available from a visitors' centre near the village of Fuente de Piedra.

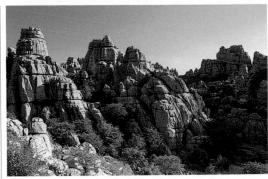
Limestone formations in the Parque Natural del Torcal

The triumphal 16th-century Arco de los Gigantes, Antequera

㉖ Antequera

Málaga. **Road map** D3. ⛰ 42,000. 🚌
🚌 Plaza San Sebastián 7 (95 270 25 05). 🅦 **antequera.co.uk**

This busy market town has long been strategically important; first as Roman Anticaria, and later as a Moorish border fortress defending Granada.

The **Iglesia de Nuestra Señora del Carmen**, with its massive Baroque altarpiece, is not to be missed. To the west of here, at the opposite end of the town, is the 19th-century **Plaza de Toros**, with its museum of bullfighting.

High on a hill overlooking the town is the **Castillo Arabe**, a 13th-century Moorish castle. Visitors cannot go inside, but can walk round the castle walls – the approach is through the 16th-century **Arco de los Gigantes**. There are fine views

from the **Torre del Papabellotas**, on the best-preserved part of the wall. In the town below, the 18th-century **Palacio de Nájera** is the setting for the Municipal Museum, whose star exhibit is a 2,000-year-old bronze statue of a Roman boy.

In the outskirts of town are three large prehistoric **dolmens** that may have been the burial chambers of tribal leaders. Two of them – Viera and Menga – stand together, the latter the oldest and most impressive of all, dated at between 4,000 and 4,500 years old. A short distance away is the Dolmen de Romeral, which has a long corridor leading to a vaulted central chamber.

🏟 Plaza de Toros
Crta de Sevilla. **Tel** 95 270 81 42.
Open Tue–Sun. Museo Taurino:
Open Tue–Sun.

🏛 Palacio de Nájera
Coso Viejo. **Tel** 95 270 83 00. **Open** 9:30am–2pm, 4:30–6:30pm Tue–Sat (to 7pm Sat), 10am–2pm Sun. 🈺 🈯
Dolmens: **Tel** 95 271 22 06. **Open** 9am–8pm Tue–Sat, 10am–5pm Sun. 🈺 🈯 Tue.

㉗ El Torcal

Málaga. **Road map** D3. 🚌 🚌 Ante-quera. ℹ Antequera (95 270 25 05).

A huge exposed hump of limestone upland battered into bizarre formations by wind and rain, the **Parque Natural del Torcal** is very popular with hikers. Most follow a network of footpaths leading from a visitors' centre in the middle; short walks (up to two hours) are

marked by yellow arrows; longer walks are marked in red. There are canyons, caves, mushroom-shaped rocks and other geological curiosities to see. The park also boasts fox and weasel populations, and colonies of eagles, hawks and vultures. It also protects rare plants and flowers, among them species of wild orchid.

㉘ Archidona

Málaga. **Road map** D3. ⛰ 8,200. 🚌
🚌 ℹ Plaza Ochavada 2 (95 271 64 79). 🈳 Mon.

This small town is worth a stop to see its extraordinary **Plaza Ochavada**. This is an octagonal square built in the 18th century in a French style, but which also incorporates traditional Andalusian features.

From the **Ermita Virgen de Gracia** on a hillside above the town are commanding views over rolling countryside.

The 18th-century, octagonal Plaza Ochavada in Archidona

29 Nerja

Málaga. **Road map** D3. 🏛 18,000. 🚌
ℹ️ Calle Puerta del Mar 2 (95 252 15
31). 🗓 Tue. **w** nerja.org

This fashionable resort at the
eastern extremity of the Costa
del Sol lies at the foot of the
beautiful mountains of the Sierra
de Almijara, and is perched on a
cliff above a succession of sandy
coves. The main area for tourist
activity in the resort centres
around the promenade, running
along a rocky promontory
known as **El Balcón de Europa**
(the Balcony of Europe). Spread
along its length is a hotel and
cafés with outdoor tables. There
are sweeping views up and
down the coast. On the edges
of town, holiday villas and
apartments proliferate.

Due east of the town are the
Cuevas de Nerja, a series of vast
caverns of considerable

The town of Nerja overlooking the sea from El Balcón de Europa

archaeological interest, which
were discovered in 1959. Wall
paintings *(see p46)* found in
them are believed to be about
20,000 years old. Unfortunately
they are closed to public view,
but a few of the many
cathedral-sized chambers are
open to the public. One of these
has been turned into an

impressive underground
auditorium large enough to
hold audiences of several
hundred. Concerts are held
there in the summer.

🏛 **Cuevas de Nerja**
Carretera de las Cuevas de Nerja.
Tel 95 252 95 20. **Open** daily. 🏛
w cuevadenerja.es

32 Málaga

Málaga. **Road map** D3. 🏛 650,000.
✈️ 🚇 🚌 ℹ️ Pasaje de Chinitas 4
(95 130 89 11). 🗓 Sun.
w malagaturismo.com

A thriving port, Málaga
is Andalusia's second
largest city. Initial
impressions tend to be
of ugly suburbs, high-
rise blocks and lines of
rusting cranes, but this
belies a city that is rich
with history, and is filled with
monuments and the vibrancy
of Andalusia. It also has many
restaurants and shops.

Malaca, the Phoenician *(see
pp46–7)* city, was an important
trading port on the Iberian
peninsula. After Rome's victory
against Carthage in 206 BC *(see
p48)*, it became a major port for
Roman trade with Byzantium.
Málaga's heyday came in the
years after 711, when it fell to
the Moors and became their
main port serving Granada. It
was recaptured by the Christians
in 1487 after a bloody siege. The
Moors left behind were expelled
(see pp54–5) after a rebellion.

Following a long decline, the
city flourished again during the
19th century, when Málaga wine

became one of Europe's popular
drinks. Unfortunately, phylloxera,
the vine disease that ravaged
the vineyards of Europe, ended
the prosperity of its
vineyards. This, however,
was when tourists began
to winter here.

The old town at the
heart of Málaga radiates
from the **catedral**. It was
begun in 1528 by Diego
de Siloé, but it is a
bizarre mix of styles. Its
construction was interrupted by
an earthquake in 1680. The half-
built second tower, abandoned
in 1765 when funds ran
out, is the reason for its
nickname: La
Manquita (the
one-armed one).

Façade detail, Málaga
Cathedral

Málaga's **Museo Carmen
Thyseen** houses a fine
collection of 13th–20th century
Spanish art. The **Museo de
Picasso**, displays works by the
native artist *(see p58)*. The **Casa
Natal de Picasso**, where the
painter spent his early years, is
now the headquarters of the
Picasso Foundation.

On the hill directly
behind the Alcazaba are

Amphitheatre

Entrance

Puerta de las
Columnas

Puerta
Principal

Plaza de Armas

㉚ The Axarquia

Málaga. **Road map** D3. **ℹ** San Antonio 1, Cómpeta (95 251 60 06).
W competa.es

The hills behind Torre del Mar and Nerja make up the pretty upland region of the Axarquia, whose main town, **Vélez-Málaga**, has a few old streets and the remains of a castle to explore.

A better base for excursions is the attractive sweet wine-producing town of **Cómpeta**, 20 km (12 miles) from the coast by winding mountain roads. From here, there is an interesting "Mudejar route" down the hill and up the valley to **Archez** and **Salares**, villages whose church towers are undisguised brick minarets dating from the 15th and 13th centuries respectively.

Two other villages worth visiting are **Frigiliana**, close to the coast and easily accessible from Nerja; and **Comares** (north east of Vélez-Málaga), perched on top of an impressive outcrop of rock from which there are superb views.

Narrow street in the Barrio de San Sebastián, Vélez Málaga

㉛ Montes de Málaga

Málaga. **Road map** D3. **🚌** to Colmenar. **ℹ** Lagar de Torrijos, on C345 at km 544,3 (95 104 21 00).

To the north and east of Málaga are the beautiful hills of Montes de Málaga. A wide area is undergoing reforestation and forms the **Parque Natural de Montes de Málaga**. Wildlife thrives in the strongly scented undergrowth of lavender and wild herbs. Occasionally, there are glimpses of wild cats, stone martens, wild boars, eagles and other birds of prey.

Walkers can follow marked trails. A farmhouse has been restored and converted into an ethnological museum. Along the C345 road between Málaga and the park, there are sensational views down to the sea.

the ruins of the 14th-century Moorish **Castillo de Gibralfaro**. Connected to the fortress by two ramparts, it can be reached through some beautiful gardens. There are views over the old town, port and Málaga bullring. The road to Parador de Málaga also leads to this hilltop.

Eastwards, on the road to Vélez Málaga, is the unspoilt beach of Rincón de la Victoria (see p37).

🏛 Museo Carmen Thyseen
Plaza Carmen Thyssen. **Tel** 90 230 31 31. **Open** 10am–8pm Tue–Sun.

🏛 Museo de Picasso
Calle San Agustín 8. **Tel** 95 212 76 00. **Open** 10am–8pm Tue–Sun (to 9pm Fri & Sat). 🏛

🏛 Casa Natal de Picasso
Plaza de la Merced 15. **Tel** 95 192 60 60. **Open** 9:30am–8pm daily. **Closed** public hols.

🏰 Castillo de Gibralfaro
Tel 95 222 72 30. **Open** 9am–6pm Tue–Sun (to 8pm summer). 🏛

🏰 Alcazaba
Calle Alcazabilla s/n. **Tel** 95 222 72 30. **Open** 9:30am–7pm Tue–Sun.

🏛 Museo Arqueológico
Calle Alcazabilla. **Tel** 95 191 19 04. **Closed** for renovations until late 2014. 🏛 **W** museosdeandalucia.es

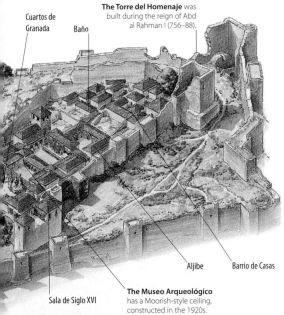

Cuartos de Granada

Baño

The Torre del Homenaje was built during the reign of Abd al Rahman I (756–88).

Aljibe

Barrio de Casas

Sala de Siglo XVI

The Museo Arqueológico has a Moorish-style ceiling, constructed in the 1920s.

Málaga's Alcazaba

Málaga's vast Alcazaba was built between the 8th and 11th centuries on the site of a Roman town. The two are curiously juxtaposed, with the Roman amphitheatre, discovered in 1951 and now almost fully excavated, just outside the entrance. The remains of Moorish walls can be seen, but the real attraction is the Museo Arqueológico, housing collections of Phoenician, Roman and Moorish artifacts, including fine ceramics.

Torremolinos, the capital of the Costa del Sol's tourist industry

❸ Torremolinos

Málaga. **Road map** D4. ⛰ 50,000.
🚉 🚌 ℹ Plaza Blas Infante
1 (952 37 95 12). 🛍 Thu.
ⓦ ayto-torremolinos.org

Torremolinos grew from a village in the 1950s to one of the busiest resorts on the Costa del Sol, where British and, to a lesser extent, German holiday-makers enjoyed their cheap package holidays. It also developed its red-light district and a raffish nightlife to provide "recreation" for sailors of the US navy in port at Málaga.

The town was cleaned up as part of a scheme that spent huge sums on new squares, a promenade, green spaces and enlarging the beach with millions of tonnes of golden sand.

Although Torremolinos still has scores of English bars run by expatriates, the atmosphere is now decidedly less downmarket, especially at Carihuela beach, towards the adjoining resort of Benalmádena.

❹ Benalmádena

Málaga. **Road map** D4. ⛰ 66,000. 🚌
🚌 ℹ Antonio Machado (952 44 24 94).

Benalmádena hosts an array of attractions, including the impressive **Castillo de Colomares** built between 1987 and 1994 as homage to Christopher Columbus. The monument reflects architectural styles that influenced Spanish culture, including Byzantine, Romanesque and Arabic, and carved into the structure are representations of Spain's history.

Europe's largest Buddhist monument, the Benálmadena **Stupa**, is also located here. It was inaugurated in 2003 by the local Buddhist community.

🏛 Castillo de Colomares
Carretera del Sol (El Viñazo). **Tel** 952 44 88 21. **Open** 10am–2pm, 4–7pm daily, (summer: to 9pm; winter: to 6pm).

🏛 Stupa
Calle Muérdago s/n, El Retamar. **Tel** 606 27 53 75. **Open** 10am–2pm, 3:30–7pm Tue–Sat; 10am–7:30pm Sun. 🅿

❸ Fuengirola

Málaga. **Road map** C4. ⛰ 53,000.
🚉 🚌 ℹ Avda Jesús Santos Rein 6
(95 246 74 57). 🛍 Tue, Sat & Sun.
ⓦ fuengirola.org

The town of Fuengirola is another package-holiday resort, although some of the wilder elements of its mostly British clientele have moved on to newer pastures. Nowadays Fuengirola attracts mainly families.

During the mild winter months, retired people from the UK come to stroll along the promenade, go to English bars and waltz the afternoons away at hotel tea dances.

Boxes of fresh fish, Fuengirola

❻ Marbella

Málaga. **Road map** C4. ⛰ 120,000.
🚌 ℹ Glorieta de la Fontanilla s/n,
Paseo Maritimo (95 277 14 42). 🛍
Mon & Sat (Puerto Banús).
ⓦ marbella.es

Marbella is one of Europe's most exclusive holiday resorts. Royalty, film stars and other members of the jet set spend

Yachts and motorboats moored in the exclusive marina of Marbella

For hotels and restaurants in this region see pp216–19 and pp228–37

Life in the Sun

The idealized image of the Costa del Sol before tourism is of idyllic fishing villages where life was always at an easy pace. It is true to say that local economies have turned away from fishing and agriculture, and that the natural beauty of this coast has been marred by development. Any measured view, however, should consider the situation described by Laurie Lee, the writer who in 1936 wrote of "… salt-fish villages, thin-ribbed, sea-hating, cursing their place in the sun". Today, few Andalusians curse their new-found prosperity.

19th-century lithograph of the harbour at Málaga

their summers here, in smart villas or at one of Marbella's luxury hotels. In winter, the major attraction is the golf *(see pp36–7)*.

As well as modern developments, Marbella boasts a well-preserved, charming Old Town. A number of streets lead from the main road, Avenida Ramón y Cajal, to Plaza de los Naranjos, the main square, surrounded by orange trees (hence its name).

The remains of the town's Arab walls loom over adjacent Calle Carmen, which leads to the 17th-century Iglesia de Nuestra Señora de la Encarnación. Nearby is the Museo del Grabado Contemporaneo (Museum of Contemporary Engravings), which contains works by Miró and Picasso.

On the other side of Avenida Ramón y Cajal is the Paseo de la Alameda, a park with benches decorated with colourful ceramics. From here, the road to the seafront, Avenida del Mar, is lined with sculptures made from designs by Salvador Dalí.

Heading west, Avenida Ramón y Cajal becomes the A7/N340. The first stretch is known as the "Golden Mile" because of its real-estate value. At the other end of the Golden Mile is Puerto Banús, the most exclusive marina in Spain.

Beyond Puerto Banús is San Pedro de Alcántara, really a separate town but officially part of Marbella. It is quiet, with a sleepy atmosphere,

especially in the Plaza de la Iglesia, the town square. Most of the smart holiday developments are located on the town's fringes, set amid a number of golf courses.

Ⅲ Museo del Grabado Contemporáneo
C/Hospital Bazan s/n. **Tel** 952 76 57 41. **Open** Mon–Sat. **Closed** public hols.

㊲ Estepona

Málaga. **Road map** C4. 46,000. 🚌 ⓘ Avda San Lorenzo 1 (95 280 20 02). 🏪 Wed & Sun. 🆆 **infoestepona.com**

This fishing village, situated midway between Marbella and Gibraltar, has been altered, but not totally overwhelmed, by tourist developments. It is not particularly attractive at first sight, with big hotels and

The leafy Plaza de las Flores hidden in Estepona's backstreets

apartment blocks fronting the town's busy main tourist area. Behind, however, there are endearing pockets of all that is quintessentially Spanish – orange trees lining the streets, and the lovely **Plaza Arce** and **Plaza de las Flores**, peaceful squares where old men sit reading newspapers while around them children kick footballs about. There are also a few good, relatively inexpensive, fish restaurants and tapas bars. The beach is pleasant enough and evenings in the town tend to be quiet, which makes the resort popular for families with young children.

Not far away from Estepona, however, is a popular nudist beach called the Costa Natura *(see pp36–7)*.

Relaxing in attractive San Pedro de Alcántara

GRANADA
AND ALMERÍA

Eastern Andalusia is dominated by the Sierra Nevada, Iberia's highest range and one of Spain's premier winter sports venues. At its foot is Granada, once a Moorish kingdom, with a royal palace, the Alhambra, straight out of *One Thousand and One Nights*. Ruined fortresses, relics of a warring past, dominate the towns of Granada province. In Almería's arid interior, film directors have put to use atmospheric landscapes reminiscent of Arabia or the Wild West.

At the point where the mountains of the Sierra Nevada meet the plain, 670 m (2,200 ft) above sea level, nestles the ancient city of Granada, founded by the Iberians. For 250 years it was the capital of a Moorish kingdom whose borders enclosed both Almería and Málaga provinces. On a ridge overlooking the city rises the royal citadel of the Alhambra, a complex of spacious palaces and water gardens.

The mountainous terrain of Granada province is starkly impressive. Amid the ravines, crags and terraced fields of Las Alpujarras on the southern flank of the Sierra Nevada, the villages seem to cling to the sheer slopes.

Along the coastal strip of Granada province, avocados and custard apples flourish in the subtropical climate. Hotels, villas and holiday apartment blocks are also much in evidence here.

East of Granada, the landscape becomes more arid. Around the town of Guadix, founded in Phoenician and Roman times, thousands of people live in cave-houses. A statue of an Iberian goddess from pre-Roman times was found at Baza, and at Los Millares, near Almería, there are traces of a 4,000-year-old settlement.

Almería, a flourishing port in the Moorish era, has been revitalized by a new form of agriculture. Plastic greenhouses now cover hectares of its surrounding province, producing fruit and vegetables all year round. Along the sparsely populated coast of Cabo de Gata, little-visited villages and bays doze in year-round sunshine.

The Renaissance castle of La Calahorra at the foot of the Sierra Nevada

◀ Street view in Alpujarras de la Sierra, with the Sierra Nevada mountains in the background

Exploring Granada and Almería

Granada and the Alhambra are the obvious highlights of this region, but are only a part of its appeal. Improved roads make it easy to reach most places within a few hours, and from Granada it is possible to explore the Sierra Nevada, plunge into the clear waters of the Costa Tropical, or wander through beautiful, spectacularly situated old towns, such as Montefrío and Alhama de Granada. From Almería it is a short hop to the Arizona-like country around Tabernas, where spaghetti westerns were made, or to the secluded beaches of the Parque Natural de Cabo de Gata. Each town and whitewashed village that lies in between has its own charm.

The Alhambra, with the snow-covered Sierra Nevada mountain range in the background

Sights at a Glance

1. Montefrío
2. Loja
3. Alhama de Granada
4. Santa Fé
5. Granada pp194–202
6. Almuñécar
7. Salobreña
8. Lanjarón
10. Poqueira Valley
11. Sierra Nevada
12. La Calahorra
13. Guadix
14. Baza
15. Vélez Blanco
16. Tabernas
17. Roquetas de Mar
18. Almería pp206–7
19. Parque Natural de Cabo de Gata
20. San José
21. Níjar
22. Sorbas
23. Mojácar

Tour
9. Las Alpujarras

Key

- ▬▬ Motorway
- ▬▬ Major road
- ▭▭▭ Minor road
- ▭▭▭ Scenic route
- ▬▬ Main railway
- ▭▭ Minor railway
- ▬▬ Provincial border
- △ Summit

For additional map symbols *see back flap*

Sierra de Segura

Sagra
2382m

Puebla de
Don Fadrique

A330

Huéscar

A317

Castillejar   Galera

María

VÉLEZ
BLANCO 15

Vélez Rubio

Guadal

A330

Embalse
de Negratín

Cúllar

Chirivel

A92N

Benamaurel

Zújar

Lorca

A327

14 BAZA

Oria

Santa Maria
de Nieva

Pulpí

A92N

Caniles

A334

Albox

Huércal-Overa

Cuevas del
Almanzora

Sierra
de Raza

Almanzora

N340

A7

Serón   Purchena   Macael

A L M E R Í A

Vera

Tetica de Bacares
2088m

Ulella del Campo

Garrucha

Fiñana

Sierra de los Filabres

A349

23 MOJÁCAR

Abla

Gérgal

22
SORBAS

N340a

Laujar de
Andarax   Canjáyar

16 TABERNAS

Carboneras

Sierra
Cabrera

A348

Gádor

A92

Sierra Albamilla

Punta de los
Muertos

Sierra de
Gádor

Benahadux

NÍJAR 21

Berja

ALMERÍA 18

Rodalquilar

Dalías

347

A7

N340a

Punta de la Polacra

19

El Ejido

Costa

de

Almería

El Cabo
de Gata

20 SAN JOSÉ

ROQUETAS
DE MAR 17

Cabo de Gata

PARQUE NATURAL DE CABO DE GATA

Spaghetti-western-style landscape near Tabernas

Avenida de Andalucía, the
main street in Lanjarón

Getting Around

The A92 runs west to Guadix and then turns
south to Almería. The A92N continues west
from Guadix towards Lorca. The N340
follows the coast via Almería and the Costa
Tropical. The N323 links the coast with
Granada and the A348 connects the villages
of the Alpujarras. There are three trains a day
between Granada and Almería, but no
coastal rail service. Frequent buses run from
both cities to towns on main routes.

Whitewashed houses on the edge of the gorge at Alhama de Granada, surrounded by olive groves

❶ Montefrío

Granada. **Road map** D3. 🏔 7,000. 🚌
ℹ Plaza de España 1 (958 33 60 04).
🗓 Mon.

Montefrío is the archetypal Andalusian town, which, approached by road from the south, offers wonderful views of tiled rooftops and whitewashed houses running up to a steep crag. The village is surmounted by remains of Moorish fortifications and the 16th-century Gothic **Iglesia de la Villa**, which is attributed to Diego de Siloé. Located in the centre of town stands the **Iglesia de la Encarnación**, in Neo-Classical design; the architect Ventura Rodríguez (1717–85) is credited with its design. Montefrío is also famed for the high quality of its pork products.

❷ Loja

Granada. **Road map** D3. 🏔 21,000.
🚉 🚌 ℹ Edificio Espacio Joven Calle Comedias 2 (958 32 39 49).
🗓 Mon. 🌐 lojaturismo.com

A ruined Moorish fort rises above the crooked streets of the old town of Loja, which was built at a strategic point on the Río Genil. The Renaissance **Templo de San Gabriel** (1566) has a striking façade, designed by Diego de Siloé. Known as "the city of water", Loja also has

some beautiful fountains. East of the town, the fast-flowing Río Genil cuts through **Los Infiernos** gorge. Sample local trout in **Riofrío**, to the west.

❸ Alhama de Granada

Granada. **Road map** D3. 🏔 6,000. 🚌
ℹ Montes Jovellar 10 (958 36 06 86).
🗓 Fri. 🌐 turismodealhama.com

Alhama is a charming, small town balanced above a gorge. It was known as Al hamma (hot springs) to the Arabs. Their baths can still be seen in **Hotel Balneario** on the edge of the town. Alhama's fall to the Christians in 1482 led to the final humiliation of the Nasrid kingdom at Granada in 1492 (see p52). The 16th-century **Iglesia de Carmen** has a number of very fine paintings on its dome, which had to be restored after damage incurred during the Spanish Civil War (see pp58–9). Narrow, immaculately whitewashed streets lead to the **Iglesia de la Encarnación**, founded by the Catholic Monarchs (see pp52–3) in the 16th century. Some of the vestments worn by the present-day priests are said to have been embroidered by Queen Isabel herself. The church

Belfry of Templo de San Gabriel at Loja

Spire-tip of the church, Santa Fé

also has a Renaissance bell tower designed by Diego de Siloé. Nearby is the 16th- century **Hospital de la Reina**, now an exposition centre for local artists housing a fine artesonado ceiling.

🏨 **Hotel Balneario**
Calle Balneario. **Tel** 958 35 00 11.
Open Mar–Nov.

🏨 **Hospital de la Reina**
Calle Vendederas s/n. **Tel** 958 36 06 43.
Open 11am–1:30pm, 4–8pm Fri.
Contact Tourist Office to visit (open 8am–3pm Mon–Fri).

❹ Santa Fé

Granada. **Road map** D3. 🏔 12,500.
🚌 ℹ Arco de Sevilla, Calle Isabel la Católica, 7 (958 51 31 10). 🗓 Thu.
🌐 lavegadegranada.es

The army of the Catholic Monarchs camped here as it lay siege to Granada (see p52). The camp burned down, it is said, after a maid placed a candle too close to a curtain in Isabel's tent. Fernando ordered a model town to be built. Its name, "holy faith", was chosen by the devout Isabel. In 1492 the Moors made a formal surrender at Santa Fé and here, in the same year, the two monarchs backed Columbus's voyage of exploration (see p131). An earthquake destroyed some of the town in 1806. A Moor's severed head, carved in stone, decorates the spire of the parish church.

❺ Granada

See pp194–203.

❻ Almuñécar

Granada. **Road map** D3. 🏚 22,000.
📧 ℹ️ Avenida Europa s/n (958 63 11
25). 🚌 Fri. **w** almunecar.info

Almuñécar lies on southern
Spain's most spectacular coast,
the **Costa Tropical** *(see p36)*,
where mountains rise to over
2,000 m (6,560 ft) from the
shores of the Mediterranean
Sea. The Phoenicians founded
the first settlement, called Sexi,
at Almuñécar, and the Romans
built an aqueduct here. When
the English writer Laurie Lee
made his long trek across
Spain in 1936, he described
Almuñécar as "a tumbling little
village fronted by a strip of
grey sand, which some hoped
would be an attraction for
tourists". On returning in the
1950s, he found a village still
coming to terms with the
Spanish Civil War *(see pp58–9)*,
which he recounts in his
novel *A Rose for Winter*.
   Almuñécar is now a holiday
resort. Above the old town is
the **Castillo de San Miguel**.
In its shadow are botanic
gardens, the **Parque
Ornitológico** and a Roman
fish-salting factory. Phoenician

artifacts are on display in the
**Museo Arqueológico Cueva
de Siete Palacios**.

🏰 **Castillo de San Miguel**
Open Tue–Sun. 🏚

🦅 **Parque Ornitológico**
Plaza de Abderraman s/n. **Tel** 958 88
26 12. **Open** daily. 🏚

🏛 **Museo Arqueológico Cueva
de Siete Palacios**
Casco Antiguo. **Open** Tue–Sun. 🏚

❼ Salobreña

Granada. **Road map** E3. 🏚 10,500.
📧 ℹ️ Plaza de Goya s/n
(958 61 03 14). 🚌 Tue & Fri.
w ayto-salobrena.org

From across the coastal plain,
Salobreña looks like a white
liner sailing above a sea of

Castillo de San Miguel, overlooking the village of Almuñécar

waving sugar cane. Narrow
streets wend their way up a hill
first fortified by the Phoenicians.
The hill later became the site of
the restored **Castillo Árabe**,
which gives fine views of the
Sierra Nevada *(see p203)*.
Modern developments, bars
and restaurants line part of this
resort's lengthy beach.

🏰 **Castillo Árabe**
Falda del Castillo, Calle Andrés Segovia.
Tel 958 61 27 33. **Open** daily. 🏚 🎫

❽ Lanjarón

Granada. **Road map** E3. 🏚 24,000. 📧
ℹ️ Avda de la Alpujarra s/n (958 77 04
62). 🚌 Tue & Fri. **w** lanjanet.com

Scores of snow-fed springs
bubble from the slopes below
the Sierra Nevada, and Lanjarón,
on the threshold of Las Alpujarras
(see pp204–5), has a long history
as a spa. From June to October
visitors flock to the town to take
the waters and, under medical
supervision, enjoy various water
treatments for arthritis, obesity,
nervous tension and other
ailments. Lanjarón bottled water
is sold all over Spain.
   The town occupies a lovely
site, but it can seem melancholic.
The exception to this is during
the early hours of the festival of
San Juan *(see p39)* when a water
battle takes place. Anybody who
dares venture into the streets
gets liberally doused.

🏛 **Balneario**
Balneario de Lanjarón. **Tel** 958 77
01 37. **Open** daily. **Closed** mid-
Dec–mid-Jan. 🏚 ♿
w hotelbalneariolanjaron.com

The village of Salobreña viewed across fields of sugar cane

❺ Granada

The guitarist Andres Segovia (1893–1987) described Granada as a "place of dreams, where the Lord put the seed of music in my soul". It was ruled by the Nasrid dynasty *(see pp52–3)* from 1238 until 1492 when it fell to the Catholic Monarchs. Before the Moors were expelled, artisans, merchants, scholars and scientists all contributed to the city's reputation as a centre for culture. Under Christian rule the city became a focus for the Renaissance. After a period of decline in the 19th century, Granada has become the subject of renewed interest and efforts are being made to restore parts of it to their past glory.

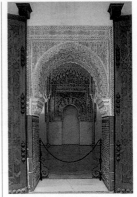
Entrance to the Moorish mihrab in the Palacio de la Madraza

Façade of Granada cathedral

🏛 Alhambra and Generalife
See pp198–202.

🏛 Catedral
C/Gran Via 5. **Tel** 958 22 29 59.
On the orders of the Catholic Monarchs, work on the cathedral began in 1523 to Enrique de Egas's Gothic-style plans. It continued under the Renaissance maestro Diego de Siloé, who also designed the façade. Corinthian pillars support his circular Capilla Mayor. Under its dome, windows of 16th-century glass depict Juan del Campo's *The Passion*. The west front was designed by local Baroque artist Alonso Cano. His grave and many of his works are housed in the cathedral. By the entrance arch are wooden statues of the Catholic Monarchs carved by Pedro de Mena in 1677.

🏛 Capilla Real
C/Oficios 3. **Tel** 958 22 92 39.
The Royal Chapel was built for the Catholic Monarchs between 1505 and 1507 by Enrique de Egas. A magnificent *reja* (grille)

by Maestro Bartolomé de Jaén encloses the mausoleums and high altar. The *retablo* by the sculptor Felipe de Vigarney has reliefs depicting the fall of Granada *(see pp52–3)*. Carrara marble figures of Fernando and Isabel repose next to those of their daughter Juana la Loca (the Mad) and her husband Felipe el Hermoso (the Handsome), both by the sculptor Bartolomé Ordóñez.

Steps lead down to the crypt where the corpses are stored in lead coffins. In the sacristy there are more statues of the two monarchs and many art treasures, including paintings by Van der Weyden and Botticelli. Glass cases house Isabel's crown and Fernando's sword.

🏛 Palacio de la Madraza
Calle Oficios 14. **Tel** 958 24 34 84.
Open Mon–Fri. ♿
Originally an Arab university, this building later became the city hall. The façade dates from the 18th century. Inside is a Moorish hall with a finely decorated mihrab. Today the Palacio is part of the University of Granada.

🏛 Corral del Carbón
Calle Mariana Pineda s/n. **Tel** 958 22 59 90. **Open** 10:30am–1pm, 5–8pm Mon–Fri; 10:30am–2pm Sat. ♿
This galleried courtyard is a unique relic of the Moorish era. Originally it was a storehouse and inn for merchants who mainly dealt in coal. In Christian times it was a venue for theatrical performances. Today it houses government offices.

🏛 Casa de los Tiros
Calle Pavaneras 19. **Tel** 600 14 31 75.
Open Jun–mid-Sep: 9am–3:30pm Tue–Sat, 10am–5pm Sun & public hols; mid-Sep–May: 10am–8:30pm Tue–Sat, 10am–5pm Sun & public hols.
This fortress-like palace was built in Renaissance style in the 16th century. It was once the property of a family who were awarded the Generalife after the fall of Granada *(see pp52–3)*; among their possessions was a sword belonging to Boabdil *(see p53)*. The sword is represented

Reja by Maestro Bartolomé de Jaén enclosing the altar of the Capilla Real

on the façade. The building owes its name to the muskets in its battlements, *tiros* being the Spanish word for shot.

🖼 Mirador de San Nicolás

From this square visitors can enjoy splendid sunset views. Tiled rooftops drop away to the Darro river, on the far side of which stands the Alhambra; the Sierra Nevada provides a suitably dramatic backdrop.

🖼 El Bañuelo

Carrera del Darro 31. **Tel** 958 22 97 38. **Open** 9:30am–2pm Tue–Sat. **Closed** public hols.

These brick-vaulted Arab baths, located near the Darro river, were built in the 11th century. Roman, Visigothic and Arab capitals were all incorporated into the baths' columns.

🏛 Museo Arqueológico

Carrera del Darro 43. **Tel** 958 22 56 40. **Closed** for renovations until late 2014.

The Renaissance Casa de Castril, with a Plateresque

Cupola in the sanctuary of the Monasterio de la Cartuja

portal, houses this museum of Iberian, Phoenician and Roman antiquities.

🏛 Palacio Carlos V

Alhambra. **Tel** 958 56 35 08. **Open** Tue–Sun (opening hours vary month by month so call ahead).

This palace in the Alhambra houses the Museo Hispano-Musulmán and the Museo de Bellas Artes. The highlight of the quite thrilling Muslim art collection is a most exquisite 15th-century vase from the

Alhambra, which has amazing blue and gold designs.

🏛 Monasterio de la Cartuja

Tel 958 16 19 32. **Open** 10am–1pm, 4–8pm daily. 🖼

A Christian warrior, El Gran Capitán, donated the land on which this monastery was built in 1516. A cupola by Antonio Palomino tops the sanctuary. The Churrigue-resque sacristy (see p29) is by mason Luis de Arévalo and sculptor Luis Cabello.

Sights at a Glance

① Mirador de San Nicolás
② Museo Arqueológico
③ El Bañuelo
④ Alhambra
⑤ Palacio Carlos V
⑥ Catedral
⑦ Capilla Real
⑧ Palacio de la Madraza
⑨ Corral del Carbón
⑩ Casa de los Tiros

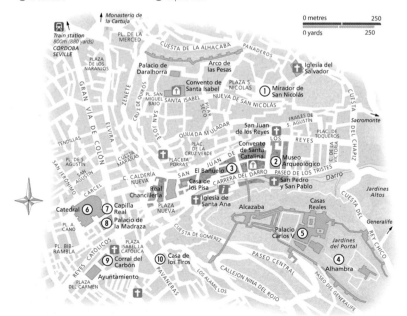

Street-by-Street: The Albaicín

This corner of the city, clinging to the hillside opposite the Alhambra, is where one feels closest to the city's Moorish ancestry. A fortress was first built here in the 13th century and there were once over 30 mosques, some of which can still be traced. Along narrow, cobbled alleys stand *cármenes*, villas with Moorish decoration and gardens, secluded from the world by their high walls. In the evening, when the scent of jasmine lingers in the air, take a walk up to the Mirador de San Nicolás. From here the view over a maze of rooftops and the Alhambra glowing in the sunset is magic.

Albaicín Street
Steep and sinuous, the Albaicín streets form a virtual labyrinth. Many street names start with *Cuesta*, meaning slope.

Real Chancillería
Commissioned by the Catholic Monarchs, the Royal Chancery dates from 1530. Its patio is attributed to de Siloé.

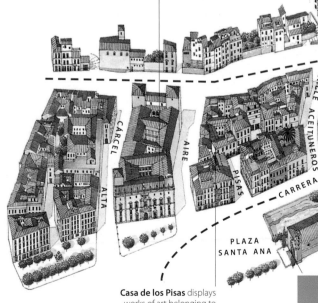

Casa de los Pisas displays works of art belonging to the Knights Hospitallers, founded by Juan de Dios in the 16th century.

Key

— Suggested route

0 metres	50
0 yards	50

★ Iglesia de Santa Ana
At the end of the Plaza Nueva stands this 16th-century brick church in Mudéjar style. It has an elegant Plateresque portal and, inside, a coffered ceiling.

Carrera del Darro
The road along the Río Darro leads past fine façades and crumbling bridges. At the top end, several bars offer views of the Alhambra.

★ Museo Arqueológico
The ornate façade of this museum has Plateresque carvings, including reliefs of mythological figures.

VISITORS' CHECKLIST

Practical Information
Granada. **Road map** D3. 🚹 250,000. ℹ️ Santa Ana 4 (958 57 52 02); C/Virgen Blanca 9 (902 40 50 45). 🗓️ Sat & Sun. 🎉 Día de la Cruz (3 May), Corpus Christi (May/Jun). 🌐 granadatur.com

Transport
✈️ 12 km (7 miles) SE of city. 🚌 Avenida de Andalucia s/n (902 24 02 02). 🚍 Carretera de Jaen s/n (958 18 54 80).

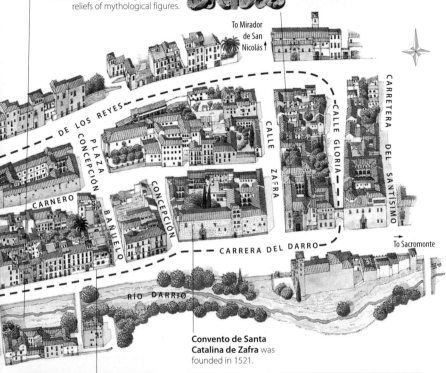

To Mirador de San Nicolás ↑

To Sacromonte →

Convento de Santa Catalina de Zafra was founded in 1521.

★ El Bañuelo
Star-shaped openings in the vaults let light into these well-preserved Moorish baths, which were built in the 11th century.

Sacromonte

Granada's gypsies formerly lived in the caves honeycombing this hillside. Travellers such as Washington Irving *(see p57)* would go there to enjoy spontaneous outbursts of flamenco. Today, virtually all the gypsies have moved away, but touristy flamenco shows of variable quality are still performed here in the evenings *(see p244)*. A Benedictine monastery, the Abadía del Sacromonte, sits at the very top of the hill. Inside, the ashes of San Cecilio, Granada's patron saint, are stored.

Gypsies dancing flamenco, 19th century

Granada: Alhambra

A magical use of space, light, water and decoration characterizes this most sensual piece of architecture. It was built under Ismail I, Yusuf I and Muhammad V, caliphs when the Nasrid dynasty *(see p52)* ruled Granada. Seeking to belie an image of waning power, they constructed their idea of paradise on Earth. Modest materials were used (tiles, plaster and timber), but they were superbly worked. Although the Alhambra suffered from decay and pillage, including an attempt by Napoleon's troops to blow it up, it has undergone extensive restoration and its delicate craftsmanship still dazzles the eye.

★ **Salón de Embajadores**
The ceiling of this sumptuous throne room, built between 1334 and 1354, represents the seven heavens of the Muslim cosmos.

★ **Patio de Arrayanes**
This pool, set amid myrtle hedges and graceful arcades, reflects light into the surrounding halls.

KEY

① **Patio de Machuca**

② **Sala de la Barca**

③ **Washington Irving's apartments**

④ **Jardín de Lindaraja**

⑤ **Baños Reales**

⑥ **The Sala de las Dos Hermanas,** with its honeycomb dome, is regarded as the ultimate example of Spanish Islamic architecture.

⑦ **Puerta de la Rawda**

⑧ **The Palacio Carlos V** *(see p54),* a fine Renaissance building, was added to the Alhambra in 1526.

Entrance

Patio del Mexuar
This council chamber, completed in 1365, was where the reigning sultan listened to the petitions of his subjects and held meetings with his ministers.

Palacio del Partal
A tower and its pavilion, with a five-arched portico, are all that remain of the Palacio del Partal, the Alhambra's oldest palace.

VISITORS' CHECKLIST

Practical Information
Granada.
Tel 958 02 79 71. Book by phone: 958 92 60 31 or online.
Open 8:30am–8pm daily (6pm in winter).
Night visits: summer: 10–11:30pm Fri & Sat; winter: 8–9:30pm Fri & Sat.
w alhambra-patronato.es.
Booking in advance is essential in high season.

Transport
2.

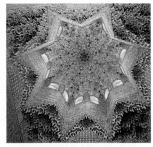

Sala de los Reyes
This great banqueting hall was used to hold extravagant parties and feasts. Beautiful ceiling paintings on leather, from the 14th century, depict tales of hunting and chivalry.

★ Sala de los Abencerrajes
This hall takes its name from a noble family, who were rivals of Boabdil (see pp52–3). According to legend, he had them massacred while they attended a banquet here. The pattern of the stalactited ceiling was inspired by Pythagoras' theorem.

★ Patio de los Leones
Built by Muhammad V, this patio is lined with arcades supported by 124 slender marble columns. At its centre a fountain rests on 12 marble lions.

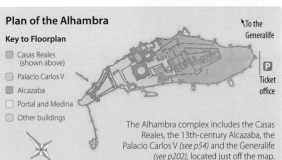

Plan of the Alhambra

Key to Floorplan
- Casas Reales (shown above)
- Palacio Carlos V
- Alcazaba
- Portal and Medina
- Other buildings

To the Generalife

P Ticket office

The Alhambra complex includes the Casas Reales, the 13th-century Alcazaba, the Palacio Carlos V (see p54) and the Generalife (see p202), located just off the map.

Granada: Generalife

Located north of the Alhambra, the Generalife was the country estate of the Nasrid kings. Here, they could escape the intrigues of the palace and enjoy tranquillity high above the city, a little closer to heaven. The name Generalife, or Yannat al Arif, has various interpretations, perhaps the most pleasing being "the garden of lofty paradise". The gardens, begun in the 13th century, have been modified over the years. They originally contained orchards and pastures for animals. The Generalife provides a magical setting for Granada's yearly International Music and Dance Festival *(see p39)*.

Patio de la Acequia
This enclosed oriental garden is built round a long central pool. Rows of water jets make graceful arches above it.

Sala Regia

Jardines Altos (Upper Gardens)

The **Escalera del Agua** is a staircase with water flowing gently down it.

Entrance

The Patio de Polo was the courtyard where palace visitors, arriving on horseback, would leave their horses.

The Patio de los Cipreses, otherwise known as the Patio de la Sultana, was the secret meeting place for Soraya, wife of the Sultan Abu l Hasan, and her lover, the chief of the Abencerrajes.

Patio del Generalife
Leading up from the Alhambra to the Generalife are the Jardines Bajos (lower gardens). Above them, just before the main compound, is the Patio del Generalife.

The majestic peaks of the Sierra Nevada towering, in places, over 3,000 m (9,800 ft) above sea level

❾ Las Alpujarras

See pp204–5.

❿ Poqueira Valley

Barranco de Poqueira, Granada. **Road map** E3. ℹ️ Plaza de la Libertad 7, Pampaneira (95 876 31 27).

Many visitors to the Alpujarras get no further than this deep, steep-sided valley above Orgiva, and it is certainly the best place to head for on a short visit. It contains three pretty, well-kept villages climbing the slope. In ascending order, they are: **Pampaneira**, **Bubion** and **Capileira**. All are perfect examples of the singular architectural style of the Alpujarras, which has its closest relation in the Atlas Mountains of Morocco. The whitewashed houses of each village huddle together seemingly randomly ("a confused agglomeration of boxes" as the writer Gerald Brenan described them), with flat grey gravel roofs sprouting a variety of eccentrically tall chimneys. The streets between the houses are rarely straight, often stepped and tapering, and they sometimes disappear into short tunnels.

The countryside between the villages makes excellent walking or horse-riding country. The slopes are still divided by dry-stone walls into terraced fields that are fed by an ingenious irrigation system that distributes the melt water from the mountains above. Dilapidated mills and old threshing floors are other signs of a vanishing way of life.

⓫ Sierra Nevada

Granada. **Road map** E3. 🚌 from Granada. ℹ️ Parque Nacional Sierra Nevada Centro de Visitantes "El Dornajo", Carretera de Sierra Nevada Km 23, Güéjar Sierra (95 834 06 25). 🌐 **sierranevadaskiguide.com**

Fourteen peaks, more than 3,000 m (9,800 ft) high, crown the heights of the Sierra Nevada. The snow lingers until July and begins falling again in late autumn. Europe's highest road (closed to traffic) runs past a ski resort at 2,100 m (6,890 ft), and skirts the two highest peaks, **Pico Veleta** at 3,398 m (11,145 ft) and **Mulhacén** at 3,482 m (11,420 ft). Its altitude and closeness to the Mediterranean account for the range of fauna and flora native to this mountain range. It is a habitat for golden eagles, rare butterflies and over 60 species of flowers unique to the area.

The Sierra Nevada was declared a national park in 1999 and access to it restricted. The park authorities run guided minibus excursions to the higher slopes from its checkpoints on the two sides of the Sierra Nevada: Hoya de la Mora (above the ski station on the Granada side) and Hoya del Portillo (above Capileira in the Alpujarras). The Sierra Nevada observatory is located on the northern slopes at an elevation of 2800 m (9,186 ft).

⓬ La Calahorra

Granada. **Road map** E3. 🚌 Guadix. ℹ️ Town Hall, Plaza Ayuntamiento 1 (95 867 71 32). **Open** 10am–1pm, 4–6pm Wed.

Immensely thick walls encircle this castle, perched on a hillock above the village. Rodrigo de Mendoza, son of Cardinal Mendoza, ordered La Calahorra to be built for his bride between 1509 and 1512, using architects and craftsmen from Italy. Inside is a Renaissance courtyard with a staircase and Carrara marble pillars.

The castle of La Calahorra above the village of the same name

Whitewashed cave dwellings in the troglodyte quarter of Guadix

⑬ Guadix

Granada. **Road map** E3. 🚗 20,100.
🚉 🚌 ℹ️ Avenida de la Constitución
15-18 (958 66 28 04).
🗓️ Sat. 🌐 guadix.es

The troglodyte quarter, with 2,000 inhabited caves, is the town's most remarkable sight. The **Museo de Alfarería** and **Cueva-Museo de Costumbres Populares** show how they live underground.

Around 2,000 years ago Guadix had iron, copper and silver mines. The town thrived under the Moors and after the Reconquest *(see pp52–3)*, but declined in the 18th century.

Relics of San Torcuato, who established the first Christian bishopric in Spain, are kept in the Cathedral museum. The **Catedral**, begun in 1594 by Diego de Siloé, was finished between 1701 and 1796 by Gaspar Cayón and Vicente de Acero. Near the 9th-century **Alcazaba**, the town's Mudéjar **Iglesia de Santiago** has a fine coffered ceiling. **Palacio de Peñaflor**, dating from the 16th century, is now fully restored.

🏛️ **Museo de Alfarería**
C/San Miguel 59 (958 66 47 67). **Open** 10am–2pm, 4–7pm daily. **Closed** Sun pm all year, Sat pm in winter). ♿

🏛️ **Cueva-Museo de Costumbres Populares**
Ermita Nueva s/n. (958 66 55 69). **Open** 9am–2pm, 4–6pm Mon–Fri, 9am–2pm Sat. ♿

⑭ Baza

Granada. **Road map** E2. 🚗 20,000.
🚌 ℹ️ Plaza Mayor s/n (958 86 13 25).
🗓️ Wed.

Impressive evidence of ancient cultures based around Baza came to light in 1971, when a large, seated, female figure was found in a necropolis. She is the Dama

---

⑨ A Tour of Las Alpujarras

Las Alpujarras lie on the southern slopes of the Sierra Nevada. The villages in this area cling to valley sides clothed with oak and walnut trees. Their flat-roofed houses are distinctive and seen nowhere else in Andalusia. Local food is rustic. A speciality is *plato alpujarreño*: pork fillet, ham, sausage and blood sausage, accompanied by a pinkish wine from the Contraviesa mountains. Local crafts include handwoven rugs *(see p242)* and curtains with Moorish-influenced designs.

④ Trevélez
Trevélez, in the shadow of Mulhacén, is built in typical Alpujarran style and is famous for its cured hams.

② Poqueira Valley
Three villages typical of Las Alpujarras in this river valley are Capileira, Bubión and Pampaneira *(see p203)*.

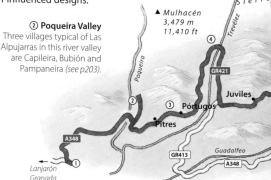

Orgiva
is the largest town of the ..., with a Baroque church ... main street and a lively market.

③ Fuente Agria
People come here from far and wide to drink the iron-rich, naturally carbonated waters.

...urants in this region see pp216–19 and pp228–37

de Baza *(see p47)*, believed to represent an Iberian goddess, and estimated to be 2,400 years old. Subsequently, she was removed to the Museo Arqueológico in Madrid but a replica can be seen in the **Museo Arqueológico** in Baza. The Renaissance **Colegiata de Santa María**, nearby, has a Plateresque entrance and a fine 18th-century tower.

During the first few days of September a riotous fiesta takes place *(see p40)*. An emissary, El Cascamorras, is despatched from the neighbouring town of Guadix to try to bring back a coveted image of the Virgin from Baza's **Convento de la Merced**. He is covered in oil and chased back to Guadix by youths, also covered in oil. There, he is taunted again for returning empty-handed.

▥ Museo Arqueológico
Plaza Mayor s/n. **Tel** 958 86 19 47.
Open 11am–2pm Tue–Sun (also 6–7:30pm Thu–Sat).

⓯ Vélez Blanco

Almería. **Road map** F2. ▨ 2,200. ▥ Vélez Rubio. ℹ Marqués de los Vélez s/n (950 41 95 85). ▥ Wed.

Dominating this pleasant little village is the mighty **Castillo de Vélez Blanco**. It was built from 1506 to 1513 by the first Marquis de Los Vélez, and its interior richly adorned by Italian craftsmen. Unfortunately for the visitor its

The village of Vélez Blanco, overlooked by a 16th-century castle

Renaissance splendour has since been ripped out and shipped to the Metropolitan Museum of New York. There is, however, a reconstruction of one of the original patios.

A blend of Gothic, Renaissance and Mudéjar styles *(see pp28–9)* can be seen in the **Iglesia de Santiago**, located in the village's main street.

Just outside Vélez Blanco is the **Cueva de los Letreros**, which contains paintings from around 4000 BC. One image depicts a horned man holding sickles; another the Indalo, a figure believed to be a deity with magical powers, still used as a symbol of Almería.

⌂ Castillo de Vélez Blanco
Tel 607 41 50 55. **Open** 10am–2pm, 5–8pm Wed–Sun (Oct–Mar: 4–6pm).

⌂ Cueva de los Letreros
Camino de la Cueva de los Letreros. **Tel** 671 99 91 29. **Open** noon–4pm daily. ▨

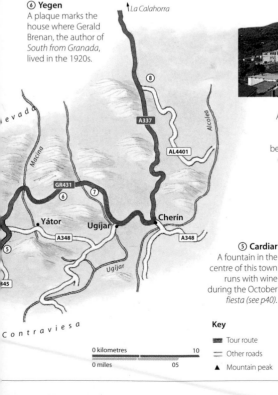

⑥ Yegen
A plaque marks the house where Gerald Brenan, the author of *South from Granada*, lived in the 1920s.

↑ *La Calahorra*

⑦ Válor
Aben Humeya, leader of a rebellion by Moriscos *(see p54)*, was born in this village. A commemorative battle between Moors and Christians is staged each year in mid-September *(see p40)*.

⑧ Puerto de la Ragua
This pass, which leads across the mountains to Guadix, is nearly 2,000 m (6,560 ft) high and often snowbound in winter.

⑤ Cardiar
A fountain in the centre of this town runs with wine during the October *fiesta (see p40)*.

Yátor
Ugíjar
Cherín

Tips for Drivers

Tour length: 85 km (56 miles).
Stopping-off points: Orgiva and Trevélez have bars, restaurants and hotels. Bubión has hotels and one good restaurant *(see p236)*. Capileira has bars and restaurants. Orgiva is the last petrol stop before Cadiar.

Key

▬ Tour route
═ Other roads
▲ Mountain peak

0 kilometres 10
0 miles 05

⑱ Almería

A colossal fortress bears witness to Almería's golden age, when it was an important port for the Caliphate of Córdoba. Known as al Mariyat (the Mirror of the Sea), the city was a centre for trade and textile industries, with silk, cotton and brocade among its chief exports. After the city fell to the Catholic Monarchs *(see pp52–3)* in 1489, it went into decline for the next 300 years. During the 19th and early 20th centuries, mining and a new port revived the city's fortunes, but this period ended abruptly with the start of the Civil War *(see pp58–9)*. Today a North African air still pervades the city, with its flat-roofed houses, desert-like environs and palm trees. North African faces are common as ferries link the city with Morocco.

The 10th-century Alcazaba overlooking the old town of Almería

🏰 Alcazaba
C/Almanzor s/n. **Tel** 950 17 55 00.
Open Tue–Sun. **Closed** 1 Jan, 25 Dec.

Fine views over the city are offered by this 1,000-year old Moorish fortress. It has been restored and within its walls are pleasant gardens and a Mudéjar chapel. It was the largest fortress built by the Moors and covered an area of more than 25,000 sq m (269,000 sq ft). The walls extend for 430 m (1,410 ft). Abd al Rahman III started construction in AD 955, but there were considerable additions later. The fort withstood two major sieges but fell to the Catholic Monarchs *(see pp52–3)* in 1489. Their coat of arms can be seen on the Torre del Homenaje, which was built during the monarchs' reign.

In the past, a bell in the Alcazaba was rung to advise the farmers in the surrounding countryside when irrigation was allowed. Bells were also rung to warn the citizens of Almería when pirates had been sighted off the coast. It is inadvisable for visitors to wander around the Alcazaba district alone or after dark.

🏛 Catedral
Plaza de la Catedral 8. **Tel** 950 234 848.
Open Mon–Sat.

From North Africa, Berber pirates would often raid Almería. Consequently, the cathedral looks more like a fortress than a place of worship, with four towers, thick walls and small windows. A mosque once stood on the site. It was later converted to a Christian temple, but destroyed by an earthquake in 1522. Work began on the present building in 1524 under the direction of Diego de Siloé. Juan de Orea designed the Renaissance façade. He also created the beautifully carved walnut choir stalls. The naves and high altar are Gothic.

🏛 Templo San Juan
C/Calle San Juan & Calle General Luque. **Tel** 950 23 30 07. **Open** 6:15–7:30pm daily.

Traces of Almería's most important mosque can still be seen – one wall of the present church is Moorish. Inside is a 12th-century mihrab, a prayer niche with cupola. The church, built over the mosque, was damaged in the Spanish Civil War and abandoned until 1979. It is now restored.

🏙 Plaza Vieja
Also known as the Plaza de la Constitución, this is a 17th-century arcaded square. On one side is the Ayuntamiento, a building with a cream and pink façade dating from 1899.

🏙 Puerta de Purchena
Located at the heart of the city, the Puerta de Purchena was

The pedestrianized 17th-century Plaza Vieja, surrounded by elegant arcades

once one of the main gateways in the city walls. From it run a number of shopping streets, including the wide Paseo de Almería. A tree-lined thoroughfare, this is the focus of city life, with its cafés, Teatro Cervantes and nearby food market.

✠ Centro Rescate de la Fauna Sahariana

C/General Segura 1. **Tel** 950 28 10 45. **Open** call ahead for an appointment.

At the rear of the Alcazaba, this rescue centre shelters endangered species from the Sahara, in particular different kinds of gazelle. Having flourished in Almería's arid climate, some animals have been shipped to restock African nature reserves.

🏛 Museo de Almería

Carretera de Ronda 91. **Tel** 950 10 04 09. **Open** Jun–mid-Sep: 9am–3:30pm Tue–Sat, 10am–5pm Sun & pub hols; mid-Sep–May: 10am–8:30pm Tue–Sat, 10am–5pm Sun & pub hols. 🖾 (free for EU citizens).

Almería's two main prehistoric civilizations, Los Millares and El Algar, are explained in this

Brightly coloured entrance to a gypsy cave in La Chanca district

archaeological museum that has 900 exhibits chosen from a collection of 80,000 pieces.

Environs

One of the most important examples of a Copper Age settlement in Europe, **Los Millares**, lies 17 km (10.5 miles) north of Almería. As many as 2,000 people occupied the site from around 2700 to 1800 BC *(see pp46–7)*. Discovered in 1891, remains of houses,

VISITORS' CHECKLIST

Practical Information
Almería. **Road map** F3. 🚊 170,000. 🛈 Parque Nicolás Salmerón s/n (950 17 52 20). 🚌 Tue, Fri & Sat. 🎭 Semana Santa (Easter), Feria de Almería (last week Aug).
w andalucia.org

Transport
🚆 Plaza de la Estación (902 24 02 02). 🚌 Plaza de la Estación (950 27 37 06).

defensive ramparts and a necropolis that contains more than 100 tombs have since been uncovered.

The community here lived from agriculture but also had the capability to forge tools, arms and adornments from copper, which was mined in the nearby of Sierra de Gador.

🏛 Los Millares

Santa Fé de Mondújar. **Tel** 677 90 34 04. **Open** 10am–2pm Wed–Sun. (Groups of 12 or more call ahead.)
w losmillares.info

Sights at a Glance

① Alcazaba
② Templo San Juan
③ Catedral
④ Plaza Vieja
⑤ Puerta de Purchena

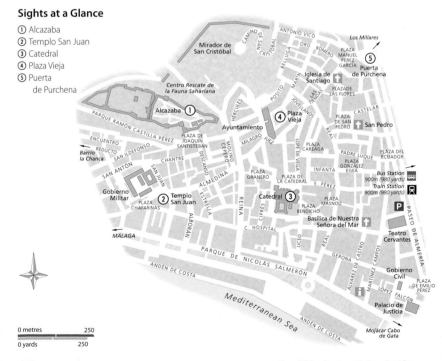

Spaghetti Westerns

Two Wild West towns lie off the N340 highway west of Tabernas. Here, visitors can re-enact classic film scenes or watch stunt men performing bank hold-ups and saloon brawls. The Poblados del Oeste were built during the 1960s and early 1970s when low costs and eternal sunshine made Almería the ideal location for spaghetti westerns. Sergio Leone, director of *The Good, the Bad and the Ugly*, built a ranch here and film-sets sprang up in the desert. Local gypsies played Indians and Mexicans. The deserts and Arizona-style badlands are still used occasionally for television commercials and series, and by film directors such as Steven Spielberg.

Still from *For a Few Dollars More* by Sergio Leone

⓰ Tabernas

Almería. **Road map** F3. 🏔 3,000. 🚌 *i* on main road: Nacional 340, km 464 (950 52 50 30). 🏪 Wed.

A Moorish hilltop fortress presides over the town of Tabernas and the surrounding dusty, cactus-dotted scenery of eroded hills and dried-out riverbeds. The harsh, rugged scenery has figured in many so-called spaghetti westerns.

Not far from Tabernas is a solar energy research centre, where hundreds of heliostats follow the course of southern Andalusia's powerful sun.

⓱ Roquetas de Mar

Almería. **Road map** F3. 🏔 34,000. *i* Avenida Mediterraneo 2 (950 33 32 03).

Much of Almería's southern coastal plain is given over to massive plastic greenhouses in which vegetables and flowers are raised for export. Interrupting the greenhouses is the resort of Roquetas de Mar, which has a 17th-century castle and a squat lighthouse, both used for exhibitions. Roquetas also has an aquarium with tropical and Mediterranean species of fish.

🔲 **Aquarium**
Avda Reino de España.
Tel 950 16 00 36. **Open** 10am–6pm Wed–Fri, 10am–7pm Sat & Sun. 🌐
🆆 aquariumroquetas.com

⓲ Almería

See pp206–7.

⓳ Parque Natural de Cabo de Gata

Almería. **Road map** F3. 🚌 to San José. *i* Centro de Visitantes de las Amoladeras, Carretera Cabo de Gata km 6 (950 16 04 35). Park **Open** daily.

Towering cliffs of volcanic rock, sand dunes, salt flats, secluded coves and a few fishing settlements can be found in the 29,000-ha (71,700-acre) Parque Natural de Cabo de Gata. The end of the cape, near the Arrecife de las Sirenas (Sirens' Reef), is marked by a lighthouse. The park includes a stretch of sea-bed about 2 km (1.2 miles) wide, which allows protection of the marine flora and fauna; the clear waters attract divers and snorkellers.

The area of dunes and saltpans between the cape and the Playa de San Miguel is a habitat for thorny jujube trees. Thousands of migrating birds stop here en route to and from Africa. Among the 170 or so bird species recorded in the park there are flamingoes, avocets, Dupont's larks and griffon vultures. Attempts are also being made to reintroduce the monk seal, which died out in the 1970s. At the northern end of the park, where there is a cormorants' fishing area, is Punta de los Muertos, ("dead man's point"); this takes its name from the bodies of shipwrecked sailors that are said to have washed ashore there.

⓴ San José

Almería. **Road map** F3. 🏔 1,000. 🚌 *i* Calle Correos s/n (950 38 02 99). 🏪 Sun (Easter & summer).

Located on a fine, sandy bay, San José is a small but fast-growing sea resort within the Parque Natural de Cabo de Gata. Rising behind it is the arid **Sierra de Cabo de Gata**, a range

Lighthouse overlooking the cliffs of the Parque Natural de Cabo de Gata

The harbour at the traditional fishing village of La Isleta

of bleak grandeur. Nearby are fine beaches, including Playa de los Genoveses *(see p37)*. Along the coast are **Rodalquilar**, a town once important for gold-mining, and **La Isleta**, a fishing hamlet.

㉑ Níjar

Almería. **Road map** F3. 3,000. ℹ️ Fundición s/n, Rodalquilar, Níjar (950 38 98 20). Wed.

Set amid a lush oasis of citrustrees on the edge of the Sierra Alhamilla, Níjar's fame stems from the colourful pottery and the *jarapas*, handwoven rugs and blankets, that are made here. The town's historic quarter is typical of Andalusia, with narrow, streets and wrought-iron balconies.

The **Iglesia de Nuestra Señora de la Anunciación,** dating from the 16th century, has a coffered Mudéjar ceiling, delicately inlaid. The barren plain between Níjar and the sea has begun to blossom thanks to irrigation.

In Spanish minds, the name of Níjar is closely associated with a poignant and violent incident that occurred here in the 1920s, and later became the subject of a play by Federico García Lorca.

㉒ Sorbas

Almería. **Road map** F3. 3,000. ℹ️ Centro de Visitantes los Yesares, Calle Terraplen, 9 (950 36 45 63). Thu.

Balanced on the edge of a deep chasm, Sorbas over-looks the Río de Aguas, which flows far below. There are two buildings in this village worth a look: the 16th-century **Iglesia de Santa María** and a 17th-century mansion said to have once been a summer retreat for the Duke of Alba.

Another point of interest for visitors is the traditional, rustic earthenware turned out and sold by Sorbas' local potters.

Located near to Sorbas is the peculiar **Yesos de Sorbas** nature reserve. This is an unusual region of karst, where water action has carved out hundreds of subterranean galleries and chambers in the limestone and gypsum strata. Speleologists are allowed to explore the caves, but only if they are granted permission by Andalusia's environmental department. On the surface, the green, fertile valley of the Río de Aguas cuts through dry, eroded hills. Local wildlife in this area includes tortoises and peregrine falcons.

㉓ Mojácar

Almería. **Road map** F3. 7,000. ℹ️ Calle Glorieta, 1 (950 61 50 25). Wed & Sun.

From a distance, the village of Mojácar shimmers like the mirage of a Moorish citadel, its white houses cascading over a lofty ridge near to the sea. The village was taken by the Christians in 1488 and the Moors were later expelled. In the years after the Spanish Civil War *(see pp58–9)* the village fell into ruin, as much of its population emigrated. In the 1960s Mojácar was discovered by tourists, giving rise to a new era of prosperity. The old gateway in the walls is still here, but otherwise the village has been completely rebuilt.

Pensión façade in the picturesque village of Mojácar

Blood Wedding At Nijar

Bodas de Sangre (Blood Wedding), a play by Federico García Lorca *(see p59)*, is based on a tragic event that occurred in 1928 near the town of Níjar. A woman called Paquita la Coja agreed, under pressure from her sister, to marry a suitor, Casimiro. A few hours before the ceremony, however, she fled with her cousin. Casimiro felt humiliated and Paquita's sister, who had hoped to benefit from the dowry, was furious. The cousin was found shot dead and Paquita half-strangled. Paquita's sister and her husband, Casimiro's brother, were found guilty of the crime. Shamed by this horrific scenario, Paquita hid from the world until her death in 1987. Lorca never visited Níjar, but based his play on newspaper reports.

The dramatist Federico García Lorca (1899–1936)

TRAVELLERS' NEEDS

WHERE TO STAY

Some of the most charming places to stay in Spain are in Andalusia. They range from restored castles to family guesthouses, and from one of the most luxurious hotels in Europe to an organic farm deep in the countryside. For budget travel there are pensions and youth hostels, and for hikers there are mountain refuges. A night or two in a B&B is an increasingly popular option in rural areas. Apartments and village houses throughout the region are let by the week for self-catering holidays. Andalusia's climate is also ideal for camping (except Nov–Mar), which can be a cheaper alternative.

The hotel listings *pp 216–19* are organized into different themes, with DK Choice entries highlighted – see Recommended Hotels on page 215 for more information.

The Monasterio de San Francisco in Palma del Río (*see p218*)

Where to Look

In Seville, the most appealing places to stay are mainly in the centre of town, especially around the Santa Cruz district (*see pp74–87*), where there is a broad range of hotels. As in most cities, the cheapest hotels tend to be small family-run pensions in the backstreets.

Parking is always a problem in the town centre, so if you drive, you may have to book into a hotel with secure private parking, or look around the city's outer suburbs. You can ask your hotel to direct you to attended car parks in the city. A reasonable alternative is to stay in a town close to Seville, such as Carmona (*see pp136–7*).

Granada has two main hotel districts: around the Alhambra (*see pp198–9*), which is quiet, and around the centre, which is livelier, noisier and usually cheaper. Central hotels make the best base for going out on the town at night.

In Córdoba the Judería (*see pp144–5*) is the most convenient place to stay if you plan to get around on foot. If you drive, you may prefer a hotel on the outskirts of the city.

Hotels in Andalusia's coastal resorts are mainly the modern chains that cater for package holiday-makers, although there are also many small, family-owned seaside hotels favoured by Spanish and foreign visitors alike. If you want somewhere more relaxing, there are good small hotels a short way inland. Look out for them in the white towns between Arcos de la Frontera (*see p179*) and Ronda (*see pp180–81*), and around Cazorla (*see p160*).

Two small private chains have a growing network of hotels in western Andalusia: the luxury Fuerte group and the budget Tugasa chain.

Hotel Grading and Facilities

Hotels in Andalusia are awarded categories and stars by the regional tourist authorities. Hotels (H is the abbreviation) are awarded between one and five stars and pensions (P) between either one and two stars. The star-rating system assesses the quantity of facilities a hotel has (such as whether there is a lift or air conditioning) rather than the quality of service to expect.

Most hotels in the region have restaurants that can be used by non-residents.

The hillside terrace of an Andalusian hotel with views across Granada

◄ Stained glass windows at Atarazanas market, Málaga

Hotel-Residencias (HR), however, do not have dining rooms, although they may serve breakfast.

Paradors

Paradors are government-run hotels that fall into the three- to five-star classifications. The best ones occupy historic monuments, such as castles, monasteries, palaces and old hunting lodges, but a number of them have been purpose-built in attractive settings. Though a parador will not always be the best hotel in town, they can be counted on to deliver a predictable level of comfort: regional dishes will always be on the menu and rooms are generally comfortable and spacious. The bedroom furniture varies little from parador to parador.

If you are travelling around the paradors during high season, or intending to stay in smaller paradors, it is wise to book ahead through agents for the paradors (see p214).

Prices

Hotels are obliged by law to display their range of prices behind the reception desk and in every room. As a rule, the more stars a hotel has, the more you pay. Rates for a double room start at €45 per night in a cheap one-star pension and can reach as high as €275 in a five-star hotel.

Prices vary according to the room, the region and season. Rural hotels are generally cheaper than city ones. All the prices quoted on pages 216–19 are based on the rates for high season. High season is usually July and August, but it can also run from April to October. City hotels charge inflated rates during major *fiestas*, such as Semana Santa (see p42) in Seville. Easter is a popular travel period for the Spanish themselves, and it is usually included in the high-season

Traditional courtyards are typical of many Andalusian hotels

price range, so be sure to enquire about availability and prices in advance.

Note that most hotels in Andalusia will quote prices per room and meal prices per person without *IVA* (VAT).

Booking and Checking In

Five-star hotel restaurant sign

You do not need to book ahead if you are travelling off-season in rural Andalusia, unless you want to stay in a particular hotel. On the other hand, it is essential to reserve rooms by phone, through a travel agent or on the Internet if you travel in high season. You will also need to book if you want a specific room, with a good view, with a double bed (twin beds are the norm), or away from a noisy road. Hotels in many coastal resorts close in the winter, so check that anywhere you want to stay is open.

Some hotels will request a deposit of 20–25 per cent for booking during peak times, or for a long stay. This can be arranged by credit card and phone, even in smaller hotels. Others will hold your booking until an agreed arrival time. Try to make cancellations at least a

week in advance, or you may lose all or some of your deposit. A reserved room will be held only until 6pm unless you can inform the hotel that you are going to arrive late.

When you book in you will be asked for your passport or identity card, to comply with police regulations. It will be returned to you when your details have been copied.

You are expected to check out of your room by noon or to pay for another night. Most hotels are happy to keep your luggage for you until later that day.

The impressive entrance of a hotel housed in a former Sevillian mansion

Mosaic tiling in the courtyard of a hostel

Paying

These days most hotels, except the most basic of bed and breakfasts, accept payment by credit card. In some large hotels you may be asked to sign a blank credit card slip on arrival. Under Spanish law it is fraudulent to ask you to do this, and you are advised to refuse to sign.

No hotel in Andalusia will take cheques, even when backed by a guarantee card or drawn on a Spanish bank.

In Spain it is customary to tip the porter and the chambermaid in a hotel by €1–2. The usual tip to leave in hotel restaurants is 5–10 per cent of the bill, although some restaurants will have included a service charge already.

Self-Catering

Villas and holiday flats let by the week are plentiful along the Costa del Sol and the coasts of Granada and Almería. Most cities will also have holiday let accommodation in central, well-furnished apartments that are cheaper than a comparable hotel. The local tourism office can supply information about letting agencies.

Inland, an increasing number of village and farm houses are now also being let all over the region. In the UK, a number of private companies, among them **The Individual Traveller's Spain**, act as agents for owners of apartments and houses. Many agents belong to an organization called the **RAAR** (Red Andaluza de Alojamientos Rurales or Andalusian Rural Accommodation Network), through which it is possible to make direct bookings.

Prices charged for self-catering accommodation sometimes vary considerably: prices are determined by location, the season and type of property. A four-person villa with a pool costs as little as €240 for a week if it is inland and over €950 per week if it is in a prime coastal location.

Another possibility is the *villa turística* (holiday village), which is half hotel, half holiday apartments. The guests can hire rooms with kitchens and use a restaurant.

Bed and Breakfast

Andalusia's 500 or more *casas rurales* offering bed and breakfast range from stately *cortijos* (manor houses) to small organic farms. Do not expect usual hotel service or a long list of facilities. However, you may

---

DIRECTORY

Hotels

Asociación de Hoteles de Sevilla
Calle San Pablo 1,
Casa A Bajo,
41001 Seville.
Tel 95 422 15 38.
W hotelesdesevilla.com

Asociación de Hoteles Rurales de Andalucía (AHRA)
C/Cueva de Viera 2.
Centro del Negocio CADI,
Edificio Málaga
3ª planta local 8,
29200 Antequera,
Málaga.
Tel 952 70 51 28.
W ahra.es

Fuerte Hotels
W fuertehoteles.com

Tugasa Hotels
W tugasa.com

Paradors

Central de Reservas
Calle Requena 3,
28013 Madrid.
Tel 90 254 79 79.
W parador.es

Keytel
The Foundry,
156 Blackfriars Road,
London SE1 8EN.
Tel (020) 7953 3020.
W keytel.co.uk

Self-Catering & Bed & Breakfast

The Individual Traveller's Spain
Tel (0800) 096 3439.
W villas4you.co.uk

RAAR
Sagunto 8-10-3,
04004 Almería.
Tel 950 28 00 93.
W raar.es

Youth Hostels

Central de Reservas de Inturjoven
Calle Miño 24, 41011
Seville. **Map** 3 A4.
Tel 90 251 00 00.
W inturjoven.com

Mountain Refuges

Federación Andaluza de Montañismo
Calle Santa Paula 23,
2° Planta, 18001 Granada.
Tel 95 829 13 40.
Opening hours: 8:30am–
2:30pm Mon–Fri (also Oct–
May: 4–6pm Wed).
W fedamon.com

Camping

Club de Camping y Caravanning de Andalucía
Calle Francisco Carrión
Mejias 13, 41003 Seville.
Tel 95 422 77 66.
W irdecampings.com

Federación Anda-luza de Campings
Tel 958 22 35 17.
W campings andalucia.es

Camping and Caravanning Club
Tel 0845 130 7631.
W campingand caravanningclub.co.uk

Disabled

IHD
EURL, Boîte Postale 62,
83480 Puget-sur-Argens,
France. **Tel** (0494) 81 61 51.

Viajes 2000
Paseo de la Castellana
228–30, 28046 Madrid.
Tel 91 323 25 23.
W viajes2000.com

Some youth hostels can be charmingly rustic

be met with a friendly welcome and be spoiled with good home cooking.

A stay at a bed and breakfast can be booked through **RAAR**, the owners' association, or directly. If you are booking from abroad you may be asked to send a 10 per cent deposit and to stay for at least two nights.

Youth Hostels and Mountain Refuges

To use Andalusia's extensive network of *albergues juveniles* (youth hostels) you have to buy an international YHA card from a hostel or show a card from your country. Bed and breakfast costs between €12 and €18 per person. You can book a bed or room in a hostel directly or through the central booking office of Inturjoven – **Central de Reservas de Inturjoven**.

If you backpack in remote mountain areas, you can stay in *refugios*, which are shelters with basic kitchens and dormitories. The *refugios* are marked on all good large-scale maps of the mountains and national parks. They are administered by the **Federación Andaluza de Montañismo**.

Camp Sites

There are more than 110 camp sites across the region of Andalusia, many of them along the coasts but there are also some outside the major cities

Logo for a five-star hotel

and in popular countryside areas. Most have electricity and running water; some also have launderettes, restaurants, shops, play areas for children and pools.

It is wise to take with you a camping *carnet* (card). It can be used to check in at sites, and it also gives you third party insurance. *Carnets* are issued by the AA, the RAC, and by camping and caravanning clubs. A map of all the region's camp sites, with links to their websites, is available from the **F.A.C. (Federación Andaluza de Campings)**.

Disabled Travellers

Hotel managers will advise on wheelchair access and staff will always assist, but few hotels are equipped for the disabled. However, some of the youth hostels are. **RADAR** *(see p256)*, the Royal Association for Disability and Rehabilitation, publishes a useful booklet

called *Holidays and Travel Abroad*, and Accessible Tourism publishes a fact sheet for disabled travellers in Spain.

In Spain, the Confederación Coordinadora Estatal de Minusválidos Físicos de España, also known as **Servi-COCEMFE** *(see p256)*, and **Viajes 2000** have details of hotels with special facilities in Andalusia.

IHD (International Help for the Disabled) arranges accessible accommodation, nurses, transport and other help for visitors to the Costa del Sol.

Recommended Hotels

The hotels listed on pages 216–9 cover the best boutique, luxury, bed and breakfast, inns and historic accommodation types in Seville and Andalusia. They are listed by price within each area. Boutique hotels are modern, with high design elements, while luxury hotels encompass the finest of Seville and Andalusia's upscale hotels. Bed and breakfasts offer a personable experience, with cozy rooms and a hearty breakfast, while inns are quaint places oozing charm. The area is also full of historic accommodation as many monasteries and mansions have been converted into hotels.

Throughout the listings, certain hotels have been marked as DK Choice. These offer a particularly special experience – either for their beautiful surroundings, excellent service, outstanding rooms, top-notch amenities, or a combination of these.

A pretty room in a bed-and-breakfast hotel

Where to Stay

Seville

El Arenal

Montecarlo €
Boutique Map 5 B3
C/Gravina 51, 41001
Tel 954 21 75 01
ⓦ hotelmontecarlodesevilla.com
Restored 18th-century mansion
with wrought-iron gates and twin
inner patios. Comfortable rooms.

Taberna del Alabardero €€
Historic Map 5 B3
C/Zaragoza 20, 41001
Tel 954 590 27 21
ⓦ tabernadelalabardero.com
The rooms here boast antiques
and stylish fabrics. Cozy central
patio with stained-glass roof.

Gran Melia Colon €€€
Luxury Map 5 B3
C/Canalejas 1, 41001
Tel 954 50 55 99
ⓦ solmelia.com
Elegant rooms and attentive
service at this centrally located
hotel. Popular with celebrities.

Santa Cruz

> **DK Choice**
>
> **Casa Numero Siete** €€
> Boutique Map 6 E3
> C/Virgenes 7, 41004
> **Tel** 954 22 15 81
> ⓦ casanumero7.com
> Discover luxury in a 19th-
> century mansion right in
> the heart of Seville's evocative
> old quarter. The furnishings
> at this small but immaculate
> boutique guesthouse include
> antiques and family heirlooms.

Hostería del Laurel €€
Historic Map 6 D4
Plaza de los Venerables 5, 41004
Tel 954 22 02 95
ⓦ hosteriadellaurel.com
An atmospheric hotel set in a
historic building in the old quarter.
The place is said to have inspired
romantic writer Zorrilla to create
the character of Don Juan.

Hotel Inglaterra €€
Historic Map 5 C3
Plaza Nueva 7, 41001
Tel 954 22 49 70
ⓦ hotelinglaterra.com
Chic hotel with superb antique
furnishings and Andalusian tiles.
Enjoy a cocktail at the rooftop
terrace bar.

La Casa del Maestro €€
Historic Map 6 E2
C/Niño Ricardo 5, 41004
Tel 954 50 00 07
ⓦ lacasadelmaestro.com
A delightful yellow-ochre guesthouse centred on a traditional
plant-filled patio. Spacious and
vibrantly decorated rooms.

Alfonso XIII €€€
Historic Map 6 D5
C/San Fernando 2, 41004
Tel 954 91 70 00
ⓦ hotel-alfonsoxiii-seville.com
A regal hotel with opulent
furnishings, crystal chandeliers
and marble columns.

EME Catedral Hotel €€€
Luxury Map 6 D4
C/Alemanes 27, 41004
Tel 954 56 00 00
ⓦ emecatedralhotel.com
Two restaurants, a panoramic
terrace, pool and spa are the main
attractions at this superb hotel.

Las Casas del Rey de Baeza €€€
Boutique Map 6 E2
Plaza Jesús de la Redención 2, 41003
Tel 954 56 14 41
ⓦ hospes.es
Stylish hotel with chic bedrooms.
Lovely open-air patio and spa.

La Macarena

Patio de la Alameda €
B&B Map 2 D4
Alameda de Hercules, 56, 41002
Tel 954 90 49 99
ⓦ patiodelaalemeda.com
Rooms at this delightful B&B are
stylishly furnished with details
such as mosaic tiled bathrooms.

Alcoba del Rey de Sevilla €€
Boutique Map 6 D4
C/Bécquer 8, 41002
Tel 954 91 58 00
ⓦ alcobadelrey.com
Intricate glassware, colourful tiles
and silk cushions define the
decor of this charming hotel.

**Hotel Boutique Casa
Romana** €€
Boutique Map 5 C2
C/Trajano 5, 41003
Tel 954 91 51 70
ⓦ hotelcasaromana.
com
Roman and
Andalusian themes
merge in this
imaginative hotel. The
elegant rooms border
a bright central patio.
The rooftop terrace
has a large Jacuzzi.

> **Price Guide**
> Prices are based on one night's stay in
> high season for a standard double room,
> inclusive of service charges and taxes.
>
> € under €120
> €€ €120 to 200
> €€€ over €200

Maestranza

Picasso €
B&B Map 6 D5
C/San Gregorio 1, 41004
Tel 954 20 18 64
Centrally located hotel with
simple, clean and comfortable
rooms grouped around a patio.

Triana

Ribera de Triana Hotel €€€
Luxury Map 3 A1
Plaza Chapina, 41010
Tel 954 26 80 00
ⓦ hotelriberadetriana.com
Upmarket hotel with modern
decor, rooftop pool and terrace
offering stunning city views, and
first-rate technological amenities.

La Cartuja

Barcelo Renacimiento €€
Luxury Map 1 C2
Avenida Alvaro Alonso Barba,
Isla de Cartuja, 41092
Tel 954 46 22 22
ⓦ barcelo.com
Geared towards business-users,
this hotel has modern decor and
a spacious convention centre
with all amenities.

La Campana

Cervantes €€
Boutique Map 6 D1
C/Cervantes 10, 41003
Tel 954 90 02 80
ⓦ hotel-cervantes.com
A charming hotel with coloured-
glass ceilings and a white,
beautifully tiled patio. Comfortable bedrooms with mellow
decor. Close to main sights.

Comfortable furnishings at Casa Numero Siete, Seville

Huelva and Sevilla

ALCALÁ DE GUADAÍRA: Hotel
Oromana €
Historic **Map** B3
Avda de Portugal, 41500
Tel *954 68 64 00*
An atmospheric and friendly
hotel set in a converted 1920s
mansion. Great on-site restaurant.

DK Choice

ARACENA: Finca Buen Vino €€
B&B **Map** B2
Carretera N-433, km 95 Los
Marines, 21293
Tel *959 12 77 78*
W fincabuenvino.com
This hilltop guesthouse, set
amidst citrus and olive groves
bordering a lovely natural park,
is famed for its cuisine and
cookery courses. All rooms are
spacious and individually
furnished. Expect great service.

ARACENA: La Casa Noble €€
Boutique **Map** B2
C/Campito 35, 21200
Tel *959 12 77 78*
W lacasanoble.net
This restored Andalusian house
has all modern comforts and
facilities. Enjoys stunning views.

CARMONA: Alcazar de la Reina €
Historic **Map** B2
C. Hermana Concepción Orellana, 2,
41410
Tel *954 19 62 00*
W alcazar-reina.es
This stately hotel has large,
elegant rooms with lovely views.

DK Choice

CARMONA:
Parador de Carmona €€€
Luxury **Map** B2
C/Alcazar s/n, 41410
Tel *954 14 10 10*
W paradores-spain.com
This is one of Spain's classic
paradors. Originally a Moorish
fortress, it has a stunning hilltop
site and majestic interiors
decorated with tapestries and
antiques. The rooms are stylish
and comfortable. Relax in
the outdoor swimming pool
(summer only).

CAZALLA DE LA SIERRA:
Las Navezuelas €
Inn **Map** B2
Crta Cazalla-Ed. Pedrosa, 41370
Tel *954 88 47 64*
W lasnavazuelas.com
A lovely *cortijo* (farmhouse) with
simple rooms and homely meals.

DK Choice

CAZALLA DE LA SIERRA:
Cartuja de Cazalla €€
Historic **Map** B2
Crta Cazalla-Constantina
km 2.5, 41370
Tel *954 88 45 16*
W cartujadecazalla.com
A unique refuge from the hassle
of modern life, this two-storey
Carthusian monastery is popular
with artists and sculptors. There
are eight rooms and a gardener's
cottage for families.

EL ROCIO: Hotel El Toruño €
Inn **Map** B3
Plaza Acebuchal 22, 21750
Tel *954 44 23 23*
W toruno.es
A whitewashed villa hotel on the
edge of the Doñana National
Park. Great location and service.

ISLA CRISTINA: Sensimar Isla
Cristina Palace €€€
Luxury **Map** A3
Avenida del Parque, s/n, 21420
Tel *959 34 44 99*
W sensimarislacristinapalace.com
Deluxe beachside hotel and spa.
All rooms have private balconies
overlooking the pool or ocean.

MAZAGÓN:
Parador de Mazagón €€
Luxury **Map** A3
Crta San Juan-Matalascañas
km 31, 21130
Tel *954 53 63 00*
W paradores-spain.com
Comfortable and well-appointed
parador in a stunning location.

VALENCINA DE LA CONCEPCIÓN:
Hotel Vereda Real €
Historic **Map** B2
Crta Gines - Valencina (SE-525) 41950
Tel *955 72 01 10*
W hotel-veredareal.com
A centrally located, picturesque
hotel with a pool, library and gym.

Córdoba and Jaén

BAEZA: Hotel Fuentenueva €
Historic **Map** E2
C/Carmen 15, 23440
Tel *953 74 31 00*
W fuentenueva.com
All rooms and apartments at this
hotel have hydromassage baths.

CAZORLA: Molino de la Farraga €
Historic **Map** E2
Camino de la Hoz, 23470
Tel *953 72 12 49*
W molinolafarraga.com
A restored 200-year-old mill with
clean rooms and traditional decor.

Stylish interiors at Hospes Palacio de Bailio
in Córdoba

CAZORLA: Parador de Cazorla €€
Luxury **Map** E2
Sierra de Cazorla, 23470
Tel *953 72 70 75*
Vintage parador located in the
heart of Cazorla National Park.
Ideal for nature lovers. Closed
mid-November to February.

CÓRDOBA:
Casa de los Azulejos €
Historic **Map** C2
C/Fernando Colon 5, 14005
Tel *957 47 00 00*
W casadelosazulejos.hotels82.com
Traditional Córdoban mansion
centred around a tiled patio.
Modern rooms with Wi-Fi.

CÓRDOBA: Hotel Maestre €
Inn **Map** C2
C/Romero Barros 4-6, 17003
Tel *957 47 24 10*
W hotelmaestre.com
A charming, traditional hotel
with a central flower-filled patio,
and clean and simple rooms.

CÓRDOBA:
Hospes Palacio de Bailio €€
Boutique **Map** C2
C/Ramirez de las
Casas Deza 10-12, 14012
Tel *957 49 89 93*
W hospes.es
Magnificently restored 17th-
century palace with elegant
furnishings and beautiful gardens.

DK Choice

CÓRDOBA: Lola €€
Boutique **Map** C2
C/Romero 3, 14001
Tel *957 20 03 05*
W hotelconencantolola.com
Set in a lovingly restored 19th-
century palace, this charming
boutique hotel is an atmospheric
place to stay in Córdoba's
labyrinthine Judería quarter.
There are eight period
furnished rooms – all named
after Arab princesses. Superb
views of the city from the terrace.

For more information on types of hotels *see p211*

CÓRDOBA:
Eurostars Las Adelfas   €€€
Luxury   Map C2
Avda de la Arruzafa, 14012
Tel *957 27 74 20*
ⓦ eurostarslasadelfas.com
Elegant hotel with a large pool
set in lovely gardens. Great service.

JAÉN: Parador de Jaén   €€
Luxury   Map D2
Castillo de Santa Catalina s/n
Tel *953 23 00 00*
ⓦ paradores-spain.com
Hilltop parador with traditional
Arabic decor and rooms that
offer panoramic views.

PALMA DEL RIO:
Monasterio de San Francisco €
Historic   Map C2
Avda del Pio XII 35, 14700
Tel *957 71 01 83*
ⓦ intergrouphoteles.com
A converted 15th-century
Franciscan monastery offering
clean rooms and organic meals.

ÚBEDA: Zenit El Postigo   €
Inn   Map E2
C/Postigo 5, 23400
Tel *953 795 550*
Modern hotel with fireplace,
pool and garden. Free Wi-Fi.

ZUHEROS: Zuhayra   €
Inn   Map D2
C/Mirador 10, 14870
Tel *957 69 46 93*
ⓦ zercahoteles.com
Friendly hotel with neat rooms and
modern amenities. Good location.

Cádiz and Málaga

DK Choice

ARCOS DE LA FRONTERA:
Casa Grande   €
Historic   Map B3
C/Maldonaldo 10, 11360
Tel *956 70 39 30*
ⓦ lacasagrande.net
A gleaming whitewashed 18th-
century mansion with a hilltop
location, offering great views of
the Andalusian countryside
below. Each room has unique
decor. Good breakfast spread.

ARCOS DE LA FRONTERA:
Parador
de Arcos de la Frontera   €€
Historic   Map B3
Plaza del Cabildo, 11630
Tel *956 70 05 00*
ⓦ paradores-spain.com
Converted magistrate's mansion
with great views from the terrace.

View from the roof terrace at Casa Grande,
Arcos de la Frontera

CÁDIZ: Pension Centro-Sol   €
Inn   Map B4
C/Manzanares 1, 11010
Tel *956 28 31 03*
ⓦ hostalcentrosolcadiz.com
A Neo-classical hostel with clean
rooms and a warm ambience.

CÁDIZ: Hotel Playa Victoria   €€
Boutique   Map B4
Glorieta Ingeniero La Cierva 4, 11010
Tel *956 20 51 00*
ⓦ palafoxhoteles.com
Eco-friendly seafront hotel with
avant-garde interior furnishings.

CAÑOS DE MECA: Las Breña   €€
Boutique   Map B4
Avda Trafalgar 4, 11160
Tel *956 43 73 68*
Simple and spacious rooms,
some with sea views. Excellent
beach location.

CASTELLAR DE LA FRONTERA:
Casa Convento La Almoraima €€
Historic   Map C4
*Ctra. Algeciras-Ronda s/n, Finca el
Almoraima, 11350*
Tel *956 69 30 50*
ⓦ laalmoraimahotel.com
A former monastery converted
into a modern hotel with antique
furnishings and an inner patio.

CORTES DE LA FRONTERA:
Casa Rural Ahora   €
Inn   Map C4
Bda El Colmenar 29490
Tel *952 15 30 46*
ⓦ ahoraya.es
A rural hideaway nestling in
a valley beside a stream. Chic
rustic furnishings and decor.

GIBRALTAR: Rock Hotel   €€
Historic   Map C4
3 Europe Road, Gibraltar
Tel *956 77 30 00*
ⓦ rockhotelgibraltar.com
A 70-year-old colonial style
cliffside hotel with a nostalgic
aura and cozy guest rooms.
Outdoor swimming pool.

DK Choice

GRAZALEMA:
Hotel Fuerte Grazalema   €
Inn   Map C3
*Baldio de los Alamillos, Crta
A-372, 11610*
Tel *956 13 30 00*
ⓦ fuertehoteles.com
A comfortable rural hotel
located inside the wooded
Grazalema Nature Reserve. Ideal
for walking, cycling or horse-
riding breaks. Good children's
facilities. The on-site restaurant
serves regional dishes.

MÁLAGA: Salles Hotel   €€
Luxury   Map D3
C/Marmoles 6, 29007
Tel *952 07 02 16*
ⓦ salleshotel.com
Well-appointed hotel in the heart
of Málaga with superb city views.

MARBELLA: El Fuerte Hotel   €€€
Luxury   Map C4
Avda. El Fuerte, 29602
Tel *952 86 15 00*
ⓦ fuertehoteles.com
Marbella's very first purpose-built
luxury hotel. Offers all modern
amenities and is close to the beach.

MARBELLA:
Marbella Club Hotel   €€€
Luxury   Map C4
Avda Principe von Hohenlohe, 29600
Tel *952 82 22 11*
ⓦ marbellaclub.com
A deluxe beachside hotel with
lush gardens, swimming pools,
world-class golf course and spa.

MIJAS: Hotel Hacienda
Puerta del Sol   €€€
Luxury   Map C3
Crta Fuengirola-Mijas km 4, 29650
Tel *952 48 64 00*
ⓦ hotelclubpuertadelsol.com
Stylish hotel with an exceptional
range of sports amenities, and
both covered and open-air pools.

NERJA: El Carabeo   €€
Boutique   Map D3
C/Carabeo 34, 29780
Tel *952 52 54 44*
ⓦ hotelcarabeo.com
A charming, British-owned hotel.
Rooms are furnished with
antiques and original artworks.

OJÉN: Posada del Angel   €
Inn   Map C3
C/Mesones 21, 29610
Tel *952 88 18 08*
ⓦ laposadadelangel.net
Traditional Andalusian hotel with
individually decorated rooms.
Enjoy breakfast underneath the
lemon tree on the patio.

PUERTO DE SANTA MARIA:
Monasterio de San Miguel €
Historic **Map** B3
C/Virgen de los Milagros 27, 11150
Tel *954 54 04 40*
[w] hotelmonasteriosanmiguel.es
A former Capuchin monastery
with many original features. Rooms
are large and simply furnished.

RINCÓN DE LA VICTORIA:
Molino de Santillan €
Historic **Map** D3
Crta de Macharaviaya km 3, 29780
Tel *952 40 09 49*
[w] molinodesantillan.es
Warm decor at this converted
former finca set high on a hilltop.
Outdoor activities are available.

RONDA: Parador de Ronda €€€
Historic **Map** C3
Plaza España, 29400
Tel *952 87 75 00*
[w] paradores-spain.com
A parador with bright, stylish
rooms – top floor suites have
fine views – and a huge garden.

SANLÚCAR DE BARRAMEDA:
Hotel Barrameda €
Boutique **Map** B3
Ancha 10, 11540
Tel *956 38 58 78*
[w] hotelbarrameda.com
Smart hotel overlooking Cabildo
Square. Some of the modern
rooms have private terraces.

TARIFA: Hurricane Hotel €€
Boutique **Map** B4
Crta N-340 Km 78, 11380
Tel *956 68 49 19*
[w] hurricanehotel.com
Laidback hotel with lush gardens,
two pools and health facilities
such as gym, sauna and massage
services. Great on-site restaurant.

VEJER DE LA FRONTERA:
La Casa del Califa €€€
Boutique **Map** B4
Plaza de España, 16 11150
Tel *956 44 77 30*
[w] lacasadelcalifa.com
An intimate and charming hotel
with individually decorated
rooms. Excellent service.

Granada and Almería

ALMERÍA: AM Husa Catedral €
Historic **Map** F3
Plaza Catedral 8, 04002
Tel *950 27 81 78*
[w] hotelcatedral.net
A converted former 19th-century
manor house with spacious and
comfortable rooms. Enjoy great
views from the roof terrace.

Light and spacious suite at La Bobadilla, Loja

GRANADA: Pension Landázuri €
Inn **Map** D3
Cuesta de Gomeréz 24, 18009
Tel *958 22 14 06*
[w] pensionlanazuri.com
A quaint pension with terraces
overlooking the city and Alhambra.

GRANADA: Posada del Toro €
Inn **Map** D3
C/Elvira 1, 18010
Tel *958 22 73 33*
[w] posadadeltoro.com
A renovated 19th-century inn
that blends old charm and modern
comforts. Wi-Fi in all rooms.

GRANADA: Casa 1800 €€
Boutique **Map** D3
C/Benalua 11, 18010
Tel *958 21 07 00*
[w] hotelcasa1800granada.com
Romantic hotel in a converted
17th-century mansion.

DK Choice

GRANADA:
Parador de Granada €€€
Luxury **Map** D3
C/Real de la Alhambra, 18009
Tel *958 22 14 40*
[w] paradores-spain.com
Lovingly restored from an old
convent, this parador enjoys an
incomparable location right
inside the grounds of the
Alhambra Palace. Elegantly-
appointed rooms. Book ahead.

LOJA: La Bobadilla €€€
Luxury **Map** D3
*Crtr Salinas-Villanueva de Tapia
(A-333), Km. 65.5, Finca la Bobadilla,
18300*
Tel *958 32 18 61*
[w] barcelolabobadilla.com
A luxurious hotel where all rooms
and suites have a unique decor.

Mecina Bombarón: Benarum €€
B&B **Map** E3
C/Casas Blancas 1, 18450
Tel *958 85 11 40*
[w] benarum.com
Plush hotel in the mountains of
Alpujarra with all modern comforts.

MOJÁCAR: Parador de Mojácar €€
Luxury **Map** F3
Paseo del Mediterráneo, 339
Tel *950 47 82 50*
[w] paradores-spain.com
Dazzling white beachside
parador with comfortable rooms
that offer Mediterranean views.

MONACHIL: La Almunia del Valle €
Boutique **Map** E3
Camino de la Umbría, 18193
Tel *958 30 80 10*
[w] laalmuniadelvalle.com
Friendly boutique hotel located
high in the Sierra Nevada. Lovely
gardens and pool (summer only).

MOTRIL: Casa de los Bates €€
Luxury **Map** E3
Crta N-340 km 329.5, 18600
Tel *958 34 94 95*
[w] casadelosbates.com
Well-furnished hotel retreat with
great sea views and pastel-hued
decor. Great service.

ORGIVA: Taray Botanico €
B&B **Map** E3
*Crta A-348 Tablete-Abuñol km 18,
18400*
Tel *958 78 45 25*
[w] hoteltaray.com
A lovely whitewashed rural hotel
with an olive and orange tree-
filled garden. Free parking.

**PECHINA: Balneario de
Sierra Alhamilla** €
Historic **Map** F3
C/los Baos, s/n, Pechina, 04259
Tel *950 31 74 13*
Well-restored 18th-century spa
hotel in the Sierra Alhamilla.
Unwind in the thermal pool with
underwater jets.

San José: Cortijo el Sotillo €€
Historic **Map** F3
Crta San Jose, 04118
Tel *950 61 11 00*
[w] cortijoelsotillo.es
A relaxing 18th-century farm-
house set in Cabo de Gata Natural
Park. Enjoy the quiet of unspoilt
beaches, just a short drive away.

For more information on types of hotels *see p211*

WHERE TO EAT AND DRINK

One of the joys of eating out in this region is the sheer sociability of the Andalusians. Family and friends, often with children in tow, start early with tapas, and usually continue eating until after midnight. The food has a regional bias – the best restaurants have grown from taverns and tapas bars serving fresh, home-cooked food. The restaurants listed on pages 228–37 have been selected for food and conviviality. There is a guide to tapas and a glossary on pages 224–5, and pages 226–7 illustrate the typical food and drink of the region.

The dining room of El Churrasco restaurant, Córdoba *(see p232)*

Andalusian Cuisine

The food of Andalusia falls into two categories: coastal and inland. Five of the region's eight provinces have stretches of coastline and a sixth, Seville, has a tidal river and several seaports (Cádiz, Sanlúcar, Barbate and Zahara among them) nearby. Coastal cooking includes a huge variety of fish and shellfish. The most famous fish dish is *pescaito frito* (fried fish). Although fish is integral to the Spanish diet, meat dishes such as veal and chops also make regular appearances on menus across the region.

Inland, rich stews with hams and sausages, and game, pork, lamb and chicken dishes are served. Vegetables and salads are excellent, as is Andalusia's signature dish, *gazpacho*, a soup made from vine-ripened tomatoes and peppers.

Meal Times

In Spain, *desayuno* (breakfast), is a light meal, often toasted bread with butter and jam and *café con leche* (milky coffee). A more substantial breakfast follows between 10 and 11am, a *bocadillo* or *mollete* (a sandwich or roll) with ham, sausage or cheese; or a slice of *tortilla de patatas* (potato omelette). *Churros* (fried dough strips) are sold mainly from stalls in autumn and winter.

It is common for Andalusians to stop in a bar for a beer or wine with tapas around 1pm. By 2 or 2:30pm offices close for *almuerzo* (lunch), the main meal of the day, eaten between 2 and 3pm, followed by a *siesta* hour. By 5:30pm or 6pm cafés, *salones de té* (tea rooms) and *pastelerías* (pastry shops) fill up for *la merienda* (tea): pastries and cakes with coffee, tea or juice.

Tapas bars become busy by 8:30pm. *La cena* (supper) is eaten from about 9pm, although some places begin service earlier for tourists. Spaniards tend to lunch out on weekdays and dine out at weekends. Sunday lunch is usually a family affair.

Standing up, enjoying a tapa

How to Dress

Spanish people dress smartly, especially in city restaurants. In the beach resorts, dress is casual, although shorts at night are frowned on.

Reading the Menu

The Spanish for menu is *la carta*. The Spanish *menú* means a fixed-price menu of the day. The day's specialities are often chalked on a board or clipped to the menu. Some finer restaurants offer a *menú de degustación*, which allows you to sample six or seven of the chef's special dishes.

La carta will start with *sopas* (soups), *ensaladas* (salads), *entremeses* (hors d'oeuvres), *huevos y tortillas* (eggs and omelettes) and *verduras y legumbres* (vegetable dishes).

Main courses are *pescados y mariscos* (fish and shellfish) and *carnes y aves* (meat and poultry). Paella and other rice dishes often come as the first course. Follow rice with meat, or start with

Bar in Calle Gerona, behind the Iglesia de Santa Catalina *(see p95)*, Seville

serrano ham or salad and follow with paella. It is quite normal to order just one or two courses from any part of the menu.

Desserts and puddings are grouped as *postres*, but fresh fruit is the preferred choice for desserts in Andalusia.

Children

Children are generally very welcome, but there are seldom special facilities for them. *Ventas*, or country restaurants, are the exception; they often have play areas.

Smoking

Smoking is not permitted inside public areas, including in restaurants, cafés and bars. Smoking on outside terraces is still allowed.

Wheelchair Access

Since restaurants are rarely designed for wheelchairs, you (or hotel staff) should call to book and to discuss access to restaurant and toilets. Spanish law requires all new-build public buildings to have wheelchair access, so newer restaurants will offer easier disabled access and facilities such as adapted toilets and wheelchair space in dining areas.

Stylish dining room of the exclusive Egaña Oriza, Seville *(see p229)*

Wine Choices

Dry *fino* wines are perfect with shellfish, *serrano* ham, olives, soups and first courses. Wines to accompany meals are usually from Ribera del Duero, Rioja, Navarra or Penedés. A tapas bar might serve Valdepeñas or La Mancha wines. *Oloroso* wines are often drunk as a digestif. *(See also What to Drink pp226–7 and The Land of Sherry pp34–5.)*

What it Costs

The cheapest places to eat are usually tapas bars and smaller, family-run establishments *(bar-restaurantes)*. A *menú del día* is offered in the majority of restaurants. It is usually three courses and priced well below choices from *la carta*.

Ordering from *la carta* in a restaurant can push your final bill way above average, especially if you choose pricey items like *ibérico* ham and fresh seafood. If you find "bargain prices" for swordfish, hake, sole and other fish, then it is probably frozen. Expect shellfish such as lobster and large prawns, and fish such as sea bass and

Relaxed ambience at the Manolo Bar in the Parque María Luisa *(see pp102–3)*, Seville

bream, to be priced by weight. The bill *(la cuenta)* includes service charges and sometimes a small cover charge. Prices on the menus do not include six per cent *IVA* (VAT), which, as a rule, is added when the bill is totalled. Tipping is just that, a discretionary gratuity. The Spanish rarely tip more than five per cent, often just rounding up the bill.

Credit cards are accepted in restaurants everywhere, but do not expect to pay by credit card in a tapas bar or café.

Recommended Restaurants

The restaurants featured in this guide have been selected for their good value, food, location and atmosphere. A wide range of establishments have been included – from no-frills dining spots, tapas bars and restaurants specializing in seafood to stylish diners featuring tasting menus prepared by leading Spanish chefs. Seville offers plenty of options for both carnivores and vegetarians alike.

Note that establishments labelled DK Choice are places that have been highlighted in recognition of an exceptional feature – exquisite food, an inviting ambience or simply for great value. Most of these places are popular with locals and visitors, so be sure to book well in advance.

The Flavours of Andalusia

Andalusia is vast, bordered on one side by the Mediterranean and on the other by the Atlantic. Inland are lofty mountains, undulating hills, endless olive groves and bright fields of sunflowers. The cuisine is as varied as the terrain, with a huge array of seafood, meat and game, and sun-ripened fruit and vegetables. The *tapeo* (tapas-bar-hopping) is a regional institution and, around Granada, these little morsels are still served free with drinks. Along the coast, especially the Costa del Sol, the influx of foreigners has brought glamorous international restaurants but, inland, traditional recipes are still the norm at old-fashioned *ventas* (countryside restaurants).

Olives and olive oil

Choosing from a selection of tapas

Tapas

The *tapeo*, or tapas crawl, is an intrinsic part of daily life in Andalusia. Each bar is usually known for a particular speciality: one might be well known for its home-made *croquetas* (potato croquettes, usually filled with ham or cod), while another will serve exceptional hams, and yet another might make the best *albóndigas* (meatballs) in the neighbourhood. Tapas are often accompanied by a glass of chilled, dry *fino* sherry, or perhaps a cold draught beer *(una caña)*. Tapas were once free, but that tradition has largely died out.

Seafood

It's not surprising, given its extensive coastline, that southern Spain offers every imaginable variety of seafood, including cod, hake, prawns, crayfish, clams, razor clams, octopus, cuttlefish, sole and tuna. Almost every seaside resort will offer *pescaíto frito*, originally a Malaga dish, made with whatever fish is freshest that day. In Cádiz, they are served appealingly in a paper cone, and in nearby Sanlúcar you must not miss the sweet and juicy *langostinos* (king prawns).

Jamón Iberico belota — Morcilla with onion — Morcilla with rice — Salchichón Iberico belota — Chorizo rosario picante — Lomo embuchado

Selection of delicious Spanish *embutidos* (cured meats)

Regional Dishes and Specialities

Andalusia embodies many of the images most closely associated with Spain – the heady rhythms of flamenco, striking white villages, bull-fighting and tapas. You can easily make a meal of these delectable treats, and most bars have an excellent range. Don't miss the mouthwatering hams from Jabugo and Trevélez which are famed throughout Spain, or the platters of freshly fried fish liberally doused with lemon juice. An ice-cold sherry (the word comes from Jérez, where most sherry is produced) is deliciously refreshing in the searing summer heat and is the most popular tipple at southern fiestas. While pork, particularly *jamon* (cured ham) remains the most appreciated local meat, duck, beef and lamb are also favourites, subtly flavoured with aromatic bay leaves.

Pomegranates

Gazpacho This chilled soup combines ripe tomatoes, breadcrumbs, cucumbers, garlic, vinegar, olive oil and peppers.

Andalusian market stall displaying fresh local produce

Meat and Game

Pork is king in Andalusia. The famous hams of Jabugo (in the southwest) and Trevélez (near Granada) are among the finest produced in Spain, and are made with free range, black-footed pigs fed on a diet of acorns. Beef is also popular; endless fields full of glossy black bulls (some

Prawns and sardines on display at the fishmarket

raised for bull-fighting but most for meat) are a common sight, and one of the most popular local dishes is *rabo de toro* (bull's tail). All kinds of cured meats are made here, often to traditional recipes that have remained unchanged for centuries. In the wild inland Sierras, you'll find an abundance of game in season, along with the traditional country staples of lamb and rabbit

Fruit and Vegetables

The undulating Andalusian fields and hillsides are densely covered with beautiful olive groves, and the best oils are graded as carefully as fine wines. Olive oil is liberally used in Andaluz cuisine, and the typical southern breakfast is toasted country bread

topped with thin slices of tomato and drizzled with olive oil – utterly delicious. The hot climate is perfect for fruit and vegetables, including luscious peaches, papayas, persimmons, and mangoes, as well as tomatoes, asparagus, aubergines (eggplants) and artichokes. The chilled tomato soup, *gazpacho*, is a classic, but *salmorejo*, which is thicker and topped with a sprinkling of chopped boiled eggs and ham, is even tastier.

ON THE MENU

Chocos con habas Cuttlefish is cooked with beans, white wine and plenty of bay leaves.

Pato a la Sevillana Succulent duck, cooked slowly with onion, leeks, carrots, bayleaf and a dash of sherry, this is a speciality of Seville.

Rabo de Toro An Andaluz classic, made with chunks of bull's tail, slowly braised with vegetables, bay leaf and a dash of sherry until tender.

Salmorejo Cordobés A creamy tomato dip thickened with breadcrumbs.

Torta de Camarones Delicious fritters filled with tiny, whole shrimp.

Tortilla del Sacromonte A speciality of Granada: omelette with brains, kidney or other offal, peppers and peas.

Huevos a la Flamenca Eggs are baked in a terracotta dish with tomato sauce, ham and chorizo sausage.

Pescaíto Frito A seaside favourite, this is a platter of small fish tossed in batter and quickly fried in olive oil.

Tocino de Cielo This is a creamy custard dessert with a caramel topping. Its name means "heavenly lard".

Choosing Tapas

Tapas, sometimes called *pinchos,* are small snacks that originated in Andalusia in the 19th century to accompany sherry. Stemming from a bartender's practice of covering a glass with a saucer or *tapa* (cover) to keep out flies, the custom progressed to a chunk of cheese or bread being used, and then to a few olives being placed on a platter to accompany a drink. Once free of charge, tapas are usually paid for nowadays, and a selection makes a delicious light meal. Choose from a range of appetizing varieties, from cold meats to elaborately prepared hot dishes of meat, seafood or vegetables.

Mixed green olives

Patatas bravas is a piquant dish of fried potatoes with a spicy red sauce.

Albondigas (meatballs) are a hearty tapa, often served with a spicy tomato sauce.

Almendras fritas are fried, salted almonds.

Banderillas are canapes skewered on toothpicks. The entire canape should be eaten at once.

Calamares fritos are squid rings and tentacles which have been dusted with flour before being deep fried in olive oil. They are usually served garnished with a piece of lemon.

Jamón serrano is salt-cured ham dried in mountain (*serrano*) air.

ON THE TAPAS BAR

Alcachofas Artichokes, typically served pickled in vinegar

Almejas Clams

Berenjenas rebozadas Battered and fried aubergines (eggplants)

Boquerones al natural Fresh anchovies in garlic and olive oil. Often served fried as well

Buñuelos de bacalao Salt cod fritters

Cacahuetes Peanuts

Calamares a la romana Fried squid rings

Callos Tripe

Caracoles Snails

Carne en salsa Meat in a thick sauce

Champiñones Button mushrooms fried and served in a light sauce with garlic and parsley

Chiporones a la plancha Grilled cuttlefish with a garlic and parsley sauce

Chopitos Cuttlefish fried in batter

Chorizo al vino Chorizo sausage cooked in red wine

Chorizo diablo Chorizo served flamed with brandy

Costillas Spare ribs

Criadillas Bulls' testicles

Croquetas Croquettes

Ensaladilla Rusa Russian salad, with vegetables and mayonnaise

Gambas pil pil Spicy, garlicky fried king prawns (shrimp)

Habas con jamón Tender broad beans fried with *jamón serrano*

Magro Pork in a paprika and tomato sauce

Manitas de cerdo Pig's trotters

Mejillones Mussels

Merluza a la romana Hake fried in a light batter

Tapas Bars

Even a small village will have at least one bar where the locals go to enjoy drinks, tapas and conversation with friends. On Sundays and holidays, favourite places are packed with whole families enjoying the fare. In larger towns it is customary to move from bar to bar, sampling the specialities of each. A tapa is a single serving, whereas a *ración* is two or three. Tapas are usually eaten standing or perching on a stool at the bar rather that sitting at a table, for which a surcharge is generally made.

Diners make their choice at a busy tapas bar

Chorizo, a popular sausage flavoured with paprika and garlic, may be eaten cold or fried and served hot.

Salpicón de mariscos is a luxurious cold salad of assorted fresh seafood in a zesty vinaigrette.

Gambas a la plancha is a simple but flavourful dish of grilled prawns (shrimp).

Tortilla española is the ubiquitous Spanish omelette of onion and potato bound with egg.

Queso manchego is a sheep's-milk cheese from La Mancha.

Pollo al ajillo consists of small pieces of chicken (often wings) sautéd and then simmered with a garlic-flavoured sauce.

Migas Breadcrumbs, fried and flavoured with a variety of savoury ingredients

Montaditos Mini sandwiches made with a variety of fillings

Morcilla Black (blood) pudding

Muslitos del mar Crab-meat croquette, skewered onto a claw

Orejas de cerdo Pig's ear

Paella Rice dish made with meat, fish and/or vegetables

Pan de ajo Garlic bread

Patatas a lo pobre Potato chunks sautéd with onions and red and green peppers

Patatas alioli Potato chunks in a garlic mayonnaise

Pescaítos fritos Fish given a light dusting of flour and fried

Pescaditos Small fried fish

Pimientos Fried green peppers

Pimientos rellenos Stuffed peppers, usually with tuna

Pinchos morunos Moorish pork kebabs

Pulpo Baby octopus

Quesos Spanish cheeses

Rabo de toro Bull's tail

Revueltos Scrambled eggs with asparagus or mushrooms

Salmonetes Red mullet

Sardinas Sardines, fried or grilled

Sepia a la plancha Grilled cuttlefish

Sesos Brains, usually lamb or calf

Truita de patates Catalan name for *tortilla española*

Verdura a la plancha Grilled vegetables

What to Drink in Andalusia

Andalusia is the third-largest of Spain's wine regions and produces some of the world's best-known wines; particularly sherry *(see pp34–5)*. Wine is such a large part of the culture that festivals celebrating the *vendimia* (grape harvest) are held all over the region *(see p40)*. Bars and cafés are an institution in Andalusia, and much public life takes place over morning coffee. Start the day with coffee at the counter in a café, have sherry or beer at midday, wine with lunch, and finish lunch or dinner with coffee and a *copa* of brandy.

Autumn grape harvest or *vendimia* celebrated all over Andalusia

Fino from Jerez

Manzanilla from Sanlúcar

Fino from Montilla

Fino

Fino is Andalusia's signature drink. Ask for *un fino*, or *una copa de vino fino*. Depending on where you are, you may be served a dry, pale sherry from Jerez de la Frontera *(see p166)*, a dry Montilla-Moriles wine from Córdoba province, or a dry Manzanilla, a sherry from Sanlúcar de Barrameda *(see p166)*. You can also ask for *fino* by name: for instance, Tío Pepe, a sherry from the González Byass *bodega* in Jerez; Gran Barquero, which comes from Montilla *(see p151)*; or Solear, a Manzanilla from the Barbadillo *bodega* in Sanlúcar. Manzanilla is the favoured drink during the Feria de Abril in Seville *(see p42)*.

Fino wine has a higher degree of alcohol than table wines (around 15 per cent). When drunk, it should have a fresh aroma and be dry and light to the palate. It is usually served chilled, in a small-stemmed glass with a rim narrower than its base. (Hold it by the base, not around the middle.) However, in some rustic bars, *fino* comes in a tall, straight glass known as a *copita* or a *vasito*.

Fino is most often drunk with first courses and tapas, and its dry taste is a perfect accompaniment to dishes such as *jamón serrano (see pp224–5)*.

Wine

Andalusia produces a few young white table wines, notably Castillo de San Diego, Marqués de la Sierra and wines from El Condado *(see p133)*. Most table wines – *tinto* (red), *blanco* (white) and *rosado* (rosé) – come from other parts of Spain. In more up-market establishments these tend to be Rioja, Ribera del Duero, Navarra and Penedés. Look for the label showing the wine's *denominación de origen* (guarantee of origin and quality). Recent vintages, or *cosecha* wines, are the least expensive; *crianza* and *reserva* wines are aged and more expensive. *Cava*, sparkling wines made by *méthode champenoise* are usually from Catalonia.

Tapas bars tend to serve ordinary Valdepeñas and La Mancha wines. People often dilute these with some *gaseosa*, a fizzy, slightly sweet lemonade. The resulting mixture – known as *tinto de verano* ("summer red wine") – is actually very refreshing.

Castillo de San Diego

Beer

Several brands of lager beers are brewed in Andalusia. These all come in bottles, though quite a few of them are available on draught, too. People often drink draught beers with tapas, especially in summer. Ask for *una caña*. One very good local beer, among the best in Spain, is Cruzcampo. Another, which may perhaps be more familiar to non-Spaniards, is San Miguel.

Una caña de cerveza

Cruzcampo in a bottle

Anise brandy
(aguardiente)

Moscatel from
Málaga

Lepanto *coñac*
from Jerez

Other Aperitifs and Digestifs

Anise brandy, which is often called *aguardiente*, the name for any distilled spirit, can be sweet or dry. It is drunk from breakfast *(desayuno)* to late afternoon tea *(la merienda)* and is sometimes accompanied by little cakes, especially during festivities. It is also drunk after dinner as a digestif.

Tinto de verano is a summer drink of red wine with ice and *gaseosa*. *Sangría* is a red-wine punch with fruit.

With tapas, instead of *fino*, try one of the mellow apéritif wines, such as *amontillado*, *oloroso* or *palo cortado* (see p35), made in Jerez and Montilla. With your dessert try a *moscatel*; the best known of these is a Málaga wine from Pedro Ximénez or muscatel grapes. Alternatively try a sweet "cream" sherry from Jerez. After dinner, have a brandy with coffee. Spanish brandy comes mainly from the sherry *bodegas* in Jerez and is called *coñac* in bars. Most *bodegas* produce at least three labels and price ranges, often displayed on shelves whose levels correspond to quality. A good middle-shelf brandy is Magno; top-shelf labels are Lepanto and Larios 1886.

If you are going on, say, to a nightclub, it is customary to switch to tall drinks – whisky with ice and water, gin and tonic or rum and soda. Rum is made on the south coast, where sugar cane is grown.

Amontillado from Jerez, an apéritif wine

Coffee

In the morning, the Spanish tend to drink *café con leche,* half hot milk, half coffee, often served in a glass instead of a cup. Children and insomniacs might prefer to have a *leche manchada* instead, prepared with just a "shadow" of coffee and lots of hot milk. Another option is a *cortado*, which is mainly coffee, with a tiny amount of milk. After dinner, you should drink *café solo*, a black espresso-style coffee, which is served in a tiny cup, though it sometimes comes in a short glass.

Café con leche

Café solo

Spanish coffee is made in espresso machines from coffee beans dark-roasted *(torrefacto)* with a little sugar to give it a special flavour.

Other Drinks

Herbal teas or *infusiones* can be ordered in most bars and cafés. *Poleo-menta* (mint), *manzanilla* (camomile), and *tila* (limeflower) are among the best. *Zumo de naranja natural* (freshly squeezed orange juice) is excellent but expensive and not always available. *Mosto* is grape juice. Tap water throughout Spain is safe to drink, but Andalusians are discerning about the taste of their water and buy it bottled from natural springs, such as Lanjarón *(see p193)*; it can be bought either *sin gas* (still) or *con gas* (bubbly). Fresh goat's milk is also available in most villages.

Mineral water
from Lanjarón

Fresh orange juice

Camomile tea
(manzanilla)

Hot Chocolate

Hot chocolate

Chocolate, originally from Mexico, was imported to Europe by conquistadors. *Tchocolatl*, a bitter, peppery drink made from cocoa, was drunk by the Aztec Indians during religious celebrations. Nuns, living in the colonies, adapted it by adding sugar to the cocoa, creating a sweeter drink more acceptable to European tastes. During the 16th century, chocolate became increasingly popular. Spain had a monopoly on the export of cocoa beans and the "formula" for chocolate was a state secret for over a century. In the 1830s, the English writer, Richard Ford, described chocolate as "for the Spanish what tea is for the English". For many Spaniards this is still the case.

Indian making
tchocolatl

Where to Eat and Drink

Seville

El Arenal

Bodeguita Casablanca €
Traditional **Map** 5 C5
C/Adolfo Rodriguez Jurado 12, 41002
Tel 954 22 41 14 **Closed** Sat eve & Sun
Traditional family-run tapas bar
with no-frills decor of tiles and
barrel tables. Very popular with
regular clientèle.

La Brunilda Tapas €
Traditional **Map** 5 B3
C/Galera 5, 41001
Tel 954 22 04 81 **Closed** Sun eve
Bright, modern bar with excellent
tapas. Try the solomillo de buey y
patatas al tomillo (ox sirloin with
thyme potatoes).

El Aguador de Velazquez €€
Fusion **Map** 5 C3
C/Albareda 14, 41001
Tel 954 22 47 20
Tucked away on a backstreet,
El Aguador is a delight. The menu
ranges from regional favourites
to adaptations of Asian and
Mexican dishes.

El Burladero €€
Traditional **Map** 5 B3
C/Canalejas 1, 41001
Tel 954 50 55 99
Set inside the 19th-century Hotel
Gran Melia Colon, with bull-
fighting memorabilia and a varied
menu. Try the cola de toro (oxtail)
in eight different ways.

El Cabildo €€
Traditional **Map** 5 C4
Plaza del Cabildo, 41001
Tel 954 22 79 70
Atmospheric restaurant with
Arabic-style furnishings, serving
traditional Andalusian dishes such
as pescaito frito (fried fish platter).

Enrique Becerra €€
Historic **Map** 5 C4
C/Gamazo 2, 41001
Tel 954 21 30 49 **Closed** Sun
Sample delicious albóndigas de
cordero a la yerbabuena (lamb
meatballs with mint) or pastel de
queso, beicon y alcauciles (cheese,
bacon and artichoke pie) at this
renovated 19th-century mansion.

DK Choice

Taberna del Alabardero €€
Traditional **Map** 5 B3
C/Zaragoza 20, 41001
Tel 954 50 27 21
Savour a flavoursome meal in
this beautiful eating spot set
in an old, refurbished mansion.
Tuck into one of the popular
dishes, such as the excellent
merluza al horno sobre fideuá
(hake on a bed of noodles).

Santa Cruz & Parque Maria Luisa

El Modesto €
Traditional **Map** 6 E4
C/Cano y Cueta 5 (Plaza de la
Carne), 41004
Tel 954 41 68 11 **Closed** Tue
A classic establishment with
tables overlooking Jardines de
Murillo. Try the paellas or gambas
al ajillo (shrimp cooked in oil with
garlic and chilli peppers).

La Albahaca €€
Traditional **Map** 6 E4
Plaza de Santa Cruz 12, 41004
Tel 954 22 07 14 **Closed** Sun
Stately 1920s mansion filled with
antique furniture and located
beside an intimate square. Quality
French-Basque specialities include
sea bass with plum and raisins.

Price Guide
Prices categories include a three course
evening meal for one including a half
bottle of house wine and all extra charges.

$ under $25
$$ $25 to 45
$$$ over $45

Albarama €€
Fusion **Map** 5 C3
Plaza de San Francisco 5, 41004
Tel 954 22 97 84 **Closed** Sun eve
Stylish but casual gastro-bar with
a commanding plaza location.
Delicious, innovative dishes, such
as hamburgesa de atún con tartar
de aguacate (tuna burger with
avocado tartar sauce).

Casa Plácido €€
Traditional **Map** 6 E4
Mesón del Moro 5, 41004
Tel 954 56 39 71
Small tapas bar decorated with
traditional tiles, bullfight posters
and hanging hams. Sample fino
from the barrel and excellent
tortillas (potato omelettes).

Casa Robles €€
Seafood **Map** 6 D4
C/Placentines 2–2a Planta, 41004
Tel 954 21 31 50
Prize-winning restaurant adorned
with statues and coloured tiles.
Great fish and shellfish selection
on the menu, plus an impressive
wine list.

Corral del Agua €€
Traditional **Map** 6 D5
Callejón del Agua 6, 41004
Tel 954 22 48 41 **Closed** Sun
Cool patio dining close to the
Real Alcazar gardens, with vibrant
decor featuring antiques and
paintings. Try the lubina en jerez
(sea bass cooked in sherry).

Don Raimundo €€
Historic **Map** 6 D4
C/Argote del Molino 26, 41004
Tel 954 22 33 55
A converted 17th-century
convent with stone walls, vivid
tiles and elegant chandeliers.
Dig into delicious perdiz con arroz
(partridge with rice) and jabali al
horno (oven-cooked wild boar).

Doña Elvira €€
Traditional **Map** 6 D4
Plaza de Doña Elvira 6, 41004
Tel 954 29 36 98
With links to the Don Juan legend,
this traditional Sevillian restaurant
offers dining indoors or al fresco
under shady trees. Serves excellent
gazpachos, paellas and frituras de
pescado (mixed fried fish).

Spacious dining area at Casa Robles, Seville

A rich selection of tapas on offer at Egaña Oriza, Seville

El Giraldillo €€
Traditional   **Map** 6 D4
Plaza Virgen de los Reyes 2, 41004
Tel *954 21 45 25*
Renowned eating spot close to the Giralda serving traditional Andalusian dishes such as *rabo de toro* (braised bull's tail) and *tortilla de camaron* (shrimp fritter). Good service.

Egaña Oriza €€
Seafood   **Map** 3 C3
C/San Fernando 41, 41004
Tel *954 22 72 54*
Elegant Basque-orientated conservatory restaurant set in an early 20th-century mansion. Sample the superb *bacalao* (salt cod) and *merluza* (hake). Also on offer are great meat dishes and desserts.

San Marco €€
Italian   **Map** 6 E4
Mesón del Moro 6, 41004
Tel *954 21 43 90*
A uniquely atmospheric restaurant located in the old Arab Baths. Come here for first-rate Italian pasta dishes. One of four branches in the city.

Santa Cruz €€
Traditional   **Map** 6 E4
Plaza de los Venerables 5, 41004
Tel *954 22 35 83*
A spacious mansion with colonnaded interiors and an open terrace. Specialities include the *rabo de toro* (braised bull's tail) and a wide range of seafood.

DK Choice

Vineria San Telmo €€
Fusion   **Map** 6 E4
Paseo Catalina de Ribera 4, 41004
Tel *954 41 06 00*
A charming establishment with tables on a pleasant square.

Innovative twists to regional favourites will delight, such as *trigo cremoso con boletus y aceite de trufa* (creamy bulghur risotto with boletus mushrooms and truffle oil), but make sure you leave room for the fabulous home-made desserts.

Berrecita €€€
Traditional   **Map** 6 D3
C/Recaredo 9, 41004
Tel *954 41 20 57*   **Closed** *Sun eve*
An intimate restaurant offering gourmet creations. Don't miss the *rape con sopeao* (angler fish in lobster and tomato sauce).

San Fernando €€€
Traditional   **Map** 6 D5
C/San Fernando 2, 41004
Tel *954 91 70 44*
A first-rate restaurant inside the Alfonso XIII Hotel. Try the marinated king prawn and quail salad or go for the *solomillo* (beef) Wellington.

Santo €€€
Fusion   **Map** 6 D4
C/Argote de Molino 29, 41004
Tel *954 56 10 20*
Creative dishes such as glazed Iberian pork with sesame sauce are served in stylish surrounds. Try the food and wine pairing menu.

La Macarena

Contenedor €€
Traditional   **Map** 2 E4
C/San Luis 50, 41003
Tel *954 91 63 33*   **Closed** *Mon eve*
Top-value eating spot serving traditional dishes using fresh market produce. Art exhibitions are held here on Mondays and Saturdays. Good service.

Eslava €€
Traditional   **Map** 1 C4
C/Eslava 3, 41002
Tel *954 90 65 68*
A no-frills, popular restaurant featuring creative Andalusian cuisine. Great seafood and salads, and an inventive choice of tapas.

Triana

Taberna Macuro €
Fusion   **Map** 3 B3
Rosario Vega 10, 41011
Tel *954 28 46 85*   **Closed** *Sun*
Eclectic bar that also functions as a gallery space for local artists. Interesting versions of hummus, falafel, ceviche and Spanish cuisine. Great selection of wine.

El Faro de Triana €€
Seafood   **Map** 5 A4
Puente Triana, 41010
Tel *954 33 61 92*
Striking yellow-ochre walled restaurant with two dining terraces overlooking the river. Come here to savour quality seafood at a great location.

Taberna Don Cecilio €€
Traditional   **Map** 3 A2
C /Manuel Pareja Obregón 2, 41010
Tel *615 08 49 38*
A small Triana gem serving delicious tapas. Highlights include stuffed pork in Pedro Jimenez sauce and goat's cheese salad with caramelized onions.

Abades Triana €€€
Seafood   **Map** 3 B3
C/Betis 69, 41010
Tel *954 28 64 59*
Enjoy superb international and Mediterranean cuisine at this riverside eating spot with stunning views.

Chic place settings at Taberna del Alabardero, Seville

For more information on types of restaurants see p221

Huelva and Sevilla

ALJARAQUE: La Plazuela Restaurante €
Seafood   Map A3
Calle de la Fuente 40, 21110
Tel *959 31 88 31*   **Closed** *Sun*
Sample fresh fish and seafood from the Atlantic coast, choice meats and a variety of fresh home-made breads.

ALMONTE: El Tamborilero €
Traditional   Map B3
C/Unamuno 15, 21730
Tel *959 40 69 55*   **Closed** *Sun; 1–15 Jul*
An atmospheric former *bodega* (wine cellar) with traditional decor and a chef who invites you into the kitchen to choose from their selections of the day.

DK Choice

ALMONTE: Aires de Doñana (La Choza del Rocío) €€
Traditional   Map B3
Avda de la Canaliega 1, 21730
Tel *959 44 22 89*
A converted *choza* (large thatched hut), this beautifully decorated restaurant enjoys splendid terrace views across the Doñana parkland's woods, reeds and waterways. Specialities served here include *revuelto marismeño* (scrambled eggs with local herbs) and *cabrito lechal* (suckling kid).

BORMUJOS: La Choza de Manuela €
Traditional   Map B2
Calle Maimónides 6, 41930
Tel *959 72 60 92*   **Closed** *Mon*
A complex of thatched roof huts and terraces, this is a charming place to come for excellent grilled meats and fish.

Bright and inviting dining room at El Tamborilero, Almonte

Unpretentious with generous portions and unbeatable prices.

CARMONA: Goya €
Traditional   Map B2
C/Prim 2, 41410
Tel *959 14 30 60*
Unassuming Sevillian eating spot off the city's main square. Try the baked lamb. The tapas bar does good tortillas.

CARMONA: El Molino de la Romera €
Traditional   Map B2
C/Sor Angela de la Cruz 8, 41410
Tel *954 14 20 00*   **Closed** *Mon*
Converted from a 16th-century Moorish mill and granary, this evocative restaurant specializes in delicious regional dishes.

CARMONA: El Ruedo €
Traditional   Map B2
C/Pastora Pavon 22, 41410
Tel *954 19 00 78*
This family-run restaurant serves traditional dishes with a twist. Try *setas con jamón a la plancha* (grilled wild mushrooms and Serrano ham).

CARMONA: Parador Alcazar del Rey Don Pedro €€
Traditional   Map B2
C/del Alcazar s/n, 41410
Tel *954 14 10 10*
Chic parador restaurant with a vaulted, antique-furnished dining room. First-rate regional dishes made with fresh market produce.

EL ROCIO: Restaurante Toruño €€
Traditional   Map B3
Plaza Acebuchal 22, 21750
Tel *959 44 24 22*
Inviting restaurant with terrace boasting excellent views. Try the *berenjenas gratinadas* (aubergine gratin), or one of the rice dishes.

Appetizing tapas at El Molino de la Romera, Carmona

GERENA: Casa Salvi Tapas €
Traditional   Map B2
Miguel de Cervantes 46, 41860
Tel *955 78 32 72*
Choose from a vast selection of tapas and plates and enjoy your meal in the shady plaza or one of the charming dining rooms. Superb value.

HUELVA: Las Meigas €€
Seafood   Map A3
Avda Guatemala 44
Tel *959 27 19 58*   **Closed** *Sun*
Top-notch restaurant serving fresh Atlantic seafood. Try the scrumptious *pulpo a la gallega con cachelos* (Galician-style octopus with sliced potato).

HUELVA: El Portichuelo €€
Traditional   Map A3
Avda Vazquez Lopez 15, 21110
Tel *959 24 57 68*
Unpretentious and centrally located, El Portichuelo dishes out traditional Andalusian fare made from the freshest market produce. Warm and friendly service.

HUELVA: Terranova €€
Traditional   Map A3
C/San Sebastian, 19
Tel *959 26 15 07*
Impeccably prepared seafood, fish, meat and vegetables with innovative twists. Try the award-winning *tapa bacalao al ajo confitado* (salt cod with garlic confit), but leave room for the tantalizing home-made desserts.

ISLA CRISTINA: Casa Rufino €
Seafood   Map A3
Avda de la Playa, 21410
Tel *959 33 08 10*   **Closed** *Jan*
A beachside haven for seafood lovers, serving a variety of fresh fish. Try the *rape en salsa de pasas* (angler fish in raisin sauce).

JABUGO: Meson Cinco Jotas €€
Traditional Map A2
Crta San Juan del Puerto, 21290
Tel *959 12 10 71*
Unpretentious eating joint in the birthplace of Spain's greatest *jamón* (cured ham). Sample the home-cured *jabugo* and cod with prawns and olives.

LA RINCONADA: El Pela €
Traditional Map B2
Plaza de Rodriguez Montes 2, 41880
Tel *954 79 70 39* **Closed** *Wed*
Simple, no-frills Sevillian restaurant where breakfast is served with delicious *pan prieto de la Algaba* (local speciality bread). Warm and friendly service.

MATALASCAÑAS: Los Pepes €€
Seafood Map A3
Sector N Parcela 43, Paseo Marítimo de Matalascañas
Tel *959 44 10 64*
Large sunny *chiringuito* (stall) with a beachside terrace. Try the *lubina en sal* (sea bass baked in salt) and *langosta* (fresh lobster), or one of the first-rate *guisos* (stews).

OSUNA: El Mesón del Duque €
Traditional Map C3
Plaza de la Duquesa 2, 41640
Tel *954 81 28 45* **Closed** *Wed, second week in May*
A fine traditional eating spot with a terrace, offering Andalusian specialities. Tapas include home-made *albóndigas* (meatballs).

OSUNA: Doña Guadalupe €€
Traditional Map C3
Plaza de Guadalupe 6-8, 41640
Tel *954 81 05 58* **Closed** *Sun eve, Mon, 1–15 Aug*
Family-run restaurant with outdoor terrace dining. Sample classic regional fare such as *perdíz con arroz* (partridge cooked with rice).

PALOS DE LA FRONTERA:
El Bodegón €
Traditional Map A3
C/Rábida 46, 21810
Tel *959 53 11 05* **Closed** *Tue; 15–30 Sep*
A homely, eco-conscious restaurant with both indoor and patio dining options. Bite into the juicy *solomillo a la brasa* (oak grilled sirloin steak).

Córdoba and Jaén

BAEZA: Casa Juanito €€
Traditional Map E2
Av del Alcalde Puché Pardo 57, 23440
Tel *953 74 00 40*
A cozy family-run eating place in a beautiful historical town. Olive oil-based dishes include *cabrito*

Landscape paintings decorating the walls of the dining room at Casa Juanito, Baeza

con habas (young goat with broad beans). Fabulous home-made desserts.

DK Choice

BAEZA: El Sarmiento €€
Traditional Map E2
Plaza del Arcediano 10, 23440
Tel *953 74 03 23*
Tucked away between the cathedral and old city wall, this charming restaurant offers both indoor and outdoor dining with abundant plates of fresh vegetables and a good variety of meats. Try the *pincho de lachazo a la brasa* (grilled skewers of suckling lamb).

BAILÉN: Zodiaco Libra €€
Traditional Map D2
Antigua Carretera Madrid-Cadiz km 294, 23710
Tel *953 67 10 58*
A popular restaurant that serves cold summer soups on a lovely garden terrace. Great shrimp and asparagus *revuelto* (scrambled egg) dishes.

CAZORLA: Meson Leandro €€
Traditional Map E2
C/Hoz 3, 23470
Tel *953 72 06 32* **Closed** *Wed & 15–30 Jun*
Michelin-recommended restaurant in a lovely Jaén village bordering a national park, and renowned for its *carne a la piedra* (stone-baked meat) dishes.

CÓRDOBA: La Almudaina €
Traditional Map C2
Jardines de los Santos Martires 1, 14004
Tel *957 47 43 42* **Closed** *Sun eve*
Excellent restaurant in a former bishop's palace. Traditional dishes include *salmorejo* (Spanish soup) and *solomillo al foie* (pork sirloin with paté).

CÓRDOBA: La Boqueria €
Traditional Map C2
C/Maria la Judia s/n
Tel *957 40 25 62*
Gourmet café-restaurant serving market-fresh dishes such as rice with lobster, *buey gallego* (Galician ox) and Jabugo ham. Great wine list and extensive menu of gin and tonics.

CÓRDOBA: Taberna Sociedad de Plateros €
Traditional Map C2
C/Maria Auxiliadora 25, 14002
Tel *957 47 03 04*
Iconic 1930s establishment frequented by celebrities. Try the *revuelto* (scrambled eggs).

CÓRDOBA: Caballo Rojo €€
Traditional Map C2
C/Cardenal Herrero, 28, 14003
Tel *957 47 53 75*
Charming eating place with a dining courtyard right next to the Mezquita. Discover Basque-, Moorish- and Sephardic-influenced dishes such as *cordero con miel* (lamb with honey) and the delicious monkfish *mozarábe*.

CÓRDOBA:
Casa Pepe de la Juderia €€
Traditional Map C2
C/Romero 1, 14008
Tel *957 20 07 44* **Closed** *last 2 weekends of May*
An enduring favourite since 1928. Dine in the flower-filled patio and savour the traditional Córdoban pork dish *flamenquin*.

CÓRDOBA: El Blason €€
Traditional Map C2
C/Jose Zorrilla 11, 14008
Tel *957 48 06 25* **Closed** *Sun*
Centrally located restaurant with an elegant tiled patio. Amazing *guisos* (stews), inventive seafood dishes and delectable home-made desserts.

CÓRDOBA: El Churrasco €€
Traditional   Map C2
C/Romero 16, 14008
Tel *957 29 08 19* **Closed** *Aug; 24 Oct; 24, 25 & 31 Dec*
Indulge in romantic patio dining under a lemon tree. Enjoy the charcoal-grilled steaks or one of a range of vegetarian dishes.

CÓRDOBA: Regadera €€
Traditional   Map C2
Calle de la Cruz de Rastro 2, 14002
Tel *957 10 14 00*
Appealingly situated, just steps from the riverfront, Regadera serves excellent food at great prices. Try the *rabo de toro con espuma de patata* (bull's tail with potato foam).

CÓRDOBA: San Miguel Casa El Pisto €€
Traditional   Map C2
Plaza San Miguel 1, 14002
Tel *957 47 83 28*   **Closed** *Sun*
Sterling family-run eating spot with tiled floors and traditional decor. Sample Iberian cured meats and *pisto* (ratatouille).

JAÉN: Antaño €
Traditional   Map D2
C/Rioja 5, 23003
Tel *953 22 46 51*   **Closed** *1 Jan, 25 Dec*
No-frills restaurant with a large summer terrace. Try the *cazuela* (fish stew) or *bacalao en alioli* (cod in garlic and mayonnaise sauce).

JAÉN: Casa Vicente €
Traditional   Map D2
C/Cristo Rey 3, 23007
Tel *953 23 22 22*   **Closed** *Sun & Mon eve*
Elegant mansion restaurant with local favourites such as *guiso de cordero* (lamb stew) and *pimientos rellenos de mariscos* (shellfish-stuffed peppers).

JAÉN: Taberna Don Sancho €
Traditional   Map D2
Avda de Andalucia 17, 23005
Tel *953 27 51 21*
Friendly restaurant with a creative take on classic dishes. Ask for the delicious cod with blueberries..

JAÉN: Casa San Antonio €€
Traditional   Map D2
C/Fermin Palma 3, 23008
Tel *953 27 02 62*   **Closed** *Sun eve, Mon, Aug*
Chic restaurant with a lovely terrace serving contemporary versions of traditional dishes. The menu changes frequently but the excellent *cochinillo* (suckling pig) features regularly. A taster menu is also available.

PALMA DEL RÍO: El Refectorio €€
Historic   Map C2
Avda Pio XII 35, 14700
Tel *957 71 01 83*
Dine in the old rectory of a converted 15th-century monastery. Traditional dishes include game in winter. Try the wild boar cooked in acorn flour.

ÚBEDA: El Seco €
Traditional   Map E2
C/Corazon de Jesus 8, 23400.
Tel *953 79 14 52*
Sink into a cozy dining room and savour homely dishes such as *bacalao el seco* (salt cod in cream sauce). Good service.

DK Choice

ÚBEDA: Parador Condestable Davalos €€
Historic   Map E2
Plaza Vazquez de Molina, 23400
Tel *953 75 03 45*
One of Úbeda's finest and most sumptuous spots, this stylish restaurant is located in a grand 16th-century parador. Savour the outstanding *cabrito guisado con piñones* (stewed kid with pine nuts) and seasonal game dishes. A wonderful historic setting, traditional decor and mouth-watering food.

Cádiz and Málaga

ALGECIRAS: Montes €
Vegetarian/Seafood   Map C4
C/Juan Morrison s/n. 11201
Tel *956 65 42 07*
Popular with locals, this simple restaurant serves a good choice of dishes. Great *sopa de picadillo* (ham, onion and potato broth).

ALGECIRAS: La Cabaña €€
Traditional   Map C4
Avda Agua Marina 5, 11203
Tel *956 66 73 79*   **Closed** *Mon*
Traditional restaurant with indoor and terrace dining, and live music some nights. Dishes include *pulpo gallego* (Galician-style octopus).

ARCOS DE LA FRONTERA: Bar La Carcel €
Traditional   Map B3
C/Marques de Torresoto 6, 11630
Tel *956 70 04 10*
A very popular restaurant with rustic decor. Ask for the aubergine with honey and goat's cheese, or try the *carne en Pedro Ximenez* (wine-marinated meat).

BENAHAVÍS: Los Abanicos €
Traditional   Map C4
C/Málaga 15, 28679
Tel *952 16 71 51*   **Closed** *Tue, Christmas*
Charming village restaurant specializing in regional dishes with excellent *paletilla de cordero* (shoulder of lamb). Popular for Sunday lunches.

BENAOJÁN: Molino del Santo €€
Traditional   Map C3
Bda Estacion 29370
Tel *952 16 71 51*   **Closed** *Dec–Feb*
With a great location amidst wooded mountain countryside, this place serves dishes prepared with fresh market vegetables and local chorizo, ham and game.

CÁDIZ: Balandro €
Seafood   Map B4
Alameda Apodaca 22, 11004
Tel *956 22 09 92*   **Closed** *Sun eve, Mon*
Set in a converted 18th-century mansion overlooking the Bay of Cádiz, this place offers excellent

Vibrant interior at El Churrasco, Córdoba

Elegant place settings at Casa Paco, Coin

boned and grilled gilthead and a good selection of meat dishes.

CÁDIZ: El Faro €€
Seafood **Map** B4
C/San Felix 15, 11011
Tel 956 21 10 68
Atmospheric seafood restaurant in the port district. Do not miss the *tortillitas de camarones* (shrimp fritters), or try one of the various taster menus available.

CÁDIZ: Freiduria Cervecería Las Flores €€
Seafood **Map** B4
Plaza Topete 4, 11009
Tel 956 22 61 12
Simple restaurant specializing in *mariscos* (shellfish) and fresh *pescaito frito* (fried fish platter) – make your choice and see it cooked on the spot.

CÁDIZ: Ventorillo del Chato €€
Seafood **Map** B4
Via Augusta Julia, 11011
Tel 956 25 00 25 **Closed** Sun eve (all day Sun in Aug)
Lovely 18th-century seaside inn specializing in local fresh fish. Try the *pasta negra fresca y frutos del mar* (black pasta with seafood).

CASARES: Venta Garcia €
Traditional **Map** C4
Crta. de Casares (MA 546) km 7, 29690
Tel 952 89 41 91 **Closed** Mon
Charming restaurant set in a scenic white roadside villa that offers great terrace views. The scallops are delicious and so is the *guiso de pescado* (fish stew).

COÍN: Casa Paco €€
Traditional **Map** C3
C/Maria Moreno 2, 29100
Tel 952 45 03 49 **Closed** Mon eve, Tue
Large country inn with a range of menus. Try the *boquerones* (fresh anchovies) and feast on *langostinos* (king prawns) and rice dishes. Popular for wedding receptions.

ESTEPONA: La Alborada €€
Seafood **Map** C4
Puerto Deportivo de Estepona, 29680
Tel 952 89 20 47
Stylish and modern marina restaurant serving tasty paellas and great *pescaito frito* (Andalusian fried fish platter). Good selection of desserts.

FUENGIROLA: Moochers €
Vegetarian **Map** C4
C/la Cruz 17, 39640
Tel 952 47 71 54
A warm and lively restaurant with soft, candlelit interiors and live music in the evening. Moochers specializes in vegetarian crèpes but seafood and chicken are also available. Rooftop terrace dining available in summer.

FUENGIROLA: Vegetalia €
Vegetarian **Map** C4
C/Santa Isabel 8, Los Boliches 29640
Tel 952 58 60 31 **Closed** Sun, Jul–Aug
Finnish-owned vegetarian restaurant with an excellent lunchtime buffet. Indulge in delicious home-made desserts.

Original wine press at La Fructuosa restaurant, Gaucin

GAUCÍN: La Fructuosa €€
Traditional **Map** C4
C/Convento 67, 29480
Tel 952 15 10 72 **Closed** Sun–Thu.
Comfortable Spanish-Moroccan-style restaurant with ceiling beams and an old wine press. Savour the views while sampling the fresh goat's cheese and honey.

GIBRALTAR: The Waterfront €€
Traditional **Map** C4
Queensway Quay, Marina Bay
Tel 350 20 04 56 66 **Closed** Good Fri; 25, 26, 31 Dec; 1 Jan
A charming waterside eating spot with idyllic sunset views. Sink your teeth into the amazing Cajun chicken, T-bone steaks and grilled sea bass. Also serves good vegetarian choices.

GIBRALTAR: Rib Room €€
Traditional **Map** C4
Rock Hotel, 3 Europa Road
Tel 350 20 07 30 00
Iconic restaurant in one of Gibraltar's most distinguished hotels, serving delicious modern British cuisine with Iberian and Moroccan influences.

JEREZ DE LA FRONTERA: Reino de Leon Gastrobar €
Fusion **Map** B3
C/Latorre, 8, 11402
Tel 956 32 29 15
Chic modern restaurant with interesting choices such as *chupa-chups cremoso de cheddar con regaliz* (creamy cheddar lollipops with liquorice). Finish with one of the inventive gin and tonics.

JEREZ DE LA FRONTERA: Bar Juanito €€
Traditional **Map** C4
C/Pascaderia Vieja 8, 11403
Tel 956 33 48 38 **Closed** Sun eve, Mon
Atmospheric tapas bar and restaurant serving exceptionally large portions of tapas; be sure to try the local artichokes.

For more information on types of restaurants *see p221*

234 | TRAVELLERS' NEEDS

Diners enjoying the seaview at Garum, Marbella

LA LINEA: La Marina €
Seafood   Map C4
Paseo Maritimo, La Atunara s/n, 11300
Tel *956 17 15 31*   **Closed** *Mon; 24,*
31 Dec
Large seaside restaurant with
nautical decor. Enjoy great bay
views while savouring delicious
chirlas marinera (clams).

LOS BARRIOS: Mesón El Copo €€
Seafood   Map C4
Calle La Almadraba 2 (Palmones),
11369
Tel *956 67 77 10*   **Closed** *Sun*
First-rate beachside restaurant
serving fresh local *urta* (sea
bream) and *gallineta* (Atlantic red
fish). Great home-made desserts.

MÁLAGA:
Antigua Casa de la Guardia €
Traditional   Map D3
Alameda Principal 18, 29015
Tel *952 21 46 80* **Closed** *Sun (except*
Holy Week, Feria & Dec)
One of Málaga's oldest and
most atmospheric wine cellar
bars. Their speciality tipple is
dark, rich Pedro Ximenez wine
served directly from the barrel.

The elegant Parador Gibralfaro restaurant,
Málaga

DK Choice

MÁLAGA: El Tintero €
Seafood   Map D3
Playa del Dedo s/n (El Palo), 29018
Tel *952 20 68 26*
Undoubtedly the noisiest
restaurant on the Costa del
Sol. However, the beachside
location, sweeping views
across the bay and magnificent
choice of fish dishes make El
Tintero a must. Go for the grilled
salmonetes (red mullet) or *rape*
(angler fish) in a rich garlic sauce.
Great value for money.

MÁLAGA: Mesón Astorga €
Traditional   Map D3
C/Gerona 11, 29006
Tel *952 34 25 63*   **Closed** *Sun*
Go to Mesón Astorga for *almejas*
(clams) and *boqueroncitos* (baby
anchovies), and try the fried
aubergine with sugar cane honey.

MÁLAGA:
Mesón Cortijo de Pepe €
Traditional   Map D3
Plaza de la Merced 2, 29012
Tel *952 22 40 71*   **Closed** *Tue*
Popular tapas bar that serves
succulent *calamares romana*
(squid fried in batter) and *gambas
a la plancha* (grilled prawns).

MÁLAGA: Café de Paris €€
Fusion   Map D3
C/Velez Málaga 8, 29016
Tel *952 00 35 88*   **Closed** *Sun,*
Mon eve
Stylish restaurant serving
modern Spanish-Mediterranean
dishes such as parmesan rice
and tasty pigeon.

MÁLAGA: Parador Gibralfaro €€
Traditional   Map D3
Castillo de Gibralfaro s/n, 29006
Tel *952 22 19 02*
Elegant restaurant in Málaga's
spectacular hilltop parador,

---

serving traditional fare such as
zoque and *gazpachelo* (standard
and fish versions of *gazpacho*).

MANILVA: Macues €€
Seafood   Map C4
Puerto Deportivo de la Duquesa s/n
Tel *952 89 03 95*   **Closed** *Mon, Sat*
lunch
Stylish place serving *dorada el sal*
(sea bream baked in salt) – a
regular favourite – and charcoal-
grilled steaks for meat lovers.

MARBELLA: Altamirano €
Seafood   Map C4
Plaza Altamirano 3, 29600
Tel *952 82 49 32* **Closed** *Wed; 8 Jan–*
15 Feb
Good value family-friendly
restaurant with a garden. Sample
the seafood specialities, such as
fritura malagueno (fried fish
platter) and *besugo a la brasa*
(barbecued sea bream).

MARBELLA: Garum €€
Fusion   Map C4
Paseo Marítimo 3, 29602
Tel *952 85 88 58*
Finnish-run restaurant with an
enclosed beachside terrace. Try
tasty pumpkin, *albóndigas* (meat-
balls), smoked lamb and steaks.

MARBELLA: Santiago €€
Seafood   Map C4
Avda Duque de Ahamada 5, 29602
Tel *952 77 00 78*
Great seafood institution dishing
out *almejas* (clams), *lubina* (sea
bass) and a variety of paellas.
Good tapas selection at the bar.

MARBELLA: El Portalon €€€
Traditional   Map C4
Crta Málaga-Cádiz km 178, 29600
Tel *952 62 78 80*   **Closed** *Sun eve*
Traditional restaurant that serves
delicious *lubina con verduras frescas*
(sea bass with fresh vegetables)
and *lechona al homo* (suckling
pig baked in a woodfired oven).

MARBELLA: Skina €€€
Fusion **Map** C4
C/Aduar 12, 29601
Tel 952 76 52 77 **Closed** Sun, Mon,
9–15 Dec, 7 Jan–3 Feb
Chic, intimate, old-town
restaurant with an eclectic mix of
dishes from rabbit terrine to sole
with artichokes and tomato.

MIJAS: El Mirlo Blanco €€
Traditional **Map** C3
Cuesta de la Villa 13, 29650
Tel 952 48 57 00 **Closed** Tue, 11 Jan–
11 Feb
Established Basque restaurant
serving dishes such as txangurro
(stuffed spider crab) and kokotxas
de bacalao pil pil (cod cheeks in
hot garlic, chilli and olive oil).

NERJA: Restaurante Jacky
International
Edificio Corona Locale 6, C/C
6, 29780
Tel 952 52 11 38
Intimate, quality restaurant
French and Mediterranear
Excellent menu de degusto
try the quail stuffed with f

PUERTO DE SANTA MA
Casa Flores
Traditional
Ribera del Rio 9, 11500
Tel 956 54 35 12
Excellent langostinos (ki
~rcebes (goose barnacles) and
doraua ~ \`ead bream) at this
family-run establishment.

PUERTO DE SANTA MARIA:
El Faro de el Puerto €€
Seafood **Map** B3
Crta de Fuentebravia km 0.5, 11500
Tel 956 87 09 52 **Closed** Sun eve
(except Aug)
Refined family-run restaurant set
in lush gardens serving delicious
lomo de pargo con berengenas (red
snapper with aubergine).

RONDA: Tragatapas €
Traditional **Map** C3
Calle Nueva 4, 29400
Tel 952 87 72 09
Cozy and unassuming, Tragatapas
offers inventive tapas such as goat's
cheese and asparagus, marinated
salmon and sautéed mushrooms,
all at a very good price.

RONDA: Mirador de La Espinela
€€
Traditional **Map** C3
Paseo de Blas Infante 1, 29400
Tel 952 87 13 67 **Closed** Sat & Sun
Smart restaurant in a converted
19th-century villa. Traditional
offerings include grilled trout and
chuletas de cerdo (pork cutlets).

RONDA: Pedro Romero €€
Map C3

soup, a
restaurant. Scintillating menu
degustación; impeccable service.

SAN FERNANDO:
Venta de Vargas €€
Traditional **Map** B4
Plaza de San Juan Vargas 11110
Tel 956 88 16 22
Former haunt of flamenco icon
Cameron de la Isla. The menu
here includes chocos de la bahia
(cuttlefish from the bay). Live
flamenco every now and then.

Subtle lighting at Tragabuches, Ronda

SANLUCAR DE BARRAMEDA:
€€
Map B3

Sun
onal
od
al

€€
Map B4
n. 79.3,

Chic restaur... across
the straits. Specializes in fresh
seafood, salads and pizzas. The
café serves great coffee and cakes.

TARIFA: Meson de Sancho €€
Traditional **Map** B4
Crta Cádiz-Málaga (N 340) km 94,
11380
Tel 956 68 81 27
Homely Andalusian inn serving
first-rate dishes. Order the sea
bream cooked in cognac or the
pierna de cordero (leg of lamb).

TORREMOLINOS:
Yate El Cordobés €
Seafood **Map** D3
Paseo Maritimo s/n (Bajondillo) 29620
Tel 952 38 49 56
Sample local seafood dishes
ranging from espetos de sardinas
(charcoal-cooked fresh sardines)
to mero en adobo (grouper with
garlic mayonnaise sauce).

TORREMOLINOS: Casa Juan €€
Seafood **Map** D3
C/San Ginés 18–24, 29620
Tel 952 37 35 12
Excellent value fish dishes at
this family-run establishment.
The bouillabaisse and fried sea-
food platter are popular draws.

The well-stocked wine cellar at El Faro del Puerto, Puerto de Santa Maria

For more information on types of restaurants see p221

TORREMOLINOS: Frutos €€
Traditional Map D3
Avda de la Riviera 80, 29620
Tel *952 38 15 40* **Closed** *Sun eve*
One of the grand old Costa del
Sol restaurants. Enjoy classic
dishes such as *judiones a la
Granja* (Castilian style white
beans) and a wide selection of
fresh fish. There is a well-stocked
wine cellar.

DK Choice

**Torremolinos:
Nuevo Lanjarón** €€
Traditional Map D3
C/Europa 10, 29620
Tel *952 38 87 74* **Closed** *Mon*
This long-established family-
run place is probably the best
value restaurant on the Costa
del Sol. Choose from a variety
of inexpensive set menus that
include fish and meat dishes.
Try the exquisite *estofado de
ternera* (veal stew) or the
generous *fritura malagueña*
(fried fish platter), followed by
home-made flan. Good service.

**VEJER DE LA FRONTERA:
Venta Pinto** €€
Seafood Map B4
C/La Barca de Vejer 11150
Tel *956 45 08 77*
Traditional restaurant with
specialities including *perdiz roja
asada* (roasted partridge) and
rodaballo al horno con alcaparras
(baked turbot with capers).

**ZAHARA DE LOS ATUNES: Casa
Juanito** €
Seafood Map B4
C/Alcalde Ruiz Cana 7, 11393
Tel *956 43 92 11* **Closed** *Wed*
Charming restaurant with terrace
dining. Sample exquisite seafood
dishes, such as the excellent local
tuna. Good tapas bar.

Granada and Almería

**ALMERÍA: Rincón de
Juan Pedro** €
Traditional Map F3
C/Federico Castro 2, 04130
Tel *950 23 58 19* **Closed** *Mon*
A very popular tapas bar, offering
pungent hams, chorizos and
cheeses, as well as local specialities
such as *trigo a la cortijera* (wheat
berry and sausage stew).

ALMERÍA: Bodega Bellavista €€
Traditional Map F3
*Urbanizacion Bellavista, Llanos de
Alquian, 04130*
Tel *950 29 71 56* **Closed** *Sun eve &
Mon*
This charming old-fashioned
restaurant is located close to the
airport. It offers classic regional
seafood – shellfish dominates
the menu – and meat dishes,
using fresh market produce.
Great wine list.

ALMERÍA: Casa Sevilla €€
Seafood Map F3
C/Rueda López, 04004
Tel *950 27 29 12* **Closed** *Sun,
Mon eve*
Sociable family restaurant serving
fresh seafood. Go for the *tempura
de bacalao sobre arroz meloso de
hongos* (cod tempura on a bed of
creamy mushroom rice). Monthly
wine tastings.

ALMERÍA: Club de Mar €€
Seafood Map F3
Playa de Almadrabillas, 1, 04007
Tel *950 23 50 43* **Closed** *Tue*
Chic restaurant with a lovely
seafront terrace in Almeria's
prestigious yacht club.
Renowned for its *zarzuela de
pescado y marisco* (bouillabaise)
and *fritura de pescado* (fried fish
platter). Excellent service.

ALMERÍA: Valentin €€
Seafood Map F3
C/Tenor Iribarne 19, 04001
Tel *950 26 44 75* **Closed** *Mon, Sep*
A very popular *marisqueria*
(restaurant specializing in
shellfish) where everything is
market fresh.

**ALMERÍA:
Torreluz Mediterraneo** €€€
Fusion Map F3
Plaza Flores 1, 04001
Tel *950 28 14 25* **Closed** *Sun,
Mon eve*
Elegant restaurant with creative
dishes such as squid with
coriander pesto. Leave room for
the chocolate soufflé with mint
sauce and orange compote.

BUBÍON: Teide €
Traditional Map E3
C/Carretera s/n, 18412
Tel *958 76 30 37* **Closed** *Second
fortnight in Jun*
Charming stone-built restaurant
with a tree-shaded garden. Serves
home-cooked food such as *migas*
(fried breadcrumbs with garlic)
and *choto asado* (roast kid).

CARBONERAS: El Cabo €€
Seafood Map F3
Paseo Marítimo 67, 04140
Tel *950 13 06 24* **Closed** *Mon*
Friendly beachside restaurant
close to Cabo de Gata National
Park. Try innovative seafood
dishes such as the squid stuffed
with spinach and pine nuts.

**GRANADA: Antigua Bodega
Castañeda** €
Traditional Map E3
C/Elvira 5, 18010
Tel *958 21 54 64*
Authentic tapas bar with barrels,
beams and colourful tiles. Feast
on Trevélez mountain ham, squid
and sardines and enjoy a chilled
fino on the side.

Seafood restaurant Casa Juan in Torremolinos

GRANADA: Chikito €
Traditional **Map** E3
Plaza del Campillo 9, 18009
Tel *958 22 33 64* **Closed** *Wed*
Attractive tapas bar-restaurant built on the site of a former Garcia Lorca haunt. Be brave and dig into the tortilla Sacromonte – omelette with marrow, brains, herbs and bull's testicles!

GRANADA: Restaurante Carmela
€
Modern **Map** E3
Calle Colcha, 13 (Corner of Pavaneras), 18009
Tel *958 22 57 94*
Cheery restaurant serving playful versions of classic Andalusian cuisine. Start with the *croquetas de morcilla concebolla caramelizada* (black pudding croquettes with caramelized onions).

GRANADA:
Carmen del San Miguel €€
Traditional **Map** E3
Plaza Torres Bermejas 3, 18009
Tel *958 22 67 23* **Closed** *Sun eve, all day Sun in summer*
Attractive terrace restaurant overlooking the Alhambra, serving up traditional dishes made from fresh market produce.

GRANADA:
Mirador de Mirayma €€
Traditional **Map** D3
C/Pianista Gracia Carrillo 2, 18010
Tel *958 22 82 90* **Closed** *Sun eve*
This delightful patio restaurant inside the Albaicín offers great city views. Try the fresh *remojón* (salad with salt cod, olives and orange) and *salmorejo* (thicker version of gazpacho).

DK Choice

Granada: Restaurante Damasqueros €€
Traditional **Map** E3
Calle Realejo 3, 18009
Tel *958 21 05 50* **Closed** *Sun eve, Mon*
An award-winning tapas bar that serves modern interpretations of traditional fare. The rack of lamb with *migas* (stuffing), grapes and melon is a tasty favourite, and you can't go wrong with one of their risottos or *guisos* (stews).

GRANADA: Ruta del Azafrán €€
Fusion **Map** E3
Paseo de los Tristes 1, 18010
Tel *958 22 68 82* **Closed** *24 Dec*
A neat, modern restaurant beside the Darro River serving an eclectic range of dishes, including seafood, vegetarian, Italian and Arabic food.

Charming outdoor seating at the popular Ruta del Veleta, Granada

GRANADA: Ruta del Veleta €€
Traditional **Map** E3
Crta Sierra Nevada 136, km 5,4. Cenes de la Vega, 18190
Tel *958 48 61 34* **Closed** *Sun eve*
Popular regional restaurant on the old road to Sierra Nevada. Feast on hearty dishes such as roast kid, seasonal game and good seafood.

GRANADA: Tragalios €€
Modern **Map** E3
Calle San Matias 21, 18009
Tel *685 19 37 41* **Closed** *15 Jan–5 Feb*
Colourful restaurant with innovative Interpretations of regional fare, including Iberian pork, aged beef, fresh fish and plenty of local produce.

HUERCAL ALMERÍA:
Cueva Blanca €€
Fusion **Map** F3
C/Churre 13, 04240
Tel *950 30 51 37* **Closed** *Sun & Mon*
Cozy cave-restaurant with imaginative dishes such as *salmon en sidra* (salmon in cider) and *setas en salsa de bacon* (mushrooms in bacon sauce).

Place settings at upmarket restaurant La Finca, Loja

LOJA: La Finca €€
Traditional **Map** D3
Hotel La Bobadilla, Autovia Granada-Sevilla, 18300
Tel *958 32 18 61* **Closed** *Sun & Mon May–Jul*
Delicious seafood, meat and vegetable dishes – all made using local ingredients – are served here.

MOTRIL: Tropical €
Traditional **Map** E3
Avda Rodriguez Acosta 23, 18600.
Tel *958 60 04 50* **Closed** *Sun, Jun*
Friendly seaside inn serving classic Andalusian fare. Try the lobster and rice stew.

ORGIVA: El Limonero €
Traditional **Map** E3
C/Yanez 27, 18400
Tel *958 78 51 57*
Popular joint serving healthy traditional dishes such as knuckle of lamb and oven baked sea bream. Fine salads and pastas.

ROQUETAS DE MAR: Alejandro
€€
Seafood/Fusion **Map** F3
Avda Antonio Machado 32, 04740
Tel *950 32 24 08* **Closed** *Mon; Sun & Tue eve*
Ultra-smart restaurant specializing in exquisite seafood fusion dishes. Splash out on the shellfish tasting menu.

SALOBREÑA: By Larius
Argentina Steakhouse €€
Traditional **Map** E3
Paseo de Velilla 9, 18690
Tel *958 63 93 58* **Closed** *Sun & Mon lunch*
Elegant restaurant right by the beach offering exquisitely prepared traditional favourites.

Vera: Terrazza Carmona €€
Traditional **Map** F3
C/del Mar 1, 04620
Tel *950 39 07 60* **Closed** *Mon*
Award-winning restaurant specializing in regional dishes.

For more information on types of restaurants *see p221*

SHOPS AND MARKETS

Shopping in Andalusia is a highly pleasurable business, particularly if you approach it in a typically Spanish manner. Here, shopping fits in with the climate, always respects the siesta and is meant to be an unhurried, leisurely activity, punctuated with frequent breaks for coffee and tapas.

While a number of European chain stores and franchises are beginning to appear all over Spain, the towns and villages of the south are refreshingly full of shops and businesses that are unique to the area. The region is renowned for its high-quality, traditional arts and crafts, and there is an overwhelming choice of ceramics, leather goods, marquetry, jewellery in filigree silver, and sweets and biscuits.

World-famous wines can be had from the *bodegas* of Jerez, Montilla, Málaga and Sanlúcar de Barrameda. A visit to a *bodega*, an experience in itself, is the best way to become familiar with the variety of wines on offer.

Many shops still provide a charming personal service. Although few assistants speak English, most are very obliging.

Calle Sierpes, one of the busiest shopping streets in Seville

When to Shop

Spanish shops tend to close during the afternoon siesta (except for department stores and touristy souvenir shops in the large towns). Most shops open at 9:30am and close at 1:30pm. They usually reopen about 4:30pm or 5pm, and stay open until around 8pm. These times will obviously vary from shop to shop; boutiques, for example, rarely open before 10am. Times also tend to vary during summer – some shops close altogether in the afternoon heat, while others will stay open later than usual, in order to take full advantage of the large numbers of visitors.

Many shops – especially if they are in small towns – close on Saturday afternoons. This practice, however, is now gradually disappearing. Sales generally take place in January and July, though shops may also sometimes offer pre-Christmas discounts or start their sales in late December.

How to Pay

It is still customary among Spaniards to pay in cash. While many shops, especially the larger stores, now accept major credit cards, few take traveller's cheques.

You are entitled to exchange goods if you can produce a receipt, although this does not apply to items bought in a sale. Large shops and department stores tend to give credit notes rather than cash refunds. It is a good idea to check the shop's policy with a sales assistant before you buy anything.

One of several styles of plate made in Seville

Vat Exemption

Visitors to Spain who come from countries outside the European Union can claim a 16 per cent refund of sales tax (*IVA*, pronounced "eeva" in Spanish) on items bought at large department stores such as **Cortefiel** and **El Corte Inglés**. For each item that you purchase costing more than 600 pesetas you need to collect a form from the store's central cash desk. You should have this stamped both as you leave Spain and on re-entering your own country. You then need to return the stamped form to the shop where the purchase was made, which, in turn, will send you a cheque for 16 per cent of the value of the articles.

An array of fans at Díaz, Calle Sierpes, Seville

Handmade Fans

A classic souvenir from Andalusia, a fan is useful in the searing heat. The most exclusive are wooden, carved and painted by hand.

Castanets

Castanets, a classic flamenco musical instrument, can be bought in a medley of sizes, made of wood or plastic.

Guitars

In the land of flamenco, guitars are a speciality. Workshops in Córdoba produce top-quality, custom-made guitars, many of which are destined for famous guitarists.

Mantillas

A *mantilla* is a headdress of lace draped over a large and ornate comb which is crafted from tortoiseshell or made in plastic.

The Flavours of Andalusia

Andalusian gastronomy reflects locally grown produce. An astonishing range of olive oils is available, and the region's grapes are made into sherry vinegars, as well as some of Spain's most distinctive wines (*see p226*). Almonds are used to make delicious sweets, such as turrón, a type of nougat.

Olive oil from the provinces of Córdoba and Sevilla

Sherry wine vinegars produced by sherry *bodegas*

Yemas, sweets produced by nuns in the Convento de San Leandro (*see p81*)

Marmalade from the Convento de Santa Paula (*see p94*) in Seville

Herbs and Spices

Almost 800 years of Moorish occupation in Andalusia left a distinctive mark on the region's cuisine. Many dishes are flavoured with fragrant spices once imported from the East, such as cumin, coriander, paprika, and strands of saffron. Markets are the best place to buy exotic spices and locally grown herbs, which are sold loose by weight.

Saffron threads

Pimentón (paprika)

Coriander seeds

Cumin seeds

ENTERTAINMENT IN ANDALUSIA

In Andalusia there is almost always a lively buzz in the streets, and activities such as bar-hopping and people-watching can provide enough entertainment in themselves to fill up any spare moment of your holiday.

But there is also plenty more going on. Southern Spain boasts a busy programme of traditional fiestas (see pp42–3), as well as a variety of annual cultural festivals (see pp38–41), bullfights (see pp30–31) and sporting fixtures. There's also music and dance in abundance – Andalusia is, after all, the home of flamenco.

Given the mild climate, many events take place out of doors; in summer, when daytime temperatures soar to up to 45°C (113°F), they don't start until late in the evening, when the air is cooler. Many cultural events and concerts start at around midnight.

Flamenco guitarist playing at a festival at the Teatro de la Maestranza, Seville

Practical Information

Tourist information offices are the best places to find out what is on locally, but there are also two useful listings magazines worth looking out for: *El Giraldillo* (published in Seville) and *Qué Hacer/What's On* (published in Málaga). Both appear monthly, cover all of Andalusia and are free.

Each major city has its own commercial websites offering a wealth of local information, but a number of websites covering the whole of Spain, notably **Lanetro** and **Guía del Ocio**, are also worth consulting; just choose the province in which you are interested from the drop-down menu.

Booking Tickets

It is usually possible to book tickets for major sports events, operas, concerts and festivals in advance at the venue's booking office, by phone or online. Alternatively, use an agency that specializes in booking tickets for all entertainments, such as **Ticketmaster** and **Entradas.com.**

Flamenco

Seville and Jerez de la Frontera claim to be the birthplaces of flamenco, the traditional music and dance of Andalusia (see pp32–3). Both cities have *tablaos*, bars and restaurants with floorshows where the admission usually includes dinner or at least a drink. In Seville, it is best to look for venues in the Barrio de Santa Cruz. A good starting point is the **Museo del Baile Flamenco** (see p79). Other reliable venues include **La Carbonería** and **La Casa de la Memoria de Al Andalus**.

Jerez has a **Centro Andaluz de Flamenco**, as well as several *tablaos*. In Granada, there are traditional flamenco venues in Sacromonte (see p197) and the Albaicín – among them, **Sala Albayzín** and **Zambra María La Canastera**. Córdoba also has a couple of flamenco bars, notably **El Cardenal** and **La Bulería**.

The two main flamenco festivals are Seville's **Bienal de Flamenco**, which is held in theatres all over the city in even-numbered years, and Córdoba's **Concurso Nacional de Arte Flamenco**, which happens every third year, the next being in 2016.

Theatre

Most drama staged in Andalusia is in Spanish, but there are occasional performances by visiting international companies or mime artists. The theatre season includes not only plays, but also classical music, dance and opera. Seville's main theatres are the **Teatro de la Maestranza** (see p72), the **Teatro Lope de Vega** (see p101) and the **Teatro Central**.

In Córdoba, the place to go is the **Gran Teatro**. Granada's two main theatres are the **Teatro Alhambra** and the **Teatro Isabel La Católica**. Málaga has the **Teatro Cánovas** and the **Teatro Cervantes**.

Gran Teatro, Córdoba, one of the city's leading venues for theatre

Rosario Flores, a famous Andalusian singing star, performing at one of her concerts

Cinema

Foreign films shown in mainstream cinemas in Andalusia are usually dubbed into Spanish. Original-version (VO for *version original*) films are shown in cinemas such as **Avenida 5 Cines** in Seville, the **Filmoteca de Andalucía** in Córdoba and the **Complejo Cinematográfico Gran Marbella** on the Costa del Sol. From June to late August, you can also attend a *cine de verano*, an open-air "summer cinema".

Opera and Classical Music

In Seville, most operas, including those by prestigious international companies, are performed at either the **Teatro Lope de Vega** or the **Teatro de la Maestranza** *(see p72)*. For something less high-brow, Spain has its own brand of operetta, *zarzuela*.

As for classical music, all the main cities maintain their own orchestras (such as the **Real Orquesta Sinfónica de Sevilla**). Granada is great for classical music. As well as having the **Centro Cultural Manuel de Falla** as a venue, it hosts the **Festival Internacional de Música y Danza** *(see p39)*, during which concerts are held against the backdrop of the Alhambra.

Other Live Music

Touring international rock and pop stars mostly play their Spanish dates in Madrid or Barcelona, but they sometimes make it to Seville or other cities in Andalusia. Such concerts usually take place in football stadiums and bullrings. Spain has its own thriving rock-pop scene. Andalusian musicians, in particular, have drawn on their flamenco roots to create distinctive fusions between musical genres. Two other great influences on the contemporary music of Andalusia are North Africa and Latin America. Jazz also has a devoted public in Andalusia: Seville has the **Naima Jazz Café** and Granada has the **Festival de Jazz**. To find out where the up-and-coming acts are playing, ask around or keep an eye out for flyers.

Another interesting musical tradition is represented by *la tuna*: groups of students dressed as minstrels playing lutes and mandolins and singing serenades in streets and squares.

La tuna, traditional singers in Santa Cruz, Seville

Nightlife

Nights out in Andalusia begin late and can easily go on until dawn. The first stop is often a *bar de copas* (also called a *pub*), which differs from a tapas bar in that no food is served and spirits replace wine and beer for drinking. Some such bars have DJs at weekends. The next stop is a *discoteca*, which may open at midnight but not fill up for a couple of hours. There are clubs in the city centres, but many are on industrial estates or outside of town, where the noise won't bother residents.

Where to go depends on your age, your musical tastes and your sexual orientation – each city has a few gay and lesbian clubs. If you aren't concerned about being seen in the hippest places, reliably fun areas to go bar-hopping in are the Santa Cruz quarter in Seville, the Judería in Córdoba and around the Plaza del Realejo and the lower Albaicín (especially the Carrera del Darro and the Paseo de los Tristes) in Granada.

The summer nightlife of the holiday resorts on the Costa del Sol is completely different from that of the cities of Andalusia. Here you'll still find *bares de copa* and *discotecas*, but also many places geared to foreign tourists.

For a smart night out, try one of Andalusia's casinos. Don't dress too casually, and take some ID with you.

A display of flamenco dancing in a bar in Seville

Real Escuela Andaluza de Arte Ecuestre, Jerez de la Frontera

Bullfighting

The **Maestranza** bullring *(see p72)* in Seville is mythical among bullfighting fans, and some of the most important bullfights in Spain are held here during the Feria de Abril *(see p42)*. Ronda *(see pp180–81)*, Córdoba and Granada also have their own bullrings and a renowned season.

The season usually runs from April to October. Booking tickets in advance is essential if the matadors are well known, and advisable if you want to sit in the shade *(sombra)*. It may be easier to get tickets for *novilladas*, fights involving matadors who are not yet fully qualified. Tickets are sold at the bullring's booking office.

Tile for Seville's Betis football club

Football

Football is the most popular spectator sport in Spain. Seville has two rival teams, FC Sevilla, based at the **Estadio Ramón Sánchez Pizjuán**, and Betis, who play at the **Estadio Benito Villamarín**.

Other successful teams in the region are Cádiz, Málaga and Recreativo de Huelva (the oldest football club in Spain).

The Spanish football league has three divisions, with league matches being played on Sunday (sometimes Saturday) evenings from September to June. During the season, teams also compete in an eliminatory tournament for the Copa del Rey (King's Cup) and for international trophies; such matches are usually played midweek. Important fixtures are televised, although some are only shown on pay-per-view channels. To see a live game, it is advisable to book ahead at the stadium or online.

Entertainment for Children

In Spain, children go wherever adults go at just about any time of day or night. If you want to take yours for a treat, there are several options. **Isla Mágica** *(see p108)* in Seville is Andalusia's

biggest theme park, while **Tivoli World** is the largest amusement park on the Costa del Sol. Every city and strip of coast has its water park designed specifically for older children *(see p249)*. A cable car, the **Teleférico Benalmádena**, takes off from beside Tivoli World to the top of Mount Calamorro, 800 m (2,600 ft) above sea level. There's another good cable-car ride in Gibraltar *(see pp176–7)*. In Seville, a boat trip down the river can be fun, as can be the trip across the Bay of Cádiz in a *vaporcito (see p169)*. Horse and carriages travel round the streets in Marbella, Córdoba and Seville, and most beach resorts also have road trains.

The desert in the centre of Almería was once used as a film set for westerns *(see p208)*, and kids love the shoot-outs staged by the small Wild West town of **Oasys Parque Tematico Mini-Hollywood**, near Tabernas. Another good show – this time of performing horses – is put on by the **Real Escuela Andaluza de Arte Ecuestre** *(see p166)* in Jerez de la Frontera. Jerez also has Andalusia's best collection of exotic animals in the **Zoo Botánico**; the safari park **Selwo Aventura**, outside Estepona, is also good. There are aquariums at Roquetas del Mar *(see p208)* in Almería and Benalmádena, a town that also offers **Selwo Marina**, Andalusia's only dolphinarium and ice penguinarium.

The port of Gibraltar from the vantage point of a cable car

DIRECTORY

Practical Information

El Giraldillo
w elgiraldillo.es

Guía del Ocio
w guiadelocio.com

Lanetro
w lanetro.com

Booking Tickets

Entradas.com
Tel 902 20 09 20.
w entradas.com

Ticketmaster
w ticketmaster.es

Flamenco

SEVILLE

Bienal de Flamenco
Tel 95 42 34 46.

La Carbonería
Calle Levies 18.
Map 1 D1 (6 E3).
Tel 954 21 44 60.

Casa de la Memoria de Al Andalus
C/ Cuna 6.
Map 3 C1 (6 D2).
Tel 954 56 06 70.

CÓRDOBA

La Bulería
Calle Pedro López 3.
Tel 957 48 38 89.

El Cardenal
Calle Torrijos 10
Tel 957 48 31 12.
w tablaocardenal.es

Concurso Nacional de Arte Flamenco
Tel 957 48 00 19.

GRANADA

Sala Albayzín
Carretera de Murcia,
Mirador San Cristóbal.
Tel 958 80 46 46.
w flamencoalbayzin.com

Zambra María La Canastera
Camino del
Sacromonte 89.
Tel 958 12 11 83.
w granadainfo.com/canastera

JEREZ DE LA FRONTERA

Centro Andaluz de Flamenco
Palacio Pemartin,
Plaza San Juan 1.
Tel 956 90 21 34.
w centroandaluzdeflamenco.es

Theatre

SEVILLE

Teatro Central
Avenida José Gálvez, Isla
de la Cartuja. Map 1 C2.
Tel 955 03 72 00.
w juntadeandalucia.es/culturaydeporte/teatrocentral/

CÓRDOBA

Gran Teatro
Avenida Gran Capitán 3.
Tel 957 48 02 37.
w teatrocordoba.com

GRANADA

Teatro Alhambra
Molinos 56.
Tel 958 02 80 00.

Teatro Isabel La Católica
Acera del Casino.
Tel 958 22 29 07.

MÁLAGA

Teatro Cánovas
Plaza de El Ejido.
Tel 951 30 89 02.

Teatro Cervantes
Calle Ramos Marín.
Tel 952 22 41 09.
w teatrocervantes.com

Cinema

SEVILLE

Avenida 5 Cines
Marqués de Paradas 15.
Tel 954 29 30 25.

CÓRDOBA

Filmoteca de Andalucía
Medina y Corella 5.
Tel 957 10 36 27.
w filmotecadeandalucia.com

MARBELLA

Complejo Cinematográfico Gran Marbella
Tel 952 81 64 21.
w cinesgranmarbella.com

Opera and Classical Music

SEVILLE

Teatro de la Maestranza
Paseo de Colón 22.
Map 3 B2 (5 C5).
Tel 954 22 33 44.
w teatrodelamaestranza.es

Real Orquesta Sinfónica de Sevilla
Tel 954 56 15 36.
w rossevilla.es

GRANADA

Centro Cultural Manuel de Falla
Paseo de los Mártires.
Tel 958 22 21 88.
w manueldefalla.org

Festival Internacional de Música y Danza
Tel 958 22 18 44.
w granadafestival.org

Other Live Music

SEVILLE

Naima Jazz Café
Calle Trajano 47.
Map 1 C5 (5 C1).
Tel 954 38 24 85.
w naimacafejazz.com

GRANADA

Festival de Jazz de Granada
Casa Morisca,
Horno del Oro 14.
Tel 958 21 59 80.
w jazzgranada.net

Nightlife

SEVILLE

Gran Casino Aljarafe
Avenida de la Arboleda,
Tomares.
Tel 902 42 42 22.
w grancasinoaljarafe.com

Metro
Calle Betis 29.

Regoneo
Calle Betis 31.

BENALMÁDENA

Casino Torrequebrada
Avenida del Sol.
Tel 952 57 73 00.
w casinotorrequebrada.com

GRANADA

Granada 10
Cárcel Baja 10.
Tel 958 22 40 01.
w granada10.com

Marbella
Casino Nueva Andalucía
Hotel Andalucía Plaza.
Tel 952 81 40 00.
w casinomarbella.com

PUERTO DE SANTA MARÍA

Casino Bahía de Cádiz
Tel 956 87 10 42.
w casinobahiadecadiz.es

Bullfighting

CÓRDOBA

Plaza de Toros
Avenida de Gran Vía
Parque.
Tel 957 23 25 07.

GRANADA

Plaza de Toros
Avenida Doctor Olóriz 25.
Tel 958 27 24 51.

Football

Estadio Benito Villamarín
Avenida Heliópolis,
Seville.
Tel 902 19 19 07.
w realbetisbalompie.es

Estadio Ramón Sánchez Pizjuán (Sevilla FC)
Avenida Eduardo Dato,
Seville. Map 4 F2.
Tel 902 51 00 11.
w sevillafc.es

Entertainment for Children

BENALMÁDENA

Selwo Marina
Parque de la Paloma.
Tel 902 19 04 82.
w selwomarina.com

Teleférico Benalmádena
Explanada de Tivoli.
Tel 902 19 04 82.
w teleferico benalmadena.com

Tivoli World
Arroyo de la Miel.
Tel 952 57 70 16.
w tivoli.es

Estepona
Selwo Aventura
Autovía Costa del Sol, Las
Lomas del Monte.
Tel 902 19 04 82.
w selwo.es

Jerez de la Frontera
Zoo Botánico
Calle Taxdirt.
Tel 956 14 97 85.
w zoobotanicojerez.com

Tabernas
Oasys Parque Tematico
Mini-Hollywood
Tabernas, Almería.
Tel 950 36 52 36.
w oasysparquetematico.com

OUTDOOR ACTIVITIES AND SPECIALIST HOLIDAYS

Andalusia has a perfect climate for enjoying a range of outdoor activities, with comparatively few cold or wet days, and reliable sunshine most of the year. Its coastline offers a great variety of watersports – from windsurfing on the Atlantic coast, to scuba diving in the clear, calm waters of the Mediterranean. Away from the seashore, there are many golf courses and some great countryside – mostly hilly or mountainous – suitable for hiking and horse riding. In winter, skiers head for Europe's southernmost winter-sport resort on the slopes of the Sierra Nevada.

Walking and Trekking

Andalusia has a huge variety of landscapes suitable for walking: from coastal fringes, through forests, to mountain ranges. Spring is the best time to be outdoors: temperatures are mild, and the landscape blossoms with wildflowers. Mid-summer is best avoided because of the extreme heat and the risk of dehydration.

Two popular areas for hiking are the Alpujarras *(see pp204–5)* and the Sierra de Grazalema *(see p178)*, but all of the region's nature reserves have marked footpaths.

Always carry a good map. The Spanish army (Servicio Geográfico del Ejercito) produces a useful series of 1:50,000 maps, but the best are the 1:25,000-series maps published by the Centro Nacional de Información Geográfica (CNIG). Wear good walking shoes, preferably boots, and long trousers to avoid lacerations from spiky Mediterranean shrubs. Bring a hat and, if you are going to be gaining altitude, a warm jacket. Always carry drinking water.

For more advice, contact the **Federación Andaluza de**

Montañismo. Companies such as **Andalucian Adventures** *(see Specialist Holidays)* and **Spanish Steps** offer guided walks through the region.

Cycling

Andalusia's terrain is mainly mountainous, which discourages all but the hardiest cyclist. Added to this, there are few quiet backroads to use as alternatives to busy main roads. However, the trend of converting disused railway lines into "green ways" (*vias verdes*) has created 12 traffic-free cycling routes, such as the 55-km (34-mile) Via Verde del Aceite (Olive Oil Green Way) between Jaén and Alcaudete. To locate green ways, see the **Fundación de los Ferrocarriles Españoles** website. If you want to go on an organized cycling holiday with accommodation arranged for you, try **Biking Andalucia**.

Fishing

Andalusia offers good seafishing off its coasts as well as rather more limited

Fishing at a beach on Andalusia's Mediterranean coast

opportunities for freshwater fishing in its scattered reservoirs and rivers, such as in the Cazorla Nature Reserve *(see p160)*. For information about where to go and permits needed, contact the regional fishing association, the **Federación Andaluza de Pesca Deportiva**.

Wildlife and Birdwatching

The best place to get close to Andalusia's wildlife is the Doñana National Park *(see pp134–5)*, but other nature reserves in the region also offer good opportunities for wildflower- and bird-spotting. Contact **Iberian Wildlife** for tours. Several companies run whale-watching trips out of Tarifa harbour *(see p174)*; among them is the **Foundation for Information and Research on Marine Mammals**.

Equestrian Sports

The horse forms a proud part of Andalusia's traditions, as can

Hiking down from the Sierra Nevada through the Alpujarras

be seen during Seville's April Fair *(see p42)*, the pilgrimage to El Rocío *(see p42)* and many other fiestas. The undisputed equestrian capital of Andalusia is Jerez de la Frontera *(see p166)*, home of the Real Escuela Andaluza de Arte Ecuestre, which stages regular shows featuring dancing horses.

A day's trek on horseback can be a splendid way to get to know the countryside of Andalusia. There are stables everywhere that will organize anything from a brief outing to an extended riding holiday. Two of them are **Dallas Love** in the Alpujarras and **Los Alamos** on the Costa de la Luz. For all things to do with horses, the organization to contact is the **Federación Andaluza de Hípica**.

Horse riding on the deserted Atlantic beach of Zahara, near Cádiz

The stunning golf course at La Cala de Mijas, near the beaches of Málaga

Golf

Andalusia boasts more than 90 golf courses, mainly concentrated on the Costa del Sol (also known as the "Costa Golf") and around the major cities. Most have 18 holes and are open to non-members on payment of a green fee; advance booking is recommended.

The largest golf club in Andalusia is **La Cala de Mijas**, which has three 18-hole courses and one six-hole course. Another outstanding course can be found at **Montecastillo**, in Jerez de la Frontera, which is used for the Volvo Masters and other important tournaments. To find your nearest golf course, consult the **Federación Andaluza de Golf**.

Tennis

Tennis is extremely popular in Andalusia. To find out where to play, ask around locally. Many large hotels have courts available for the use of guests, and there are also private clubs you can join. An inexpensive option is to book a court at the local sports centre. For more information, contact the **Federación Andaluza de Tenis.**

Watersports

Watersports such as kayaking and waterskiing are available at all major resorts along the coast. Sea-going boats can be hired at most of the marinas. For information about sailing in the waters off Andalusia, contact the **Real Federación Española de Vela**.

Tarifa *(see p177)* has ideal conditions for wind- and kite-surfing; Hotel Hurricane *(see p219)* will point you towards lessons and equipment rental. The headlands at La Herradura, on the coast of Granada province, and around the Cabo de Gata in Almería are known for their scuba diving. The **Federación Española de Actividades Subacuáticas** will direct you to the nearest dive school, where you can try an introductory dive or sign up for an intensive course.

Andalusia also has ten water parks *(parques acuáticos)* especially aimed at children, with slides and wave pools. They are at Torre del Mar, Torremolinos, Granada, Mijas, Córdoba, Seville, Almuñecar (on the coast of Granada), Puerto de Santa Maria, Huelva and Vera (in Almería).

Air Sports

To find out where and how to hang-glide, balloon or parachute over Andalusia, contact the **Federación Andaluza de los Deportes Aéreos**.

Because of its normally reliable weather conditions, Andalusia is considered a good place for parachuting: **Skydive Spain** has its own drop zone near Seville and runs beginners' courses as well as taking clients on tandem jumps. For balloon trips, check the **Balloon Flights Spain** website for details.

Skiing

The **Sierra Nevada** *(see p203)* is Europe's southernmost skiing resort. Its base station is at 2,100 m (6,890 ft), and its highest run starts from 3,300 m (10,800 ft). The resort has 80 pistes, with a longest continual run of almost 6 km (4 miles) down the Pista del Águila.

Kite-surfing, a popular activity on the beaches of windy Tarifa

The impressive and atmospheric Turkish baths in Granada

Naturism

Topless bathing is tacitly accepted at all resorts, most of which have one or more discreet, officially recognized naturist beaches in a cove away from the main beach. **Vera Playa Club** in Almería is a hotel specifically for nudists, and **Costa Natura** near Estepona is a residential "village" also dedicated to naturism. For further information about naturism, contact the **Asociación Naturista-Nudista de Andalucía**.

Spas and Arab baths

Andalusia's traditional spas are mainly small, out-of-the-way towns where springs of thermal or medicinal waters supply hotels-cum- sanatoriums that treat patients with a range of ailments. The main ones are Alhama de Almería, Sierra Alhamilla (Almería), Alhama de Granada, Alicun de las Torres (Granada), Graena (near Guadix), Lanjarón (in the Alpujarras), San Andrés (Jaén), Carratraca (Málaga), Fuente Armaga at Tolox (Málaga) and Fuente Amarga at Chiclana in Cádiz. Contact the **Asociación Nacional de Estaciones Termales** for further details.

Spa hotels have seen a huge growth in popularity over the past few years. These hotels tend to be larger, luxury properties and are often beachside or complemented with a golf course. The spa facilities are normally reserved for the use of hotel guests and tend to focus more on pampering and beauty treatments rather than providing health-enhancing therapy.

The spa at **Gran Hotel Guadalpin Banus** (Puerto Banus, Marbella coast) specializes in Oriental Spa treatments, with Japanese and Chinese influences as well as meditation, yoga and pilates classes. Guests at the **Hotel La Fuente de la Higuera**, in Ronda, can choose from a range of facials, wraps and massages or have a soak in the Turkish baths. **Hotel Villa Padierna Palace** in Marbella focuses more on well-being, offering slimming and anti-stress treatments. The serenity spa at **Las Dunas**, in Estepona, uses Ligne St Barth products from the French Caribbean in all of its pampering treatments. The **Marbella Club Hotel** *(see p218)* has a beachfront spa that offers 99 thalasso, body and beauty treatments, including the seashell facial massage. The Elysium Spa at **NH Sotogrande** (Sotogrande) offers treatments such as hydromassage and a colour-therapy relaxation room.

When Andalusia was under the sway of the Moors, it had many public bathhouses – the equivalent to Turkish baths. The last one closed in the 17th century, however private companies have been recreating their own "Arab baths", with hot and cold rooms and massages available, in the cities of Seville, Córdoba, Málaga and Granada. Sessions need to be reserved – and, in some cases, paid for – in advance.

Specialist Holidays

A good way to spend a week or two in Andalusia while learning something useful at the same time is to go on a special-interest holiday. If you want to get deep into the heart of Andalusia, you could try a residential flamenco dancing workshop at **Cortijo del Caño** in Granada, for example.

Cooking is another way to learn something about your surroundings. **Annie B's Spanish Kitchen** runs residential courses in Mediterranean cooking, while at **L'Atelier** in the Alpujarras you'll be taught vegan and vegetarian cuisine.

Learning to speak Spanish is another obvious way to make a holiday yield tangible benefits, but be warned: you may pick up an Andaluz accent rather than the more neutral pronunciation of central Spain. Many private companies run courses in Spanish lasting from a week to several months, but a safe option is to make arrangements with the organization in charge of promoting the Spanish language, the **Instituto Cervantes**.

Other subjects on offer are not directly related to Andalusia. **Authentic Adventures** will teach you painting, photography, as well as taking you for guided walks, and the **Complejo Turístico Salitre** in the mountains behind Estepona will introduce you to the delights of the night sky from its observatory.

An artist painting the coastal scene at Nerja, on the Costa del Sol

DIRECTORY

Walking and Trekking

Federación Andaluza de Montañismo
Calle Santa Paula 23,
2° Planta,
Granada.
Tel 958 29 13 40.
🆆 fedamon.com

Spanish Steps
Calle Carretera 6,
Cómpeta (Málaga).
Tel 952 55 32 70.
🆆 spanish-steps.com

Cycling

Biking Andalucia
Apartado de Correos 124,
Orgiva (Granada).
Tel 676 00 25 46.
🆆 bikingandalucia.com

Fundación de los Ferrocarriles Españoles
🆆 ffe.es/viasverdes

Fishing

Federación Andaluza de Pesca Deportiva
Calle Paraíso 4,
Edificio Jerez 74,
2ª Planta, Oficina 6m
Jerez de la Frontera
(Cádiz).
Tel 956 18 75 85.
🆆 fapd.org

Wildlife and Birdwatching

Foundation for Information and Research on Marine Mammals
Pedro Cortés 4, Tarifa.
Tel 956 62 70 08.
🆆 firmm.org

Iberian Wildlife
Apartado de Correos 59,
Potes (Cantabria).
Tel 942 73 51 54.
🆆 iberianwildlife.com

Equestrian Sports

Los Alamos
Apartado 56,
Barbate (Cádiz).
Tel 956 43 10 47.
🆆 losalamosriding.co.uk

Dallas Love Stables
Bubión (Alpujarras).
Tel 608 45 38 02.
🆆 spain-horse-riding.com

Federación Andaluza de Hípica
Tel 954 21 81 46.
🆆 fah.es

Golf

La Cala Resort
La Cala de Mijas,
Mijas Costa.
Tel 952 669 016.
🆆 lacala.com

Federación Andaluza de Golf
Tel 952 22 55 90.
🆆 rfga.org

Montecastillo Barceló Golf Resort
Carretera de Arcos,
Jerez de La Frontera.
Tel 956 15 12 00.
🆆 barcelomontecastillo.com

Tennis

Federación Andaluza de Tenis
Tel 954 44 44 33.
🆆 fatenis.com

Watersports

Federación Española de Actividades Subacuáticas
Tel 932 00 67 69.
🆆 fedas.es

Real Federación Española de Vela
Tel 915 19 50 08.
🆆 rfev.es

Air Sports

Balloon Flights Spain
🆆 balloonflightsspain.com

Federación Andaluza de los Deportes Aéreos
Estadio de la Cartuja,
Seville.
Tel 954 32 54 38.
🆆 feada.org

Skydive Spain
Apartado de Correos 66,
Bolullos de la Mitación.
Tel 955 76 60 56.
🆆 skydivespain.com

Skiing

Sierra Nevada
Tel 902 70 80 90.
🆆 sierranevadaski.com

Naturism

Asociación Naturista-Nudista de Andalucía
Tel 628 80 62 50.
🆆 anna-nudismo.es

Costa Natura
Carretera de Cádiz
km 151, Estepona.
Tel 952 80 80 65.
🆆 costanatura.com

Vera Playa Club
Carretera de Garrucha a
Villaricos, Vera (Almería).
Tel 950 62 70 10.
🆆 veraplaya.info

Spas and Spa Hotels

Asociación Nacional de Estaciones Termales
Tel 902 11 76 22.
🆆 balnearios.org

Las Dunas Beach Hotel & Spa
Urb. La Boladilla Baja,
Ctra de Cadiz km 163.5,
29689 Estepona, Marbella.
Tel 952 80 94 00.

Gran Hotel Guadalpin Banus
C/Edgar Neville s/n,
Nueva Andalucía,
Puerto Banus, Marbella.
Tel 952 41 01 51.
🆆 tgsguadalpinbanus.com

Hotel La Fuente de la Higuera
Partido de los Frontones,
29400 Ronda, Málaga.
Tel 952 16 56 08.
🆆 hotellafuente.com

NH Sotogrande
Autovía A-7, Salida 130,
11310 Cádiz.
Tel 956 69 54 44.
🆆 nh-hotels.com

Villa Padierna Palace Hotel GL
Carretera de Cádiz,
km 166, Benahavís.
Tel 952 88 91 50.
🆆 hotelvillapadierna.com

Arab Baths

Córdoba
Calle Corregidor Luis de
la Cerda 51.
Tel 957 48 47 46.
🆆 hammamspain.com

Granada
Calle Santa Ana 16.
Tel 958 22 99 78.
🆆 hammamspain.com

Málaga
Plaza de los Mártires 5.
Tel 958 80 54 81.
🆆 hammamspain.com

Seville
Calle Aire 15.
Tel 955 01 00 25.
🆆 airedesevilla.com

Specialist Holidays

Annie B's Spanish Cooking
Casa Alegre, Vejer de
la Frontera.
Tel 620 56 06 49.

L'Atelier
Calle Alberca 21, Mecina
Fondales (Alpujarras).
Tel 958 85 75 01.
🆆 ivu.org/atelier

Authentic Adventures
Tel 01453 823 328
(in the UK).
🆆 authenticadventures.co.uk

Complejo Turístico Salitre
Tel 952 11 70 05.
🆆 turismosalitre.com

Cortijo del Caño
Lanjarón (Alpujarras).
Tel 958 77 12 44.
🆆 alpujarrasinfo.com/dance

Instituto Cervantes
Tel 91 436 76 00.
🆆 cervantes.es

SURVIVAL GUIDE

PRACTICAL INFORMATION

The economy of Andalusia is heavily dependent on tourism. The rich variety of natural attractions and its cultural heritage draw visitors to the area throughout the year. Many have even settled in this evocative region, home of all things quintessentially Spanish: rich terracotta landscapes, olive groves, flamenco dancing, and *corridas* (bullfights).

Andalusia has successfully staged high-profile sporting events such as the Sierra Nevada Ski Championships, the UEFA Cup final and the European Grand Prix, which have led to an increase in the number of tourist facilities and an improved infrastructure. The *Junta de Andalucía* has tourist offices across the region, offering a wealth of brochures, maps and leaflets.

Try not to do too much at once, but savour the particular delights of one or two places. Adjust to the slower pace and, in summer, do your sightseeing early in the day before the heat becomes unbearable.

Guided horse-drawn carriage tours operate in Andalusia's main cities

When to Go

Any season is perfect for a visit to Andalusia. Spring boasts balmy weather and numerous festivals, including the Holy Week processions and Feria de Abril *(see p38)*, as well as local fairs in all towns, and the start of the bullfighting season. Summer is hot in the region's interior so it is the perfect time to head to the vast coastline, while autumn offers pleasant weather for sightseeing or rural excursions. Winter weather is mild in most areas, except in the Sierra Nevada *(see p203)* where you can hit the ski slopes.

Visas and Passports

Visitors from the US, Canada, Australia and New Zealand do not need a visa for stays of up to 90 days. For longer visits, apply to your Spanish Consulate for a permit *(visado)* several months in advance. Visas are not required for citizens of EU countries. Visitors from all other countries are legally required to obtain a visa before travelling to Spain. Please check the requirements before travel with your Spanish Consulate.

On arrival, your hotel will take your passport details. If you lose your passport, or need legal advice or other help while in Spain, contact your embassy or consulate.

Tourist Information

All of Andalusia's major cities have several *Oficinas de Turismo* (tourist offices). *Turespaña* provides information on Spain at a national level, while offices run by the *Junta de Andalucía* cover Andalusia as a region. Local tourist offices usually have details only of their environs.

Most tourist offices are well organized, offering brochures covering all kind of services. They have a range of leaflets listing local festivals and can also offer suggestions on nightlife and shows, as well as outdoor activities. For guided tours, the tourist office will be able to direct you to a number of multilingual agencies, such as *El Legado Andalusi* ("The Legacy of Al-Andalus"), which highlights Andalusia's heritage through exhibitions and self-guided cultural tours *(see p272)*.

Admission Charges

Many sights offer free entry to Spanish residents and members of the European Union. Others charge a moderate fee (with relevant ID, seniors, students and children receive discounts). Large groups should make advance reservations, and may be offered a discount. In Granada, Córdoba, Baeza, Ubeda and Jaén, a *bono turístico* (tourist pass) allows entrance to various monuments and

Many monuments and museums offer free or discounted entry

museums for a discounted fixed rate. At many sights, credit card payments are not accepted.

Opening Hours

The majority of museums and monuments are operated by the *Junta de Andalucía* and are open 10am–8:30pm from mid-September to May, and 9am–3:30pm from June to mid-September, staying open during the siesta. Most are open Sunday and public holidays 10am–5pm, but close all day Monday. Ticket offices close an hour before the sight closes.

Many churches open only for Mass, but in small towns a caretaker will often let visitors in between religious services. Hours for Mass vary, but are usually held every Sunday to 8pm, and between 7–9pm on weekdays.

Language

Along the Costa del Sol you will find many multilingual residents and establishments. In major city centres many people working in the service industry will have at least a basic level of English, but in rural towns you are likely to hear mainly Spanish. Most people are very accommodating and will try their best to communicate with you.

Etiquette and Smoking

In Spain strangers usually greet each other on meeting in doorways or lifts – and even when passing on the street in small towns. When introduced to someone, expect to shake hands. Once they are familiar, men embrace and pat each other on the shoulder, and female friends greet each other with a hug or kiss on both cheeks.

Spaniards rarely drink alcohol without nibbles until after dinner. The waiter will not bring the bill until you ask for it, and generally the bill for a round of drinks is not shared. The Spanish tend to dress smartly, so wearing very casual clothes and shoes will readily identify you as a tourist.

Visitors outside a church in El Rocío, Andalusia

However, few venues have a strict dress code so smart casual attire is accepted.

Smoking is not allowed in any public indoor space except in designated areas of bars and restaurants.

Visiting Churches

In most towns, tourists are welcome in the church during a service as long as they are quiet and respectful.

Dress codes in Spanish churches are not as strict as in other Catholic countries, but visitors should avoid skimpy shorts and bare shoulders and arms. There is usually no admission charge, except in larger cathedrals, although a donation may be expected. Tourist offices and hotels are usually able to provide details of churches holding services in English.

Public Conveniences

Public toilets are scarce. However, there is a bar on virtually every corner that is legally bound to allow you to use its toilets. Another option is to head to department store, El Corte Inglés. Ladies should look for a "D" *(Damas)* or "M" *(Mujeres)* on the door; while men's rooms are marked with a "H" *(Hombres)* or a "C" *(Caballeros)*.

Carry a pack of tissues when travelling to rural areas as toilet paper is a rare find. This should not be a problem in city centres and at major tourist sights. Watch out for signs in public toilets within older buildings that state *"No tirar papel al WC"* (do not flush paper or other objects down the toilet).

Taxes and Tipping

If you are not a European Union resident, you can reclaim the VAT *(IVA* in Spanish) paid on goods bought in any authorized shop in Spain. When you spend a minimum of €90.15 in the same shop on the same day *(see p238)*, ask for information on how to claim your refund. See www. premiertaxfree.com

Tipping tends to be an issue of discretion in Spain. A service charge *(servicio)* is usually included *(see p221)* in the bill, but in more upmarket restaurants you are expected to tip around five per cent in addition. It is also common to round up the fare for taxi drivers.

Upmarket restaurants in Seville will expect a tip in addition to the bill

Travellers with Special Needs

Modern buildings generally have adequate provision for disabled visitors, with lifts, ramps and special toilet facilities. However, entry to some historical monuments may be restricted so check ahead with the local tourist office or monument staff. Some historic centres have pedestrian zones and bicycle lanes, which can be used, with caution, by wheelchairs.

RADAR a UK based charity, and the **Oficina de Turismo para Personas Discapacitadas** in Seville can provide travel information for disabled users. In Madrid, **Servi-COCEMFE** advises on suitable accommodation *(see p215)*.

All public transport in Seville is wheelchair accessible, with electronic ramps or same-level entry onto buses and Metro-Centro trams.

Senior Travellers

There are many options for both leisurely and more active holidays for senior travellers. Health spas have become popular choices as are walking holidays. There are substantial discounts for travellers over the age of 55 staying in four-star hotels, during the off-peak season. US-based **Road Scholar** specialises in offering group travel experiences for seniors.

Gay and Lesbian Travellers

In general, Spain openly accepts gays and lesbians. However, discretion is still advisable in

A Gay Pride Parade weaving its way through the streets of Málaga

Local market stall with a colourful display of fresh produce

rural towns and public places. Spain has a dynamic gay scene, with clubs, bars, hotels and associations throughout Andalusia, particularly in the larger cities.

One association that promotes gay and lesbian rights is **Colegas**, while the **International Gay & Lesbian Travel Association** has an online directory of gay- and lesbian-friendly travel businesses and tour operators.

International Student Identity Card

Travelling on a Budget

Most large towns have a **Centro de Documentación e Información Juvenil**, which provides information for students and young people. A valid International Student Identification Card (ISIC card) entitles you to some price reductions, including museum entrance fees and travel.

Many museums and monuments offer free entry one day a week so check in advance.

To dine on a budget, order the *menú del día* (a 2–3 course meal at a fixed price) or choose tapas instead of from *la carta*. Another saving would be to opt for locally brewed beer or house wines.

Youth hostels provide shared minimal facilities for a bargain price, while family-run budget hotels offer more privacy.

Responsible Travel

There are a growing number of hotels and guesthouses with an emphasis on green tourism. **Andeco** promotes ecotourism in Andalusia, while **Acentorural** and **Top Rural** list accommodation throughout the countryside. **Glamping Hub** offers a glamorous but green way of camping, offering 14 destinations in Andalucia.

Every town and city has local markets and shops that promote their regional produce, and local activities and festivals to provide entertainment. Local farmers belong to cooperatives, which sell their produce in the markets *(Mercado de Abastos)*. Locally grown meats and fresh fish from regional waters are also sold here, but there will also be some imported produce.

Organically grown produce is referred to as *ecológico*; while organic meats are defined as *de corral*, *ecológica* or *organica*, and will be marked as such in stores and markets. Market stalls that exclusively sell organically grown goods are very difficult to find, even in bigger cities.

Every town and city has local artisan shops. On Sunday mornings, Seville's Art Market features works from local professional artists. Seasonal markets also feature regional artisans, with one of the most impressive being the *Mercado de Belenes* (Market of Nativity Scenes), held every December in the Plaza de San Francisco. Here you will find numerous stalls offering intricately detailed, handmade nativity characters. Local activities and festivals such as Holy Week processions, annual fairs and music festivals promoting local artists provide unique entertainment.

Time

Spain is one hour ahead of Greenwich Mean Time (GMT) and British Summer Time, except for brief periods in spring and autumn when clock changes are not synchronized.

The 24-hour clock is used for written and official purposes but not in speech. The morning is referred to as *por la mañana* and the afternoon, *por la tarde*. Afternoon starts after siesta time, at around 5pm.

Electricity

The current in Spain is 220V- AC with two-pin, round-pronged plugs. Adaptors can be found in many local hypermarkets, supermarkets and electrical stores. If you can, take one with you to be on the safe side. Many hotels now use the key/card system for switching on the electricity supply in rooms.

Conversion Chart

Imperial to Metric
1 inch = 2.54 centimetres
1 foot = 30 centimetres
1 mile = 1.6 kilometres
1 ounce = 28 grams
1 pound = 454 grams
1 pint = 0.6 litres
1 gallon = 4.6 litres

Metric to Imperial
1 centimetre = 0.4 inches
1 metre = 3 feet, 3 inches
1 kilometre = 0.6 miles
1 gram = 0.04 ounces
1 kilogram = 2.2 pounds
1 litre = 1.8 pints

DIRECTORY

Embassies and Consulates

Australian Embassy
Torre Espacio, Paseo de la Castellana 259D, Planta 24, 28046 Madrid.
Tel 913 53 66 00.
W spain.embassy. gov.au

British Consulate
Edificio Eurocom, Calle Mauricio Moro Pareto 2, 29006 Málaga.
Tel 902 10 93 56.
W ukinspain.fco. gov.uk

Canadian Consulate
Edificio Horizonte, Plaza de la Malagueta 2, 1st floor, 29016 Málaga.
Tel 952 22 33 46.
W international.gc.ca

US Consulate
Plaza Nueva, 8-8 dupl, 2nd floor, Seville.
Map 3 B1 (5 C3).
Tel 954 21 85 71.
W embusa.es

Tourist Information

Oficinas de Turismo
W andalucia.org

Almería
Parque Nicolás Salmerón s/n.
Tel 950 17 52 20.

Córdoba
Calle Torrijos 10.
Tel 957 35 51 79.

Granada
Calle Santa Ana 4.
Tel 958 57 52 02.

Málaga
Pasaje de Chinitas 4.
Tel 951 30 89 11.

Seville
Avenida de la Constitución.
Map 3 C2 (5 C4).
Tel 954 78 75 78.

Plaza San Francisco, Edificio Laredo 19, Seville.
Map 3 C3 (5 C3).
Tel 954 59 52 88.
W turismo.sevilla.org

Spanish Tourist Office (UK)
64 North Row, London W1K 7DE.
Tel 020 7317 2011.
W spain.info

Travellers with Special Needs

Oficina de Turismo para Personas Discapacitadas (CEADIS)
Calle Fray Isidoro de Sevilla 1, Seville.
Tel 954 91 54 44.
W valinet.org

RADAR
12 City Forum, 250 City Road, London EC1V 8AF, UK.
Tel (020) 7250 3222.
W radar.org.uk

Servi-COCEMFE
C/Luis Cabrera 63, 28002 Madrid.
Tel 917 44 36 00.
W cocemfe.es

Senior Travellers

Road Scholar
11 Avenue de Lafayette, Boston, MA 02111-1746.
Tel 1 800 454 5768 (outside US 1 9/8 323 4141).
W roadscholar.org

Gay and Lesbian Travellers

Colegas
Tel 954 50 13 77.
W colegaweb.org

International Gay & Lesbian Travel Association
W iglta.org

Travelling on a Budget

ALMERÍA

Centro de Información Juvenil
C/ Marín 1.
Tel 950 21 13 67.
W injuve.es

CÓRDOBA

La Casa de la Juventud
Campo Madre de Dios s/n, 14010.
Tel 957 76 47 07.
W injuve.es

GRANADA

Centro de Información Juvenil
Avenida de Madrid 5, Granada.
Tel 958 20 46 52.
W injuve.es

MÁLAGA

Centro de Información y Asesoramiento Juvenil (INFOJOVEN)
Calle Roger de Flor 1, Málaga.
Tel 951 92 60 67.
W juventud.malaga.eu

SEVILLE

Instituto Andaluz de la Juventud
Calle Bilbao, 8–10, Seville.
Tel 955 03 57 16.
W informajoven.org

Responsible Travel

Acentorural
C/Puerta del Osario 3, 2nd floor, Seville.
Tel 954 95 61 73.
W acentorural.com

Andeco
Avenida Ramón y Cajal nº4, Marbella (Málaga).
Tel 952 77 09 54.
W ecoturismo enandalucia.org

Glamping Hub
Marion St, Denver, Colorado.
Tel (415) 800 3004.
W glampinghub.com

Top Rural
Paseo de la Castellana 79, Madrid.
Tel 902 10 97 11.
W toprural.com

Personal Security and Health

Andalusia is, by and large, a safe place for visitors. Women travelling alone tend not to be hassled, but may have to put up with so-called compliments from men of all ages. Pickpockets and bag-snatchers, however, are very common in cities, so be cautious around tourist spots and on crowded transport. If you must carry valuable items, avoid putting them all in the same place. Wear a money belt and do not keep your wallet in an easily accessible place. If you become ill during your stay, go to a pharmacy, where someone should be able to advise you. Organize travel insurance before leaving for Spain as it is difficult to obtain and more expensive once there.

Mounted police officers from the *Policía Nacional*

Police

There are three types of police in Spain – the *Guardia Civil*, the *Policía Nacional* and the *Policía Local*. When approaching police on the street, remember that it is illegal to be without ID.

In rural areas you will usually encounter the green-uniformed *Guardia Civil*, who patrol the country highways and will help if your car breaks down *(see p271)*. They also set up random road blocks to check for drink driving or other infractions. The *Policía Nacional*, who wear a

Ambulance displaying the emergency number

Marked car of the *Policía Nacional*

Fire engine marked with contact number

dark blue uniform, have many responsibilities, such as dealing with visitors' permits and documentation, they are also the best to turn to when reporting a crime.

The *Policía Local* handle the day-to-day traffic policing of towns and cities.

What to Be Aware of

The abundance of street-life means that you will rarely find yourself alone or in a position to be harassed.

There are no particularly notorious areas of Seville to be avoided. Just act streetwise: do not use maps late at night and try to look like you know where you are going.

When visiting the Sacromonte caves in Granada to see flamenco performances *(see p197)*, go in a group and keep an eye on your belongings. In cities such as Seville, Granada and Córdoba, beware of gypsies who will try to read your palm or offer a sprig of rosemary, then demand compensation (petty change doesn't suffice). Your refusal to pay results in their outrage, and you can have a difficult time getting away from them. Make sure that you take official taxis displaying a licence number, although illegal cabs are rare.

In an Emergency

The telephone number for medical emergency services is **061**. Report all serious crime to the local police and for the fire brigade dial **112**.

Lost and Stolen Property

Pickpockets are common in crowded areas. Beware of people trying to distract you while someone else snatches your bag or wallet. Wear bags and cameras across your body, not on your shoulder, and take special care of mobile phones and laptops. At ATMs be cautious of loitering strangers. Take a photocopy of your passport and leave the original in the hotel safe. Park in a secure car park, storing valuables out of view.

Report any incident to the police *(poner una denuncia)* as soon as possible (within 24 hours), particularly if you wish to obtain a statement *(denuncia)* for an insurance claim.

Health Precautions

Beware of the sun, particularly in the summer months when temperatures can reach up to 45° C (113° F). Try to avoid walking in the midday sun and stay in the shade whenever possible. Use sunscreen, wear a hat and be sure to drink plenty of water.

In rural areas, take any signs showing a bull or saying *toro bravo* (fighting bull) seriously. These bulls are extremely dangerous animals and should not be approached.

Hospitals and Pharmacies

For minor ailments, visit a pharmacy *(farmacia)*, where pharmacists can dispense a wide range of medication over the counter, but for many drugs you will need a doctor's prescription.

Farmacias have a green or red neon cross outside and are found in most towns. A few are open 24 hours, but most open 12 hours a day. Some close for *siesta*. At least one will be *de guardia* – ready to dispatch out of hours. The opening rota is posted on the door of all *farmacias* and also in local newspapers.

For urgent medical assistance, go to the nearest *Urgencias* – the emergency ward of a hospital or clinic.

Spanish pharmacy signs

All the cities have several hospitals each, while the Costa del Sol has a hospital situated on the main coastal highway (N340) just east of Marbella. For private care, contact your insurance company for a list of centres covered by your plan.

Most hospitals will have volunteer interpreters who speak English and occasionally other languages.

The Cruz Roja (Red Cross) has an extensive network throughout Spain and runs an ambulance service.

Your hotel and embassy or consulate can provide a list of English-speaking doctors and dentists. Dental procedures are safe and are generally cheaper than the UK and US.

Travel And Health Insurance

All EU nationals are entitled to Spanish social security cover. Before travelling, you must obtain the **European Health Insurance Card** (see www.ehic.org.uk). Show your card or policy to receive medical care. In some cases you may have to pay first and be reimbursed later. For private medical care, make sure you have your policy on you when you request assistance.

Travel insurance is advisable, and should be arranged before your trip. Carry all documentation with you.

If you need a lawyer, ask your embassy or consulate *(see p257)* to recommend one. Not all lawyers speak English, but police stations may be able to offer a volunteer interpreter *(intérprete)*. Otherwise you may need to hire a *Traductor Oficial* or *Jurado* to state your case and undertake legal work.

DIRECTORY

Local Police Stations

Almería
Tel 950 62 30 40.

Córdoba
Tel 957 29 07 60.

Granada
Tel 958 248 211.

Málaga
Tel 952 06 18 70.

Seville
Tel 954 37 84 96.

In an Emergency

Ambulance
Tel 061.

Fire Brigade
Tel 112.

Police
Tel 112.

Lost and Stolen Property

Almería
Oficina de Objetos Perdidos,
C/ Santos Zarate 15.
Tel 950 62 14 98.

Córdoba
Comisaria de Policía
Avenida Doctor Fleming 2.
Tel 957 59 45 00.

Granada
Ayuntamiento
Plaza del Carmen 5.
Tel 958 24 81 03.

Málaga
Victoria nº 15.
Tel 951 92 61 11.

Seville
Oficina de Objetos Perdidos
Manuel Vázquez Sagastizábal 3.
Map 6 F5.
Tel 954 21 50 64.

Hospitals

Cruz Roja
Hospital Victoria Eugenia, Avenida de la Cruz Roja, Seville. **Map** 2 E4.
Tel 954 35 14 00.

Hospital Costa del Sol
Autovia A-7 km 187, Marbella, Málaga.
Tel 951 97 66 69.

Hospital General
Avenida de las Fuerzas Armadas 2, Granada.
Tel 958 02 00 00.

Hospital Reina Sofía
Avenida Menéndez Pidal s/n, Córdoba.
Tel 957 01 00 00.

Hospital Torrecardenas
Paraje de Torrecardenas s/n, Almería.
Tel 950 01 60 00.

Hospital Universitario Virgen del Rocio
Avenida Manuel Siurots s/n, Seville.
Tel 955 01 20 00.

Pharmacies

Almería
Carretera de Ronda 325.
Tel 950 25 35 57.
Open 24 hours.

Córdoba
Calle Lope de Hoces 7.
Tel 957 29 35 70.

Granada
Calle Reyes Catolicos 5.
Tel 958 26 26 64.

Málaga
Calle Mesonero Romas 2.
Tel 952 61 08 36.

Seville
María Auxiliadora 6.
Tel 954 41 62 61.
Open 24 hours.

Travel and Health Insurance

Asociación Profesional de Traductores e Intérpretes
Plaza de los Mostenses 1, 28615 Madrid.
Tel 652 15 54 06.
W aptij.es

European Health Insurance Card (EHIC)
PO Box 1114, Newcastle upon Tyne NE99 2TL, UK.
Tel 0845 605 0707 (from abroad +44 191 212 7500).

Banking and Currency

Finding a bank is not a problem, as there are usually one or two even in small towns (but not necessarily in villages). Other options for changing currency include *casas de cambio*, hotels and travel agents. Changing money in Spain is best attempted in larger cities, where banks have the best exchange rates. Alternatively, credit cards are widely accepted across Andalusia.

You can take any amount of foreign currency into Spain, but sums worth over €6,000 should be declared at customs when you enter the country.

Changing Money

Most banks have a foreign exchange desk *casas de cambio*, and in building societies a *cajas de ahorros*. While Málaga airport has 24-hour exchange facilities and at Seville airport the Iberia Airlines information desk offers money changing, the rates are generally higher in airports. You can change money at El Corte Inglés department stores, travel agents and hotels, although their rates are not favourable and fees vary.

It is better to take enough euros for your initial needs before travelling, and to shop around for the best rates at your leisure after you arrive.

You must show your passport or driver's licence to change money. To enter a bank you must ring a bell and wait to be buzzed in.

Banking Hours

Banks open from 8:30am to 2pm Monday to Friday. Few banks open on Saturdays. During a town's annual *feria* week *(see pp42–3)* banking hours are reduced, and on public holidays they remain closed *(see p41)*.

ATMs

ATMs are readily available in Andalusia. Look for the logo on your card to find an appropriate machine. ATMs have various language options. Check with your bank regarding foreign transaction fees and inform them prior to travel. Spanish banks may impose a fee (€2–3 per transaction), but exchange rates are better.

Debit and Credit Cards

Credit cards such as **Visa**, **American Express** and **MasterCard**, as well as debit cards bearing the Cirrus or Maestro logo are widely accepted all over Spain. Most payment transactions require identification (passport or driving licence). With your PIN number you can withdraw money from ATMs. Traveller's cheques are rarely accepted and difficult to cash.

Wiring Money

To wire money, you can use a bank or an international service such as **Western Union** or **MoneyGram**. If using a bank, use a large central office where they may have more experience. To receive money through a bank you will need a local bank account.

For both sending and receiving money, Western Union is available at all central **Correos** post offices. MoneyGram is available at select stores or public telephone offices *(locutorios)*.

A branch of the BBVA bank, Seville

The Euro

The euro (€) is the common currency of the European Union. It went into general circulation on 1 January 2002, initially for 12 participating countries. Spain was one of those countries.

EU members using the euro as sole official currency are known as the Eurozone. Several EU members have opted out of joining this common currency.

Euro notes are identical throughout the Eurozone countries, each one including designs of fictional architectural structures and monuments. The coins, however, have one side identical (the value side), and one side with an image unique to each country. Both notes and coins are exchangeable in each of the participating countries.

Bank Notes

Euro bank notes have seven denominations. The €5 note (grey in colour) is the smallest, followed by the €10 note (pink), €20 note (blue), €50 note (orange), €100 note (green), €200 note (yellow) and €500 note (purple). All notes show the stars of the European Union.

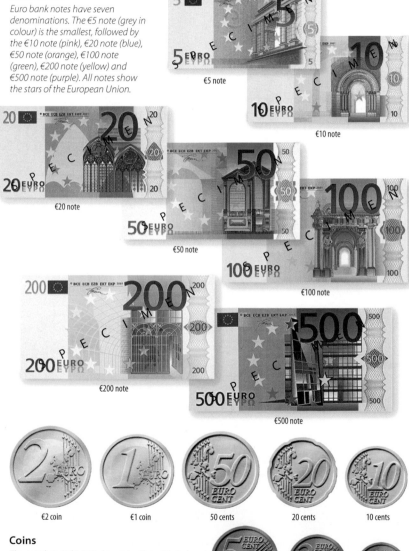

€5 note

€10 note

€20 note

€50 note

€100 note

€200 note

€500 note

€2 coin

€1 coin

50 cents

20 cents

10 cents

Coins

The euro has eight coin denominations: €1 and €2; 50 cents, 20 cents, 10 cents, 5 cents, 2 cents and 1 cent. The €2 and €1 coins are both silver and gold in colour. The 50-, 20- and 10-cent coins are gold. The 5-, 2- and 1-cent coins are bronze.

5 cents

2 cents

1 cent

Communications and Media

The telephone system in Spain is run by Telefónica. It is efficient, but one of the most expensive in Europe. Public telephones are available on the street and at *locutorios (public telephone call centres)*. Spain also has a good network of Internet cafés.

Spain's postal service can be slow but letters posted at central post offices will arrive at their destination faster. Digital TV and radio provide options for regional and international programmes. Newspapers, both in hard copy and online, are plentiful in Andalusia.

International and Local Telephone Calls

There are plenty of phone booths *(cabinas telefónicas)* on the streets of Spain, as well as at *locutorios*, where you buy a phonecard *(tarjetas telefónicas)* to place a call. Public phones use coins and phonecards, which are available from most tobacconists *(estancos)* and newsstands. They are priced by their value in call units.

It is easiest to make long-distance calls *(conferencias de largas distancias)* at *locutorios*. A call made from a *cabina telefónica* or *locutorio* costs 35 per cent more than from a private phone. Calls from hotel telephones are also more expensive. Calling abroad is cheapest between 10pm and 8am daily.

Logo of Spanish telecom system, Telefónica

Mobile Phones

A 3G broadband mobile (or mobile operable in frequency GSM 900/1800) will work in Spain, but check first with your provider regarding costs. If you plan to make frequent calls, it will probably work out cheaper to get a Spanish number. You can have your phone unlocked and get a prepaid SIM card, or buy a pre-pay phone that comes with a number of minutes included. **Orange**, **Vodafone**, **Movistar**

and **Yoigo** are common suppliers, and their products can be found at El Corte Inglés stores *(see p241)* or **Phone House**. Average costs with a pre-pay card for national calls are €0.35/min; a national SMS costs €0.15.

Internet

Internet cafés can be found scattered across all cities and in some small towns. The average price per hour is €2. In Seville, the central post office has a small *locutorio* with Internet access and the tourist office near Plaza Nueva offers free Internet access for 10 minutes. Most local libraries also offer computers with free Internet access. Wi-Fi is available in nearly all hotels, although some still charge excessive rates. It is also available in many bars and cafés, and also in some parks and plazas. **Starbucks** can be found in nearly every major city, offering free Wi-Fi.

Postal Services

The Spanish postal service between major cities is fairly efficient, but between smaller towns it can be slow. Letters posted at a central post office usually arrive in reasonable time; although for important or urgent mail use the *certificado* (registered) and *urgente* (express) mail services.

Reaching the Right Number

When dialling within a city, province or to another province, dial the entire number – the province is indicated by the initial numbers: Seville 954, 955; Málaga 951, 952; Córdoba 957; Cádiz 956; Granada 958; Huelva 959; Jaén 953; Almería 950.

- International calls: dial 00, wait for tone, dial country and area codes and number.
- Telefónica directory enquiries are on 11818.
- International directory enquiries are on 025.
- Operator assistance for calls to Europe and North Africa is on 1008. For the rest of the world, dial 1005. If you want to know the cost, ask the operator beforehand.
- To connect directly with the operator in your country dial 900 followed by the country code 990061 (Australia); 990015 (Canada); 990011 (USA); or 990044 for the UK.

Main post offices open all day Monday to Saturday; local post offices open mornings only. A *poste restante* service in central offices enables you to collect letters or parcels. A passport or other form of identification is needed but there is no collection fee.

Buy stamps *(sellos)* at any post office and at *estancos* (state-run tobacconists), displaying a yellow and blue sign.

International couriers such as **DHL** and **UPS** guarantee urgent delivery worldwide. Call the central office to arrange a pick up.

A DHL delivery truck on a street in Seville

Kiosk selling newspapers and magazines

Addresses

In speech, on maps and in written information, Spaniards often drop the *Calle* in street names, so that Calle Mateos Gago becomes Mateos Gago. Other terms, such as *Plaza (Pza)*, *Callejón*, *Carretera (Ctra)* and *Avenida (Avda)*, remain unchanged.

In addresses, a *s/n (sin numéro)* after the street name indicates that the building has no number. Outside towns, an address may say "Carretera Córdoba–Málaga km 47" – this means the sight is on the highway near to the kilometre sign.

Newspapers and Magazines

The most important national papers are *El País* (the socialist paper with a daily Andalusian version), *ABC* (conservative), and *El Mundo* (independent). Local papers such as *Ideal* in Granada, *Diario de Sevilla*, the *Córdoba Diario*, *Almería Diario*, or the *Málaga Sur*, have extensive listings of local cultural and sporting activities. An English version of *Sur* is distributed free in Málaga, Granada, Almería and Cádiz on Fridays or is viewable online at **w suringlish.com**.

The English paper *Costa del Sol News* can be purchased weekly in kiosks along the Málaga coast. Almería province also has an English newspaper, *Costa Almería News*, published on Friday.

The local listings magazines are the *Giraldillo* in Seville and the *Guía del Ocio* in Granada *(see p244)*. FIND has complete cultural listings and nightlife for the Costa del Sol and *La Tribuna*, Córdoba's weekly free sheet, publishes useful practical information. Málaga has *Qué Hacer/What's On*. The online guide **w guiadelocio.com** has current listings of events and activities for all provinces of Spain.

Television and Radio

In 2010, Spain eliminated the use of all analogue TV signals, and changed completely to digital TV as the standard signal, providing around 30 TV channels for free. Two are state channels, TVE1 and TVE2, and the main private ones are Antena 3, Cuatro and Telecinco. In addition, Andalusia has Canal Sur and Canal 2 Andalusia. Canal Plus is a cable TV company showing films, sport and documentaries. Subtitled foreign films are listed by the letters V.O. *(Versión Original)*.

Canal Sur logo

The best radio news programmes are broadcast on Radio Nacional de España. BBC World Service frequencies and listings can be found on their website, **w bbc.co.uk/worldservice**. With the all-digital signal, most programmes are available in their original language simply by changing the TV language setting.

DIRECTORY

Mobile Phones

Movistar
w movistar.es

Orange
w orange.es

Phone House
w phonehouse.es

Vodafone
w vodafone.es

Yoigo
w yoigo.com

Internet

Biblioteca Central
Centro Cívico Centro, Plaza de la Corredera, s/n, Córdoba.
Tel 957 49 68 82.

Correo
Avenida de la Constitución 32, Seville. **Map** 3 C2 (5 C4).
Tel 954 22 47 60.

Cybercafe Abakan
Calle Marcos 19, Almería.

Locutorio Duquesa
Calle Duquesa, Granada.

Meeting Point
Plaza de la Merced 29, Málaga.

Starbucks
Av Constitucion 11, Seville.
Tel 954 21 80 05.

Postal services

General Information
Tel 902 19 71 97.
w correos.es

Almería
Av San Juan Bosco 35.
Tel 950 28 15 12.

Córdoba
Calle Cruz Conde 15.
Tel 957 49 63 42.

Granada
Puerta Real 2.
Tel 958 22 11 38.

Málaga
Avenida Andalucia 1.
Tel 952 36 43 80.

Seville
Avenida de la Constitución 32.
Map 3 C2 (5 C4).
Tel 954 22 47 60.

Couriers

DHL
Tel 902 12 24 24.
w dhl.es

UPS
Tel 902 88 88 20.
w ups.com

TRAVEL INFORMATION

Andalusia is well served by a wide range of transport. Each year sees the arrival of thousands of flights, mostly from European countries, though some are from further afield. Most flights from beyond Europe stop in Madrid or Barcelona before arriving at Andalusia's busiest airport, Málaga. Located a short plane or ferry ride from Morocco, Málaga serves as a gateway to Africa. Seville airport also caters to international flights.

Seville and Málaga have good rail links, and the AVE high-speed train between major cities will often be quicker than flying (including checking-in time). There are coaches from northern Europe and regional services in Andalusia. Ferries sail from Plymouth and Portsmouth to Santander and Bilbao; with a 10-hour drive to Andalusia. Driving is not recommended in summer when the number of cars on the road peaks.

One of Andalusia's increasing number of biodiesel-fuelled buses

Green Travel

In Andalusia, awareness about environmental issues is improving. Recycling initiatives, solar and wind energy, and biodiesel-fuelled buses are all on the rise. An efficient network of public transportation makes it fairly easy to get around Andalusia without a car. Trains and coaches are modern and comfortable, with extensive and reliable services. Many historic city centres have very limited access for vehicles, with large pedestrianized zones, bicycle lanes and a bike hire scheme *(see p273)*.

Rural Andalusia has a large network of natural parks and trails as well as rivers and lakes for water sports, although depending on your itinerary a car may be necessary.

Arriving by Air

Most of Europe's major airlines, as well as some Middle Eastern and American lines, run scheduled flights to Málaga, Andalusia's main airport. A large portion of the traffic, however, is made up of budget airlines and cheap charter flights, which

bring in thousands of holiday-makers. Over-booking can be a problem in summer and flights are often delayed. Seville airport is much less busy and is convenient for travellers staying inland. Granada and Almería offer limited domestic and international flights too.

Tickets and Fares

Fares vary widely and peak travel depends on the destination: May, June, September and October for Seville; June to August for the coast, and December to February for the Sierra Nevada. You can book directly through an airline, or via online search engines such as www.kayak.co.uk or www.momondo.com, which compare numerous

servers to get the best deal, or for a complete service visit your local travel agent.

Almost all package deals to Andalusia focus on beach holidays. However, some tour operators also offer city breaks, which can be cheaper in the winter. **Tour Andalusia** offers small group tours originating in Málaga and **Euro Adventures (EA Tours)** offer food and wine package holidays starting in Costa del Sol, then following an itinerary, travelling by coach along the Costa del Sol to Seville, Córdoba, Granada and Cádiz. Low-cost airlines also offer cheap deals.

Seville Airport

Seville airport is 4 km (2.5 miles) north of the city centre. **Iberia** and **Air Europa** fly to numerous domestic and international destinations. **Ryanair** and **Vueling Airlines** offer low-cost flights, and charter flights also operate out of Seville.

Los Amarillos runs a daily bus service between Prado de San Sebastián and the airport, approximately every 30 minutes from 5:15am (6:15am Sundays) to midnight. Taxis to the city centre cost €20–24.

Seville airport, conveniently situated just outside the city

Modern interior of the ticket hall, Seville airport

Malaga Airport

Málaga airport has links to about 120 international destinations and receives around 10 million passengers each year. It is particularly busy from June to September. Scheduled flights are available from British Airways, Iberia, **Easyjet**, Ryanair, Virgin, **BMI Baby** and Vueling.

The *tren de cercanías (see p266)* runs into Málaga and down the coast to Fuengirola, departing every 20 minutes from 6am to 11pm.

The No. 19 bus, which runs every 30 minutes from 6:30am to midnight, also travels into Málaga.

Granada Airport

Granada's airport is 17 km (10.5 miles) southeast of the city on the main road to Málaga. Facilities and flights are rather limited, but there are regular flights to Palma de Mallorca, Barcelona, and Madrid, as well as limited services to Melilla, Milan and Bologna. There are car hire facilities in the terminal.

Gibraltar Airport

This airport can be a useful arrival point when visiting the southwest of Andalusia. Flights are operated by British Airways, **Monarch Airlines** and Easyjet, with services from Heathrow, Gatwick, Luton and Manchester. The airport has few amenities.

Almeria Airport

Located 9 km (6 miles) west of the city, Almería's airport has limited facilities. Flights are offered to Barcelona, Madrid, Seville, Palma de Mallorca, Brussels, Manchester and Melilla with Air Europa, Air Berlin, BMI Baby, Easyjet, Ryanair and Monarch Airlines.

Airport Car Hire

The major airports are well served with international car hire companies such as **AVIS**, **ATESA**, **Hertz** and **Europcar**, as well as local companies. **Holiday Autos** is a budget option, best booked online. Hire your car prior to your visit during high-season. Many UK travel agents are able to organize fly-drive deals.

An FRS fast ferry on the Tangier–Tarifa route

Getting to North Africa

Most nationalities need only a valid passport to visit Morocco for a stay up to 90 days. For further information contact the **Consulate of Morocco**. Morocco time is 1 hour behind Spain.

Acciona Trasmediterranea, **FRS** and **BALEARIA** operate ferries from Algeciras to Ceuta; FRS, Baleária and **COMARIT** ferries run from Algeciras to Tangier. FRS and COMARIT have fast ferries (35–45 mins) from Tarifa to Tangier. Acciona Trasmediterranea runs from Almería to Melilla in 8 hours. FRS also has a high-speed Gibraltar–Tangier route.

By air, Iberia, **Royal Air Maroc (RAM)**, Air Europa and Air Nostrum operate from Spain's mainland to various destinations in North Africa. **Helicópteros Inaer** runs a helicopter shuttle service between Málaga and Ceuta.

DIRECTORY

Arriving by Air

Air Europa
w aireuropa.com

BMI Baby
w bmibaby.com

Easyjet
w easyjet.com

Iberia
w iberia.com

Ryanair
w ryanair.com

Vueling Airlines
w vueling.com

Package Deals

Euro Adventures (EA Tours)
w euroadventures.net

Tour Andalusia
w tourandalusia.co.uk

Car Hire

Avis
w avis.es

ATESA
w atesa.es

Europcar
w europcar.es

Hertz
w hertz.com

Holiday Autos
w holidayautos.co.uk

Getting to North Africa

Consulate of Morocco
Camino de los Descubrimientos, Isla de la Cartuja, Seville.
Tel 954 08 10 44.

Acciona Trasmediterranea
w trasmediterranea.es

BALEARIA
w balearia.com

COMARIT
w comarit.es

FRS
w frs.es

Helicópteros Inaer
w inaer.com

Royal Air Maroc (RAM)
w royalairmaroc.com

Travelling by Train

Owing to the natural bottleneck of the Pyrenees, train connections between Spain and the rest of Europe are a little restricted. However, a subsidiary of Spain's national network, **RENFE**, runs a service that links Madrid and Barcelona to France, Italy, Austria and Switzerland. RENFE offers routes throughout the country, on a variety of trains, and at a high level of service. The high-speed AVE *(Tren de Alta Velocidad Española)* linking Seville, Córdoba and Madrid, and Málaga to Madrid (via Córdoba) has cut down journey times by almost half, and is extremely efficient.

AVE high-speed trains at Santa Justa railway station, Seville

Arriving by Train

Trains coming from other European countries to Spain terminate in either Madrid or Barcelona. From Barcelona it is about 5 hours to Seville by high-speed AVE; from Madrid it takes around 3 hours travelling by AVE.

Andalusia's most important stations are Málaga, Seville's Santa Justa *(see p267)* and Córdoba. Connections to major Andalusian towns and with Barcelona and Madrid (including 20+ AVE high-speed trains) run daily.

European and American rail passes, including EurRail and Inter-Rail, are accepted on the RENFE network, subject to the usual conditions. However, on certain trains you may find a supplement is payable.

All major stations are accessible to disabled passengers. Passengers can arrange in advance for assistance in the station, through RENFE's subsidiary company, **Atendo**.

Train Travel in Spain

The train network in Spain is very extensive with services suited to every budget. Travelling on the AVE is the fastest option, with a money-back guarantee that the train will reach its destination no more than 5 minutes late. They have drastically cut their prices, now making them a very attractive travel choice.

Other long-distance train services, known as *larga distancia*, are divided into *diurnos* (daytime) and *nocturnos* (night-time). *Talgos* trains are slightly more luxurious and expensive,

offering both day- and night-time travel. Night trains offer the option of private cabins with beds. *Media distancias* run daytime from city to city within a limited area. *Cercanías* are commuter trains running from large towns to the suburbs.

Bookings and Reservations

Train tickets can be booked online or in travel agencies with the RENFE logo. It is advisable to book long-distance journeys in advance; booking is essential if you travel on public holidays *(días festivos)* or long weekends *(puentes)*. You can book a ticket up to 60 days in advance. Alternatively, use an auto check-in machine at major stations up to 15 minutes before travelling. Auto check-in machines can also be used for making changes to your scheduled itinerary. Discounts are usually given for advance bookings, last-minute bookings and round trips.

More information is available on RENFE's website.

Tickets

Train travel in Spain is fairly reasonably priced. *Larga distancia* and *media distancia* have first and second class *(preferente/turista)*. The tickets on Spanish trains always show a number for your seat (or bed on sleepers). Tickets are sold online, at main line stations, at some *cercanías* stations and in RENFE-authorized travel agencies. *Cercanías* tickets may be bought in the ticket office or by using self-service machines. Credit cards are accepted at all stations.

The ticket counter at Córdoba railway station

Spain's Principal RENFE Network

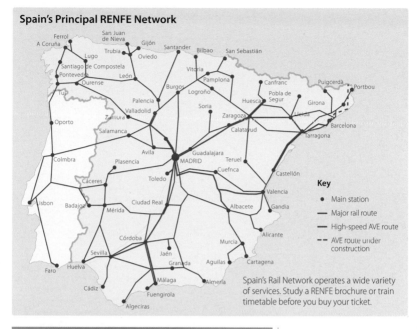

Ferrol
A Coruña
San Juan de Nieva
Gijón
Santander
Bilbao
San Sebastián
Lugo
Trubia
Oviedo
Santiago de Compostela
Pontevedra
León
Vitoria
Pamplona
Canfranc
Puigcerdà
Portbou
Tuy
Ourense
Burgos
Logroño
Pobla de Segur
Huesca
Girona
Palencia
Valladolid
Soria
Zaragoza
Lleida
Barcelona
Oporto
Zamora
Salamanca
Calatayud
Tarragona
Avila
Guadalajara
MADRID
Teruel
Castellón
Colmbra
Plasencia
Toledo
Cuenca
Cáceres
Valencia
Lisbon
Badajoz
Ciudad Real
Albacete
Gandia
Mérida
Alicante
Córdoba
Murcia
Sevilla
Jaén
Aguilas
Cartagena
Faro
Huelva
Granada
Cádiz
Málaga
Almería
Fuengirola
Algeciras

Key

● Main station
— Major rail route
— High-speed AVE route
-- AVE route under construction

Spain's Rail Network operates a wide variety of services. Study a RENFE brochure or train timetable before you buy your ticket.

Santa Justa railway station, Seville

Timetables

The punctuality rating of trains in Andalusia is quite high, particularly for the AVE. Brochures with prices and timetables are distributed free and are easy to follow. Information for *laborables* (weekdays) and *sábados, domingos y festivos* (Saturdays, Sundays and public holidays) is at the bottom of the timetable.

Seville

Santa Justa is a modern and user-friendly station, located about 5 minutes by car or bus from the city centre.
    Use the self-service ticket machines to buy *cercanías* tickets *(see p266)*. The auto check-in machines allow you to print out tickets reserved online *(see p266)*.
    Numerous amenities include a café, tourist office, car hire agencies, shops, newsstands, ATMs and money-changing facilities. For lost property, ask at the office marked *Atención al Cliente*.
    Bus stops and taxi ranks are located in front of the station.

Córdoba

Córdoba has a grand, modern station. Located in the northwest of the city, it is just a few minutes by car or taxi to the city centre. The AVE to Madrid takes just 2 hours; to Seville 45 minutes. The station is well served with cafés, shops, auto check-in machines and a tourist office. Outside, there are bus stops, a taxi rank and car hire agencies. The coach station is adjacent.

Platforms at Córdoba railway station

Platform at Granada railway station

Granada

Small and provincial, the station in Granada is housed in an old building and has few amenities. There is a small café-cum-restaurant and a taxi rank outside. Most trains that pass through are regional or *cercanías* but long-distance trains do run to Madrid, Seville, the Costa Blanca, Barcelona, Almería, Córdoba and Málaga. Storage lockers are available.

Málaga

Málaga's Maria Zambrano station expanded when the AVE line was added, making it the largest in Spain. There is a direct daily train to Barcelona and a connection to Madrid (via Córdoba). There is also a high-speed AVE line direct to central Seville under construction. A *cercanías* train connects to Málaga airport and the station will soon be linked to major towns through a Metro connection.

Málaga's station has many amenities, including auto check-in machines, luggage storage, car-hire agencies and a tourist office. Outside, there are bus stops and a taxi rank. A four-star hotel and large shopping centre are conveniently attached.

Almería

Almería's *Estación Intermodal* train and coach stations share the same building. Direct trains connect to Granada and Seville; to reach Córdoba you will need to make a connection in Granada; for Málaga, change at Antequera.

The station is small, with limited services such as a café, bank, newsstand, some shops and car hire agencies. Outside are bus stops and a taxi rank.

Scenic Routes

Travel by *cercanías* trains offers some very scenic routes. The most remarkable is a lengthy ride from Bobadilla (50 minutes north of Málaga), which heads south through gorges and mountains, passing through picturesque villages, before arriving in Algeciras. It takes about 3 hours and costs from €17.50.

A shorter ride, from Málaga to Fuengirola (30 minutes from the airport; 45 from Málaga station) provides stunning views of the Mediterranean from the mountains above for just €2.65.

Málaga's Maria Zambrano railway station at night

Travelling by Coach

The major coach links between Andalusia and the rest of Europe are with France, Holland, Belgium, Switzerland and Austria. Within the region itself, coach travel is very popular and has improved enormously. Most coaches now run on bio-diesel and most have air conditioning and toilet facilities. Travelling by coach is very economical and thanks to Andalusia's improved roads, it can be quick and enjoyable. However, around the many holidays in the Spanish festive calendar, travelling can be difficult: coach stations tend to be over-crowded, coaches slow to depart and the roads busy.

Arriving by Coach

The major coach stations in Andalusia are in Seville, Córdoba, Granada, Málaga and Almería. Coaches run frequently between major cities and towns, and may provide the only public transport to and from small villages, offering a chance to experience local regions.

The main departure hall of Plaza de Armas coach station in Seville

Tickets and Reservations

Reservations for medium to long-distance travel can be made at bus stations, online via Movelia (ww.movelia.es), or on the websites of individual bus companies. You can buy tickets on board regional buses, but during peak seasons it is wise to purchase them in advance. Discounts are given for round-trip tickets and there may be online reductions.

"Supra" coaches operated by **Alsa** on popular routes are direct and boast leather seats, extra legroom, free Wi-Fi, and on-board refreshments.

Seville

Seville has two coach stations in the centre of town, Plaza de Armas and Prado de San Sebastián. Buses from Prado de San Sebastián head mainly south, with destinations such as Cádiz, Jerez and Algeciras. Both stations have a café and newsstand, plus at Plaza de Armas there is Metro and Metro-Centro access outside.

Córdoba

The main coach station in Córdoba is run by a regional branch of Alsa, Alsina Graells. It is basic, with a small waiting area, café, newsstand and lockers. Coaches depart regularly for Granada, Cádiz, Almería, Málaga and Seville.

Granada

In Granada, travellers may be confused by the choice of coach companies, each with a variety of destinations. Alsa is the largest coach company, and its station is referred to as the central coach station. This station offers routes all over Murcia and Andalusia. Coaches for Madrid leave from the main train station.

Málaga

Málaga coach station is located in the centre of town, behind the train station. Coaches depart daily to all of Spain, as well as some international destinations. The station has a café, newsstand, shop, Internet café and money exchange. A taxi rank and bus stops are located outside.

Almería

Almería's coach and train stations share a building. It has little in the way of amenities (see p268), but does provide transport to destinations across Andalusia and Murcia.

DIRECTORY

Coach Stations

Almería
Estación Intermodal
Plaza de la Estación s/n.
Tel 950 26 20 98.

Córdoba
Terminal Alsina Graells
Glorieta de las Tres Culturas.
Tel 957 40 40 40.

Granada
Terminal Alsina Graells Sur
Carretera de Jaen, Granada.
Tel 958 18 54 80.

Málaga
Estación de Autobuses
Paseo de los Tilos.
Tel 952 35 00 61.

Seville
Estación Plaza de Armas
Plaza de Armas.
Map 1 B5 & 5 A2.
Tel 954 90 80 40.

Prado de San Sebastián Estación
Map 4 D3.
Tel 954 41 71 11.

Coach Companies

Alsa
ⓦ alsa.es

Damas
ⓦ damas-sa.es

Leda
ⓦ leda.es

Socibus
ⓦ socibus.es

Transportes Generales Comes
ⓦ tgcomes.es

Regional coach operated by the Alsa company

Driving in Andalusia

Many of the main roads and motorways in Andalusia are new and in very good condition. The road network is continually expanding, so always check a recently published map. Fold-out maps can be obtained at airports or tourist offices. You should also bear in mind that the number of accidents on Spanish roads is quite high, due to the confusion in road rules. Always drive with caution, but particularly in July and August when the roads are packed with holiday-makers who do not know the area. When visiting towns and villages, it is best to park your vehicle away from the centre and then walk in.

Typically narrow Andalusian street blocked by a parked car

Arriving by Car

Visitors bringing their own vehicles from other countries will need documentation in Spain. You should always make sure you have your driving licence, vehicle registration document and insurance. Your insurance company should be able to arrange an overseas extension of your car insurance. To hire a car in Spain you need a current driving licence and be over 18 years of age.

If you are travelling from the UK you will need your pink plastic photocard and an International Driving Permit, obtain this from the RAC or the AA.

Most Spanish motorways are well equipped with an SOS network of telephones, which provide instant access to the emergency and breakdown services. Ask for *auxilio en carretera*.

Rules of the Road

In Spain people drive on the right, so you must give way to the right. At intersections and roundabouts always proceed with caution.

The speed limits are 50 km/h (30 mph) in built-up areas; 90–100 km/h (55–60 mph) outside them and 120 k/h (75 mph) on motorways. Seat belts are compulsory both in the back and front; motor cyclists must wear crash helmets. Drivers must always carry two warning triangles and a reflective vest, as well as a first-aid kit.

Road Signs

Standard European road signs are used in Andalusia. However, signposting is often confusing and inconsistent, so be especially attentive when navigating in or out of cities. When leaving a town, scan the road for direction signs to other towns. Some are small and easily missed. If you need to change direction, look for signs, which say *Cambio de Sentido*. They generally lead to bridges or underpasses where you can turn around.

Local Drivers

Many drivers in Andalusia ignore road signs and speed up at amber traffic lights. It is common for drivers to come up close to the car in front to signal that they want to overtake. Indicators are not necessarily used by Spanish drivers, so be alert to the movements of nearby vehicles.

Motorways

In Andalusia almost all the motorways (*autovías*) are toll-free; except for the A4 *autopista*

Road Signs in Andalusia

Look out for the following road signs: *Peligro*, indicating danger, *Obras*, meaning roadworks ahead, *Ceda el Paso*, showing that you should give way and *Cuidado*, advising caution.

A road sign showing major routes at a crossroads

Overhead sign indicating the road is a motorway

Be alert to the fact that bulls may be on the road

Warning of the likelihood of snow or ice

(toll motorway) that connects Seville and Cádiz, and the AP7 along the Costa del Sol, which has some sections with tolls.

When driving on the *autopista*, the toll booths are at sporadic intervals. At the booths a sign posts the corresponding fare. Drive into one of the lanes with a green light indicating the method of payment you wish to use.

Driving in the Sierra Nevada along one of the highest roads in Europe

Driving in the Countryside

Only head off the major "N" roads *(rutas nacionales)* if you are not in any hurry. Some of the minor roads in Andalusia wind and climb, and their surfaces will often be in poor condition. In addition, although diversions may be marked, when you take them you may find they are inadequately signposted. Taking a minor road may add hours to a journey.

Buying Petrol

Many petrol stations in and around Andalusia still have attendants. Petrol stations out of town, tend to remain open 24 hours a day.

At self-service stations you generally have to pay for the petrol before it is dispatched. *Gasoil* (diesel) and *sin plomo* (unleaded) are usually available. Credit cards are widely accepted.

Driving in Town

Driving in the towns and cities of Andalusia can be difficult. The centres of Seville and Córdoba have streets that are narrow, labyrinthine and hard to negotiate in a car. Coupled with the often inconsiderate driving

of the residents, this can make it quite stressful to drive. Additionally, parking access is time-limited in Seville and completely restricted to city residents in some parts of Granada's centre.

Breakdown Services

If you breakdown, pull to a safe location at the side of the road. Put on the reflective vest (required to be carried in your car at all times) and place one reflective triangle in front and another approximately 50 m (165 ft) behind the car. If necessary, call for assistance, from breakdown services such as **ADA**, **Europ Assistance** or **RACE**.

Parking

In Seville, on-street parking is extremely difficult to find and is metered for a maximum stay of 1–2 hours. The best option for visitors is a parking garage – a few public garages operate, otherwise some hotels offer parking for guests.

There are few car parks in Córdoba and parking costs €1.50-2.50 per hour in Seville, Granada, Córdoba & Málaga.

Logos for AVIS and Hertz, popular car rental companies

Car Rental

In all major cities, car hire agencies are located near the train stations. Cars can be returned to the same location, or dropped off in another town, although there may be a surcharge for this. Local companies such as **Atesa**, **Avis** and **Hertz**, provide good bargains, but be wary of anyone asking for a large credit card deposit. Most rental cars are manual; automatics cost more to hire.

DIRECTORY

Parking

Almería
Garage Belén
Avenida Federico García Lorca 42.
Tel 950 25 30 60.

Córdoba
Aparcamientos Isolux Corsan Córdoba S.L.
Avenida Custodius 2.
Tel 957 29 96 19.

Granada
Parquigran
Plaza de San Agustín s/n.
Tel 958 29 60 33.

Málaga
La Marina
Plaza de la Marina 4.
Tel 952 21 88 31.

Seville
Aparcamientos Magdalena
Méndez Núñez 1.
Tel 954 22 83 33.

Breakdown Services

ADA
Tel 915 19 33 00.
w ada.es

Europ Assistance
Tel 902 15 85 85
(outside Spain 34 915 149 900).
w europ-assistance.com

RACE
(affiliated to the RAC in the UK)
Tel 902 40 45 45.

Car Rental

Atesa
w atesa.es
Jerez (Cadiz) Airport
Tel 956 18 68 14.
Málaga
Tel 952 35 65 50.
Seville
Tel 954 41 26 40.

Avis
w avis.es
Córdoba
Tel 957 40 14 45.
Granada
Tel 958 44 64 55.
Málaga
Tel 952 33 68 81.
Seville
Tel 954 44 91 21.

Hertz
w hertz.es
Córdoba
Tel 957 40 20 61.
Granada
Tel 958 20 44 54.
Málaga
Tel 952 23 30 86.
Seville
Tel 954 51 47 20.

Getting Around Towns and Cities

Many of Andalusia's cities, towns and villages have small, historic centres, characterized by narrow streets and tiny squares. Walking is an excellent and practical way of getting around the sights, especially as entry by car is restricted to residents in parts of many towns. For the same reason, city buses are generally not much good for travelling between monuments, but they are useful to get to shopping areas or from your hotel into the centre of town. Buses are very cheap, clean and safe, and generally only crowded at rush hours.

Typical *circulares* bus, operating around Seville

In Granada, buses are less useful except for Nos. 31, 32 and 34, which run from the centre of the city to Albaicín, Alhambra and Sacromonte.

In Córdoba the Nos. 3 and 16 take passengers from the historic area to the more commercial centre of the city.

Málaga's L3 services the town hall area and train station, while in Almería the No. 1 bus operates around the Old Town.

Metro

Seville's Metro system was designed to aid transport between the outer areas of Seville and the city centre. Line 1 is useful for getting from the historical centre (Puerta Jerez) to shopping centers (Nervión or Ciudad Expo's MetroMar). The system will eventually consist of four Metro lines, which will provide easy access to bus and train stations and include a line to the airport (Line 4).

Place your card (see Tickets section) over the reader to pass through barriers, and press the green button by the train door to open it. On-board overhead monitors announce the stops.

Metro-Centro

The Metro-Centro tram opened in 2008 in Seville city centre. It provides climate-controlled, rapid transport between San Bernardo station and Plaza Nueva in an otherwise pedestrian-only zone. Other lines are planned over the next few years, extending the network to Puerta Osario and Santa Justa train station.

Pay at the machine at tram stops (or pass your card over the reader on board); press the green button to open the door.

Guided tour visiting the Patio de las Doncellas at Seville's Real Alcázar

Walking

In many Andalusian towns, major sights are often only a short walk from where you are likely to be staying – at most just a short bus or taxi ride away. One of the joys of Andalusia's cities is to lose yourself in their narrow streets and to stumble upon the sights as you go.

Drivers in Spain tend not to respect pedestrians, even where pedestrians have the right of way. Crossings with pedestrian signals often have only a flashing amber light showing to oncoming drivers, even when the signal pedestrians see shows a green man; therefore it is advisable to be very cautious.

Red signal for wait; green for walk with care

Guided Tours

There is no better way to soak up the ambience of Andalusia's fine cities than from the seat of an old-fashioned, horse-drawn carriage. Drivers wait in line with their carriages near major monuments. They take up to four people and cost from €30–40 for 40 minutes. For tours on foot, consult local tourist offices about multilingual walking and cultural tours with **El Legado Andalusi**.

In Seville, **Bici 4 City** can rent you a bike that comes complete with an MP3 guided tour.

A more relaxing option is a cruise up the Guadalquivir River on a riverboat, with spectacular views of the city. Open-topped double-decker **City Sightseeing** buses offer hop-on-hop-off tours complete with audio guides, available in Seville, Granada, Cádiz and Málaga.

City Buses

City buses are most useful for getting to outlying sights because the historical centres are mostly pedestrianized. In Seville, the useful lines for visitors are the *circulares*, numbered C1 to C6, which run around the city centre.

Stops are announced on overhead monitors. Metro-Centro trams pass every 3–5 minutes and stop briefly at all stops.

Tickets

A *billete sencillo* or *univiaje* (single ticket) can be purchased on buses, but be sure to carry small change.

In Seville, the *tarjeta multiviaje* (multi-trip pass) and *tarjeta turística* (1–3 day pass) are valid on all TUSSAM means of transport (city bus, airport bus and Metro-Centro).

Cards can be purchased and topped up at newsstands or Tussam information kiosks, and are also rechargeable at Metro and Metro-Centro stops. Metro cards can be purchased in the entrance of stations and are for use exclusively on the Metro.

Tarjeta multiviaje and *tarjeta turística* electronic passes

Taxis

Spanish towns and cities are generously supplied with taxis, so there is not usually a problem

Standard, white Seville taxi, with its logo and official number

finding one, day or night. Taxis are always white and have a logo on the doors, which displays their official number. Drivers rarely speak any English, so learn enough Spanish to explain where you are going. The meter marks up the basic fare; however, supplements are added for *tarifa nocturna* (night-time driving), *maletas* (luggage) or *días festivos* (public holidays). If you are in doubt of the correct price, ask for the *tarifas* (tariff list).

Cycling

There are cycle lanes in most cities. Seville has pedestrianized a main throughfare in the centre, creating a wide promenade, which allows for bikes. Helmets are recommended.

SEVICI is a self-service bike rental programme in Seville, with 2,500 bikes available 24 hours a day. Bikes can be hired free for 30 minutes and are charged per hour after that. A €150 credit card deposit is paid and refunded on return of the bike.

Motorists tend to treat cyclists as a nuisance and city traffic can be dangerous for cyclists. **Andalucian Cycling Experience** offer trails into the country on mountain bikes.

Bicycles lined up ready for hire at SEVICI docking stations, Seville

DIRECTORY

Guided Tours

City Sightseeing
w city-sightseeing.com

El Legado Andalusi
w legadoandalusi.es

City Buses

ALMERÍA

Surbus
Calle Freniche s/n.
Tel 950 62 47 35.
w surbus.com

CÓRDOBA

Aucorsa
Plaza de Colón s/n.
Tel 957 47 64 50.
w aucorsa.es

GRANADA

Transportes Rober
Acera del Darro 30.
Tel 900 71 09 00.
w transportesrober.com

MÁLAGA

EMT
Camino de San Rafael 97.
Tel 902 52 72 00.
w emtmalaga.es

SEVILLE

Autobuses Urbanos Tussam
Avenida de Andalucia II.
Map 4 D3. **Tel** 902 45 99 54.
w tussam.es

Metro

Metro
w metro-sevilla.es

Metro-Centro
w tussam.es

Taxis

Almería
Tele-Taxis **Tel** 950 25 11 11.

Córdoba
Radio Taxi **Tel** 957 76 44 44.

Granada
Tele Radio Taxi **Tel** 958 28 06 54.

Málaga
UniTaxi **Tel** 952 33 33 33.

Seville
Tele-Taxis **Tel** 954 62 22 22.

Cycling

Andalucian Cycling Experience
w andaluciancyclingexperience.com

Bici 4 City
w bici4city.com

SEVICI
w sevici.es

General Index

Page numbers in **bold** refer to
main entries

Acknowledgments

Dorling Kindersley would like to thank the following people whose contributions and assistance have made this book possible.

Main Contributors

David Baird, resident in Andalusia from 1971 to 1995, has written many articles and books on Spain, including *Inside Andalusia*.
Martin Symington is a travel journalist and author who has written extensively on Spain. He is a regular contributor to *The Daily Telegraph* and also worked on the *Eyewitness Travel Guide to Great Britain*.
Nigel Tisdall, contributor to the *Eyewitness Travel Guide to France*, is the author of many travel publications, including the *Insight Pocket Guide to Seville*.

Additional Contributors

Louise Cook, Josefina Fernández, Adam Hopkins, Nick Inman, Janet Mendel, Steve Miller, Javier Gómez Morata, Clara Villanueva, John Gill, Mari Nicholson.
Additional Illustrations
Richard Bonson, Louise Boulton, Brian Cracker, Roy Flooks, Jared Gilbey, Paul Guest, Christian Hook, Mike Lake, Maltings Partnership, John Woodcock.
Additional Cartography
James Anderson, DK Cartography, Uma Bhattacharya, Mohammed Hassan, Jasneet Kaur.
Revisions and Relaunch Team
Asad Ali, Emma Anacootee, Lynnette McCurdy Bastida, Claire Baranowski, Marta Bescos, Francisco Bastida Cabaña, Hilary Bird, Eugenia Blandino, Greta Britton, Maggie Crowley, Cathy Day, Niki Foreman, Vinod Harish, Kaberi Hazarika, Tim Hollis, Claire Jones, Vincent Kurien, Colin Loughrey, Francesca Machiavelli, Nicola Malone, Susan Mennell, Michael Osborne, Rakesh Kumar Pal, Sachida Nand Pradhan, Ellen Root, Olivia Shepherd, Azeem Siddiqui, Sylvia Tombesi-Walton, Priyansha Tuli, Catherine Waring, Conrad van Dyk, Nikhil Verma, Word on Spain.

Index

Helen Peters.

Additional Photography

Lynnette McCurdy Bastida, Rolando Naranjo Campos, Patrick Llewelyn-Davies, David Murray, Martin Norris, Ian O'Leary, Rough Guides/ Demetrio Carasco, Clive Streeter, Peter Wilson.

Photographic and Artwork Reference

Concha Moreno at Aeropuerto Málaga; Fanny de Carranza at the Area de Cultura del Ayuntamiento, Málaga; Tere González at Oficina de Turismo, Ayuntamiento, Cádiz; and staff at Castillo San Marcos, El Puerto de Santa María, Itálica, Seville cathedral and the Museo Bellas Artes, Seville.

Special Assistance

Dorling Kindersley would like to thank all the regional and local tourist offices, *ayuntamientos* and *diputaciones* in Andalusia for their valuable help, and especially the Oficina de Turismo de Sevilla de Junta de Andalucía and other departments of the Junta de Andalucía. Particular thanks also to: Javier Morata, Jose Luis de Andrés de Colsa and Isidoro González-Adalid Cabezas at Acanto Arquitectura y Urbanismo, Madrid; Juan Fernández at Aguilar for his helpful comments; Robert op de Beek at Alvear, Montilla; Francisco Benavent at Fundación Andaluza de Flamenco, Jerez de la Frontera; staff at the Locutorio, Granada; Paul Montegrifo; Amanda Corbett at Patronato Provincial de Turismo de Sevilla; José Pérez de Ayala at the Parque Nacional de Doñana; Gabinete de Prensa, RENFE, Sevilla; Graham Hines and Rachel Taylor at the Sherry Institute of Spain, London; Dr David Stone; Joaquín Sendra at Turismo Andaluz SA; *6 Toros 6* magazine, Madrid.

Photography Permissions

The publisher would like to thank all those who gave permission to photograph at various *ayuntamientos*, cathedrals, churches, galleries, hotels, museums, restaurants, shops, transport services and other establishments too numerous to thank individually.

Picture Credits

a = above; b = below; c = centre; f = far; l = left; r = right; t = top.

Works of art have been reproduced with the permission of the following copyright holders: (c) Suceesion Picasso/ DACS, London 2006 56clb; DACS, London 2011 58cb; © **Patrimonio Nacional Madrid**: 51ca, 54bl.
Photos taken with the assistance of **Al-andalus, Casa-museo Fg Lorca**, Fuentevaqueros, Granada: 199b; **Teatro de la Maestranza**, Seville: 244cla; **Canal Sur**, Sevilla: 263cb.
The publisher would like to thank the following individuals, companies and picture libraries for permission to reproduce their photographs:
Adif: 226br, 267cl, 267br, 268tl, 268bl; **Aena**: 264br, 265tl; **Aisa Archivo Iconográfico**, Barcelona: 4tr, 27bl, 27br, *Juanita Cruz*, A Beltrane (1934) 30bc (d); Biblioteca Nacional Madrid/Museo Universal, *La Spange de C Davillier*, Gustavo Doré 32cl (d); 46c, 46br, 47cr, 48ca; Cathedral, Seville, *San Isidoro y San Leandro*, Ignacio de Ries (17th century) 49crb; Universidad de Barcelona, *La Corte de Abderramán*, Dionisio Baixeres (1885) 50cr–51cl; 51tc, 51bl, 52bc, 52br, 53bl, 54bl; Museo Naval Madrid, *Retrato de Magallanes*, 54br; 56cl; Casón del Buen Retiro, *La Rendición de Bailén*, J Casado del Alisal (1864) 57tl; Greenwich Museum, *Battle of Trafalgar*, G Chamberg 57ca (d); 56cr–57cl, 59br, 125bl; Museo-Casa de los Tiros, *Gitanos Bailando el Vito*, Anonymous 197br (d); Algar 48bc, 50clb; Servicio Histórico Nacional, *Alfonso XII*, R de Madrazo 57br (d); 59ca; © DACS 1996 Museo Nacional d el Teatro, Almagro, Ciudad Real, poster "Yerma" (FG Lorca) by José Caballero y Juan Antonio Morales (1934) 59cb; D Baird 40br, 43cl; Bevilacqua 49bl, 53c; JD Dallet 46clb; Dulevant 54clb; J Lorman 37ca; M Ángeles Sánchez 42t; Sevillano 43tr; **Alamy images**: Jerónimo Alba 210-11; dbimages/Allen Brown 272cla, blickwinkel 249br; Luis Dafos 200-1; Danita Delimont/ Alan Klehr 175tr; David Sanger Photography/ Sam Bloomberg-Rissman 173tl; Kathy deWitt 111cr; Mark Eveleigh 170tr; Rolf Hicker Photography 104; Jose Antonio Jimenez 173br; Jon Arnold Images/ Jon Arnold 110cla; John Kellerman 2-3; Chris Knapton 248bl; Lightworks Media 249tr; Melvyn Longhurst 171tc; Stefano Politi Markovina 12tc; Barry Mason 250br; Rod McLean 68; Geoffrey Morgan 246br; Robert Harding Picture Library Ltd/ Michael Jenner 223cl; Pascal

Saez 260bl; SAS 182tc; Carmen Sedano 249cl; Alex Segre 225tr; Gordon Sinclair 170bl; 170cla; Peter Howard Smith 256tr; image broker/Karl Heinz Spremberg 263tl, Renaud Visage 222cla; Ben Welsh 248cra; Ken Welsh 144cl; Peter M. Wilson 171br, 172bl. **Alsa Groups S.L.L.C:** 269bl; **Arenas Fotografía Artística,** Seville: 53cr, 120cl, Monasterio de la Rábida, Huelva, *Partida de Colón*, Manuel Cabral Bejarano 131br (d), **Avis Budget Group:** 271c; **La Belle Aurore,** Steve Davey & Juliet Coombe: 23c; **La Bobadilla:** 219tr; **Bridgeman Art Library/Index:** *The Life and Times of Don Quixote y Saavedra* (1608), Biblioteca Universidad Barcelona 55cb. **Casa Grande:** 218tc; **Casa Juan:** 236b; **Casa Juanito:** 231tr; **Casa Museo F. Garcia Lorca:** 209br; **Casa Numero Siete:** 216br; **Casa Paco:** 233t; **Casa Robles:** 228bl; **Cephas:** Mick Rock 24tr, 34tr, 34cl, 35cr, 35br, 163; **Cerámica Santa Ana:** 239c; **El Churrasco:** 232br; **Bruce Coleman:** Hans Reinhard 25crb; Konrad Wothe 161crb; **Colegas:** 256bl; **Dee Conway:** 33cr; **Corbis:** Michele Falzone 74; Owen Franken 223tl; Calle Montes 138; Scheufler Collection 8–9; Sylvain Sonnet 66; **Giancarlo Costa, Milan:** 31bc (d), 45b. **JD Dallet, Málaga:** 22bl, 36clb, 36br, 39br, 40cla, 150cr. **Dreamstime.com:** Arenaphotouk 13tl; Fotomicar 15b; Neirfy 12br; Sidqi 14tr; Nikolai Sorokin 10tl; Tupungato 122-3; Asier Villafranca 14bl; **Agencia EFE, Madrid:** 60clb, 60b, 61bl, 61cr; **Egaña Oriza:** 229tl; **Empresa Pública de Emergencias Sanitarias:** 259ca; **Equipo 28 Seville:** 33tl; **Mary Evans Picture Library:** 100br, 181br (d); **El Vapor de el puerto:** 169br. **El Faro de el Puerto:** 235bl; **La Finca:** 237bc; **Fotolia:** Artur Bogacki 20; citylights 96; **La Fructuosa:** 233bc. **Garum:** 234t; **Getty images:** AFP 31cr; marcp_dmoz 11br; Chris Sattiberger 62–3; Andrés Valdaliso Martinez 15tc; Visions Of Our Land 13br; **The Roland Grant Archive:** *"For a Few Dollars More"*, United Artists 208tl; **Giraudon, Paris:** 46cr; Flammarion-Giraudon 47c; **Robert Harding Picture Library:** Sheila Terry 53crb; **Hemispheres images:**Jean du Boisberranger 111tl; Patrick Frilet 250tl; Bertrand Gardel 111bl; Hervé Hughes 111crb; Stefano Torrione 172cra; **Hertz:** 271cb; **Hospes Palacio de Bailio:** 217tr; **Hulton Deutsch:** 58cr–59cl, AM/Keystone 61tl, 175bc. **Incafo Archivo Fotográfico, Madrid:** 161ca; A Camoyán 161cb; JL Glez Grande 161cla; Candy Lopesino/Juan Hidalgo 161cb; JL Muñoz 161bl; **Index, Barcelona:** 47cb, 48br, 50cla, 50bl, 50br, 51cb, 56br, 57crb, 57clb (d), 57cb; Image/Index Private Collection, *Sucesos de Casaviejas*, Saenz Tejada 59tl; Iranzo 48clb; **The Image Bank:** © Chasan 65bc; Stockphotos inc © Terry Williams 188; **Images:** 4b, 24b, 25tl, 25bl, 36tr, 38br; AGE Fotostock 30tr, 30cl, 31c, 32br, 35cl, 41cla, 41br, 141tr, 161c, 226tr, 246tl; Horizon/Michele Paggetta 30c–31c; courtesy **Isla Magica:** 108tl, 108bl. **JCDecaux Spain:** 273bl; **Pablo Juliá, Seville:** 245br. **Anthony King:** 25tr. **Life File Photographic Library:** 152bl; **José Lucas, Seville:** 86br, 169tc, 246c, 258clb, 272tr; **Neil Lukas:** 134clb, 134bc.

Arxiu Mas, Barcelona: 30br; Museo Taurino, Madrid, poster for a bullfight featuring Rodolfo Gaona, H Colmenero 31bl; 49tc, 52c, 52cr–53cl; Museo América, Madrid, *View of Seville,* Sánchez Coello 54cr–55cl; © Patrimonio Nacional Madrid 49br, 52cl, 52cb, 53ca; **Magnum**/Jean Gaumy 61cb; **El Molino de la Romera:** 230tr. **NHPA:** Vicente Garcia Canseco 135ca; **Naturpress, Madrid:** Jose Luis G Grande 135bc; Francisco Márquez 25br; **Network Photographers:** 35tl; Rapho/Hans Silvester 38cl. **Oronoz Archivo Fotográfico, Madrid:** 30cla, 168tr; Private Collection *Reyes Presidiendo a una Corrida de Toros* (1862), Anonymous 31br, 42c, 46b, 47tl, 47ca, 47cl, 47crb, 47br, 47tl, 49tl; María Novella Church, Florence, *Detail of Averroes,* Andrea Bonainti 51tl; 51crb, 51bc, 53tl, Diputación de Granada, *Salida de Boabdil de la Alhambra,* Manuel Gómez Moreno 53clb; 54cla; Museo del Prado, *Cristo Crucificado,* Diego Velázquez 55ca (d); Museo de Prado, *Expulsión de los Moriscos,* Vicent Carducho 55c (d); Musée du Louvre, Paris, *Joven Mendigo,* Bartolomé Murillo 55bc (d); © Patrimonio Nacional Madrid, Palacio Real, Riofrio, Segovia, *Carlos III Vestido de Cazador,* F Liani 56bl; © DACS London 1996, Sternberg Palace, Prague, *Self-Portrait,* Pablo Picasso 58clb; Private Collection, Madrid, *Soldados del Ejército Español en la Guerra de Cuba* 58br; 59crb, 59bl, 61tc, 76bl, 87bl, 147tr; Private Collection, Madrid, *Patio Andaluz,* Garcia Rodríguez 150cl; Museo de Bellas Artes, Cádiz, *San Bruno en Éxtasis,* Zurbarán; 197bl; 227br. **Eduardo Paez, Granada:** *Porte de la Justice,* Baron de Taylor 44; **Paisajes Españoles, Madrid:** 93tc; **Parador Gibralfaro:** 234bl; **Jose M Perez de Ayala, Doñana:** 134tr, 134cla; **Pictures:** 43br; **Prisma, Barcelona:** 55tl, 139b; *Vista desde el Puerto* Nicolás Chapny (1884) 183t; 245tl; Hans Lohr 165br; Anna N 178ca; Sonsoles Prada 47crb. **Ruta del Veleta:** 237tr. **M Ángeles Sánchez, Madrid:** 242tr, 242tc; **STA Travel Group:** 256c; **Tony Stone Images:** Robert Everts 86cla. **Visions of Andalucía Slide Library, Málaga:** M Almarza 25cr; Michelle Chaplow 23br; 32cr–33cl, 166br; A Navarro 40clb; **SOL.com:** 110bl; **Superstock:** age fotostock 88, 162; Jacobo Hernández 126; Felipe Rodríguez 252–3; Greg Stechishin 188. **Taberna del Alabardero:** 229br; **El Tamborliero:** 230bl; **Telefonica:** 262clb; Tragabuches 235tr; **Tussam:** 264cla, 273cl, 273clb; **Peter Wilson:** 39cla, 65crb, 178tr, 178bl, 183tr.

Front Endpaper: **Corbis:** Michele Falzone Rtr; Calle Montes Ltr; Sylvain Sonnet Rcla; **Fotolia:** citylights Rcra; **Superstock:** age fotostock Lbl ,Rtl; Jacobo Hernández Ltl; Greg Stechishin Rbr.

Jacket Images: Front and Spine – **Corbis:** Jean-Pierre Lescourret.

Map Images: **Corbis:** Jean-Pierre Lescourret.

Special Editions of DK Travel Guides

DK Travel Guides can be purchased in bulk quantities at discounted prices for use in promotions or as premiums. We are also able to offer special editions and personalized jackets, corporate imprints, and excerpts from all of our books, tailored specifically to meet your own needs.

To find out more, please contact:
in the United States **SpecialSales@dk.com**
in the UK **TravelSpecialSales@uk.dk.com**
in Canada DK Special Sales at
general@tourmaline.ca
in Australia
business.development@pearson.com.au

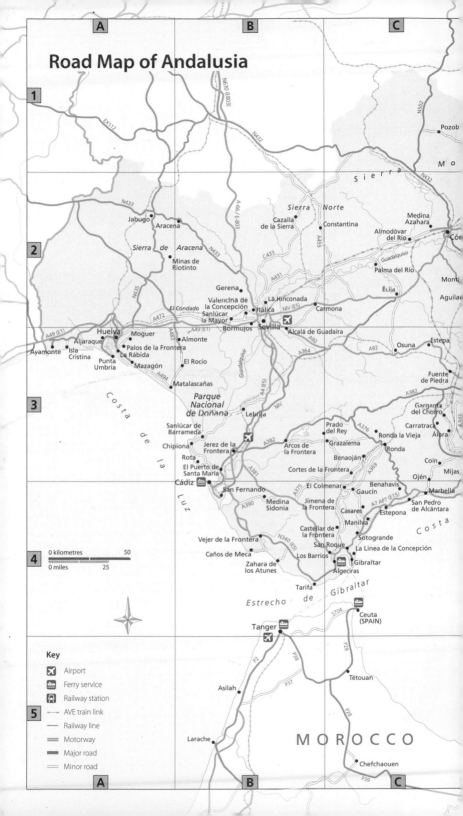

twin room	habitación con dos camas	ah-bee-tah-thee-yohn kohn dohs kah-mahs
single room	habitación individual	ah-bee-tah-thee-yohn een-dee-vee-doo-ahl
room with a bath	habitación con baño,	ah-bee-tah-thee-yohn kohn bah-nyoh
shower	ducha	doo-chah
porter	el botones	ehl boh-toh-nehs
key	la llave	lah yah-veh
I have a reservation.	Tengo una habitación reservada.	tehn-goh oo-na ah-bee-tah-thee-yohn reh-sehr-vah-dah

Eating Out

Have you got a table for …?	¿Tienen mesa para …?	tee-yeh-nehn meh-sah pah-rah
I want to reserve a table.	Quiero reservar una mesa.	kee-yeh-roh reh-sehr-vahr oo-nah meh-sah
The bill please.	La cuenta por favor.	lah kwehn-tah pohr fah-vohr
I am a vegetarian	Soy vegetariano/a	soy beh-heh-tah-ree-yah-na/na
Waitress/waiter	Camarera/camarero	kah-mah-reh-rah kah-mah-reh-rah
menu	la carta	lah kahr-tah
fixed-price menu	menú del día	meh-noo dehl dee-ah
wine list	la carta de vinos	lah kahr-tah deh bee-nohs
glass	un vaso	oon vah-soh
bottle	una botella	oo-nah boh-teh-yah
knife	un cuchillo	oon koo-chee-yoh
fork	un tenedor	oon teh-neh-dohr
spoon	una cuchara	oo-nah koo-chah-rah
breakfast	el desayuno	ehl deh-sah-yoo-noh
lunch	la comida el almuerzo	lah koh-mee-dah ehl ahl-mwehr-thoh
dinner	la cena	lah theh-nah
main course	el primer plato	ehl pree-mehr plah-toh
starters	los entremeses	lohs ehn-treh-meh-sehs
dish of the day	el plato del día	ehl plah-toh dehl dee-ah
coffee	el café	ehl kah-feh
rare	poco hecho	poh-koh eh-choh
medium	medio hecho	meh-dee-yoh eh-choh
well done	muy hecho	mwee eh-choh

Menu Decoder

al horno	ahl ohr-noh	baked
asado	ah-sah-doh	roast
el aceite	ah-theh-ee-teh	oil
las aceitunas	ah-theh-toon-ahs	olives
el agua mineral	ah-gwa mee-neh-rahl	mineral water
el ajo	ah-hoh	garlic
el arroz	ahr-rohth	rice
el azúcar	ah-thoo-kahr	sugar
la carne	kahr-neh	meat
la cebolla	theh-boh-yah	onion
la cerveza	thehr-veh-thah	beer
el cerdo	therh-doh	pork
el chocolate	choh-koh-lah-teh	chocolate
el chorizo	choh-ree-thoh	red sausage
el cordero	kohr-deh-roh	lamb
el fiambre	fee-ahm-breh	cold meat
frito	free-toh	fried
la fruta	froo-tah	fruit
los frutos secos	froo-tohs seh-kohs	nuts
las gambas	gahm-bahs	prawns
el helado	eh-lah-doh	ice cream
el huevo	oo-eh-voh	egg
el jamón serrano	hah-mohn sehr-rah-noh	cured ham
el jerez	heh-rehz	sherry
la langosta	lahn-gohs-tah	lobster
la leche	leh-cheh	milk
el limón	lee-mohn	lemon
la limonada	lee-moh-nah-dah	lemonade
la mantequilla	mahn-teh-kee-yah	butter
la manzana	mahn-thah-nah	apple
los mariscos	mah-rees-kohs	seafood
la menestra	meh-nehs-trah	vegetable stew
la naranja	nah-rahn-hah	orange
el pan	pahn	bread
el pastel	pahs-tehl	cake
las patatas	pah-tah-tahs	potatoes
el pescado	pehs-kah-doh	fish

la pimienta	pee-mee-yehn-tah	pepper
el plátano	plah-tah-noh	banana
el pollo	poh-yoh	chicken
el postre	pohs-treh	dessert
el queso	keh-soh	cheese
la sal	sahl	salt
las salchichas	sahl-chee-chahs	sausages
la salsa	sahl-sah	sauce
seco	seh-koh	dry
el solomillo	soh-loh-mee-yoh	sirloin
la sopa	soh-pah	soup
la tarta	tahr-tah	pie/cake
el té	teh	tea
la ternera	tehr-neh-rah	beef
las tostadas	tohs-tah-dahs	toast
el vinagre	bee-nah-greh	vinegar
el vino blanco	bee-noh blahn-koh	white wine
el vino rosado	bee-noh roh-sah-doh	rosé wine
el vino tinto	bee-noh teen-toh	red wine

Numbers

0	cero	theh-roh
1	uno	oo-noh
2	dos	dohs
3	tres	trehs
4	cuatro	kwa-troh
5	cinco	theen-koh
6	seis	says
7	siete	see-yeh-teh
8	ocho	oh-choh
9	nueve	nweh-veh
10	diez	dee-yehz
11	once	ohn-theh
12	doce	doh-theh
13	trece	treh-theh
14	catorce	kah-tohr-theh
15	quince	keen-theh
16	dieciséis	dee-eh-thee-seh-ees
17	diecisiete	dee-eh-thee-see-yeh-teh
18	dieciocho	dee-eh-thee-oh-choh
19	diecinueve	dee-eh-thee-nweh-veh
20	veinte	beh-yeen-teh
21	veintiuno	beh-yeen-tee-oo-noh
22	veintidós	beh-yeen-tee-dohs
30	treinta	treh-yeen-tah
31	treinta y uno	treh-yeen-tah ee oo-noh
40	cuarenta	kwah-rehn-tah
50	cincuenta	theen-kwehn-tah
60	sesenta	seh-sehn-tah
70	setenta	seh-tehn-tah
80	ochenta	oh-chehn-tah
90	noventa	noh-behn-tah
100	cien	thee-yehn
101	ciento uno	thee-yehn-toh oo-noh
102	ciento dos	thee-yehn-toh dohs
200	doscientos	dohs-thee-yehn-tohs
500	quinientos	khee-nee-yehn-tohs
700	setecientos	seh-teh-thee-yehn-tohs
900	novecientos	noh-veh-thee-yehn-tohs
1,000	mil	meel
1,001	mil uno	meel oo-noh

Time

one minute	un minuto	oon mee-noo-toh
one hour	una hora	oo-na oh-rah
half an hour	media hora	meh-dee-a oh-rah
Monday	lunes	loo-nehs
Tuesday	martes	mahr-tehs
Wednesday	miércoles	mee-ehr-koh-lehs
Thursday	jueves	hweh-vehs
Friday	viernes	bee-yehr-nehs
Saturday	sábado	sah-bah-doh
Sunday	domingo	doh-meen-goh

Phrase Book

In Emergency

Help!	¡Socorro!	soh-**koh**-roh
Stop!	¡Pare!	**pah**-reh
Call a doctor!	¡Llame a un médico!	yah-meh ah **oon** meh-**dee**-koh
Call an ambulance!	¡Llame a una ambulancia!	yah-meh ah **oonah** ahm-boo-**lahn**-thee-ah
Call the police!	¡Llame a la policía!	**yah**-meh ah lah poh-lee-**thee**-ah
Call the fire brigade!	¡Llame a los bomberos!	**yah**-meh ah lohs bohm-**beh**-rohs
Where is the nearest? telephone	Dónde está el teléfono más próximo?	**dohn**-deh ehs-**tah** ehl teh-**leh**-foh-noh **mahs prohx**-ee-moh
Where is the nearest hospital?	Dónde está el hospital más próximo?	**dohn**-deh ehs-**tah** ehl ohs-pee-**tahl** **mahs prohx**-ee-moh

Communication Essentials

Yes	Sí	see
No	No	noh
Please	Por favor	pohr fah-**vohr**
Thank you	Gracias	**grah**-thee-ahs
Excuse me	Perdone	pehr-**doh**-neh
Hello	Hola	**oh**-lah
Goodbye	Adiós	ah-dee-**ohs**
Good night	Buenas noches	**bweh**-nahs noh-chehs
Morning	La mañana	lah mah-**nyah**-nah
Afternoon	La tarde	lah **tahr**-deh
Evening	La tarde	lah **tahr**-deh
Yesterday	Ayer	ah-**yehr**
Today	Hoy	oy
Tomorrow	Mañana	mah-**nya**-nah
Here	Aquí	ah-**kee**
There	Allí	ah-**yee**
What?	¿Qué?	keh
When?	¿Cuándo?	**kwahn**-doh
Why?	¿Por qué?	pohr-**keh**
Where?	¿Dónde?	**dohn**-deh

Useful Phrases

How are you?	¿Cómo está usted?	**koh**-moh ehs-**tah** oos-**tehd**
Very well, thank you.	Muy bien, gracias.	mwee bee-**yehn grah**-thee-ahs
Pleased to meet you.	Encantado de conocerle.	ehn-kahn-**tah**-doh deh koh-noh-**thehr**-leh
See you soon.	Hasta pronto.	ahs-tah **prohn**-toh
That's fine.	Está bien.	ehs-tah bee-**yehn**
Where is/are …?	¿Dónde está/están …?	**dohn**-deh ehs-**tah**/ehs-**tahn**
How far is it to …?	¿Cuántos metros/ kilómetros hay de aquí a …?	**kwahn**-tohs **meh**-trohs/kee-**loh**-meh-trohs eye deh ah-**kee** ah
Which way to …?	¿Por dónde se va a …?	pohr **dohn**-deh seh vah ah
Do you speak English?	¿Habla inglés?	**ah**-blah een-**glehs**
I don't understand	No comprendo	noh kohm-**prehn**-doh
Could you speak slowly please?	¿Puede hablar más despacio por favor?	pweh-deh ah-**blahr** mahs dehs-pah-thee-oh pohr fah-**vohr**
I'm sorry.	Lo siento.	loh see-**ehn**-toh

Useful Words

big	grande	**grahn**-deh
small	pequeño	peh-**keh**-nyoh
hot	caliente	kah-lee-**ehn**-teh
cold	frío	**free**-oh
good	bueno	**bweh**-noh
bad	malo	**mah**-loh
enough	bastante	bahs-**tahn**-teh
well	bien	bee-**yehn**
open	abierto	ah-bee-**ehr**-toh
closed	cerrado	thehr-**rah**-doh
left	izquierda	eeth-key-**ehr**-dah
right	derecha	deh-**reh**-chah
straight on	todo recto	toh-doh **rehk**-toh
near	cerca	**thehr**-kah
far	lejos	**leh**-hohs
up	arriba	ah-**ree**-bah
down	abajo	ah-**bah**-hoh
early	temprano	tehm-**prah**-noh
late	tarde	**tahr**-deh
entrance	entrada	ehn-**trah**-dah
exit	salida	sah-**lee**-dah
toilet	lavabos, servicios	lah-**vah**-bohs, sehr-**vee**-thee-ohs

more	más	mahs
less	menos	**meh**-nohs

Shopping

How much does this cost?	¿Cuánto cuesta esto?	**kwahn**-toh **kwehs**-tah ehs-toh
I would like …	Me gustaría …	meh goos-tah-**ree**-ah
Do you have?	¿Tienen?	tee-**yeh**-nehn
I'm just looking.	Sólo estoy mirando, gracias.	**soh**-loh ehs-**toy** mee-**rahn**-doh **grah**-thee-ahs
Do you take credit cards?	¿Aceptan tarjetas de crédito?	ah-**thehp**-tahn tahr-**heh**-tahs deh **kreh**-dee-toh
What time do you open?	¿A qué hora abren?	ah **keh** oh-rah **ah**-brehn
What time do you close?	¿A qué hora cierran?	ah keh oh-rah thee-**yehr**-rahn
This one.	Este	**ehs**-teh
That one.	Ese	**eh**-seh
expensive	caro	**kahr**-oh
cheap	barato	bah-**rah**-toh
size, clothes	talla	**tah**-yah
size, shoes	número	**noo**-mehr-oh
white	blanco	**blahn**-koh
black	negro	**neh**-groh
red	rojo	**roh**-hoh
yellow	amarillo	ah-mah-**ree**-yoh
green	verde	**vehr**-deh
blue	azul	ah-**thool**
antique shop	la tienda de antigüedades	lah tee-**yehn**-dah deh ahn-tee-gweh-**dah**-dehs
bakery	la panadería	lah pah-nah-deh-**ree**-ah
bank	el banco	ehl **bahn**-koh
book shop	la librería	lah lee-breh-**ree**-ah
butcher	la carnicería	lah kahr-nee-theh-**ree**-ah
cake shop	la pastelería	lah pahs-teh-leh-**ree**-ah
chemist	la farmacia	lah fahr-**mah**-thee-ah
fishmonger	la pescadería	lah pehs-kah-deh-**ree**-ah
greengrocer	la frutería	lah froo-teh-**ree**-ah
grocery	la tienda de comestibles	lah tee-**yehn**-dah deh koh-mehs-**tee**-blehs
hairdresser	la peluquería	lah peh-loo-keh-**ree**-ah
market	el mercado	ehl mehr-**kah**-doh
newsagent	el kiosko de prensa	ehl kee-**yohs**-koh deh **prehn**-sah
post office	la oficina de correos	lah oh-fee-**thee**-nah deh kohr-**reh**-ohs
shoe shop	la zapatería	lah thah-pah-teh-**ree**-ah
supermarket	el supermercado	ehl soo-pehr-mehr-**kah**-doh
tobacconist	el estanco	ehl ehs-**tahn**-koh
travel agent	la agencia de viajes	lah ah-**hehn**-thee-ah deh vee-**ah**-hehs

Sightseeing

art gallery	el museo de arte	ehl moo-**seh**-oh deh **ahr**-teh
cathedral	la catedral	lah kah-teh-**drahl**
church	la iglesia	lah ee-**gleh**-see-yah
	la basílica	lah bah-**see**-lee-kah
garden	el jardín	ehl hahr-**deen**
library	la biblioteca	lah bee-blee-yoh-**teh**-kah
museum	el museo	ehl moo-**seh**-oh
tourist information office	la oficina de información turística	lah oh-fee-**thee**-nah deh een-fohr-mah-**thee**-yohn too-**rees**-tee-kah
town hall	el ayuntamiento	ehl ah-yoon-tah-mee-**yehn**-toh
closed for holiday	cerrado por vacaciones	thehr-**rah**-doh pohr vah-kah-thee-**yoh**-nehs
bus station	la estación de autobuses	lah ehs-tah-thee-**yohn** deh owtoh-**boo**-sehs
railway station	la estación de trenes	lah ehs-tah-thee-**yohn** deh **treh**-nehs

Staying in a Hotel

Do you have a vacant room?	¿Tiene una habitación libre?	tee-**yeh**-neh **oo**-nah ah-bee-tah-thee-**yohn** lee-breh
double room	habitación doble	ah-bee-tah-thee-**yohn** **doh**-bleh
with double bed	con cama de matrimonio	kohn **kah**-mah deh mah-tree-**moh**-nee-oh